RICHARD THOMPSON

RICHARD THOMPSON

The Biography

PATRICK HUMPHRIES

Schirmer Books
An Imprint of Simon & Schuster Macmillan
New York

Prentice Hall International
London Mexico City New Delhi Singapore Sydney Toronto

Extract from Nick Hornby's *High Fidelity* reproduced by kind permission of
Victor Gollancz Ltd.

Copyright © 1997 Virgin Books

First published as *Richard Thompson: Strange Affair* in Great Britain in 1996 by Virgin
Books, an imprint of Virgin Publishing Ltd., 332 Ladbroke Grove, London, England W10
5AH. British copyright © Patrick Humphries 1996.

All rights reserved. No part of this book may be reproduced or transmitted in any form
or by any means, electronic or mechanical, including photocopying, recording, or by any
information storage retrieval system, without permission from the Publisher.

Schirmer Books
An Imprint of Simon & Schuster Macmillan
1633 Broadway
New York, NY 10019

Library of Congress Catalog Card Number: 96-37826

Printed in the United States of America

Printing Number
1 2 3 4 5 6 7 8 9 10

Library of Congress Cataloging-in-Publication Data

Humphries, Patrick.
  [Richard Thompson, strange affair]
  Richard Thompson : the biography / Patrick Humphries.
    p.   cm.
  Originally published: Richard Thompson, strange affair. London : Virgin Books, 1996.
  Discography: p.
  Includes bibliographical references and index.
  ISBN 0-02-864752-1
  1. Thompson, Richard, 1949– . 2. Rock musicians—England—Biography. I. Title.
ML419.T47H86   1997
782.42166'092—dc21
[B]   96-37826
                                                                                   CIP
                                                                                    MN

This paper meets the requirements of ANSI/MOSP 739.48-1992 {Permanence of Paper}.

All of this is for Sue Parr. Without her, there wouldn't be any of it. This book is sincerely dedicated to her, with all my love. She, more than anyone, knows what it took to get here. Chorus: 'I'm so tired of working every day ...'

Contents

Acknowledgments	ix
Introduction	1
Part 1	
Fairport	9
Part 2	
Richard and Linda	119
Part 3	
Solo	219
Afterword	341
Discography by Colin Davies	347
Bibliography	372
Lyric Permissions	373
Index	374

Acknowledgments

Unless otherwise indicated, all quotations are from my own interviews, the vast majority undertaken during 1995 specifically for this book. In a few cases I have also drawn on interviews conducted for my history of Fairport Convention.

In the course of writing this book, I conducted interviews with dozens of Richard's friends, associates and family. They were all pleased to talk about a man they value as a friend, a musician and a songwriter. All were as generous with their time as their memories.

Otherwise, everything else is my fault. Apart from the music, for which I hold Richard solely responsible.

So sincere thanks, really, to the following:

Perri Blackburn for telling me all about her shy baby brother.
Joe Boyd for reconstructing the fables.
Colin and Anita Davies for transcribing, discographing and generally Thompsoning in such good order, for so long.
Fred Dellar for being a rock of ages.
Bernard Doherty for putting the Rolling Stones on hold for an afternoon.
Pat and Elizabeth Donaldson for coffee on a hot summer's day in Hampstead.
Marc Ellington for a' things Scottish.
Pete Filleul for being on the mark about Hard Cash and Sweet Talker.
Clive Gregson for not being in Nashville, and talking so long and affectionately about his association with Richard.
Ed Haber for Flypaper and collating all that "Doom and Gloom" onto tape.
Peter Hogan for the British title, and for many years of friendship, opinion and advice. With thanks for commissioning *Meet on the Ledge* all those years ago, and for the same enthusiasm carried on into the 90s.
Ken Hunt for playing with such a straight viz Thompo. Many,

Acknowledgments

many thanks for staunch support and advice on this project over the years.

Ashley Hutchings for Tim Turner's Narration, Dr K, Ethnic Shuffle, Fairport, Steeleye, Albions and The Guv'nor.

John Hyde for having the good sense to insist on BBC Radio Two commissioning him to undertake a documentary series on Richard Thompson.

Johnny ('Jonah') Jones for all those Cropredy announcements. (And Big Pete and Aitch, for being on the door at 'The Moon'. Happy, smoke-filled days).

John Kirkpatrick for morris-ing on, and on.

Barry Lazell for invaluable chart info.

Jo Lustig for managing all these years.

Paul McGuire for sustained interest and advice.

John Martin for reminiscing, and the joy of bagpipes.

Dave Mattacks for time keeping and keeping time.

Sian Morphet for being such a Richard Thompson fan.

And not forgetting her special chum, Lawrence.

Pat Naylor for plugging the gaps.

Simon Nicol for Fairport. We'll always have Hounslow.

Mal Peachey for extending and extending and extending the hand of kindness.

Dave and Chris Pegg for memories, tickets, encouragement and wood-worm down the years.

Richard Roberts-Miller ('Big Muldoon'), for teaching a young Richard to play the guitar, which really led to this book.

Paula Shutkever for help, long after the event, even if she does think that Henry Rollins makes better records than Richard Thompson.

John Sugar for letting me hear his full unedited BBC World Service interview with Richard from 1994.

David Thomas for being so thoroughly Shand-tastic.

Danny Thompson for his thoughts on 'the governor', and thanks Sylvia, for the photos.

Joan Thompson for finding time in her hectic schedule to talk about her 'beautiful baby'.

Linda Thompson for interrupting a busy new life, with memories of an old life.

Muna Thompson for putting up with my questions about her dad.

John Tobler for a helping hand.

Vox for largely, happy days: Roy, Stan, Shaun, Mike, Ian, Phil C, Phil S, Sue, Kevin, Gary, Paul A, Paul C, Paul D, Norma, Alan, Susie, Neil . . .

Acknowledgments

Loudon Wainwright III for the time spent talking about his tennis partner.

Richard Williams for taking time off from Ayrton Senna, and driving back 20 years to Island.

Sian Wynne for being so close.

Pete Zorn for a rewarding morning near Crystal Palace.

Above all, many thanks to Richard and Nancy Thompson for finding time in their lives, and sitting down to answer all the pages of questions I kept flinging their way. Richard's reluctance at being interviewed is well known, but he breezily put up with my probing.

If the ensuing pages only hint at it, I would like to put on record my total admiration for Richard's work. For nearly 30 years he has carved himself a unique place in the annals of, phew, rock'n'roll. Long may he run.

So, Richard and Nancy, thanks again. You can have your lives back now.

PATRICK HUMPHRIES
January 1996

Some to misery are born;
Every morn and every night
Some are born to sweet delight.
Some are born to sweet delight,
Some are born to endless night.

William Blake,
Auguries of Innocence

Introduction

IT WAS ONE OF THOSE HEAVY, limp days in London during the summer of 1995. One of those chokingly hot days, as July eased into August, as surely as a slow-spun ball delivered down the crease. The humid air hung like a blanket over the suburbs of the capital. It was a day for lazing and lying, watching the cats languidly flick their tails as they slipped into a more comfortable position to while away another sleepy afternoon.

The summer had stretched interminably on. There was no end in sight, and all the good-natured, Blitz-spirit indomitability of the English had evaporated as the temperature hammered into the high 80s and just wouldn't let go. The weather was firmly back on the agenda as the great British conversational gambit.

It was a summer that sunk its claws into you and clung tightly on. It was the day the earth caught fire, and the man *Rolling Stone* magazine called 'one of the great buried treasures of English rock', had drains on his mind.

Richard Thompson apologised for the smell, he assured me it wasn't always like this. It was the weather. The perfect host, Thompson had shooed his bubbly young son away to be with his mother upstairs, and with the help of a stylish cappuccino machine, crafted a frothy coffee which he carried out into the garden. He pished the cats away and settled down to be interviewed.

With his thinning hair and diffident manner, Thompson passes convincingly as a shy and retiring English middle-class, middle-aged man. But, like the characters who populate his songs, all is not quite what it seems. Something about the face draws you. The eyes are piercing and blue, familiar but undeniably distant. The face is lined, the hair which coiled Medusa-like and Dylan-esque during the 60s, is now a memory.

There is a hesitancy to Thompson's speech, the vestige of a childhood stutter, which only emphasised the boy's natural reticence and reinforced his dreamy nature. While Thompson talks, he may appear to

Introduction

fumble for words, blink, avoid the conversational artery, nevertheless he is a riveting talker, because in his words are so many of your own memories and lodestones.

All this flicks through your mind like a home-movie projector. And all the while Thompson chats and self-destructs his own myth. When he wants to make a point, he'll turn his face to meet yours, and quite disconcertingly, the eyes have it.

A career away from the bright lights of rock'n'roll has seen Thompson rarely impinge upon the world at large. Even today, booking rehearsal rooms 'for Richard Thompson' – or indeed writing his biography – elicits a puzzled response. Fairport Convention might just strike a chord, particularly in those of a certain generation who recall Fairport's peripatetic gigging of the late 60s and early 70s. Distant bells may be rung in the ageing brains of the survivors of the great festivals. Like survivors of the Great War, the 'old contemptibles' who march in serried and steadily diminishing ranks past the Cenotaph each 11 November, festival veterans grow misty-eyed and proud at the litany: Isle Of Wight 1969; Bath 1970; Bickershaw 1972 . . . Thompson's got his campaign medals. He served, even if at times he only stood and waited.

A quarter of a century on from the 1970 Bath Festival, where I first saw Richard Thompson play, the man himself settles on the floor opposite me, uneasily eying the cassette player and the flickering red light which reminds us both that this is no casual conversation. Unfailingly courteous and amiable, Thompson's antipathy to interviews is nonetheless legendary. He recognises that, as part of the process to help shift more product, he will have to sit and be interviewed. And then be interviewed again. And again. And again . . .

Thompson is good-natured and surprisingly affable about the whole process, resigned to the fact that, however good his new album, what the interviewer wants on his cassette are memories of other people, of other times. Of Sandy Denny. Of Fairport Convention. Of Linda. Of Nick Drake . . . all warp and weft of Thompson's lustrous past. But all undeniably past. Polite but soon tiring of the exhumation, Thompson will endeavour to please, all the while trying to fast-forward the conversation to the present.

Thompson is better able than most to compartmentalise his life. He is surrounded by a network of efficient and capable people who look after him. His record company may not have many Richard Thompson gold discs hanging alongside Blur and the Beatles, but they recognise the man's true contribution. There are business managers and tour managers, who devote time to the necessary day-to-day routines, freeing Richard to do what he does best, writing remarkable songs.

Introduction

As he edges closer to his 30th anniversary as a professional musician, it's a well-trodden route for Richard Thompson. Keen to talk about the dismantling process he proudly undertook on his recent album, *Mirror Blue*, there is still the chill realisation that this, after all, is the man who wrote 'Meet On The Ledge' while still a teenager.

While he deftly froths the cappuccino, there is no escaping his role as the man responsible for some of the most haunting and durable songs the English rock'n'roll scene has ever produced. But then, 'rock'n'roll' is only the half of it. A large part of Thompson's enduring appeal is his ability to creatively span and straddle the parameters of popular music: he can cut you to the quick as he takes his '1952 Vincent Black Lightning' solo, fusing his tale of a Hell's Angel's death to a traditional ballad melody; then set your pulses racing with a big-band version of 'Tear Stained Letter', embracing some of the most angry and eloquent electric guitar you're ever likely to hear.

Then, just when you think you've got him bang to rights, just when you think that, like Van Morrison, Thompson has got into a bit of a groove, he'll hit you with something so breathtaking and audacious as 'From Galway To Graceland', and you'll be right back up there with him, as he takes you off on another sort of journey. You don't know where it's going to end, and keen to keep it fresh for himself, Thompson's not too sure either.

Over the years and down the days, Thompson has spun a web, weaving together traditional folk, jazz, cajun and rockabilly. But his has not been a quick, passport-stamped package tour around the world of music to fulfil an album quota. Thompson has lived and breathed music all his life, he has never had another career. Since he was a teenager, Richard Thompson has made a living from his own music.

Geographically he hasn't moved far from his north London roots. All of Richard Thompson's London residences are within bus rides of each other, from his birthplace off Ladbroke Grove, to Archway. From the flat he shared with Fairport's Simon Nicol and Ian Matthews to the Hampstead home he made with Linda during the early 70s, to the Muslim squat in Maida Vale. Thompson's present London home sits cosily between Finchley and Hampstead Heath. An unassuming residence, suburban and similar to the dozens of others which surround it, yet a stroll up the gentle hill and the whole of the Heath stretches out before you.

Hampstead Heath features prominently in the landscape of Richard's early memories. Thompson remembers with affection annual visits to the fair held on the Heath; Brian Wyvill has pointed out the tree on

Introduction

Hampstead Heath, with a branch they knew as 'The Ledge' when he and Richard were intrepid schoolboy tree-climbers; Thompson's composition, 'Jack Straw's Castle' (later retitled 'King of Bohemia') took its name from a pub which has stood on the Heath since the eighteenth century when as a coaching inn it was patronised by Dickens, Thackeray and Wilkie Collins. It was at the yearly fair on Hampstead Heath that Thompson recalls seeing motorcycle riders tackle the 'Wall of Death' . . .

Despite the distances travelled since then, it's still this familiar north London urban environment, with the escape of the Heath close at hand, where Richard seems to feel most at home. Or maybe, as he himself would have it, it simply 'saves you having to find a new Tesco's'.

For all the journeys he has made, all the roads and freeways travelled, Richard Thompson still scratches at his ankle, where the ball and chain of his first group chafes. The name of a house in north London and 'a general agreement on social behaviour etc by implicit consent of the majority'. Ladies and gentlemen, the greatest folk-rock band in the world . . .

It was, as ever, a closely packed Cropredy that blistering Saturday afternoon during August 1995. But Fairport's yearly reunion at the quiet Oxfordshire village unifies and divides fans in almost equal measure. Part of the audience, the ones right by the bar, swilling into the Wadworth's, couldn't give a 6X who's up there on stage, it could be Oasis in a blur.

The militant, diehard folkies want folk, or nothing at all. A quarter of a century after *Liege & Lief*, they have come to terms with bands utilising electricity onstage, but they're wary of any further developments.

Then there are visitors – earnest Germans, baffled Americans, marauding passing Celts. For them, Fairport are a venerable English rock institution, the very stuff of myth. The Americans particularly are bemused later that night by the riotous welcome accorded Joe Brown, one of the best first generation British rock'n'rollers. Brown's chirpy Cockney chappie persona, as lively offstage as it is on, prompts much scratching of heads, particularly when he delivers an authentically skiffling 'Midnight Special'.

More head scratching when Roy Wood brings on an all-girl backing band in the middle of Fairport's set, and delivers a storming Greatest Hits package ('Fire Brigade', 'Blackberry Way', 'California Man'). Some hadn't noticed, but Fairport Convention and 'folk' music long since ceased being married – now they are just good friends for the sake of the children.

Introduction

The blurring of the marriage lines had much to do with Richard Thompson. It was Thompson's songs, many written in collaboration with violinist Dave Swarbrick, which saw Fairport sever their links with the American-dominated 'underground' scene of the late 60s. While Sandy Denny's infusion and original bassist Ashley Hutchings' championing of traditional British folk, had first helped Fairport find its identity, it was Thompson and Swarbrick compositions like 'Crazy Man Michael', 'Doctor Of Physick' and 'Poor Will And The Jolly Hangman', which saw Fairport forge English folk-rock, almost singlehandedly inventing a whole new genre of popular music.

If the Wadworth's hadn't already done the trick, further blurring occurred midway through Fairport's set, when Thompson joined Roy Wood, and used his brass section for a stirring and resolutely upbeat 'I Want To See The Bright Lights Tonight', the title track of his second post-Fairport outing, and his first with then-wife Linda. Thompson rarely performs the song these days. One he had never performed, but was itching to try as soon as he knew he could get to play with Wood's brass section, was Marvin Gaye's 'I Heard It Through The Grapevine'. One of the magnificent Motown classics, which Berry Gordy's label seemed to produce with production-line efficiency during the 1960s. For all its maverick cross-fertilisation, and for all Thompson's own enthusiasm, Fairport Convention had never hitherto essayed Tamla Motown.

The evening concluded, as every Fairport reunion has done since its inception, with Thompson's anthemic 'Meet On The Ledge'. It's a song for which the composer has little real affection, but he is clearly in the minority. Everyone on the site joined in, singing the words which have come to mean so much to so many. A song which somehow seems to sum up the hopes and fears of all the years. Richard Thompson was still a teenager when he wrote the song.

Richard: 'There's a nostalgic aspect to [Cropredy] which I don't really care about, I don't need nostalgia in my life, unless it's trams or *Round the Horne*, that'll do me nicely ... I'm proud of Fairport, I always thought it was an extremely intelligent band that did absolutely the right thing. I'm very proud to be associated with them.

'Cropredy has a nostalgia element to it – that doesn't mean it's not great music, because sometimes it really is – but it can be a nostalgic event, it's certainly a sentimental event – and one wouldn't have it any other way, because people come back every year and they want to take part in the cycle. So it's moving, but in a different way. There's a kind of stillness that goes with really moving music. It's a very still place, it just grabs you.'

Introduction

'Meet On The Ledge' is a song of parting, a song of premonition and of eerie foreboding, inextricably linked with the death of Martin Lamble barely six months after its release. It has come to symbolise the bleaker side of Fairport. Sung unforgettably on record by Sandy Denny, its mournful lyrics seem to suggest the tragedy waiting around the corner not only for Fairport, but for all the youthful idealism of the 60s. Yet in its chorus there is finally hope and a belief that death is not the end:

Meet on the ledge, we're gonna meet on the ledge,
When the time is up, I'm gonna see all my friends.
Meet on the ledge, we're gonna meet on the ledge,
If you really mean it, it all comes round again.

For Fairport's legions of fans, it all comes round again in a field in Cropredy every August. Without fail, arms linked and lit by the moon, even the beeriest become momentarily sober as the baleful lyrics and poignant melody strike home one more time.

'Meet On The Ledge' offers a time for reflection, Cropredy a home to which you can return. It's pop music made popular myth; memories enshrined in the grooves of an old, pink-labelled Island single or any one of half-a-dozen Cropredy reunions, as the voices join together and strike up the chorus, until the final notes fade, and it's gone, for another year.

Any appreciation of what Richard Thompson is, has to begin with what he was, and the land he comes from.

Imagine a landscape, flat and barren. A blistering and cracked place by day, wind-whipped and lonely by night. As bare as the surface of the moon, it is an arid and featureless place. The only sound comes from the wind playing through the de-tuned telegraph wires, which stretch on poles, limitless, as far as the eye can see, reaching further than the imagination can stretch.

It is the haunted and desolate landscape of the Lone Star State, the wildlands of west Texas. A bleak and inhospitable tract made magic by the names, which read like a rosary. Dark and Catholic places – San Antonio, El Paso, Clovis, Lubbock . . . all edging towards the border of New Mexico.

Cruising along the eight-lane highways, a slab of raw-boned rockabilly punches from the radio and slices the night air with whoops and yells, as fresh as a lone coyote, baying somewhere in the blackness, in that place far away. The place beyond, far from where the car head-

Introduction

lamps reach. A lonely, solitary sort of place. Beyond reach, beyond reason ...

If Richard Thompson had been born somewhere on those desolate west Texas plains, it's a fair bet that by now, his name would be so much better known. If Thompson had cut his musical teeth in the bars of Amarillo or Austin, tribute albums from epicine young men and seraphic young women would occupy mall space.

Thompson is denied such legend, his formative years spent in the sprawling north London suburbs. Richard Thompson cut his musical teeth off the bustling Portobello Road and around the closely packed suburbs of Archway. He learned his craft in and around Totteridge and Whetstone. His musical apprenticeship was forged in a London still bearing the scars of the Blitz, twenty years before. Thompson began playing in the church halls of Golders Green and Barnet, not the smoky clubs of Clovis or Lubbock.

It's a mighty long way down rock'n'roll.

Part 1
Fairport

Chapter 1

TO BEGIN BEFORE THE BEGINNING.
Richard Thompson's mother spent all her early life in and around Notting Hill, west London, where she was born Joan Rawlins in 1920. Her mother was housekeeper to a Mr Calow at 19 Ladbroke Crescent. As Joan recalls: 'In those days, there were gates, it was a private road, and Mr Calow was taken to the City in a horse and carriage, it was so gracious ... My mother was there as housekeeper and was left the house, a Victorian house ... and everything in it. Richard has the table – a very nice table – that was left. Unfortunately, my father gambled, so jewellery, money, everything else went ... but we had a wonderful mother.

'I had to go to work when I was thirteen years old. I worked at Dorothy Perkins in Newman St, just off Oxford Street and I was there for many years.

'My husband John was a joiner in Scotland and when he was quite young he came down to London to join the police. One night, I was with a friend of mine and we thought we'd go to the local dance and I was sitting there with this friend when a man came over – which of course was John – and danced with me, and from that moment, it was like magic. So he saw me onto the bus and the bus was moving away and he said "Oh where do you work" and I yelled out "Dorothy Perkins head office" and I didn't know if he'd heard, but obviously he did, and the next day the phone rang in my lunch hour and that's how our romance began. And we had a wonderful, very romantic, a real love affair.'

Richard: 'My dad was one of those people from the lowlands of Scotland, I think they had a recruiting drive up there. John Kirkpatrick's dad was exactly the same, he was from the Borders and he got recruited into the Met. In the late 30s I think they decided that that was a good place to get people, probably there wasn't much in the way of opportunities in the Lowlands, so it was a chance to nip off to the big

Richard Thompson

city ... My dad apprenticed as a joiner up there, then came down and joined the Met. He was in uniform for a bit, then he was in the army during the war.'

Joan: 'We married in 1943 when I was twenty-three, he was just a year and a bit older than me. We had a very simple wedding, people rallied round, you know, and got food and made a cake. Things were difficult in those days. The honeymoon was very brief. We went down to Midhurst in Sussex and I've got the receipt for the hotel, which was ridiculous when you look back – shillings I think. Just a couple of days leave, that was all he had, and then he went back to Canterbury.

'John, of course, was in the army all this time – he was a sergeant instructor in Canterbury and then, being a policeman, he went into the special branch in the army. He had many commendations. He was very brave always, very, very brave. He ended up in the British army of the Rhine in Germany. Then he came home and we had a second honeymoon. I didn't want an only child, so of course Richard was conceived. We were somewhere up North, we were staying with friends of my sister. I think we stayed at the Bull, anyway we had a little holiday up there and the following April, Richard was born.'

Richard: 'Uh ... I can't remember if I was born at home. Or in hospital ... Probably at St Mary's ... Or I think it might have been at home ...' Joan smiles fondly, familiar with her son's vagueness: 'He was born at home, at Ladbroke Crescent, Notting Hill.'

Richard John Thompson was born on 3 April 1949. The only son of John and Joan Thompson who already had a daughter, Pamela known to everyone as Perri.

Joan: 'He was a most beautiful baby. I remember when he was first born, the doctor held him up and said "What a wonderful head", which I didn't think anything of, I just thought he was a lovely looking baby. His sister looked as though she'd been squashed, my father said "you look as though you sat on her". But Richard was a beautiful baby, a handsome little boy.'

Richard's musical genes seem chiefly to have come through his father's side. Three of John's uncles (Richard's great uncles) Allan, Harold and Jim played in a dance band called the Arcadians, between 1928 and 1935. In a *Folk Roots* feature from 1986, A. C. Thompson provided an exhaustive history of the Arcadians.

The group played at dances in and around Dumfries. Half their engagements consisting of waltzes, foxtrots and charlestons, played to popular tunes of the time, while the other half were country and square dances. Richard's great-grandfather – father of the three Arcadians –

one John Templeton Thompson, did much to fuel the myth of Scots parsimony. He ordered an expensive brass name-plate for his front door and when it was delivered with the name misspelt, canny John Templeton altered the spelling of the family name to match, rather than waste the plate. Younger offspring born post-plate, including Arcadian drummer Jim, were christened 'Thomson' without a 'p'.

Richard: 'Yes it's a sort of family tradition – I never heard them play – they played around the thirties – they were just a jobbing Borders dance band who had to play everything: the dance music – the reels and the jigs – and they had to play swing as well – they had a violin and a saxophone and a piano. It sounds like it would have been great fun.'

Joan recalls another musician in her husband's family: 'John had a cousin, who was a genius on the piano, he could play anything, any tune, and he never read a note of music ... And when I was courting, my husband was playing guitar in a police band – so Richard's father actually played the guitar, nothing brilliant, but enough to get a tune out.'

Richard's mother is very fond of music: 'I love music – I'm always playing music. I don't play any instrument. I would have loved to learn piano as a child. My mother was left a German framed piano, which she had to sell and I used to look at pianos and think I'd have given anything if I could play.'

The London into which Richard was born four years after the end of the Second World War, was pockmarked and scarred, although Richard himself only remembers the fun of playing on bomb-sites: 'War seemed kind of fun, coming after it anyway, I don't know what it was like being in it, that was probably fun if you were a kid as well, being bombed was probably alright if you were a kid, if you're five years old and you don't know what death really means. So that was all great, playing war was a good thing, things like guns had absolutely no reality because you never ever saw a real one. It was just complete fantasy.'

In the three months between the surrender of Nazi Germany in May 1945, and the bombs which razed Hiroshima and Nagasaki, Prime Minister Winston Churchill, the architect of victory, had been booted out of 10 Downing Street. The first Labour government since 1931 had been elected on a landslide of servicemen's votes. The soldiers were determined that the Conservatives who had led them into war would not do so again. Clement Attlee's brief was to lay the foundations for the new Jerusalem.

The Labour government was determined not to repeat the mistakes of 1918 when dazed troops, returning from the charnel-house of the

Richard Thompson

Great War, were told that they were coming back to a 'land fit for heroes'. The truth was more prosaic. It proved to be a land fit only for forgotten men, dole queues and the Means Test. Attlee, Labour's notoriously taciturn leader commented on the dismissal of Churchill and the wind of change which came in the immediate, heady aftermath of victory: 'I think the general feeling was that they wanted a new start. We were looking towards the future. The Tories were looking towards the past.'

In the introduction to his compelling overview of post-war Britain, *Never Again*, Peter Hennessy captures the feeling which was abroad during the first years of that troubled post-war Labour government: 'Never again would there be war; never again would the British people be housed in slums, living off a meagre diet thanks to low wages or no wages at all; never again would natural abilities remain dormant in the absence of educational stimulus.' Years later Richard Thompson would use the same title for one of his songs.

Swingeing social changes would form a backdrop to the lives of Richard Thompson and his contemporaries in the post-war 'baby boom'. That first Labour government inaugurated the landmark 1944 Education Act and created Britain's proudest peacetime achievement, the National Health Service. But victory in 1945 had not brought the expected fruits and the winter of 1946–47 was one of the worst ever. Rationing was still strictly enforced and queueing remained the national pastime. It was not until July 1954, nine years after the end of the war, that rationing was finally abolished. Richard's father John returned late from his wartime service with the Royal East Kent Regiment ('The Buffs'), and went back into the Metropolitan Police.

Richard: 'He went into the CID, he did various bits of it ... they move you around a lot to stop you becoming corrupt. So he did his bit on the Murder Squad and the Vice Squad and the Flying Squad and the various regional crime squads. Fabian of the Yard stuff, great old Wolseys screeching to a halt with proper bells on front. But it was a world I didn't see. My dad worked ridiculously long hours – sixteen hours a day – and I never saw him.'

Richard's early childhood was spent in the house in Ladbroke Crescent where he had been born and this is the setting for his earliest memories: 'It was a bit run down, I think it had a bomb in the street during the war. What I remember was that all the paint was peeling on both sides of the road, but I used to get pushed in the pram down to Wormwood Scrubs for a good time. I remember Portobello Market quite well as a kid, going down there with my mum or going to Cullens, you remember Cullens when they used to look after you, like a real shop, you'd go in and you'd sit down and somebody would serve you.

'I've a strong memory of actually being inside a pram and I've got one of looking up at the ducks, the row of ducks. I've got another memory of walking down Ladbroke Crescent with reins on, so I guess I must have been a toddler, so that must have been very early.'

The coronation of Queen Elizabeth II in 1953 was a welcome opportunity for the bruised and battered nation to rejoice. The demand for television sets was enormous, everyone wanted to witness the crowning of the glamorous young queen, in all its heraldic pageantry. The centuries-old ceremony made quite a different impression on the four-year-old Richard: 'I remember the Coronation street party and I remember the Coronation as well in fact. I was there. I remember as the Queen went past, I remember seeing the Queen in her coach, and at that moment I was seized by a bowel movement, and so I said I've got to go to the toilet, so I sort of defecated in the direction of the Queen as she went past, which has been held against me ever since.'

Joan: 'He was very ill when he was five. He started school, which unfortunately was a bit rough and he got dysentery straight away. He was so desperately ill he almost died. And that's when he started to stutter and the doctor thought it was the shock of the illness that brought it on. But he was always very, very intelligent as a child, even as a very young child.'

Richard: 'I think I was was a very shy child, really shy and really nervous, so I didn't talk very much I don't think. And when I did I stuttered, all the way from about the age of five. I'm not sure how you start stuttering, I think it's a kind of a nervous thing that isn't necessarily triggered by anything in particular. But it gives you a kind of social impediment which reinforces whatever was there in the first place. I still have a problem with it, especially on the telephone. Sometimes doing telephone interviews I just seize up.'

Perri (Richard's sister): 'I think all of that – the speech impediment and the shyness – came from the home environment, because it was a time when you were not encouraged to express yourself. Nowadays everyone is talking about psychology and expressing yourself and terrible teenagers, but it was all new then. There was definitely a very secure but bland atmosphere. Everything we were doing was so different to our parents and what our parents believed in.'

When Richard was around seven years old, the Thompson family moved to Dartmouth Park Hill, between Tufnell Park and Archway in north London. It was an area which had enjoyed its heyday in the

Richard Thompson

Victorian era, but by the 1890s, social reformer Charles Booth was already concerned that 'the poor and the rough will press in ... from all sides'.

Richard: 'We moved into a block of flats specifically for police families, which was a strange place to live. It was all police families, but you wouldn't have known it by the kids, who were generally slightly more lawless and irresponsible than normal kids. It was nice being in a block of flats actually, I think for kids they're rather fun, because you have a large pool of children and it was a big social thing. It was about five or six storeys high with a communal garden, footballs through the windows, the usual stuff.'

Richard Thompson grew up the only son of a policeman in the austere post-war Great Britain of the 1950s. Prior to rock'n'roll and James Dean, the phrase 'Generation Gap' hadn't been heard in the land. If it had, it would have echoed around the Thompson household in Dartmouth Park Hill.

Joan: 'Well he had a very strict father – I mean normally, in a family, you'd say "Oh here's daddy" – whereas he was a dour Scot and if everything wasn't perfect – it was difficult. But he had the other side – a very clever man – wonderful brain but he had a very gruff manner.'

It was Perri who bore the brunt of any parental disapproval. Her individuality and pursuit of her own life helped pave the way for Richard's subsequent rebellion, although she admits that her strength of character didn't help young Richard's painful lack of confidence: 'He was quiet and shy ... and I think this sister thing was quite strong – the extrovert sister who dominates the house and brother retreats ...

'He really was very quiet, he and I used to play together very happily, we played great games, making trains out of kitchen chairs, we had no problems at all – we were very good at inventing games and that kind of thing. But I was always the extrovert – I was the show-off, always leaping around the room with Fred Astaire records on, practising jiving and all that kind of thing and to my younger brother – he must have been taking it all in.'

Richard: 'Perri was more outgoing and she had more head-on collisions with my dad who was a Presbyterian Scot, a Scottish policeman, heaven help us all – and there was a kind of moral backdrop to life that you had to kick at and rebel against – so my sister was probably the big rebel. I think by the time my parents got to me they were just after an easier life, so I got a bit more leeway. My sister was definitely a seriously independently minded, headstrong, very good-looking teen-aged girl who wanted to do what she wanted to do.'

Fairport

Perri: 'A lot of the books around the house were poetry and literature – prizes father had won. He was very bright, obviously, and could have been an academic. He was very good at painting – quite an artistic, creative man, but coming from a small Scottish town there was no room for an artistic man. So he was channelled into – well of course the war – and then into London and joining the police. He was a very distant authoritarian figure – he suddenly had these two children who were quite creative and we were both probably quite incomprehensible to him. Richard was a creative son rather than a son who wanted to do a sort of Action Man thing.'

Despite his long days spent at Scotland Yard, John Thompson (who died in September 1992 in Hythe) retained a fondness for music all his life. He was an enthusiastic amateur guitarist and a keen listener to music on the family's radiogram. Richard remembers his father had 'some reasonable jazz records – Django Reinhardt, Fats Waller, Les Paul, Duke Ellington, Louis Armstrong . . . as well as the dross – a lot of Perry Como, Pearl Carr and Teddy Johnson, Billy Cotton Band Show.'

The first record Richard remembers owning was the children's favourite 'Four-Legged Friend' by the singing cowboy, Roy Rogers. He also remembers that later on, his sister Perri was a close friend of Mandy Miller, who sang 'Nellie The Elephant' ('one of the great children's records ever,' affirms her brother).

Perri: 'We didn't have a piano – there wasn't music going on all the time – there was no encouragement to learn instruments. The radio was the big thing in our house. The influence coming into the house was that of my boyfriends because absolutely everybody had a guitar – a Spanish-type guitar at that stage. Father thought we were all a bunch of layabouts.'

During the war years radio had been the great uniter, morale booster and provider of information; and it kept this central place in homes of all kinds throughout Britain for at least a decade afterwards. Radio entertainment catered for the whole family. The children were enchanted by 'Uncle Mac' and his Children's Favourites. They listened, baffled but intrigued, to Spike Milligan's *Goon Show*. And at weekends, the whole family gathered round to listen to the BBC's lunchtime comedies – *Round the Horne*, *The Navy Lark*, *The Clitheroe Kid*.

Like many of his generation, Richard's memories are of radio favourites, not television. When the Thompson family finally obtained their first black and white television, Richard's clearest memory was the influence of his dad's job: 'We had to watch all the police programmes –

Richard Thompson

Highway Patrol, Dixon of Dock Green – it was rubbish, but the American stuff was definitely more glamorous and pacy – in the great Edward G. Robinson tradition of hard-nosed detectives.'

There was only one television channel prior to 1955, and BBC radio would only rarely play the brash and invigorating new American rock'n'roll. To get to hear it, you either had to splash out your precious pounds, shillings and pence on cumbersome old 78 rpm discs, or sit, ear pressed to the radiogram, and through the crackle and static, pick out the new music on Radio Luxembourg.

Along with all his contemporaries reared on rock'n'roll, Richard never missed the BBC Light Programme's Sunday evening hit parade round-up, *Pick of the Pops*, hosted by Alan ('not 'arf!') Freeman. Then, inevitably as night followed day, *Sing Something Simple* took over the airwaves, and the weekend was truly over.

Richard: 'Sundays used to be torture in our house – from about four o'clock it was the Sunday teatime of the soul – just incredible depression. It was dark, it was always winter, always raining. Eventually, when we became teenagers, we found ways around it, ways to avoid it.'

Very occasionally, the stern mask of 'Auntie' BBC might slip and there was a perception that, very slowly, things were beginning to change.

Richard: 'There was also Peter Clayton's and Humph's jazz programmes on the radio. I'd stay up and listen under the covers in the Radio Luxembourg tradition.'

Richard's earliest rock'n'roll memories didn't come courtesy of the radio, but from his sister's record collection, the records Perri herself bought, or those she borrowed from boyfriends, and played endlessly 'on the old radiogram'.

Richard: 'Basically, a lot of Buddy Holly, and eventually I think, due to a couple of her boyfriends who were fairly musical, she had the first Dylan album and a Lightning Hopkins record very early on, and Sonny [Terry] and Brownie [McGhee] stuff – which was nice.'

Before he became enchanted by those long-playing folk and blues records, Richard was captivated by the remote, but intensely enticing, American rock'n'roll music, which was a rare, but welcome, visitor on the English airwaves.

Richard: 'I remember rock'n'roll being like something really illegal. I get that feeling now, if I go and play snooker – there's a snooker club I go to in Kentish Town. I think: this is so good, it must be illegal. There must be something wrong with it, I'm having such a good time. It was like that, you'd hear it on the radio in between Pearl Carr and Teddy

Johnson and Dennis Lotis and think wow – unbelievable, this is fantastic. Why can't it all be like this. I remember having my ear to my sister's bedroom hearing "Great Balls Of Fire" – Jerry Lee, you know – wonderful.'

Perri: 'In a way, the kind of music that was around at the time for us was so different. The main thing about our generation was that we just wanted to be totally different to our parents. And of course, this new music that came along from those early years was, I suppose, originally coming out of America with Elvis and stuff and it was just very different.'

Richard: 'She certainly was doing something when rock'n'roll hit – I think she was very young – about eleven or twelve – but she had Elvis all over her school pencil box as people did. She then became a fairly serious beatnik, that was her next big phase, she was influenced by French cinema and she smoked a lot of those funny smelling French cigarettes and dressed in a lot of black with white lipstick.

'I was six years old and I couldn't say what I was really into. Life happened to you at that age – you did what you were told – went to school – and went through the processes, you know. Musical trends and fashion trends aren't necessarily as interesting as train spotting or *Champion the Wonder Horse* on TV or something or a game of cricket out back with the lads.'

The impact of rock'n'roll was all the more marked in Britain. Ten years after the end of the war, from which Great Britain had emerged victorious, the nation showed few obvious benefits. There was a greyness, a drabness in the air. There wasn't the money to rebuild the wasteland. Bankrupted by the war, Britain could only afford to import the necessities, luxuries would have to wait. 'Austerity' was the byword.

Richard: 'I remember it as being kind of grey – but I always remember the fifties as being a great time. It had the right smells, the smells of steam trains, the smell of buses and shops. There was a conformity to dress. I think British people, male and female, dressed older in those days. If you look at a *Vogue* from the late 40s and early 50s, women are dressed in a pretty matronly way and the men are dressed in hats and with pipes, almost like granddads already. It's an old way of dressing which has pretty much been overthrown. Twenty- and thirty-year-olds dress a lot younger these days. Everyone conformed to a certain look.

'Post-war England was kind of depressed, I'm not sure that Europe ever recovered from World War I, a kind of pessimism set in after the First World War and it's still that way in a sense, still quite pessimistic

Richard Thompson

– if you go to America everything is optimistic and strident and outgoing. In America there was a new culture happening, there was a lot of wealth after the war. America came out of World War II exactly twice as wealthy as it went in, selling lots of tanks to people. America went in during a depression and came out on an incredible boom, so that 50s' culture was just wealth and trying out new ideas without anyone saying you couldn't do it.'

Rock'n'roll arrived in Great Britain in October 1955, when Bill Haley and the Comets broke through with 'Rock Around The Clock'. Elvis Presley's first UK hit was 'Heartbreak Hotel' in May 1956, and suddenly, there seemed more to life for British teenagers than *Dixon of Dock Green*.

Richard: 'I remember we used to go to Scotland every year for our holidays up to my dad's folks – we had a little hut at the seaside and I remember the juke box from the cafe in Dumfries, down the road. You could lean out of the bedroom window and you could hear the music coming across – just a couple of streets away – hearing Buddy Holly drifting across, it was just fantastic, it sounded so unbelievably good.

'The other great place to hear it was the fair – I suppose Hampstead Fair which I would have gone to since I was about four or five, hearing them play rock'n'roll loud on the dodgems – fantastic. I still feel that way about vintage rock'n'roll – it still has that thing that kind of makes me want to slash cinema seats and wear Edwardian clothes.'

The American rock'n'rollers made an immediate impact on all the young dudes, not only Richard Thompson, but also John Lennon, Paul McCartney, Keith Richards. In the stark and austere post-war Britain of the mid-50s, Elvis and that first generation of American rock'n'rollers didn't just seem to come from another country, they looked and sounded like they came from another world.

Britain's home-grown rock idols were, at best, second-best. Marty Wilde and Tommy Steele couldn't hold a candle to Eddie Cochran and Gene Vincent. Only Lonnie Donegan, the grinning monarch of the skiffle boom, had any real influence. It was Donegan's home-grown, three-chord skiffle which inspired a generation to pick up a guitar, or nail together a tea-chest bass and make their own music. Long before he ever picked up a guitar, the shy and withdrawn young Richard was busy pretending with 'a tennis racquet, so there was obviously some need to perform . . . if only in front of the mirror'.

Perri: 'My father would have loved to have had his own big band – he was a great music fan and occasionally played big band music and Django Reinhardt and he also had a great sense of humour which I think

Richard has inherited – there was a lot of humour in our household from Hancock and the Goons – all those early radio things because we always had the radio on at home – and father had a good sense of humour, although he was strict and everything, he had a good sense of humour.

'For Richard it must have been all brewing there – it's like any creative person – you've got to get your right structure to express yourself in, I think it's the same for a musician, you've got to get the right structure and the right things fall into place. At home all of that was probably stewing around and it was all completely in there but it had no voice. Because he really never said a word at home.

'We bought "Rock Around the Clock" with 2s 6d that we were given by my great aunt Laura. It was on a 78, so Richard would only have been about ten or something, so that would have been the first real record to come into the house. I suppose it was like a shaft of light coming from the outside world that we were both really waiting to get out into.'

Prior to becoming a prisoner of rock'n'roll, Richard still retained an interest in the chief hobby from his schooldays. Before he ever picked up a guitar, Richard revelled in railway trains. Today, any reference to a 'train spotter' is inherently pejorative, but then back in the 1950s, trains were worth getting hot under the collar about. Great big loud steaming beasts, which ate up the miles between London and the North, spewing smoke, and rattling along the tracks, like dragons freed from their caves.

Joan: 'He had two friends and David, Malcolm and Richard were three absolute devotees to trains. Malcolm had his room with trains running all the way round it, wonderful, absolutely wonderful, and they'd spend an awful lot of time there. And then, of course, when they were older, off they would all go train spotting. That was really his biggest hobby.'

Richard: 'I was a train spotter, a serious anorak, writing down train numbers. I just like railways. I still like railways, I'd like to run British Rail. There's something rather mathematical about them that I like. I used to love steam trains because they were kind of working antiques, some of them were so incredibly old, 1860 or something, and still chugging around. I'd always been a bit of a history buff, so I liked the historical aspect of railways as well. The fact that this ancient stuff was still rolling around, and you could get in this carriage . . . The smell, and the personality of railways was wonderful, these fire-breathing things that were alive . . .' But sometime during 1959, the trains took a back seat:

Richard Thompson

Joan: 'I remember one day I opened the front door and Richard was in his bedroom, I'd only been next door, and I thought he's playing my favourite record – and of course it was Richard. I couldn't believe it. And I said "Good heavens, I thought you were the record". He said: "I can't play all of it, you know", but he was doing very, very well – it was really great.'

Richard: 'I always remember a guitar around the house. Dad had a big old jazz thing – which in the early days I didn't get to see much because it was locked away from the kids. At some point, I think when I was ten, he brought home a Spanish guitar which he'd been given – he had an old army pal at one of the music shops in Denmark Street and they were throwing this guitar away and my dad said, "Oh, it's got a little crack in it, I'll take it home and fix it". So he glued it up and that was really my first guitar.'

Chapter 2

RICHARD: 'I just picked it up and kept picking it up, that was all it was and I'm indebted to a couple of my sister's boyfriends – you know, when they were around the house waiting to pick her up – my sister was notoriously slow at being ready for anything – she'd be two hours getting ready to go out, so I'd get a guitar lesson.'

Richard Roberts-Miller attended Westminster City School. He had a schoolfriend who lived in Camden Town, and who went out with Richard's sister Perri. It was Roberts-Miller who first taught the young Richard to play the guitar. He had acquired his technique on a £3.00 guitar his mother brought back from Spain in 1959 and from a source familiar to all British would-be Hank B. Marvins: Bert Weedon's *Play in a Day* tutor. Richard Roberts-Miller would later be immortalised as 'Big Muldoon' on the sleeve of Thompson's 1972 debut solo album.

Muldoon: 'I lent him the guitar and on a piece of ruled school paper, drew D-A-D, the basic Buddy Holly chords, and he mastered those almost instantly. He asked me if I knew any more, and I didn't, so that was my actual influence on his guitar playing – one weekend and he was ahead of me.'

Richard Roberts-Miller began going out with Perri Thompson, and together, they helped with the young Richard's musical apprenticeship.

Muldoon: 'It was a great time to be around London, 1958–1962. There was so much going on, and every year just seemed better than the year before ... Eel Pie Island, 100 Club, the Marquee, the Troubadour ... All the great musicians were between the West End and Richmond. It was like a mini renaissance. When I discovered you could borrow records from my local library, well ... Sonny Terry and Brownie McGhee, Lightning Hopkins ... Snooks Eaglin I discovered that way, and I introduced Richard to Snooks Eaglin that way. We were talking about it the other day, and he said he remembered me bringing that record round one day in 1963.

Richard Thompson

'When the first Bob Dylan album came out, I was at university, in this chap's digs, and he said you *have* to listen to this. Perri and I saw him in 1964, just amazing, and we were sitting there, and there were the Beatles in a box behind us. The entire London music scene was there.'

Richard's first 'guitar hero' was James Burton. Ten years older than Thompson, Burton first came to fame as an 18-year-old on Dale Hawkins' 1957 'Suzie Q'. Though it was his six-year spell with Ricky Nelson which made Burton the idol of a whole generation of British guitarists.

Burton's distinctive solos which enlivened saccharine Nelson material, can be heard to great effect on the hits 'Hello Mary Lou', 'Never Be Anyone Else', 'It's Late' and 'Believe What You Say'. Quitting Nelson in 1964, Burton went onto the session circuit, before emerging in Elvis Presley's touring band in 1969. Since then, Burton's name and guitar have made memorable contributions to albums by Gram Parsons, Emmylou Harris and Elvis Costello.

Richard: 'I don't know James Burton that well, but I've met him a few times and he came to dinner at my house once and I left a guitar strategically placed – and James is a real show-off and eventually he picked up the guitar and played all these licks off all the Rick Nelson records. He went through everything. He has all these fantastic stories about hanging out with Rick Nelson, Gene Vincent and Eddie Cochran – every Sunday they'd all get their Harleys out and ride along Mulholland Drive and the mountain roads outside Los Angeles.'

Richard found something he could intuitively grasp about the guitar. A dreamy, shy child, he soon mastered the fingerings and chords, and persevered with his practice. Not long after Muldoon had drawn the Buddy Holly chords on lined paper for the young Richard, his pupil sensed there was more to be gained from the instrument.

Richard: 'When I was around twelve I did a year or two of classical guitar, which was great for a lot of things. It really helped you develop. There were three of us who used to hang round a lot, Malcolm Fuller, David Roberts and myself, we were chums, grew up together, from about the age of five until fifteen or sixteen. Malcolm could play the guitar as well, and his mum decided we should get lessons.

'She found us a teacher, an interesting guy, Pete somebody, who lived in a squat, which was really exciting. He lived in the basement of a condemned building on the end of a terrace on Caledonian Road. Wow! He used to have girlfriends up there, there used to be slightly risqué girlie magazines around and strange flatmates, it was all rather bohemian. We used to go on the bus after school on Tuesday nights with our little guitars. We took lessons until – the word was – he got sent to prison for something, bypassing the gas meter or something ridiculous.'

The transition from being a dreamy, if efficient, strummer in front of his bedroom mirror, to a real convert came when Richard acquired his first electric guitar.

Richard: 'Through my dad's old Army pals again, I got an electric guitar when I was eleven or twelve, a Hofner V3 and an amp for a tenner. You could sound more like the record with an electric, strings like railway lines. The nylon-strung guitar was not the ideal rock, or folk instrument, really. Every Saturday morning from when I was about twelve I'd go down to the music shops on Charing Cross Road and just ogle the gear. If you could get to try something out, great, but I just used to go and look for years.

'Around that time I started getting my *Melody Maker* religiously every week. It was a great education. People like Max Jones performed a great public service, they had a three-page jazz spread, a folk page. Because you bought it, you might as well read it, get your money's worth. You'd end up reading the whole thing, you'd find out who Chu Berry was.

'Like a lot of kids I'd go and listen to records in those old listening booths – "No, it's not quite what I was expecting" – after you've listened to a whole side of an album. Records were expensive.'

Taking his train-spotting chums Malcolm Fuller and David Roberts along with him, Richard dipped his toe in the shallow waters of schoolboy pre-Beatle pop.

Richard: 'I was in an instrumental group doing Shadows and Duane Eddy stuff when I was about eleven. Myself and my friend Malcolm, and his schoolfriends – he went to St Aloysius Catholic School up on Highgate Hill – so it was his school chums, and me. We rehearsed every Sunday for a year, I think we played at the St Aloysius school dance as the interval band, and I think that broke us! I think we were so bad that we never played again. It was the classic thing of rehearsing for an hour, then spending three hours trying to think of a name.'

In England at the time, the eleven-plus examination decided your child's schooling future. A pass was a ticket to grammar school and the possibility of a university education.

Joan: 'When he got to the eleven-plus, the teacher called me in and said "I'm delighted to tell you that your son had the top marks in the whole school and he can go to any school he likes" and she said his

Richard Thompson

English was so interesting. She said whenever she was handed the books, she always picked Richard's out first because he had a way of the words flowing. Then of course, he chose the best school, which was William Ellis.

'I was so thrilled. Because he had been so ill, I thought she was going to tell me he was bottom of the class, instead of which, he had the highest marks in the whole school.'

William Ellis School has over the years made quite a contribution to rock'n'roll – record producer and co-writer of 'Shipbuilding' Clive Langer attended the school, as did Sex Pistols' director Julien Temple, and later on, Mark Bedford of Madness. And it was where Richard Thompson spent his formative teenage years, but although recognised as one of north London's leading schools, Richard rather drifted through William Ellis.

Richard: 'English was always my best subject. I really liked poetry. There were always a lot of books at home, they might have been my granddad's books, the whole of Walter Scott, Burns, Shelley. And comics, I loved *The Eagle, War Picture Library* – "Ach, you Englanders are too good for us!" '

Richard's mother thinks that he inherited his love of reading from his father: 'My husband was always an avid reader and was very interested in history – we had all the historical books – wonderful books we had, and Richard read every single book in the house, he just loved reading ... and yes he used to write songs. He was a bit of a loner.'

Richard: 'I was a serious, serious dreamer. I still am. But I used to be unbelievable – totally out of the window and gone – just a complete fantasy world. The world of imagination should get kicked out of you when you're three years old but it seemed to stay with me a little longer – until I was twenty-five! I had a really great ability to not pay attention to things. I don't think I lack concentration because I can concentrate very well on ... dreaming. Nebulous I think would be the state I found myself in, and confused as well. I often get confused about things or I just grasp things from the wrong end.'

While Richard was drifting through his early schooldays, sister Perri had moved out of the family home and into the peripatetic world of flat sharing.

Richard: 'My sister went from her beatnik phase into a kind of post-beatnik Bardot thing, skiffle, she did all that, and then trad jazz. The Trad Boom was a big thing. I remember her being very into that. Kenny Ball records next to Sidney Bechet. She was at Hornsey Art College and the Kinks were the local band. She had the first Dylan album, I remember seeing Peter, Paul and Mary on *Sunday Night at the London Palladium*. I must be the only man who can't remember where he was when Kennedy was shot. But I remember being in line for school dinners during the Cuban Missile Crisis.'

Muldoon: 'He had this group at school, all of whom called themselves "Muldoon", which wasn't very helpful, because when you called "Muldoon", three people looked round. My name's Richard, his name's Richard, so that wasn't very helpful either. So I became "Big Muldoon", he became "Little Muldoon" and this third chap, Malcolm I think, was just "Muldoon" ... Years later I was working on market research for Times Newspapers, and Richard was going to dedicate a track ("Shaky Nancy") to me with my real name, but being a bit of a coward I thought it might jeopardise my career, so I asked to be remembered as "Big Muldoon".'

Today Richard's London home is near the Finchley Road. Featured prominently in the goings-on of his beloved *Goon Show*, Finchley was home to both Spike Milligan and Peter Sellers while they were recording the seminal show during the 50s, and featured much in the language of Goon-ography, particularly from the mouth of the tiny, querulous Bluebottle.

Thompson is convinced that the ubiquitous 'Muldoon' nickname from his adolescence originated from *The Goon Show*. I can exclusively reveal: he is wrong. Bill Horsman, Chairman of The Goon Show Preservation Society wrote to tell me: 'I can remember "Spotty Muldoon" but he was most certainly not a Goon character. So there you are folks ...'

The only Muldoon featured in classic British comedy is the character created by Peter Cook for the TV series *Not Only ... But Also* in the mid-60s. Cook's 'The Ballad of Spotty Muldoon' was a 1965 hit single for the late comic genius, but this would be too late to explain Thompson's nickname of the early 60s.

Just as he was settling into his fourth year at William Ellis, Richard was inspired by the Beatles to try and do something with his obvious abilities on the guitar, which he still practised assiduously.

Richard: 'Eddie Cochran was dead, Buddy Holly was dead, Gene Vincent was crippled, they'd all gone. And it was only the "Bobbys" left – Bobby Vee, Bobby Rydell. It was all the bland stuff left. The industry had found a way to make it marketable, predictable, profitwise. It was pretty bland until the Mop Tops came along in, what, 1963.'

Perri: 'I was at Hornsey and I booked the Rolling Stones for our

Richard Thompson

college dance for fifty pounds – a good bargain – so it was just, absolutely at the beginning of everything that time.'

It was while still attending William Ellis School that Richard made his first real efforts at forming a group with a life beyond the school hall.

Richard: 'Hugh Cornwell (ex-Strangler) and I were pals at William Ellis. He and I used to jam together . . . then we looked around for other recruits. Nick Jones came from a whole other world, the son of *Melody Maker*'s wonderful Max Jones. Nick was urbane and sophisticated; Hugh and I were a couple of angular, awkward, nerdish young lads.

'So when Nick joined us he said "we need some material, I'll go through my demos", 'cos Max used to get all the stuff on pre-release demos in those days. So that's where we found "Jack Of Diamonds" by Ben Carruthers and the Deep, funny Kiki Dee B-sides. We got all this weird material that nobody else had. Nick was just one of those people who looked very cool behind a drum kit, and played really well until it came to a drum fill, in which case, the time would disappear. It was fun for a while.'

Talking to Peter Hogan in an early interview for this book, Hugh Cornwell remembered: 'While I was there, Richard Thompson taught me how to play bass. I used to play bass in this group he had. We were in the fourth and fifth form. We used to play at all the Hornsey College of Art dances, because Richard's sister was the Social Sec. Richard was a marvellous guitar player, and we'd play blues from his collection. We were doing "Smokestack Lightning", Chuck Berry songs, old rhythm and blues really. Nothing new. We didn't write any songs then. When Nick left school – I wanted to do my A-levels, and Richard wanted to carry on, so he left and made Fairport up.'

Going back 30 years, everyone's memories of those school days are vague. Hugh Cornwell thought their trio was called the Germs, while other schoolfriends remember Richard passing through William Ellis outfits named the Rotations and Emil and the Detectives. Perri recalls Richard's first group as A Rubber Band. Whatever the names, it's certain that they were beginning to play further afield.

Joan: 'Yes, they used to go off, I think, and play all over the place – and I didn't know anything about it – I think he used to creep out at night, which he only told me recently. We had no idea.'

Richard: 'My parents had given up on discipline at some point, I was always getting back from darkest Soho two hours later than I said I would. But they were asleep and didn't seem to worry as much as they did about having a daughter out, so I got away with things.'

Fairport

It was while he was still attending William Ellis that Richard began writing songs in the style of Bob Dylan and Phil Ochs. To the author's immense relief, time has erased that juvenilia: 'It was real dross, all drivel really, I'm happy to say I can't remember titles, I think sometimes they didn't even get that far.' A schoolfriend however does recall Richard's note-perfect rendering of Dylan's 'Mr Tambourine Man' as 'Mr Margarine Man'.

It was *probably* with Hugh Cornwell and Nick Jones that Richard first ventured out 'seriously' onstage. Nobody concerned is absolutely certain, but it seems likely to have been sometime during 1965, when Richard was sixteen.

Muldoon: 'I remember there was a party, Perri's birthday party, she was at Hornsey College by then, and Richard's band played, I can't remember what they were called, pre-Fairport ... I was most impressed. He had the range you had to acquire ... He did "Heatwave", a real Motown number, and this was young Richard, and here he was, bashing this stuff out really well.

'Richard's taste in music was always eclectic. Going back to his dad, his Scottish background, Jimmy Shand, bagpipe music – plus the jazz, and the really well arranged big band stuff. Plus this huge influx of pop. Richard's father could be intimidating, but musically, he had fairly broad tastes. I'd be sitting there listening to Buddy Holly, waiting for Perri, and Richard's dad would say "What are you listening to that rubbish for? You should be listening to Django."

'But then Richard started getting into stuff that I really hadn't looked at, like the Motown stuff. He just went on and on, looking at everything. With Fairport, you could see this great chunk of folk music had got welded into early rock, a cleaned-up R&B mixture. I used to annoy him, on "Meet On The Ledge", I'd say, "Oh that bit sounds like Duane Eddy, that big deep, bent note on the bottom string." You can hear those early influences in Fairport, but after that, his stuff seems to be completely original, to have gone off on his own. Not just musically, but the topics, which are fascinating. He seems to have the visual images which the music conjures up.'

Perri: 'The earliest time I remember Richard playing – was I think when father got him booked at some funny pub or something in north London – Tufnell Park or somewhere like that and father was always furious because Richard would never play what everyone wanted to hear. Father thought he should change his style and he should play good old dance numbers – he should be, in other words, more commercial – he should do what the audience wanted.'

Richard Thompson

Despite the boy's obvious talents on the guitar, formal music studies at William Ellis left Richard cold: 'I didn't like doing music at school – I didn't understand it. Formal music just kind of baffled me – I think I must have missed the first lesson! What's a note? How does that sound become that note and what's the point?

'I think I did have a really good ear – I think that's why I didn't understand written music very well at the time. Even when I was younger I had a good ear, I could remember arrangements of jazz records from when I was a kid and twenty years later I could think about it and sit down and write it out – so I think I had a good musical memory – I could pick up tunes quite easily.'

As a teenager, Richard followed Perri into a school holiday job, working in the cafeteria of London Zoo, down the hill in Regent's Park. It was an experience Richard drew on years later, when he remembered the animals in their cages as far neater eaters than the humans in the cafeteria, in the final verse of 'Fast Food' on *Mirror Blue*.

For as long as he can remember, Richard Thompson has been typecast as a 'folk' musician. But it wasn't until his pioneering work with Fairport Convention that 'folk' really made an impact. Like so many of his generation, he believed folk music was a dull and boring interlude in the musical curriculum; all recorder lessons and polite renderings of gentrified traditional songs.

The initial contact with American 'folk' music came from Bob Dylan, courtesy of sister Perri and Muldoon's record collection.

Richard: 'I'd never heard Woody Guthrie, if you'd grown up in that American folk music scene, Dylan wouldn't have seemed that surprising. To contemporaries, he did seem like a Woody Guthrie impersonator, more than a great original talent at the time of the first two albums. But hearing it over here, it was like, a white guy singing the blues. Really crude.

'I was influenced by what people liked at school. You were a Beatles or a Stones person. Alan Freeman's *Pick of the Pops* on Sunday night, not 'arf. We used to play snooker and listen to that. Folk music, you got a bit of Steve Benbow or Shirley Abicair ... Thinking about it, it wasn't something I'd ever go out and look for, it was just something I could play on an acoustic guitar.'

By the early 60s, Britain had already enjoyed calypso, skiffle and trad jazz booms, but folk didn't really make any indentation until the first album from Bob Dylan arrived in the UK early in 1963, when suddenly it was alright to play the acoustic guitar. From all over the country, aspiring singer-songwriters flocked to the capital – Al Stewart, Bert

Fairport

Jansch, Davy Graham, Shirley Collins, Leon Rosselson, Mike Heron, Robin Williamson, John Renbourn. All slipped in under the door marked 'folk' simply because they played the acoustic guitar.

Not all of them were by any means enamoured of folk music. The acoustic 'folk' background all too often simply an opportunity to get a gig. Many of them felt about folk as Raymond Chandler did about Hollywood: 'If my work had been any better, I would not have come; if it had been any worse, I would not have been asked.' Many of the fledgling folkies, had they been able to land a gig playing electric guitar in a rock'n'roll band, would not have bothered with Bunjies, Cousins or the Troubadour.

Even for Richard, folk 'definitely wasn't hip and cool. If you had a band you had to play something that was a bit more marketable, a bit more up to the minute. If you had to choose between Ian Campbell and the Who, you'd probably want to do Who covers.' His induction to the folk scene was far from revelatory: 'I'd go to the odd folk club occasionally. It was just another place where you'd hear music, you'd even perform sometimes. Some of the first places I ever played were folk clubs, usually with somebody else for a bit of moral support, 'cos it's pretty unnerving playing acoustic ... the usual stuff Leadbelly, Tom Paxton ... the Black Bull at Whetstone, the Starting Gate in Bounds Green.

'We didn't have that horror of folk clubs – it was just a place where you could get up and have a go, or you could sit and watch a good headliner and a bunch of amateurs having a go. By 1966–67 you could see some interesting people in folk clubs, the Rev Gary Davis, Jesse Fuller, the Watersons, Lou Killen, Derroll Adams. Interesting people, again without really thinking: "This is folk music". Folk clubs were social places, where you could hear music, or even play music. It was just another place to listen to live music.'

While Richard was a teenager, Joan and John Thompson decided to leave their rented flat in Dartmouth Park Hill for something more permanent: 'We decided that we wanted to buy a house then for when my husband retired. So we got this house in Friern Mount Drive in Whetstone, a gorgeous house, the end of the garden was Hertfordshire, it had a gorgeous garden. Richard found it very difficult then, moving there, but he insisted on staying on at his school – so he used to travel, but it was a rather long journey.'

Despite the long journey from Whetstone to William Ellis, Richard studied hard for his O- and A-Level exams. These were the certificates which ensured that crucial first rung on the job ladder. Richard's father

Richard Thompson

had grown up on the Scottish Borders during the Great Depression of the 30s. For him and all his generation, the spectre of unemployment posed a very real threat, and he was determined that his children should have qualifications to keep them off the dole queue.

Richard was by now equally determined to pursue a career in music, despite further clashes between him and his father, who felt his son's studies were suffering with all his late nights: 'I left school at eighteen – I did A levels – I was doing gigs during A levels – this isn't the way you're supposed to do it – popping up to Bradford for the evening just before the French exam! I didn't really know what I wanted to do and I suppose I thought I could go to Hornsey Art College – my sister had been there, or I could work a bit harder and study English at university. It was a way of putting off the decision of what I was going to do. In retrospect it would have been horrible to have been an art student – I'm sure I would have been the worst kind of pseudo-bohemian layabout – it would have been three years down the tube and probably the same at university. Because I really didn't know what I wanted to do, I was unmotivated in that way.'

To date – and this seems unlikely to change – Richard's only full-time, non-musical job was as apprentice to a local design partnership, a job he took straight after leaving school: 'Hans Unger and his partner were local designers who lived in Muswell Hill. They just wanted an apprentice and I thought that would be fun for a while. They worked in mosaic and stained glass, that was what they were mostly known for. Hans was a fairly well known designer – he designed a couple of those famous London Transport posters – and did a lot of advertising work for Rothmans. We'd do these strange all-night projects sometimes for the tobacco industry and they'd come along at ten o'clock in the morning with cigars and say "No".

'All that time I was there, for six or nine months – we were working on one very large stained glass project for St Columbus Church in Chester which has got glass right down both sides and at the end as well. So that was a huge job and I was helping out on that.

'They were big classical music fans so we had records or Radio Three all day, so actually I learned a lot of music. I also learned what I didn't like which was Wagner – which they played endlessly – they played the whole Ring Cycle and then started Record 1 again. I forget how many sides it was – an incredible number. So I really developed a strong dislike for Wagner.'

Joan Thompson was convinced that whatever Richard turned his hand to, he would be a success. While happy to see him settled at Hans

Fairport

Unger's, she knew that her son's evening engagements were taking him in another direction entirely: 'I mean he could have gone to university, no question about it, but he just upped and left home. He said he wanted to go off and I never wanted my children to do what they weren't happy doing. I wouldn't want someone who was artistic to have to sit in a bank, or do anything, he loved music and he was in this group with the Fairport and always being a sensible boy, I never really worried about Richard, I always felt that he would look after himself, you know. What he got up to I've no idea!

'I remember Ashley Hutchings coming to the front door and that was the first sign of Fairport Convention. And then I suppose they met Simon, and they used to rehearse – and then they went off and lived in north London somewhere.'

Chapter 3

AT THE JUNCTION of Fortismere Avenue and Fortis Green Road in north London, stands a large, three-storey Edwardian house set slightly back from the road. Built at the turn of the century, it is an unremarkable example of suburban architecture. Fortis Green was rural, quiet and undisturbed until the transport boom of the mid-Victorian era saw new railway stations pepper the landscape all around London. By the end of the nineteenth century, the area was expanding to accommodate middle-class office workers who travelled by train from the growing suburb into the City. As the twentieth century dawned, developers were casting avaricious eyes over the remaining green fields around London, impatient to replace the trees with houses.

The house survived the Blitz of 1940 and 1941, unharmed by the Nazi V1 and V2 rockets which tumbled randomly onto the capital during the final stages of the War. In 1901 the old London County Council began placing blue plaques on residences which had been occupied by distinguished persons known to 'the well-informed passer-by'. There is no blue plaque adorning this house. There are, however, occasionally visitors of a certain age who are in the know and come to stand and stare at the house.

It is not the building itself which draws the plump, casually dressed, grey-haired visitors from around the world. It is the small wooden plaque to the right of the front door as you stand facing it. Such decorations are not unusual on houses in the London suburbs. Decorative plaques are placed by doorbells or on front gates to mark individuality, bolstering the belief that an Englishman's home is his castle. Such plaques are lost symbols from a bygone age – 'Peacehaven', 'Tintagel', 'Dunroamin'.

The house in question has a carving of a little wooden trawler entering harbour. A ship returning safely home from a voyage, having survived the dangers of the sea. It is the scene from which the house takes its name – 'Fairport'.

Fairport

To fans of British folk-rock, the 'Fairport' house is the equivalent of a grassy knoll to conspiracy theorists. While the house is not up there with that other north London rock landmark, the zebra crossing on Abbey Road, Fairport House marks for many, the end of a long road tracing the beginnings of one of the most influential and long-lasting British bands.

Record sales are rarely a true register of a band's impact: Brian Eno said that the Velvet Underground may only have sold a few thousand albums, but that everyone who bought one went out and immediately formed a band.

Fairport Convention couldn't make that claim, but it is true that everyone *in* Fairport Convention went off and formed a band. The legacy is apparent on the second weekend in August every year, when tens of thousands of fans descend on Cropredy for Fairport's yearly get-together. It is also evidenced by the myriad offshoot groups which sprang from the Fairport oak – Steeleye Span, Fotheringay, the Albion Band, Matthews Southern Comfort.

Fairport's influence is also discernible in other bands who took up the folk-rock baton. Outfits such as Gryphon, Five Hand Reel, Amazing Blondel, Moving Hearts, the Strawbs, Fairground Attraction, Planxty, the Home Service, Runrig, all owe a tip of the fedora to Fairport. The influence extended far beyond those north London streets. The Pogues, 10,000 Maniacs, Any Trouble, The Men They Couldn't Hang, Los Lobos, the Waterboys, Martin Stephenson and the Daintees and the Bangles whose bassist Michael Steele's dream band was 'the Yardbirds with Fairport Convention vocals'. And all thanks to that big house in Fortis Green.

Fairport House was the home of Simon Nicol from his birth in 1950. Simon's father was a doctor and used the family home as his surgery up until his death in 1964. Simon and his mother then moved into a smaller flat, 50 yards up the road and turned the sprawling Fairport House into bedsits which were rented out to a series of transient nurses and students. One of the residents from 1965 onwards was a 19-year-old journalist, Ashley Hutchings. By day, mild-mannered Ashley was employed by Haymarket Press on titles such as *Furnishing World*. But by night, he was a one-man music industry.

Ashley had begun playing bass guitar in 1961 when he was sixteen and has remained faithful to the instrument ever since. It was Ashley who was the powerhouse of the early Fairport. His 1994 album *Twangin' 'n' a-Traddin'* features a wonderful blend of folk-rockers – including Richard Thompson – tackling late 50s and early 60s rock'n'roll instrumentals. In the poignant sleevenotes, Ashley conveys the musical flavour of the time:

> This album is fondly dedicated to every group of fledgling musicians who ever played in a draughty church hall to a dozen uninterested teenagers who don't appreciate how difficult it is to keep the back-up guitar pattern in 'Pipeline' going when your wrist ached and your equipment was sub-standard and practice time after finishing homework was short and girls were such a distraction . . . and any long-suffering teacher who had to put up with the simulated drum breaks in 'Wipe Out' tapped out on a classroom desk, and to any long-suffering sometime sweetheart who had to share her fella with three furry-faced boys with Hofners and one creep with a Vox continental.

Ashley had taken the King's Shilling of pop music early on. Like so many of his generation, he sat up night after night, his ear glued to Radio Luxembourg. He remembers hearing 'Heartbreak Hotel' when it became Elvis' first British hit in 1956, and being captivated by the mystery and promise offered by the first wave of American rock'n'roll: 'I suppose the root forms of rock'n'roll, jazz and blues, led me to pursue that type of music. I bought very, very little English music at all – Lonnie Donegan, Tommy Steele – but I considered myself to be quite well up on it. I always bought the original versions – Dion and the Belmonts "Teenager In Love" rather than Craig Douglas! My week might very often be taken up with six nights out, and each night a different musical form – jazz clubs, folk clubs, classical concerts; rock clubs like the Ferry Inn, the Flamingo, the Marquee.'

Using the North Bank Youth Club in Muswell Hill as his stage, Ashley paraded a series of one-off bands to bemused teenage audiences. The bands' names often seemed longer than the gigs: Tim Turner's Narration (named after the chap who breathlessly narrated 'Look At Life' at the cinema), Dr K's Blues Band, the Still Waters, the Electric Dysentery. It was in the murky waters of the Ethnic Shuffle Orchestra, Ashley's final pre-Fairport ensemble, that a faint but nonetheless recognisable outline of Fairport Convention began to take shape.

It was Ashley's enthusiasm that fuelled the early Fairport and his determination not to stay on the same musical spot which gave the group its dazzling repertoire and inventiveness, ensuring their longevity, long after their flowery contemporaries in the Summer of Love had wilted by the wayside. In keeping with the times, and in homage to William Blake, Ashley nicknamed himself 'Tyger'.

Richard: 'At some point Ashley quit his job and he was the first one to become a full-time musician. It was Ashley's band I think, he was always the moving force behind the direction and the policy all the way into folk-rock and into the traditional revival. So all credit to Ashley, he was really the man with the vision.'

Simon Nicol had acquired his first guitar aged eleven. Having left school in 1965, he was working as a projectionist at the Highgate Odeon when his interest in music took him along to the North Bank Youth Club, where he watched a procession of Ashley's bands: 'Ashley was always the mastermind behind these various outfits, which were, in the main, urban R&B bands, but even then he was prone to come up with obscure material. He was always a bit of an *eminence gris*, so the first time he asked me in, I was a little bit chuffed.'

The Ethnic Shuffle Orchestra is a footnote in the Fairport history, providing the transitional link between teenage larks and professional musicians. Their version of 'Washington At Valley Forge' circa 1966, can be found on Ashley's 1994 retrospective album, *The Guv'nor, Volume 1*. This washboard-fuelled shuffle is of historic interest as the only official pre-Fairport release currently available and as the only Fairport song recorded at Fairport House.

Even with *Sgt Pepper* ... still on the horizon, Ashley appreciated there wouldn't be much demand in 'Swinging London' – officially christened thus by *Time* magazine in April 1966 – for a group playing washboards and kazoos, a style which harked back to the skiffle boom of the 50s. The group were musical featherweights in the exploding and fiercely competitive London music scene of the mid-60s.

Ashley: 'I was the assistant to the managing director of Haymarket Press, and it was during that period it suddenly dawned on me that I could actually try to make a living out of music. It must have been the winter of 1966, I thought, I'm going to give up the job and try to make a go of it. There was very little work for the band, and I thought you're not actually going to get any work unless you go out there and tout for it, so that's what I did. It was a struggle to start with, until Joe Boyd took us under his wing and put us on a wage . . . but it was a struggle for six to nine months for me.'

Simon Nicol, still only sixteen, gave up his job as a projectionist too and was supported by his mother while he devoted all his energies to music which was 'wonderful of her, because the only gigs we were doing were friends' weddings and barmitzvahs at £10 a time'. Simon remembers Richard turning up to dep on an Ethnic Shuffle session at the Fairport house, where the group used to rehearse, while Richard has dim memories of his last-minute substitution as guitarist with one of Ashley's early outfits.

Richard Thompson

Richard: 'I know I filled in for Doctor K's Blues Band once – their guitarist was Jeff Kribbet who used to play with Rush and John Mayall for a while – one of those unsung guitar players. Somewhere in between Peter Green and Eric Clapton there was Jeff Kribbet. I filled in and Ashley must have liked me and said why don't you play with us, so I started playing with him and Simon and various drummers. We didn't fix on a drummer for a while. The legendary Shawn Frater, he played drums in a cravat, that's always a bad sign. Until Martin Lamble showed up, we didn't have a regular.'

Simon: 'Bryan Wyvill, who was a friend of mine, lived two doors away from Tyger in Durnsford Road, and was at school with Richard. Brian used to go on about his wizard friend, who was just as good a guitarist as Hank Marvin. After Richard came there were no more guitarists. Number one in a field of one, Richard made a huge difference, because you couldn't say "Okay, let's do the Shads medley". He would come out with this free-form, liberated music.'

Richard: 'Folk was there in the background, and among the formative Fairport bands there was an occasional acoustic band which was myself and Simon, Ashley and Judy – I think it was a four piece – and we'd do the odd folk club like that around 1966.'

Simon had another friend, Richard Lewis, who had an enormous record collection, which Simon and Ashley frequently rifled in search of material for the Ethnic Shuffle repertoire, and it was Lewis who coined the name Fairport Convention. 'It just seemed to be time for obscure names,' Thompson told *Q* in 1988. 'Hapsash and the Coloured Coat were rearing their ugly heads, so it seemed necessary to get a name with at least eight syllables.'

American journalist Langdon Winner hyperbolically called 1 June 1967, release date of the Beatles' *Sgt Pepper*, 'The closest Western civilisation has come to unity since the Congress of Vienna in 1815'. Well, not in Golders Green it wasn't. History has Richard, Ashley, Simon and Shawn Frater at St Michael's Church Hall, Golders Green on 1 June 1967, making their debut as Fairport Convention. Hire of the hall: £5; Celebratory Chinese meal afterwards: £5; Fairport's fee: £10.

That week's *Melody Maker* had the gig advertised under the banner: 'Become Converted!!! Fairport Convention happen at St Michael's Hall, Golders Green, opp. Woolworths. Adv. tickets 5s'. No one can be absolutely certain what was played that night, but certainly included were Love's 'Seven And Seven Is', Hendrix's 'Hey Joe' and Dylan's 'My Back Pages', courtesy of the Byrds. Simon recalled the demise of the Ethnic Shuffle Orchestra thus: 'By the time we started doing the Byrds' stuff, the washboards had been put away.'

Fairport

Ashley remembers that among the twenty or so people watching Fairport find their feet were Kingsley Abbott and Martin Lamble, from faraway Harrow-on-the-Hill: 'Martin came up to us after the gig and said he played better than our drummer, which set us against him – who is this upstart? But we said, well we'll have a play together, and he was good. Very good.'

And so it was that 18-year-old Martin Francis Lamble became Fairport Convention's second drummer, on the band's second-ever gig. Neil Raphael, a schoolfriend of Martin's at University College School remembered the teenage Lamble as a mature player: 'As someone who hadn't played drums for long, he did a lot of extemporizing . . . I think he would have been a fine drummer.'

All the early Fairport Convention gigs consisted of cover versions, no one was writing original material in 1967. Mind you, there was plenty of good material out there to be covered. Ashley, Simon and Richard put their heads together and came up with a selection of songs – mostly obtained from the record collections of Big Muldoon and Richard Lewis – from which Fairport drew their set lists. As Ashley recalls: 'We were quite derivative, but our sources were pretty obscure for those days.'

Martin Lamble's friend, Kingsley Abbott, for example, had Jim and Jean's *Changes* album of 1966, which contained the duo's covers of 'Flower Lady', 'Lay Down Your Weary Tune' (Dylan's own version remained officially unavailable until 1985) and Emitt Rhodes' 'Time Will Show The Wiser', the opening track of Fairport's eponymous debut the following year.

Otherwise, if you'd paid out your five shillings to see Fairport Convention during 1967, chances are, this is what you'd have heard:

'Reno, Nevada'
'The Bold Marauder' (both Richard Farina)
'Flower Lady' (Phil Ochs)
'Messin' With The Man' (Buddy Guy)
'Plastic Fantastic Lover' (Jefferson Airplane)
'East/West' (Paul Butterfield)
'Get Together' (Dino Valenti)
'Walk Away Renee' (Left Banke)
'My Back Pages'
'Lay Down Your Weary Tune'
'Chimes Of Freedom'
'Absolutely Sweet Marie' (All Bob Dylan)

Richard Thompson

Like so many other areas of pop music, the changes had been rung by the Beatles. Following the group's UK breakthrough in 1963, and their global KO of 1964, the Beatles had put across the concept of an independent, self-servicing unit, with 'their own built-in tunesmith team of John Lennon and Paul McCartney'. Prior to the Beatles, the homegrown pop talent of the day (Cliff Richard, Adam Faith) had relied on cover versions of American hits, or material supplied by the professional songwriters of Denmark Street. The Beatles had, at a stroke, shattered Tin Pan Alley's stranglehold on pop music.

The Beatles' only competitors on the world stage were the Rolling Stones, and early on in their career, manager Andrew Oldham realised that any real durability had to come from within the Stones camp, rather than relying on R&B covers. Oldham tackled the problem in typically Svengali fashion, locking Mick Jagger and Keith Richards in their kitchen and refusing to let them out until they'd written a song.

From the mid-60s on, pop groups – who would soon become rock bands – had to include their own built-in genius, capable of producing a steady stream of hits. If the pressure proved too much, you could come off the road, have your breakdown, then stay at home and write. Pink Floyd tried it with Syd Barrett. After all, it had worked for Brian Wilson and the Beach Boys, hadn't it?

But this was the pre-bootleg, post-pirate radio era, and without a 'built-in tunesmith', new material was a problem. Denied access to John Peel's *Perfumed Garden* show – which showcased the new music emerging from San Francisco – by Postmaster General Tony Benn who closed down Radio London in August 1967 – Fairport were forced to sift through the well-thumbed record collections of friends for inspiration.

BBC Radio One launched in September 1967, but it wasn't offering much outside the Top 40. The nation's bright and breezy pop network was hampered by Musicians Union needle-time restrictions, a system designed to keep union members busy, while keeping records off the airwaves. It worked fine if you were a union member, like Elvis Costello's dad Ross McManus, who kept to a breakneck schedule, learning and performing live versions of popular hits of the day on air, to help Radio 1 comply with MU demands.

Instrumentally, Fairport were finding their feet. Richard was already contributing a willowy and distinctive lead guitar, but was a shy and retiring figure onstage, hiding at the back behind the amps. Simon happily played a mean rhythm guitar, made the between-song announcements and kept up a breezy line of patter, all of which he has energetically kept on doing for 30 years. The rhythm section of Ashley and Martin was solid, but Fairport were crucially weak in the vocal department.

Richard: 'I used to sing, Ashley would sing, Simon would sing, we all used to have a go. I'm not sure we're that good now, but in those days it was pretty bad. So we thought we had to get a singer and Ashley suggested Judy Dyble who lived up the road . . .'

Judy Dyble was an 18-year-old librarian who lived in Bounds Green and had flitted through some of Ashley's pre-Fairport line-ups, principally singing a few gigs as part of Tim Turner's Narration. So when Fairport's vocal deficiencies became increasingly obvious, Judy was called in to bolster the front rank.

Richard: 'Judy used to sing in folk clubs and she played the autoharp – which with us being fans of Jim and Jean and Mimi and Dick Farina – autoharps were extremely lingua franca at the time, so we were happy to have her, plus she had sort of Mary Travers-ironed hair – which was very important. She was a sweet girl, I used to go out with Judy for a while – a very nice girl.'

Slowly Fairport were making their way through the swirling mists of the London 'underground' music scene. Barely two months after their inauspicious debut in Golders Green, Judy Dyble made her debut singing with Fairport who were supporting Pink Floyd at the UFO club on Tottenham Court Road.

Simon: 'All through that summer, we were playing gigs, mainly all-night efforts. Richard would rattle about in the van afterwards, then turn up at the stained-glass place. He was always slicing his hand on razor-sharp edges of glass because he was so tired.'

Fairport were kept busy. John Penhallow, a friend of the band, took over from Ashley as the manager and booked the gigs. Work wasn't hard to find during the summer of 1967, there was a frisson in the air, a genuine belief in the possibility of harnessing rock'n'roll, free love, dope and sex into one coherent, if slightly hazy, revolutionary manifesto. Alongside Dylan, the most quoted wordsmith that summer was Plato: 'When the mode of the music changes, the walls of the city shake.' Musicians were seen as messengers, the ones behind the Fender Strats who knew what's shakin'.

Richard: 'I don't remember doing that many gigs with the Floyd – but we did a lot of universities with them. They were contemporaries – but already that rung higher up, that bit ahead, they were the most famous underground band – and actually had things like production values – they had about three lights and a light show – that was pretty amazing stuff at the time and they had bigger amps than anybody else.'

Richard Thompson

Fairport were also part of the underground scene, albeit standing slightly to one side: 'Basically,' said Richard in retrospect, 'I think the underground embraced anyone that wasn't doing Otis Redding riffs.' The band played the same haunts with the same bunch of 'alternative' acts: 'There was a slew of bands that we did see a lot of, Blossom Toes we used to play a lot with, Arthur Brown, Edgar Broughton, Duster Bennett, Family, Incredible String Band. There was a kind of camaraderie between the bands and a lot of those people became good friends. You used to see them all the time and if your van broke down there was always somebody to tow you. It was the opposite of what I later discovered about the folk scene – which was incredible bitchy and everybody hated everybody else and was really jealous of success – real backbiting place. But the rock scene, just the nicest people, and really friendly.'

There was a genuine split between 'underground' or 'alternative' acts of the period and those who supplied the toothy, singalong fodder for Radio One and *Top of the Pops*. The Beatles were, of course, above it all, benign monarchs, surveying it all from their Olympian height through a haze of marijuana and LSD. The Stones were spending more time in chokey than they were in the recording studio. Which band you liked was a statement of intent. While today it's possible to like Oasis and Supergrass, back then it was inconceivable that anyone could give squat space to both Pink Floyd and the Tremeloes. The battle lines were drawn: commercial success was anathema to the spirit of the times.

The feeling flourished for a brief six-month period, during which – like punk a decade later – the genuine commitment and street-level enthusiasm of the hippies shone on. The first flowering of flower power in London was touchingly engaging, but it was soon swamped by the usual avarice. By the end of August 1967, a bunch of session singers, unhappily clad in kaftans, were on *Top of the Pops* singing 'Let's Go To San Francisco'.

It was all a long way away from the spontaneous enthusiasm of the 24 Hour Technicolour Dream at Alexandra Palace a mere four months before. Richard remembers being there: 'We didn't play but I went. Bands at either end and in the middle – at least three things going on at the same time – people were smoking banana skins and stuff like that.'

Undeniably 1967 was a transitional year. But as with punk, the music press was keeping its options open. *NME*'s review of *Sgt Pepper* ran along the lines of 'Blimey, bit of a change for the Fab Four here. Maybe they're running short of ideas, they even repeat the title track!' Despite

Fairport

honourable exceptions like *Melody Maker*'s Chris Welch, Richard's old band mate Nick Jones, and *NME*'s Keith Altham and Richard Green, the innate conservatism of the UK press survived that year of changes more or less intact.

While history characterises 1967 as the year the barricades tumbled and the tumbrilles rolled towards a rock'n'roll revolution, it was not so clear at the time. *Melody Maker*'s last issue of the year was headlined 'The Year of Engelbert!' Recognition that Engelbert Humperdinck's 'Release Me' had kept the Beatles double A-sided 'Penny Lane/Strawberry Fields Forever' (still regarded by many as the greatest pop single ever made) off the no. 1 slot. This hiccup interrupted the group's otherwise seamless run of Number Ones from 1963–1970.

In a quietly dogged and determined, very English sort of way, Fairport was trickling along. The gigs were coming in, but Richard kept his options open by maintaining his day job with Hans Unger. His mother remained strongly supportive. 'We didn't stop him in any way because I knew he was talented; I'd heard him play at home and I thought he was wonderful. Right from the word go I wouldn't stand in his way. But my husband was very bitter really – he wished Richard was in a bank or anything, he was dead against it. I'm afraid I was just the opposite, I thought well if they have a talent they have to use it.'

It took a 24-year-old American to elevate Fairport to full professional status and land them that crucial record deal. By the summer of 1967, Joe Boyd was already a bastion of the London alternative scene. Born in Boston, Boyd was friendly with musicians Tom Rush and Geoff Muldaur, and while still in his teens was promoting blues and folk concerts around Boston. The summer of 1965 had found him as production manager at the landmark Newport Folk Festival.

That was the year Bob Dylan divided the folk fraternity with his blitzkrieg electric set with the Paul Butterfield Blues Band and nothing would ever be quite the same again. Boyd came across Butterfield's band while working for George Wein at Elektra and notified the label's Paul Rothchild of the band's abilities. So 'as kind of a reward for leading Elektra to Paul Butterfield, I was given the job of running the London office of Elektra'. Boyd arrived in London in November 1965.

One of the first bands to come Boyd's way was Pink Floyd, whose debut single 'Arnold Layne', Boyd produced with John Wood (later a Fairport and Richard Thompson stalwart) as engineer. Boyd was scheduled to produce the Floyd's debut album but EMI insisted on a staff producer, one Norman 'Hurricane' Smith.

There was enough to keep Boyd busy that summer apart from Pink

Richard Thompson

Floyd. He was a founder member, along with John 'Hoppy' Hopkins, of the Notting Hill Free School, which soon ran into financial problems and led to the pair putting on benefit concerts to raise funds. By the end of 1966, Boyd and Hopkins had taken over an Irish dance hall on Tottenham Court Road, and turned it into UFO, London's first and most fondly remembered underground venue. Membership was fifteen shillings (75p) a year, and ten shillings (50p) on the door got you in. UFO's house bands were Pink Floyd and Soft Machine; regular visitors included Procol Harum, the Bonzo Dog Doo-Dah Band, Tomorrow and the Crazy World of Arthur Brown.

Joe Boyd had already started his own company Witchseason, which numbered the Incredible String Band among its first clients, and was keeping his eyes and ears open for new sights and sounds. In the wake of UFO, 'psychedelic' clubs had sprung up all over London, and Boyd's first sighting of Fairport was at Happening 44, in Gerrard Street, Soho, sometime during the late June or early July of 1967. Boyd recalled the venue to Jonathon Green: 'We had Jack Braceland, 50 years old, doing a light-show at UFO. He came from Watford, where he ran a nudist colony and had Happening 44 on Gerrard Street, the place I first saw the Fairport Convention. It was a strip club in the daytime, just a little hole in the wall.'

Joe Boyd: 'The thing about Fairport – when I first went down to see them at the strip club – it wasn't Judy, and it wasn't the band, and it wasn't the music that interested me. It was Richard. That was what interested me from the very beginning. To see this seventeen-year-old kid playing incredibly mature guitar solos. I didn't want to make it particularly apparent for obvious reasons, but essentially my primary interest in the Fairport Convention was Richard, because he was obviously the most talented.

'My point of view was always that it was Richard's group. And if there was any taking of sides, or arbitrating of disputes to be done, I would try gently to push the group in the direction of doing what Richard wanted to do, and doing Richard's material and following Richard's suggestions because I thought that his instincts were always the best, and the biggest problem was trying to draw him out and get him to write more.'

Boyd put Fairport into the coveted New Bands spot at UFO, where they must have done something right, because following their 5 a.m. debut, Boyd signed the band to Witchseason. Boyd was forever touting his Witchseason roster around interested parties, which explains why Fairport's early records were spread over three labels (Track, Polydor and Island) in barely twelve months.

Impressed as Boyd was by the band, he still felt there were deficiencies on the vocal front: 'Judy and Richard did the vocals, and Richard didn't feel he was a good enough singer. He really wanted to concentrate on playing the guitar, but they wanted to have that Jefferson Airplane idea – they were very influenced by all the West Coast bands, by the Youngbloods, Jefferson Airplane – so they were looking for a male vocalist, and I mentioned this to Denny Cordell, who was producing a group called the Pyramid. I went down with Richard, Judy and Ashley, I think, to some gig at a stupid boutique in Fulham Road that Pyramid was playing.'

The singer with the Pyramid was one Ian Matthews, who landed the Fairport gig, swelling the band to a six piece. With Judy and Ian as upfront singers and Ashley, Richard and Simon providing harmonies, Fairport were beginning to sound like a proper band.

There was a lot of competition out there, Fairport were underground regulars, playing the same venues as Pink Floyd, Yes, Brian Auger, Family and Soft Machine. Live work and 'Happenings!' passed the time, but the real indication that you had arrived, the litmus test which elevated you from your contemporaries, was landing a record deal.

While the spirit of the thriving underground may have been sex & drugs & rock & roll, the rock and the roll element was strictly controlled by the major record labels of the time. Aside from mavericks like Joe Meek, the British record industry had been dominated by EMI (the Beatles) and Decca (the Stones). Cracks were beginning to appear in the hegemony though: Chris Blackwell's Island Records was making its slow transition from a novelty Bluebeat label to a leading independent, while Track Records had been established by the Who's managers Kit Lambert and Chris Stamp, who were very excited about their first signing, the Jimi Hendrix Experience.

Hendrix himself was no stranger to Fairport. Arriving in the UK late in 1966, within weeks Hendrix had established himself as *the* guitarist. In the quarter century since his death, the miasma surrounding Hendrix has grown into myth. But back then, in an incredibly short four-year career, Hendrix proved himself probably the most innovative electric guitarist ever.

Film maker Peter Neal (director of *Experience*, the only Hendrix film released during the guitarist's lifetime) told me once that he witnessed an early Hendrix performance in London, and the word was obviously out, as there in the front row sat Eric Clapton, Pete Townshend, Jimmy Page and Jeff Beck, all open-mouthed, and watching Hendrix's every fretful move.

Richard Thompson

The Speakeasy just off Oxford Circus, in Margaret Street, was the club where the rock'n'roll aristocracy hung out. DJ Jeff Dexter told Jonathon Green: 'It arrived on the trail of all the great late-night clubs: the Scotch, the Crazy Elephant, the Revolution, the Cromwellian, the Bag O'Nails. A lot of the new bands would play there and all the stars would get up and jam. It was a great melting pot for the old and new styles.' Fairport played the Speakeasy several times (including 27 August and 12 December 1967) and it was here that Hendrix got up to jam with the boys and girl from north London.

Richard: 'Hendrix got up a few times at the Speakeasy. Jimi'd come in after his gig, he'd be on the road somewhere and he'd drive back and at two in the morning it'd be time to have dinner. So he'd be in quite a lot for dinner and we weren't especially privileged, most nights he'd get up to jam with whoever was playing. He used to get up and jam – he played guitar, he played bass sometimes, he just liked playing. It was kind of intimidating when you're young herberts trying to look cool and this extremely urbane and very bizarre looking, very handsome black man comes up to the stage and says do you mind if I sit in.

'When he used to sit in with us, he'd play a guitar which for him was strung the wrong way round and still play pretty well even though it was upside down. I think he just played whatever we were playing, whether it was "Absolutely Sweet Marie" or "East-West" or something, he just seemed to want to be one of the boys for a few seconds.'

When it came to jamming, Hendrix was by no means selective. During 1967, and at the Speakeasy alone, Hendrix got up and jammed with Georgie Fame, Ben E. King, Amen Corner, Eric Clapton, Eric Burdon and the New Animals, José Feliciano and Alan Price. So Fairport weren't exactly the chosen ones, but it was the sort of thing which guaranteed the band a namecheck in the influential Raver column in *Melody Maker*. Fairport are also known to have jammed with Hendrix on a half-hour version of Dylan's 'Like A Rolling Stone', a song which the guitarist had used to electrify the Monterey audience at his American debut with the Experience during June 1967.

Witchseason put Fairport on a weekly wage of £10 each, later upped to £12 10s. Stressing its underground credo, the company promised in an advert in *Oz*: 'Witchseason takes care of your head'. Within weeks of signing to Boyd's company and barely three months after their Golders Green debut, Fairport were installed at Sound Techniques Studios in Chelsea to begin their recording career.

Breathlessly, the news was broken to the world in the pages of *The Finchley Press* of 29 September 1967: 'A Muswell Hill pop group, the

Fairport Convention, who got their name from Fairport House, Fortis Green, where they rehearse, went to a recording studio last week to make their first record. The group is comprised of four entertainers, two of which come from Fortis Green – Simon Nichol [sic] and Tyger Hutchins [sic] – and one from Whetstone, Richard Thompson.'

Judy Dyble had found a copy of jazz singer Maxine Sullivan's 1936 song 'If I Had A Ribbon Bow' in Joe Boyd's record collection. As with much of the early Fairport repertoire, somebody else's song from somebody else's record collection seemed as good a place as any to begin.

Simon Nicol remembers those sessions: 'We had a terrible time recording it. We learnt it, arranged it and recorded it in four sections, then poor John Wood had to snip it all together on an Ampex four-track vertical machine. He was less than enthusiastic about our prospects.' As far as Fairport's debut single went, John Wood was right. On its release in November 1967, 'If I Had A Ribbon Bow' left the world largely unmoved.

Richard had started going out with Judy Dyble during the summer of 1967. But there was precious little time for any intimacy, as Fairport were eternally gigging, and Richard was still living at home. But romance is found in the most unlikely places and Judy told *Hokey Pokey*: 'I can remember playing at the Electric Garden, before it was Middle Earth, and Richard and I wandered outside and we saw what must have been the last lamp-lighter lighting those gas lamps in Covent Garden.'

Richard: 'Middle Earth was a club in Covent Garden, which was just a basement right off the square, when it was a fruit and veg market. On Saturday night we'd do a set at eight o'clock and then hang around for the next one at six in the morning, as one used to in those days – the lowest band got the biggest gaps between sets. And we'd go to the sausage sandwich stall – they used to do a mean sausage sandwich – and there was this incredible collision of cultures – freaks in their long hair and kaftans, market workers with their flat caps and the leather and people coming out of the opera in evening clothes and taffeta. Bizarre collision of three cultures coming at you, it was like acid without the acid.'

Despite Richard being less than impressed by Pink Floyd, Fairport were back supporting Britain's leading psychedelic ensemble and the Incredible String Band at Brian Epstein's Savile Theatre on 1 October 1967. As the year wound down, Fairport spent their time gigging around London, picking up occasional crumbs of comfort from the music press, but largely waiting for something to happen.

Chapter 4

'BEING IN THE STUDIO for the first time is really exciting and a challenge,' recalls Richard. 'We were saying what does this do? Let's do a song based on this knob, so it was extremely experimental and a lot of it misfired – it's a very eclectic album.'

Fairport had their debut album in the can by the end of 1967, although its release would be delayed for over six months, while Joe Boyd shuffled his Witchseason roster – which now included John and Beverly Martyn – around various record labels. Although the addition of Judy Dyble and Ian Matthews had boosted Fairport's line up, the band still tended to sound thin and tinny. Essentially a covers band, Fairport was beginning to attract attention, largely thanks to the curly-headed guitarist.

By the beginning of 1968, Fairport were consolidating their appeal. Tony Wilson reviewed a Middle Earth gig of 3 February for *Melody Maker*: 'One of the most interesting features about the Fairport Convention is their choice of material. Instead of the more stereotyped numbers they have widened their horizons to include compositions by writers like Leonard Cohen and the late Richard Farina ... Richard Thompson, excellent guitarist, showed well on instrumentals which included "Chill Beans, Warm Nights" and "Ghetto".'

Richard was still painfully shy, though, in true Hollywood fashion, once on stage he became visibly more assured and confident. Judy Dyble suffered the same shyness as her boyfriend, so Simon Nicol was very much Fairport's focus. Richard's 'stagecraft' consisted of standing quietly at the back, firing off long and fluent solos, which lifted the band's cover versions into something approaching originality. 'I started out as a much shyer performer, I'd be the JJ Cale figure hiding behind the Marshall stack. Coming forward to do a vocal was like walking through flames.'

While their contemporaries on the underground scene were making some sort of impact outside the usual gig circuit, Fairport were still plugging away, going out for £75 a night, and just about making ends meet. Richard had by now moved into a flat in St Mary's Road, just off the North Circular Road in Barnet, which he shared with Simon and Ian Matthews.

Muldoon: 'I can remember meeting Richard for a curry in north London one evening, and he took me back to the house on the North Circular somewhere, and the rest of the Fairports were sitting there and Richard introduced me as the man who taught him to play guitar. And they all go "wow", and every one of them handed me a guitar, four guitars thrust in my hand. It was so humiliating, all I could think up was "Living Doll" or some such rubbish.'

Perri: 'There was a period when Richard first left home when all I ever saw of him – was that I would keep a vague tab on him – and there would be a pile of T-shirts and a guitar in the corner and that was Richard in some room somewhere . . . He had to choose between working in stained glass with Hans Unger and the guitar. When he started – he was out there with his T-shirts, wandering about, forming little groups – and then suddenly at the age of about twenty-one he was at the Festival Hall with the Fairport, and that was all quite staggering from the point of view that he had always been so shy and so quiet.'

The Fairport van would come to the flat collect Richard and the others and they'd set off to yet another gig. Talking to Colin Irwin in *Melody Maker* in 1978, Thompson recalled with fondness the early days of Fairport: 'It was very enjoyable. I remember when I was about eighteen, and I'd been travelling for a year, and we were playing at universities round the country, and I'd see all the people I'd known from school at university. It was as if they'd stood still.'

Ian Matthews: 'We used to go out on the college circuit. We played up in Leeds and Sheffield, and down at Essex University, and down to Southampton and Bristol. There was a whole university thing . . . at that time it was really happening. It was a really healthy scene. There were maybe ten or a dozen bands that you would see all the time, and you'd never know who you were going to play with . . . At York University, I can remember, not knowing who was going to be there, and it turned out Family was headlining, Fairport were second on the bill and the opening act was Joe Cocker and the Grease Band.'

The band's set at this point consisted almost entirely of cover versions of new as well as old songs. Fairport were quick learners, they swiftly worked Leonard Cohen's 'Suzanne' into their stage act. The source was his debut album *The Songs of Leonard Cohen*, which was only released in the UK in February 1968. Ian Matthews brought a couple of Tim

Richard Thompson

Hardin songs to the Fairport roster ('Lady Came From Baltimore', 'Hang On To A Dream') and Bob Dylan proved, as ever, a fertile source, 'Dear Landlord' from 1968's *John Wesley Harding* album was regularly included.

Ashley: 'I remember very clearly the turnover of material around 1968 was incredible. We would learn new songs and perform them onstage almost weekly ... The material that we got through was incredible ... There were country things, "Tried So Hard", a Gene Clark song; "I Still Miss Someone" by Johnny Cash. A version of "My Dog Blue", which The Byrds recorded ... Glen D. Hardin's "Things You Gave Me", "Morning Glory" by Tim Buckley ...'

Fairport were among the first acts anywhere to feature material by a new female Canadian singer-songwriter. Joe Boyd met Joni Mitchell during the summer of 1967. 'I'd met her at Newport, and she visited England that year. George Hamilton IV had had a hit with her song "Urge For Going" ... She was looking for a publishing deal over here. I introduced her to David Platt at Essex Music, who made her some kind of advance. Anyway, at one point, she left him a tape of all her songs ... and so I played them to Fairport.'

Among the songs on the tape were 'Marcie' and 'Night In The City' – Fairport's versions can be heard on Ashley Hutchings' 1995 *The Guv'nor Volume 3*; 'Both Sides Now' – which Fairport demo-ed at the sessions which produced their debut single; and 'I Don't Know Where I Stand' and 'Chelsea Morning', both of which Fairport included on their debut album.

Richard: 'We were very lyric conscious as a band – we thought Dylan was very cool, and Phil Ochs, Richard Farina, that kind of stuff. We were very into lyrics and the place to find the good singer-songwriters at that time was America. We did some pop stuff. It was a very eclectic mixture at the start. You could say we didn't have a direction except that it was kind of folk-rock, or soft-rock in the American sense, and we liked lyrics.'

While eclectic in their choice of material and never relying on the obvious choice of covers, Fairport were undeniably, even proudly, derivative. But it is worth recalling that even at this time, when the band were at their most magpie-like, seven of the twelve songs on their debut album were in-house, with only five cover versions included.

Richard: 'I remember saying to Ashley after a gig, that I was kind of embarrassed about doing the material we were doing, because it seemed that we should have outgrown doing covers – even though it was only 1967 – it somehow wasn't good enough and other bands were writing their own stuff and we should too. I remember being angry and saying to Ashley this isn't good enough, we've got to get some original material. I don't know if it was immediately after that or when, but stuff started to trickle through.'

Fairport Convention's eponymous debut album was released by Polydor in the UK in June 1968 – though the American release was delayed until 1970. There is little on *Fairport Convention* to suggest that here was a band which would cast its shadow over folk, rock and folk-rock for the next 30 years. Desperate to make their mark, Fairport unsuccessfully essay jazz, 'zany' instrumentals, folkie doodlings ... On this evidence, the band would be lucky to last the year.

'Time Will Show The Wiser' opens with some fiery Thompson guitar, the amp cranked all the way up to eleven. Judy Dyble's vocal style could best be described as 'wistful', and in that mode, she charmingly discharges the two Joni Mitchell songs, 'I Don't Know Where I Stand' and 'Chelsea Morning'. But 'One Sure Thing' (from a 1966 Jim and Jean album) is not enhanced by Judy's rather unemotive delivery.

Richard Thompson had begun writing 'highly derivative' songs at school, but characteristically lacked the confidence to push any of his original material into the Fairport chowder, relying instead on collaboration with either school friends or band members. His first efforts – 'Sun Shade' and 'Decameron' – were written with two school friends, Paul Ghosh and Andy Horvitch. 'Decameron' retains a certain wistful charm, sensitively sung by Ian Matthews.

'The Lobster' had music from Richard and Ashley and words from a poem by George Painter, taken from the Penguin Modern Poets series. 'If (Stomp)' was credited to MacDonald–Thompson – the MacDonald in question being Ian, who later changed his name to Ian Matthews and admitted: 'I didn't have a very big involvement in that song. Richard already had the song, but it wasn't long enough, he needed two more verses, and I just wrote those for him.'

Fairport were very keen to experiment with all the state-of-the-art studio technology 1967 had to offer. It was considered essential to try and imitate the sound effects which George Martin had utilised so brilliantly for the Beatles. Since *Sgt Pepper* ... every band was determined to show they too could play that game. Fairport's own modest attempt came on the album's closing track, 'M1 Breakdown', on which Ian Matthews is credited as playing jew's harp. He later told *Zigzag*'s John Tobler: 'That was the studio thing, they just wanted me to look good, because I didn't play anything else at the time. I did play it on "M1 Breakdown", and I really cut my mouth open too. I went to listen to the playback with blood dripping down my face.'

Richard Thompson

The most interesting thing about 'It's Alright Ma, It's Only Witchcraft' was its punning debt to Bob Dylan's 'It's Alright Ma, I'm Only Bleeding'. Fairport get hip on this 'Hutchings–Thompson' composition, and true to the spirit of the times, the chorus makes repeated use of the word 'man'.

Dylan was also responsible for the album's most intriguing track, 'Jack O'Diamonds', not the 1957 Lonnie Donegan hit of the same name, but rather a chunk of Dylan's sleeve notes from 1964's *Another Side of Bob Dylan* set to music by American actor Ben Carruthers. Carruthers had appeared in a BBC TV Play For Today, *Man Without Papers* in 1965, which featured the song. It was released as a Parlophone single later that year by Ben Carruthers and the Deep. It came into the Fairport repertoire courtesy of Richard's old William Ellis band-mate, Nick Jones, from whose father's record collection it originated.

Polydor's marketing of the Fairport album could best be described as 'low-key'. An advert the label placed in *Melody Maker* didn't suggest the record company were brimming over with optimism at the band's sales potential. The advert called the album: 'One put together by unusual personalities for that insignificant minority of seekers to whom real music, oddly enough, seems to matter.'

By the time the album was in the shops, the first of the familiar 'Fairport To Split Shock!' headlines had appeared in the music press. The first split in the Fairport ranks occurred when the band felt that Judy Dyble's singing wasn't up to scratch, and she was asked to leave. Ashley Hutchings, the man who had asked Judy to join Fairport, drew the short straw: 'I took her for a walk and told her. It was very difficult, and very sad. I think the band was getting stronger, heavier, and Judy's voice, which has always been light, was suffering because of it.'

Talking to *Hokey Pokey* in 1991, Judy Dyble retained fond memories of her twelve-month stint with Fairport Convention: 'You were with friends and you were playing and it was just fun ... we giggled and laughed a lot ... That was why it was probably so hard when they eventually asked me to leave – and I had just broken up with Richard at the time. It was very traumatic, because they were friends, and it was like them saying "Sorry, but you can't be in our gang".'

Ashley Hutchings remembers Joe Boyd advising him 'very strongly' against asking Judy to leave. What little reputation Fairport had at the time was based on their image as the 'English Jefferson Airplane' – a phrase coined by DJ Tommy Vance. It was that precarious reputation Boyd was keen to cling on to, and without a Grace Slick-style frontperson, Fairport would be just another one of many all-chaps bands ploughing the underground circuit.

The five-man Fairport persevered for about half a dozen gigs during mid-1968, but according to Simon Nicol: 'We felt it could be okay, but everybody who came to see us wanted to know where the girl was. We hadn't realised just how much of an impression she had created, and we didn't want to go cap in hand to Judy.'

So Fairport held auditions for a new vocalist, and in the incongruous location of the Eight Feathers Boys Club in Fulham, first heard the singer whose name was to become inextricably linked with theirs. Alexandra Elene Maclean Denny was already a 21-year-old veteran of the folk scene by the time she attended the Fairport audition.

Sandy Denny had established a formidable reputation in and around the London clubs. She performed solo, with guitar accompaniment, but despite the courage it took to sing to a room full of strangers, offstage Sandy found herself living in the shadow of her boyfriend, the elusive American folk singer-songwriter, Jackson C. Frank.

Working as a nurse during the day, Sandy had met Frank while he was living in exile in London in 1965. Jackson C. Frank only released one album, his eponymous debut produced by Paul Simon with Al Stewart on second guitar and Art Garfunkel as the tea boy. Sandy regularly featured Frank's best-known song, 'Blues Run The Game' at her club dates, and his 'You Never Wanted Me' was a part of Fairport's stage set – the band's version from a 1968 BBC broadcast can be heard on the 1985 Sandy retrospective box set, *Who Knows Where the Time Goes*.

While still working as a nurse, Sandy was out most nights, her tiny frame lugging an enormous guitar case around the booming mid-60s' London folk circuit, gigging regularly at the Scots Hoose, Bunjies, Les Cousins and the Troubadour. 'The Troubadour in Earls Court was the 'in' place to be in the late sixties,' Dave Cousins remembered in his sleeve notes for the 1991 CD release of *Sandy Denny and the Strawbs*. 'I dropped in at the singers' night one Tuesday and suddenly, there was the best voice I'd ever heard. She was sitting on a stool playing an old Gibson guitar, about eighteen, wearing a white dress, a white straw hat, with long blonde hair and singing like an angel . . .'

Recorded in Denmark in 1967, *Sandy Denny and the Strawbs* contains an early version of her best-known song 'Who Knows Where The Time Goes', but wasn't released in the UK until 1973. Sandy's debut solo album was released here in 1967, a nine-track effort which was basically a distillation of her folk club set – Jackson C. Frank's 'You

Richard Thompson

Never Wanted Me' and 'Milk And Honey', Tom Paxton's 'Last Thing On My Mind' and the traditional 'Make Me A Pallet On Your Floor'.

So with two albums already to her name, the idea of Fairport Convention auditioning Sandy Denny was ironic. Linda Peters (later Linda Thompson) met Sandy during 1968 when they were both struggling to make it as singers and clearly remembers Sandy telling her about the audition: 'Like a lot of people, Sandy thought that Fairport were an American band, it was the name I suppose. She had already established quite a reputation in the folk clubs, so when Fairport said "What are you going to sing?" Sandy said, "Well, I'd like you to play something for *me* first"!' Sheepishly, Fairport shuffled through a Tim Buckley song, which met with Sandy's approval, and she graciously consented to join their little group.

Simon: 'She stood out like a clean glass in a sinkful of dirty dishes.'

Joe Boyd: 'I'd been concerned when Sandy Denny joined the group that she would take over, because she was such a strong personality, compared to all of them. They were much meeker, she was by far the most assertive person with the most experience, the most aggressive. But my impression was that as soon as she joined the group, she quickly became completely in awe of Richard, and deferred to his taste – "What do you think Richard?" that sort of thing.'

Richard: 'We went on a wage at some point, it must have been 1968. We had a hard time finding a manager so we asked Joe Boyd to manage us – which was possibly not such a good move, Joe being financially probably even more inept than we were. I think we started on £12 a week, Joe asked us what was the absolute minimum we could live on and so we thought £12 a week. Then when Sandy joined the band it was too embarrassing for everybody to be on that little, Sandy couldn't possibly live on under £20 a week, so it went up to £20, because Sandy used to take cabs and drank champagne. So we thought "Wow, gosh, she's really something isn't she!". So that was a bit of a shock.'

The arrival of Sandy Denny gave Richard the confidence to begin writing. She had the sort of voice which could handle the wide variety of material the band was assimilating during 1968 and early 1969, but Sandy also brought with her a wealth of knowledge about traditional folk material gained from years spent round the clubs. Slowly, they realised that if Fairport was to have any real future, it had to come from the dynamics within the group, rather than relying on material from outside.

Sandy's singing voice was immediately and noticeably stronger than Judy's. Sandy's voice was purer, and sounded stronger on the higher register, so she was able to make herself heard over and above the increasing electricity which Fairport favoured. But Sandy's singing also conveyed a smoky quality, a 'voice of experience' which suited the strong, narrative, character-driven traditional songs which Fairport were tentatively introducing into their repertoire. Sandy's singing suggested experience, which was transparently absent from the other members of the band. She had the same kind of versatility in her voice that Fairport were beginning to muster instrumentally.

It was to be a full six months before Sandy appeared on a Fairport album, but she was already consolidating her reputation with live appearances, and Fairport were featured on plenty of sessions for BBC Radio 1 during its early years. These radio sessions were an important opportunity to gain access to a wider audience than could ever be reached by their endless trawls up and down the M1 motorway.

Richard: 'I remember Ashley saying after the first BBC sessions we did with Sandy, which was the first thing we recorded with her: "at last that's something that we can be proud of", we had actually waxed something that was worthwhile – even though it was only BBC mono, it just had some quality to it.'

The needletime restrictions still held sway during the early days of Radio 1, there was a daily total of just seven hours of needletime which had to be shared with its easy-listening rival Radio Two. This limit on the number of records played on the 'nation's Number One' (and, lest we forget *only*) pop radio station ensured a healthy number of live sessions which were then relayed over Radio One.

Then as now, Radio One's champion of new music was DJ John Peel. A former pirate DJ, Peel was the main outlet for these sessions, his was the prime slot for 'underground' bands. Alongside Peel in the late 60s, DJs such as the late Stuart Henry and David Symonds also gave house room to acts such as Fairport, as well as their contemporaries Family, Soft Machine, Colosseum, and Jeff Lynne's Idle Race.

Back then, every act who appeared regularly on BBC radio had to have their audition tape passed by the Corporation's Talent Selection Group. Fairport had already made their radio debut on John Peel's *Top Gear* in December 1967, performing 'Let's Get Together', 'One Sure Thing', 'Lay Down Your Weary Tune' and 'Chelsea Morning'. Producer Bernie Andrews submitted Fairport's second *Top Gear* session, of March 1968, to the Talent Selection Group. The band received an 'enthusiastic, unanimous pass', finding themselves favourably compared to the close-harmony American group, Harpers Bizarre.

The best of Fairport's Radio One sessions from 1968/69 are collected

Richard Thompson

together on the *Heyday* album, released on CD in 1987. As with most acts then and now, Fairport used the radio sessions as an opportunity to try out new material, tinker around with something different or as a showcase for material from their current album. Thanks to what John Peel called 'a work of almost lunatic scholarship', *In Session Tonight: The Complete Radio One Recordings* by Ken Garner (BBC 1993), we know that just prior to the release of *What We Did On Our Holidays*, Fairport Convention appeared on David Symonds' show playing 'She Moves Through The Fair' and 'I'll Keep It With Mine'.

Heyday captures Fairport at ease on the radio, and also acts as a souvenir of their early live shows, just after Sandy joined. *Heyday* has a richer sounding version of a track from Fairport's debut ('I Don't Know Where I Stand') with Sandy's fuller voice replacing Judy Dyble's tentative effort. There is also a stunning version of Leonard Cohen's 'Suzanne', which highlights Martin Lamble's abilities as a drummer. The rest of the material would be familiar to anyone who had witnessed Fairport live during 1968 and early 1969 – Richard Farina's 'Reno, Nevada', Cohen's 'Bird On A Wire', Johnny Cash's 'I Still Miss Someone', Eric Andersen's 'Close The Door Lightly When You Go' and a brace of Everly Brothers' 'Gone, Gone, Gone' and 'Some Sweet Day'.

There are some engaging oddities from Fairport's radio sessions which have yet to officially surface – Thompson's laconic reading of Dylan's basement tape 'Open The Door Homer' – Dylan only knows why 'Homer', as the chorus runs 'Open the door, Richard'. Family and Blind Faith's Rik Grech became a temporary Fairporter, joining the band on violin on a storming 'Cajun Woman'. I'm only sorry I haven't had the opportunity to hear Fairport's no doubt sincerely moving and heartfelt 'Billy The Orphan Boy's Lonely Christmas' from December 1968. Other Fairport numbers from Radio 1 sessions have appeared on Ashley Hutchings' *Guv'nor* series – notably a beautiful version of 'Sir Patrick Spens', with Sandy replacing the Simon vocal familiar from *Full House*.

The most extraordinary moment of all from Fairport's BBC sessions of the 60s, comes in September 1969, when an incredulous Peel introduces Thompson cutting through 'The Lady Is A Tramp' ('Was that *really* Richard Thompson singing?' he asks afterwards). Giving it his best Frank Sinatra, and emboldened by Sandy's jazz piano, Thompson swings like a hanged man from a gallows in a strong breeze. Fairport's Radio One sessions are a footnote to the band's history, but nevertheless a revealing footnote. Their debut album is sadly unrepresentative of how quickly the band had developed, and by their second album, with Sandy fully assimilated in their ranks, many of the much-loved cover versions had been dropped from their set.

Bernard Doherty, who went on to work closely with Richard and Linda Thompson during the 1970s, remembers seeing Fairport around this time, soon after Sandy joined: 'I saw Fairport with Sandy three or four times, at the Roundhouse and somewhere in Dagenham. I remember her being very drunk at one gig, bottles of brandy on the piano, and not thinking she was very good. But she was hailed as the Grace Slick of that scene. And I didn't really think they were very good. They were very sloppy.

'The sound was so bad in those days. Everyone was into sound back then, but it wasn't really very good. So you could remember the guitar solos, but it was all a bit muffled. It was Simon who did most of the talking, and because he had long, straight hair, and he looked like he was out of the Byrds, I honed in on him, because he seemed to control the band. Richard was up at the back hugging the amps. Because I wasn't really a "guitar hero" person, I didn't really go to listen to Richard Thompson. And at that time I didn't look closely at the labels to see that they were all Richard Thompson songs.

'The thing about Fairport was, of all the bands you saw in those days – Edgar Broughton, Clouds, Traffic – Fairport had a sense of humour. Simon had this dry wit, and Richard would throw in little asides, but Simon was the frontman. Drunkenness, all over the place, but also a sense of humour.'

By August 1968, *Beat Instrumental* magazine was calling Fairport a 'shattering live experience', which Simon Nicol borrowed for the title of a composition which was to turn up years later on *Heyday*. The feature went on to call Thompson 'one of the best lead guitarists in the country ... whose sleepy-looking face belies the complexity and inventiveness of his work'.

That same inventiveness was being applied to writing as well as guitar-playing. The first fruit of Fairport's collaboration with Sandy was a single, which Island released right at the back end of 1968. 'Meet On The Ledge' remains the one song most associated with Fairport Convention; its air of weary acceptance and resigned fatalism buoyed by a chorus of something nestling next to optimism ('When the time is up, I'm gonna see all my friends').

The composer is notoriously dismissive of his first recorded solo composition: 'I suppose if it is a good song then it will say different things to different people and it'll say different things at different times. I'm still not convinced it's a good song. But if it means things to people then I'm glad. I feel some sense of achievement.'

Richard Thompson

He is, however, in the minority. There is something about the song which is forever Fairport. 'Meet On The Ledge' is, of course, tied up with the sense of loss (Martin Lamble, Sandy) which stalked the band. But it's also a song which bids a weary adieu to the idealism and optimism which were so much a part of the late 60s underground scene, a scene to which Fairport was so allied.

Hearing Sandy sing of 'too many friends who tried, blown off this mountain with the wind' remains poignant. Or listening to Ian singing Richard's line: 'And now I see, I'm all alone, but that's the only way to be' at a time when community was still considered the answer. There is a sense of some bigger picture evoked by Thompson's economical lines, from its opening 'come the day, we'd all be making songs', until the world-weary aspect of Thompson's songwriting knocks such sweetness and light right out of whack: 'These ideas never lasted long'.

Yet finally, beneath the sad and wistful lines, the chorus ends with a promise, a hope, an intention, that if you really mean it, 'it all comes round again'. There is a will to believe that it isn't all over at the end, that there is the prospect of a life after this, which gives 'Meet On The Ledge' its affectionate place in the hearts of Fairport fans, nearly 30 years on from when they first heard it.

Richard himself dismisses such interpretation and analysis. Talking to *Flypaper*'s Frank Kornelussen in 1984, Thompson grimaced: 'I just don't think much of it ... perhaps I'm still overreacting to 1969, when we got sick to death of playing it, it was asked for at every gig, along with Leonard Cohen's "Suzanne".'

'Meet On The Ledge' is a crucial part of the Fairport legend, and as such, merits some sort of appreciation. The most convincing explanation of the song's origins came from Richard's schoolfriend Brian Wyvill. It was Brian Wyvill who had provided the initial link between Richard Thompson and Fairport Convention.

Wyvill is convinced the song was written in memory of Thompson's friends from William Ellis School – Thompson was, after all, still in his teens when he wrote the song, and his schooldays were fresh in his mind. Brian recalls spending hours with Richard and another schoolfriend, Mick Quartermain, climbing the Pothole Tree on Hampstead Heath.

During those schoolboy tree-scaling exercises, Wyvill and Quartermain managed to get to the top of the tree, but Richard could only ever manage to make it halfway up. The three schoolboy chums set a reunion date of 1 April 1972, to see how time had rung its changes, but Wyvill was abroad at the time, and is certain the reunion never took place. Looking back nearly twenty years to the Pothole Tree, Brian Wyvill remembered the name of the branch which always thwarted Richard Thompson. It was known to the three of them as . . . 'The Ledge'.

Ian Matthews, whose voice is the first to be heard on 'Meet On The Ledge' thought at the time 'that song was going to be our first hit record. We were going round the circuit and seeing all the bands, and they were all saying "Yes, that's a great single, that's going to do it, that's going to be the one" . . . I think that was my first disappointment when "Meet On The Ledge" didn't happen.'

In the snappy popspeak of the time, Chris Welch in *Melody Maker*, wrote that 'Meet On The Ledge' was: 'A stand-out performance by a most underrated group. Better than many American groups of the same style, it is startling they have not received more recognition . . . This is one for the discerning.' *Disc & Music Echo*'s reviewer said of the song: 'It's a hit with me personally, but could get lost in the Christmas chart rush.'

In one of those weird pop twists, one of the songs which ensured 'Meet On The Ledge' did get 'lost in the Christmas chart rush' was Leapy Lee's unspeakable 'Little Arrows'. Eerily while I was writing this book, the most recent cover of a Richard Thompson song was 'Waltzing's For Dreamers' by Leapy Lee.

As well as marking Fairport's Island debut, 'Meet On The Ledge' appeared on the budget *You Can All Join In* sampler, for many people their first exposure to the Island roster. The 14s 11d album was Island's answer to the CBS budget taster *The Rock Machine Turns You On*. *You Can All Join In* introduced not only Fairport, but the original Nirvana, Traffic, Jethro Tull, Free and King Crimson, all seen shivering on the sleeve which was photographed at the crack of dawn in Hyde Park.

Joe Boyd had installed all his Witchseason acts at Island; as well as the Incredible String Band and John and Beverly Martyn, Boyd now added a new signing. Fairport's Ashley Hutchings had gone to see Country Joe McDonald at a Peace In Vietnam event at the Roundhouse one afternoon in 1968, and been particularly impressed by a young singer-songwriter. It was on Ashley's recommendation that Boyd signed up 20-year-old Nick Drake.

From the high point of 1967, the underground had broken cover during 1968. But bands like Fairport had little to do with the demonstrations and fighting in the streets.

Richard: 'I think Fairport was quite cynical about the drug culture

Richard Thompson

and about the whole 60s psychedelic culture – I think we really felt a bit on the fringe of it and not particularly involved. I think we probably felt quite isolated actually, in terms of what we were trying to do as a band, musically in terms of direction.

'I think I tried everything really, except heroin – but I didn't do much of anything. By the time I took acid I think it was just rubbish, I think it was basically speed. So I didn't have any revelatory acid experiences. Bit of this, a bit of that.'

During that heady summer of 1968, with student revolutions in France, Italy, Japan, Czechoslovakia, America and Mexico, it really did seem that politics was being bypassed, and that the revolution was up for grabs in the streets and on the barricades.

Joe Boyd's partner 'Hoppy' Hopkins recalled a conversation of the time: 'I remember meeting Jennie Lee at the London Arts Lab. She sat down with us, the Minister of Culture, and she said "Nye (Bevan) and me worked all our lives to make a better society, and I think we did it. We've got the National Health Service, free education, so on and so forth ... why do you say politics is pigshit?" It was an unbelievable insult to her ...'

Fairport were certainly in sympathy with all the right causes, properly anti-Vietnam and pro-*International Times*, but never wore their revolution on the sleeves of their patched denim jackets.

Richard: 'In America there was a real polarisation between the liberals and the intelligentsia – who were the folk singers and activists – and electric music was pop music, there wasn't anything else, it was just pop.

'It was Dylan who broke all that down and kind of invented modern rock music and gave it credibility, because at that time the Rolling Stones were a pop band – everybody was a pop band. There wasn't this thing called rock. That was the reason he was booed more than anything else, people thought he was betraying the whole political movement as well.

'There didn't seem to be any interest in any of that stuff over here, it didn't really apply, there wasn't a political dimension to grasp, only really the psychedelic dimension of alternative lifestyles or youth lifestyles, that people could get hold of.'

With the failure of 'Meet On The Ledge', Fairport buckled down to the recording of their second album, *What We Did On Our Holidays* late in 1968. The title comes from one of those deathless essay subjects so beloved of school teachers at the time; the cover was a blackboard in Fairport's dressing room, after the band had given it some of the primitive prior to a gig at Essex University.

Fairport

Ashley: 'I think *Holidays* is the first album with a real Fairport stamp on it. Sandy came in, and it was the first appearance of a couple of traditional songs on a Fairport record ... As a band, it was really coming together ... There was a lot of good material around, increasingly more available to us, and the guys were writing, and Sandy was bringing material in, so that there was a lot of competition for the material on that album to be good.'

Chapter 5

FAIRPORT CONVENTION'S SECOND ALBUM, *What We Did On Our Holidays* was released in January 1969. It was the album which saw Fairport begin to shake off the American influences which had dominated the band from its inception. It was the album which marked Sandy's debut with the band. And it was the album which saw Richard Thompson's emergence as a songwriter in his own write – *Holidays* featured three solo Thompson compositions as well as two collaborations.

Talking to *Beat Instrumental* in 1968 about the new direction Fairport were heading at the time of recording their second album, Thompson began with the inevitable comparisons between Fairport and the American West Coast bands: 'There are similarities . . . but there's one big and basic difference. They all seem to be doing a sort of cross between rock and soul – look at Big Brother, Country Joe and Jefferson Airplane – it's not all that far from the sock-it-to-me thing, and very American. We think of ourselves as a folk-based band. This is even more pronounced now that Sandy Denny is with us . . . She really knows what the folk tradition is all about, and the group as a whole are drawing from the English roots. The fact that we're electric doesn't make any difference.'

What We Did On Our Holidays is the transitional Fairport record, and an integral part of that transition was the inclusion and development of the traditional folk tunes which Sandy brought with her from the folk clubs, as much as Thompson's development as a songwriter.

Richard: 'When Sandy came into the band we started to do more English stuff, songs that Sandy knew from singing the folk scene. She knew Alex Campbell and Bert Jansch and everybody, so we started to meet some of these people.'

Fairport were a three-strand band at the time of *What We Did On Our Holidays*: they were developing their own in-house songwriters; they were cherrypicking the best – and usually most obscure – cover versions from the new American singer-songwriters. And, perhaps most tellingly of all, they were keenly expanding their own adaptations of traditional folk tunes.

Richard's belief in the possibilities of Fairport as an electric band tackling folk songs refers to one of the key musical issues of that period. Nearly three years on from Bob Dylan's watershed tour with the Band in 1966, opinion was still divided about the legitimacy of marrying 'folk' with 'pop'. Essentially, the late 60s argument ran along the lines that 'folk' music was by its very nature, sacrosanct. Handed down from generation to generation it was, and must remain, authentic and pure. Its value and uniqueness lay in the fact that it was unaccompanied or, if necessary, performed with acoustic accompaniment. 'Pop' or 'rock' music was popular, but it was also amplified and therefore was ephemeral, superficial and insincere.

While 1967 is remembered as rock's great year of experiment, with *Sgt Pepper* . . . in the ascendant, and debut albums from the Jimi Hendrix Experience, Pink Floyd and the Velvet Underground, 1968 was the year that retrenchment took place. The major albums of the year – Dylan's *John Wesley Harding*, the Beatles' *White Album* and the Rolling Stones' *Beggars Banquet* – were uniformly back to basics, return to roots efforts. Psychedelia was marginalised, old-style rock'n'roll and blues back on the map, even country and western was suddenly hip.

No one knew what 1969 would hold, and *What We Did On Our Holidays* was one of the first albums out of the traps that year. The album opened with Sandy's own beautiful 'Fotheringay', written after she visited the castle in Northamptonshire where Mary Queen Of Scots was executed in 1587.

Ashley Hutchings' 'Mr Lacey' was his tribute to professional eccentric and inventor, 'Professor' Bruce Lacey, who was a neighbour of Ashley's in Durnsford Road. The real 'Mr Lacey' was the man who organised regular 'Evenings of British Rubbish', and can still be seen as the Beatles' indoor gardener in *Help!*, trimming the Fabs' lawn with electric teeth. Ian Matthews remembers Ashley bringing the professor down to the studio to play the song's 'solo', which consisted of three home-made robots walking around, supervised by Lacey clad in a space suit.

Although credited as a joint Matthews/Thompson composition, Ian Matthews already had the lyrics and melody of 'Book Song', Thompson simply wrote the chords for the song.

Thompson's first solo composition on the album is the accordion-led 'No Man's Land', a swinging nightmare of a song, the melodic

Richard Thompson

jauntiness offset by the lyrical melancholy. 'No Man's Land' became one of the first Thompson songs to be covered, when it appeared on *New Colours* in 1971, sung by that band which typified the British Underground movement at its crazy, capering best – the New Seekers.

Richard: 'I thought great, now I'll make some money, but of course it was their big flop album.'

It's a little known fact that as well as being a dashed-fine guitar-player, spiffing songwriter and all-round good egg, Richard Thompson can also add accordion-playing to his CV: 'I've always thought the only accordion worth learning is the four-button one that John Kirkpatrick plays – it's like playing the uilleann pipes and the pedal steel guitar at the same time. Don't try this at home!'

The accordion on 'No Man's Land' is played by Thompson, who also used it to beef up 'Cajun Woman' on *Unhalfbricking* and in 1969 featured the instrument on his only *Top of the Pops* appearance, with 'Si Tu Dois Partir'. Thompson also played the accordion on Ian Matthews' 1972 album *Tigers Will Survive*, guesting – for some inexplicable reason – as 'Wolf J. Flywheel' (the name of Groucho Marx's character in *The Big Store*). As well as his guitar, vocal contributions to Sandy Denny's first post-Fairport solo album, *The North Star Grassman and the Ravens*, Thompson played accordion on 'Blackwaterside' and later toyed with the instrument on *Shoot Out the Lights*.

Thompson's other contribution to *What We Did On Our Holidays* was 'Tale In Hard Time', ushered in by some spiky Thompson guitar and a characteristic opening rhyme: 'Take the sun from my eyes/Let me learn to despise . . .' This time, the only covers were Joni Mitchell's 'Eastern Rain' and Dylan's 'I'll Keep It With Mine'. The Dylan song is remarkable for one of Sandy's finest vocals and some stirring ensemble playing from Fairport. It is a salutary reminder that recording covers never stopped Fairport making their own mark on a song.

Joe Boyd: 'I think we went into Feldman Music and listened to the Dylan songs. I didn't have very much to do, except for playing them the Joni Mitchell stuff. At that time, when they were in their American period, I didn't have a lot to do with finding songs for them. They were very adept at finding their own songs, they had vast record collections and knew every American singer-songwriter's works backwards and forwards.'

Two songs which formed the foundation of *What We Did On Our Holidays*, and signposted the direction the band was to take later that year, were 'Nottamun Town' and 'She Moves Through The Fair'. Both songs came to the band courtesy of Sandy Denny, although Ashley remembers 'Nottamun Town' from Shirley Collins and Davy Graham's seminal 1964 *Folk Roots, New Routes* album. The Fairport version is by no means radical, Thompson's solo is acoustic, and Ian Matthews' congas strike an incongruous Eastern note. But they remain significant as the first songs to feature the familiar credit 'Trad. Arr. Fairport'.

'She Moves Through The Fair' is a clear indication of where Fairport was going. Erroneously credited as a traditional song, 'She Moves Through The Fair' is a traditional Gaelic poem, rewritten by Irish poet Padraic Colum to a musical setting by Herbert Hughes. It was first popularised in 1909, and Fairport's version came from the Irish singer Margaret Barry. Looking back, Simon felt 'it was a bit of a nothing arrangement'.

Ashley: ' "She Moves Through The Fair" was basically Sandy's working, and us just fitting in around her. If you took out the tracks with the drums, electric bass and electric guitars, you would have Sandy doing it exactly as she would do it in the clubs.'

'The Lord Is In This Place ... How Dreadful Is This Place' was a Fairport reworking of Blind Willie Johnson's 'Dark Was The Night, Cold Was The Ground'. Recorded at St Peter's Church, Westbourne Grove, it is a slight, if atmospheric piece. Added poignancy comes from the faint sound of footsteps disappearing on the track, which belonged to 19-year-old Martin Lamble.

Fairport always enjoyed a close relationship with the landmark British rock monthly, *Zig Zag*. They were featured on the cover of the first issue in April 1969 and when the magazine ran into financial problems, it was Fairport who organised a benefit concert at the Roundhouse to keep it going. Founder Pete Frame wrote an enthusiastic profile of Fairport proclaiming that *What We Did On Our Holidays* 'towers like an aardvark in an ant colony compared with all 1969's other releases ...' Frame then zeroed in on 'the pilot of their conglomerate genius ... lead guitarist Richard Thompson, who steers the group with a film director's vision ... Thompson also wrote "No Man's Land", an exuberant accordion-dominated romp, which, despite the despondent lyric, conjures up visions of leather-trousered dancing Germans spilling beer ...'

What We Did On Our Holidays attracted precious little notice elsewhere with sales levelling out at around 20,000, so Fairport went back on the road to try and whip up some interest. Ian Matthews was clearly unhappy with the direction they were heading: ' "Book Song" was definitely an indication of where I wanted to go ... That was the direction that I thought the band was going to go, and that was what I was working on ... I didn't have any input on the songs we did. That was

Richard Thompson

Richard and Ashley ... Richard's a unique kind of person. He could tie all that stuff in, the traditional side of it and the contemporary side, and make it all sound like one thing, like it all belongs in the same place.'

Growing further apart, Matthews was dismissed in the second 'Fairport Split' shock: 'I never enjoyed going into that traditional stuff. There was no place for me to take part in something like that, because I didn't have any kind of traditional roots, like Sandy, and I didn't have any traditional sense like Richard or Ashley ... The first time we did "A Sailor's Life" onstage, I remember they worked it up in the dressing room, and I had never worked up in the dressing room in my life, it had always been done at rehearsal. That was my first foray into it, and it didn't appeal to me at all. I think it became increasingly clear that there was really no place for me in a band playing that type of music ... and the next thing I knew, Joe Boyd told me that they wanted me to leave the band.'

Following Matthews' departure, the focus of the band was even more firmly on Sandy. Rock bands of the time were all-boys-together, a gang thing, and Sandy's singing was unparalleled. On record she dominated a song, but never quashed it. She was vibrant and throaty. Visually, Sandy offered a counterpoint to the scruffy oiks either side of her – Simon's long, straight hair framed his face, while Ashley stood stock still playing the bass and rarely smiling. Richard still tended to lurk at the back, emerging into the limelight only to let rip a solo of astonishing power and intensity.

Against all the odds, it was Thompson though who began to gain the ascendant in the Fairport hierarchy. Ashley Hutchings may have laid the Fairport foundations and Sandy may have provided the charisma, but it was Richard who was now powering the group. At that stage it was still largely as a guitarist that Thompson was making his mark, but he was already scratching at the surface of songwriting. In rock music, it's always the songwriter to whom a band gravitates. It is the songwriter who builds the power base. Singers and rhythm sections can be replaced, but the real power lies in the hands of the person who writes the songs. Neither Richard nor Sandy were by any means prolific writers yet, so that strand in the Fairport history would have to bide its time.

By the middle of 1969 Fairport Convention were just another band in one of the dozens of Ford transits ploughing up and down the M1. From Mothers in Birmingham, to the Van Dike in Plymouth, from the Marquee in Soho to the Oxford Polytechnic. Or more conveniently for Simon and Richard, a quick trip down Haverstock Hill from the Brent flat for a gig at the Roundhouse. Fairport were pulling in around £600 for each show. They had even gigged abroad, in Rome and Geneva. It was too early to think seriously of America, but once the follow-up to *Holidays* was in the can, inevitably Fairport would utilise Joe Boyd's contacts, and aim to make an impact on the lucrative American market.

It was during those endless trawls up and down the motorway spine of the United Kingdom that Fairport came up with the title of their third album. *Unhalfbricking* is not the name of some traditional rural custom like 'beating the bounds', but a word which Sandy made up and contributed to a word game called Ghosts which the group played in the back of their van on the long journeys between gigs.

The couple featured on the cover of *Unhalfbricking* are Sandy Denny's parents, photographed in the garden of their Wimbledon home while the group take their tea in the background. Fairport's American record label A&M considered this image too weird for a potential US audience and replaced the offending shot with a troupe of performing elephants.

With Fairport on the road, and the all too evident generation gap, Richard was not seeing much of his own parents, his father particularly was kept at arm's length. 'At that time I just didn't see him that much really. It must have been difficult for him because he really liked guitar playing – that was the great softener I suppose. Whatever he felt about hippiedom and the lifestyle or even the music, it was still guitar playing and he really liked guitar playing and he was always saying: "Dinah" that's a great song – you should think about that one. This was somewhere in the middle of Fairport – you can just see "Dinah" fitting into the repertoire!'

Unhalfbricking received better reviews than its predecessor. Lon Goddard in *Record Mirror* hardly got any further than the title ('the word looks curiously pornographic if you stare at it long enough'). In *New Musical Express*, Nick Logan wrote: 'It's not so much that they're such skilled craftsmen that makes Fairport Convention one of the most listenable groups there are but the almost indefinable quality about their music that suggests youthfulness and vitality. Even on the sad songs the feel that permeates through is one of a joy of being alive . . .' *Melody Maker* noted: 'Even at their most rocking, Fairport maintain a gentle, tasteful approach, and should they ever seem to be too steeped in sadness, humour bubbles through . . .'. In America, *Fusion* magazine simply called *Unhalfbricking* 'perfect', and compared its impact favourably to Van Morrison's *Astral Weeks* and the Band's *Music From Big Pink*.

Richard Thompson

In his 'Now! Underground, Blues, Progressive and Pop' column in *Disc & Music Echo*, John Peel announced 'Fairport Convention, we love you!', before going on to give *Unhalfbricking* a rave review. 'This group has brought me more joy during the past two years than any other I can think of . . . It is true, therefore, that any review I write will be coloured with love. Suffice to say then that the record made me feel warm and comfortable and part of them. It is an LP that you will want to hear daily for a very long time.'

It is the album of a band at the crossroads, Fairport's own *Beatles For Sale*. The album contains three Dylan songs, two Sandy songs (including her best-loved, 'Who Knows Where The Time Goes?'), two Richard compositions and just one traditional.

Thompson's 'Genesis Hall' was named after a London squat which the police had recently busted. The knowledge that Thompson's father was still a serving police officer lends the opening lines of the song added poignancy: 'Oh my father he rides with your sheriffs/And I know he would never mean harm . . .' It is Thompson's chilling ability to ally the style of a seventeenth-century Scottish Border ballad with a rock'n'roll sensibility which still astounds. Solemn and stately, the song proceeds with tragic inevitability. And all the while, Richard and Sandy's voices blend on the heart-breaking chorus, 'Oh, oh, helpless and slow/And you don't have anywhere to go . . .'

Richard was on a cajun jag during the recording of *Unhalfbricking*, which influenced his other contribution, 'Cajun Woman'. It is notable for at least acknowledging the existence of cajun music, at a time when most people thought that zydeco was just a word you made up to cheat at Scrabble.

Richard: 'I was always into Cajun. I think I had a Clifton Chenier record in 1967 – I thought that was really great – wow, listen to this, accordion – great and all that Arhoolie stuff, you could actually find some of that in London in 1967. Ashley had a Rusty and Doug album which was great, it had all those songs on: "Alligator Man" . . . good stuff. I think the story was supposed to be the Greek story of Electra translated to the swamps of Louisiana.'

Joe Boyd had appointed Brenda Ralfini to oversee Warlock Music, the song publishing arm of Witchseason. During 1968, she had worked for Bob Dylan's publishing company, hawking the artist's latest recordings around UK song publishers. This was the original 'basement tape', the reel-to-reel from which Manfred Mann obtained 'Mighty Quinn', Julie Driscoll and Brian Auger got 'This Wheel's On Fire' and, lest we forget, the Tremeloes lifted 'I Shall Be Released'.

It was from the same fertile source that Fairport obtained 'Million Dollar Bash'. Fairport's version of Dylan's front-porch philosophy is still well worth a listen, though largely for their cornball American accents. You are also heartily recommended to seek out the version of 'Million Dollar Bash' which Ashley re-wrote for Fairport's 25th Anniversary concert. Aside from some serious Thompson electric playing, you can get to hear the austere and academic Mr Ashley Hutchings going demented before a delighted Cropredy crowd:

> You can meet all your friends,
> You can meet on the ledge,
> You can meet at the bar,
> You can meet Percy Sledge!
> Well, maybe not this year,
> But see the stars flash,
> They're all gonna be there,
> At that million dollar bash

Unhalfbricking also contained 'Percy's Song', a much earlier Dylan song about bitter injustice, which Fairport transformed into something epic and immensely moving. Just listen how Sandy's voice dips and soars, growing in outrage and indignity. For John Peel, the Fairport version built with 'the same mantric, mystic force that you found on "Hey Jude"'.

Simon: 'It needs a voice like Sandy's to get the shades of emotion across, from moodiness to compassion to outright fury. There's not many singers can do that.'

'If You Gotta Go, Go Now' had inexplicably appeared in 1967 as the B-side of a Bob Dylan single released only in the Benelux countries. Thompson's cajun fascination was further evidenced by the group's tongue-in-cheek attempt at rendering the song into French for *Unhalfbricking*. Richard remembers the band in the dressing room at Middle Earth thinking it would be fun to do the song in pidgin French, and asking over the PA if there was a Frenchman in the house. 'About three people turned up, so it was really written by committee and consequently ended up not very cajun, French or Dylan!'

'Si Tu Dois Partir' was of course The Hit. It leapfrogged all the way to no. 21 in the UK singles chart in July 1969. Fairport had strong competition, from the likes of such classics as 'The Ballad Of John and Yoko', Creedence Clearwater Revival's 'Proud Mary', Simon and Garfunkel's 'The Boxer', 'Give Peace A Chance', 'Honky Tonk Woman' . . . Surprising then that the result of a stoned French translation of an obscure Dylan B-side by a wonky English folkie band should even get within a sniff of the Top Twenty.

This was the song which landed Richard Thompson his only *Top of the Pops* appearance, although Fairport did appear on the programme again, during its short-lived album slot. To help promote 'Si Tu Dois Partir' and emphasise its Gallic roots, Ashley appeared clad in a beret, while roadie Steve Sparks sat swaddled in onions.

The last track on side one of *Unhalfbricking*, 'A Sailor's Life' was certainly a signpost, undeniably a seminal fusion of folk and rock. Unfortunately it is also a tad dull. Sandy sings it beautifully, of course, and Richard's guitar is as spellbinding as ever. But it does go on slightly longer than the career of Frank Sinatra, with precious little in the way of pacing or dynamics. In his *Rolling Stone* review of *Unhalfbricking*, John Mendelsohn concurred: 'There's an over-long traditional [song] on *Unhalfbricking*: "A Sailor's Life", which seems capable of being done without nicely.' It remains however, a minority opinion.

'A Sailor's Life' began life as an eighteenth-century ballad coming into Fairport's repertoire after Sandy had learned it from A. L. (Bert) Lloyd, doyen of the English folk revival. At the same time, Ashley Hutchings was burrowing through the library at the headquarters of the English Folk Song and Dance Society at Cecil Sharp House in London, where he unearthed further verses. All concerned with the band were enchanted with 'A Sailor's Life'. They saw it as a breakthrough for them, a way to tackle the old by fusing it with the new.

Ashley: 'We were at Southampton University waiting to go on stage, and Sandy was playing around in the dressing room, and picked up a guitar, and sang "A Sailor's Life". We loved it ... and busked along. Then the time came to go on stage. We made an instant decision. I mean, we were all buzzing with that because we enjoyed doing it so much.'

Joe Boyd: 'It was clear to me that this was a new departure for them ... I remember being quite impressed and amazed by it.'

For nearly 25 years, the only version of 'A Sailor's Life' was the one featured on *Unhalfbricking*, with Fairport's memorable inclusion of violinist Dave Swarbrick. Then in 1993, a pre-Swarbrick version appeared on the Thompson retrospective *Watching the Dark*, which gives even fuller flavour to Thompson's florid guitar.

Swarbrick had initially been approached by Boyd to add a fiddler's dram to 'Cajun Woman'. Joe recalls: 'I figured he would be delighted at the chance to play on a rock album and get the session fee.'

Richard: 'I think Ashley, as long as he was in the band, had his hand on the tiller – steering the band. It was a reasonably democratic band but probably the stronger personalities were myself and Sandy, and then Swarb came into the band and he was a strong force. So you had a lot of fairly up-front people with ideas and creativity. I think by the time Swarb joined there were probably too many and the band started to pull apart just in terms of egos. But as long as Ashley was in the band I think he was really controlling the direction.'

Swarbrick came to Olympic Studios in Barnes, west London to play on 'A Sailor's Life' one Sunday afternoon. Fairport were tired. They'd already recorded three songs earlier that day and Sandy was isolated in the booth with a streaming cold. As Simon Nicol recalls of that landmark moment: 'It didn't look auspicious.'

The importance of Swarbrick's presence on *Unhalfbricking* cannot be over-estimated. By the end of the 1960s, Swarbrick was already a major figure on the English folk scene, initially in the Ian Campbell Folk Group, but primarily in partnership with Martin Carthy. Joe Boyd remembers Fairport being overawed by the prospect of Swarbrick joining them on record: 'They were all very impressed with Swarbrick, very much "Could we really get the Great Swarbrick to play?" . . .' With Swarbrick only too keen to clamber aboard, Fairport were ready to undertake the voyage.

Ashley: 'They set the tape rolling and we did it, and the energy and adrenalin were incredible. When we finished, we knew what we had done . . . we went into the box to hear it . . . Joe and John (Wood) were almost speechless . . . we *knew* we had done something different. We knew that there was a path open to us.'

Fairport weren't looking to jump on the folk-rock bandwagon. It didn't exist. What Fairport were doing at the time was creating something entirely new. 'A Sailor's Life' and the subsequent *Liege & Lief* album may sound tepid today, but in 1969 the fusion which Fairport achieved was nothing short of revolutionary.

Simon: 'We were beginning to realise what an asset Sandy was, with her access to traditional material . . . and I felt very honoured that Swarb came in – it lent folk authenticity.'

Such was the zeal of Fairport's conversion to electric folk, that not only did the band ask Swarbrick to join, but according to Nicol they also considered approaching his partner Martin Carthy, long considered the outstanding singer of the English folk revival: 'We did discuss the possibility of Martin Carthy joining at the time, but we thought it would be too top heavy, too many people involved . . . I didn't like the idea of *three* guitarists, particularly two like Martin and Richard!'

Richard Thompson

Keen to spread the word, Fairport were back on the road in the spring of 1969 to build up interest in their forthcoming album, which was scheduled for a June release. The band set off on the familiar circuit of gigs, Birmingham, Plymouth, Oxford, Enfield, Sunderland ... The usual round of late nights and long hauls back down the motorway to north London.

Richard had begun travelling to gigs with his new girlfriend, a 26-year-old American clothes designer, Jeannie Franklyn, who had come over from her home in Los Angeles to spend some time with him. Jeannie was a cousin of Phil Ochs, which was her entrée into the world of rock'n'roll. She had a boutique in Los Angeles, and numbered Maria Muldaur and the Doors among her clients.

Joe Boyd: 'I vaguely remember a shop Jeannie Franklyn had on Santa Monica Boulevard, a little place where she did custom-made things ... She was a rather assertive, American West Coast girl. I think in some way, there's a part of Richard that's always been more comfortable with that sort of a person, somebody who leaves him alone to do music while she deals with the rest of the world ... That may have been one of the problems with Linda: he thought she was like that, but she really wasn't.'

It was while returning from a gig at Mother's in Birmingham, early on the morning of 12 May 1969, that the van carrying Fairport Convention crashed on the M1.

Eclection had been supporting Fairport at the gig, and Sandy had already driven back to London with her boyfriend, Eclection's singer Trevor Lucas. Fairport's roadie Harvey Bramham was driving the group's transit van; Simon, Ashley and Martin were in the back, while Richard and his girlfriend Jeannie were seated in the front.

Bramham who was driving, apparently fell asleep at the wheel, causing the van to drift and cartwheel. Simon Nicol was fast asleep in the back: 'I can remember waking up while the van was actually somersaulting ... When I woke up, I was the only one in the vehicle – everyone else had gone through the windows and doors.'

The van had smashed into the central reservation on the M1 near Mill Hill, and then plunged 40 feet down an embankment, before finishing upside down on a golf course. Harvey Bramham had gone straight through the windscreen. Richard and Ashley were wandering around dazed, 90 feet away from the upturned vehicle. Martin was lying very still in the distance.

Simon managed to flag down a lorry and the driver called for an ambulance which seemed to take an age to arrive. Eventually, the band were taken to the Royal National Orthopaedic Hospital in Stanmore, Middlesex.

The *Evening Standard* reported in its first edition that: 'The four injured were the group's road manager, Harvey Brahan [sic] of Purser's Cross Road, Fulham (broken leg and concussion); guitarists Simon Nicol (concussion) and Richard Thompson (broken ribs and concussion), both of St Mary's Road, Golders Green, and Ashley Hutchings (facial lacerations) of Donovan Avenue, Muswell Hill.'

Simon: 'I remember hours and hours of waiting in casualty, where they were struggling with Martin. Jeannie was already dead when they put her in the ambulance . . . Richard just sat looking at the wall, Hutch couldn't see because he had so much blood on his face . . . They only had to pick one tiny piece of glass out of my arm.'

Ashley: 'I had a broken nose, a broken cheek bone. I couldn't see immediately after the crash, both my eyes were closed up . . . When Ian (Matthews) came to visit us in hospital, the first time he saw my face, he fainted on the next bed.'

Richard's sister Perri remembers rushing to the hospital and seeing an enormous bouquet of flowers from the Rolling Stones. His parents took longer to get to Stanmore as they were on holiday at the time. His mother recalls: 'His foot was injured. It was such a shock when we went into the ward, poor Ashley Hutchings, his face was ghastly. The driver was all strung up – his legs were broken. And Richard had hurt his ankle, but we couldn't get near the beds – we could not get anywhere near Richard – we just said "Hello Richard, we're here, are you alright dear". And all these fans – some had walked from Cornwall – they'd hitch-hiked to come and see Richard – they were all round the bed – so we chatted to the people opposite – a man had broken his leg.'

Martin Lamble was still a teenager when he died in the operating theatre at Stanmore. On Fairport Convention's first press release, under 'Previous Occupation', Martin Lamble had written simply 'Child'.

METROPOLITAN POLICE

No. 994

NOTICE TO WITNESS TO ATTEND BEFORE A COURT OF SUMMARY JURISDICTION

To Mr. Richard Thompson,
33, St Mary's Road,
N.W.11.

'S' Division.
West Hendon Station.
2nd November, 1969.

Sir/~~Madam~~

I am directed by the Commissioner of Police of the Metropolis to request you to attend

HENDON ~~Metropolitan~~ Magistrates' Court

situated at The Hyde, Colindale, N.W.9.

at 10 a.m. on Tues day, the 25th of November, 1969.

to give evidence in the case of Mr. H. Bramham

{summoned for} causing death by dangerous driving

on 12th May, 1969,

your evidence being material to the proceedings.

The receipt of this communication should be acknowledged by completing the detachable slip below and returning it in the accompanying stamped and addressed envelope. (Note. This envelope must not be sealed).

If you incur expenses in connection with your attendance at Court the police officer in charge of the case should be informed when you attend. The Commissioner is authorised to refund expenses on the scale laid down [...] osts in Criminal Cases Act, 1952, and for your in- [...] ances will be forwarded by postal draft as soon as [...] dance at Court, you can avoid delay in payment by [...] that will be deducted (e.g. day's pay, half day's pay

Your obedient Servant,

P. Dooling Insp.
for Chief Superintendent

[...] for the prosecutor complainant or defendant, who will not [...] rates' Court Act, 1952, Sec. 77).

POP MEN IN M1 CRASH—TWO DIE

Two people died and four were injured, when a mini-bus carrying the Fairport Convention pop group crashed on the M1 today.

The minibus crashed into a central reservation and then plunged 40ft. down an embankment near a service station at Mill Hill.

It finished upside down on a golf course.

The two who died were Martin Lamble, the group's 19-year-old drummer, of Radnor Road, Harrow, and an American girl, Jeannie Franklin.

She was known in the pop world as "The Tailor".

She was due to return to her home in Los Angeles, where she ran a business producing stage clothes for pop groups.

MARTIN LAMBLE

engagement at a Birmingham club.

The group are well known in the Underground pop world. The group's girl singer, 21-year-old Sandy Denny, escaped.

The four injured were the group's road manager, Harvey Brahan, of Purser's Cross Road, Fulham (broken leg and concussion; guitarists Simon Nicol (concussion) and Richard Thompson (broken ribs and concussion), both of St. Mary's Road, Golders Green and Ashley Hutchings (facial lacerations and concussion) of Donovan Avenue, Muswell Hill.

Their condition was said to be comfortable at the Royal National Orthopaedic Hospital, Stanmore.

The Golders Green-based group was returning from an

Chapter 6

RICHARD HAD SUFFERED ONLY 'lacerations and a few cracked ribs', but, barely 20 years old, the crash left a terrible emotional scar. 'It was a shock, a real shock. To see people die that young. To see Martin die, he was like 17 or 18 years old. Jeannie was my girlfriend – I hadn't known her that long just a few weeks. But it was devastating for me. I felt in a state of shock for a couple of years – it was very hard to put stuff into perspective. It broke my perspective for a while – I couldn't get an overall picture of something, it was like being on a drug – seeing the world piecemeal instead of as a whole thing. I felt terribly restless, it was hard to settle down after that.'

The survivors were in a state of shock following the crash, not helped by a visit from the Drug Squad while they were still recuperating in hospital.

The bottom had fallen out of Fairport's world; the band were still incredibly young, and the simultaneous deaths of two close friends were the first fatalities among their contemporaries that they had experienced.

The music world was stunned by the Fairport tragedy. Benefit concerts were immediately organised. Van Dike's in Plymouth had a Fairport Benefit on 29 May, featuring King Crimson, Eclection, Bridget St John, and Yes, while the London Roundhouse held theirs on 25 May, with Pink Floyd and Family headlining. Following Martin Lamble's death in the crash, *Melody Maker* devoted a full page to the dangers 'Behind the Bright Lights of Pop': 'When a group hits the highway to drive hundreds of miles to yet another one-night stand, there's always a silent, unseen passenger riding along in the bandwagon. Death ... The pop world is not all laughter and light. The eternal shadows also lie in wait.'

At the time of the crash, Joe Boyd – Fairport's manager and record producer – was in America with the finished tapes of *Unhalfbricking*,

Richard Thompson

arranging Fairport's American debut at the 1969 Newport Folk Festival. 'I felt at the time the group, as it was constituted for *Unhalfbricking*, was going to do very well in America. In fact, I was on my way to the West Coast to see Bill Graham about putting them on at the Fillmore when I got the call about the crash, and I turned around and flew back to London.'

Richard responded soon after the crash by writing 'Never Again', in memoriam to Jeannie, but it was never recorded by Fairport and first appeared, sung by Linda, on *Hokey Pokey* six years later. John Kirkpatrick, who worked closely with Richard during the 1970s, is convinced that Richard's still unreleased 'Bad News Is All The Wind Can Carry' came from the same shocking event.

John Kirkpatrick: 'I came across the song when I was with The Albion Band at the National Theatre doing *Lark Rise* . . . and Ashley had a recording of it. We used it in the second play, *Candleford*, and I was just absolutely knocked out with the song, and we started doing it with Brass Monkey . . . And either somebody said, or I guessed, but it certainly comes from the time of just after the Fairport crash when Richard's girlfriend was killed . . . As usual with Richard, when you ask him "was that song about anything particular?" He'll say "Oh I don't know, it's just a song". Just fob it off. He came to a Brass Monkey gig somewhere, and somebody said that during that song he had tears pouring down his face . . .'

By the time the remaining members of the band reconvened, the shock of the tragedy and the sense of loss was beginning to fade. Simon affirms: 'The band had been through the worst thing that could have happened to them.'

Fairport's American label, A&M Records arranged for Sandy and Richard, along with Simon and his then-girlfriend Roberta, to fly over to the States for a fortnight to recuperate. Richard spent part of the time at the house of Phil Ochs in Los Angeles.

Richard: 'We went over with Joe – I'm not sure what the idea of it was – perhaps to take our minds off it or something. We were about to do an American tour and Joe thought it would be therapeutic to go and have a look at it so that when we finally did go over there we had some idea what it was like and we'd know a few people.'

This was Thompson's first visit to the city which is now his home. His impressions are preserved in a postcard he wrote to a friend at the time: 'This is the strangest place. Spent the first three days in Los Angeles, which is just absolutely utterly unbelievable. Try to imagine a starry, warm, tropical night. You are standing at the window of Phil

Ochs' house several hundred feet up Laurel Canyon or thereabouts, and stretching out beneath you for fifteen or twenty miles in all directions, laid out in squares as far as the eye can see is L.A., Hollywood, Monterey etc, which are really all one enormous city. The city of the motor car. There are no pedestrians, but it is so beautiful and so ultimately decadent . . .'

Richard: 'It was very strange. A lot of chlorine in the water and really bad air – that's all I remember, I think it was summer when we went and it just seemed really hot, muggy and humid – we'd never seen weather like that before. And the people we met were Joe's friends from Harvard – we met Mimi Farina and went to her house and we started jamming around and she'd bring out Dick's dulcimer. Geoff and Maria Muldaur in Boston. We saw Little Feat play – that was quite fun – opening for Esso Steel Band which at that point was arranged by Van Dyke Parks – he did all the arrangements, a big sponsored steel band that did "River Deep, Mountain High" and Bach and stuff. It was interesting. We went up the Big Sur coast which was nice.

'I think we flew to Los Angeles and the first night we were there we were all jetlagged and half asleep and we went to a big party at Phil Ochs' house – lots of drink, women everywhere – just fantastic. He was an old mate of Joe's, he was a funny guy – kind of pretentious in some ways – very politically motivated, maybe too politically motivated. We used to see Phil a lot, he was always at the A&M lot – he had his own office there. He used to give us an audience in his office sometimes!'

While in LA, Thompson made his American debut, he and Sandy and Simon appeared as a trio at the Troubadour in June 1969. Memories are deliberately hazy, but if pushed, Richard will admit that 'it was terrible'. Returning to the Brent flat he still shared with Simon, Richard and the remainder of Fairport had to consider what the future held for the band.

Ashley: 'It came to the point of actually sitting down and deciding what we were going to do. And this I remember clearly, we had a meeting at Trevor's flat with the survivors – Sandy, Richard, Simon and myself. We made a decision that we were going to reform.'

For Fairport, the only way forward was to pursue the direction indicated on 'A Sailor's Life', recorded just a few months before. Richard's confidence as a writer had been shaken, and none of 'the survivors' could see any future, or, indeed, any point in going back to being a British band covering the work of American singer-songwriters. Martin Lamble's death effectively cut off the avenue of the past.

Traffic had pioneered the rock'n'roll, William Morris, back-to-roots, country idyll trip way back in 1967. Steve Winwood remembered the 'Berkshire Poppies' vibe when I interviewed him in 1994: 'It was a gamekeeper's cottage, near Lambourn in Berkshire ... There was no electricity when we first went there, so we had a generator ... It was fantastic out there, cooking over an open fire, very primitive, all chocolate biscuits and tea. Just like William and the Outlaws!'

The Band, Fairport's American idols, had after all accomplished the same journey; their return to Eden took place in the tiny artistic community of West Saugerties in upstate New York. The house, known distinctively, if ungrammatically, as 'Big Pink', is now a part of rock iconography. It was here – during Bob Dylan's sabbatical year of 1967 – that the Band and he were 'in the basement, mixing up the medicine', unwittingly producing what would become rock'n'roll's first bootleg – The Great White Wonder (aka *The Basement Tapes*).

It was the Band's ability to forge a community, to swim against the tide of non-conformity, with their suits and shaggy 'Shall-We-Gather-At-The-River?' look ('We were rebelling against the rebellion,' Robbie Robertson said) which so impressed Fairport. Not to mention the music they created at the time, which made an enormous impact on Fairport Convention when it appeared on the Band's 1968 debut *Music From Big Pink* and 1969's eponymous second album with its leathery brown cover.

Richard: 'It was *the* record for us – because it was so rootsy and so unpretentious – the drums were just drums, there was no echo on it, they did it at home, it all just sounded great, the songs were fantastic, the musicianship was unbelievable. There were a lot of subtle things about the Band that we didn't really grasp – their sense of time and swing was kind of elusive to us, we didn't really have those reference points. Levon probably sat and watched loads of old black jazz drummers for ever, it had touches straight out of the 1940s.

'There was that kind of elusiveness to the rhythmic stuff that we didn't grasp. Rhythmically, Fairport and indeed British Rock generally was pretty four-square to the beat – maybe that's the way it has to be. There was a lot we admired about the Band – great songwriting, which had a nice historical perspective, good guitar playing wonderful singers, good everything.

'They were completely out of time and they made no concessions to having long hair. When we saw them at the Albert Hall they had drainpipe jeans on, turned up at the bottoms and really short hair – we hadn't seen anybody for years with short hair – even Jason King had long hair then.'

The Band were not to be conned by 'erotic politicians' like Jim Morrison; they weren't taken in by the nirvana promised by bogus gurus and bad acid. The Band were like rugged pioneers on a John Ford wagon train, snaking through Monument Valley, and on into the far distance, forging ever onward to the very edge of the known world. And by night, the pioneers would gather around the smoking fire and sing. At a time when violent revolution was in the air, the Band clung to their roots and drew strength from their families.

As Jim Morrison led the Doors through his Oedipal fantasy on 'The End', the Band wept Bob Dylan's keening 'Tears Of Rage', a song which ached for the very parental values which rock'n'roll was in the process of tearing apart.

Music From Big Pink was the album that Fairport Convention wanted to make. But theirs was to be an album of tradition and community viewed from the calm of the English countryside, rather than the hills of upstate New York. Fairport withdrew to a Queen Anne mansion in Hampshire. Joe Boyd rented the house in the village of Farley Chamberlayne near Winchester, so that Fairport could live, rehearse and work together during the summer of 1969.

Richard: 'It was the perfect place at the right time – it was a nice summer – a bit of football on the lawn and a bit of rehearsal, kite flying on Farley Mount. It was good and it was very creative. We'd be on the phone to Bert Lloyd saying "we've got to find a better 32nd verse for 'Tam Lin', you must know one..." Isn't that how Lord Arnold became Lord Darnell in "Matty Groves"? – somebody misheard it down the phone. There was stuff that Swarb knew that he wanted to do but we didn't realise that he'd pinched some of it off Martin [Carthy] at the time – but we did it anyway. Swarb had done all the folk stuff – he'd done it all, knew everybody – so for him to be electrified was really exciting, he was really having a good time, very stimulated.'

Swarbrick was now officially enrolled as a member of Fairport Convention, and drummer Dave Mattacks, a Londoner born in 1948, was recruited to replace Martin Lamble. Mattacks' pre-Fairport groups included the Pioneers, Andy and the Marksmen and nine months with a Belfast dance band.

Simon: 'I think when Swarbrick came into the band, he'd just made a very strong album with Carthy (*Prince Heathen*), which played back to back with *Liege & Lief*, is like listening to an acoustic version of the same record ... Everyone got to know each other much better at Farley Chamberlayne, and that was where Swarb and Richard ... defined their relationship.'

Dave Mattacks: 'They went from being the English Jefferson Airplane to the English Fairport Convention.'

Richard Thompson

Fairport needed an opportunity to regroup following the trauma of the crash and the increased pressure from their growing success. London had become a melting pot at the tail end of the 1960s. There were just too many distractions in the capital.

Fairport were energised by what they had accomplished on 'A Sailor's Life' earlier in the year. With the input Sandy and Swarbrick brought from the traditional side, the fruits of Ashley's research combined with Richard's writing, Fairport Convention – during the long, hot summer of 1969 – were well equipped for their future together.

Men had walked upon the moon that summer. It is hard to believe now, but at the time, the moon walk seemed an important part of the overall optimism of the period. There was a feeling that, hurtling into the unknown and setting foot on another planet, really was the dawning of the age of Aquarius. While back on earth, whole new nations seemed to be forged at Woodstock, Hyde Park and the Isle of Wight.

The first issue of the short-lived UK *Rolling Stone*, in October 1969, sported Fairport Convention on the cover – though hard at work at the time, creating the album which was to define English folk-rock – Eric Hayes' pictures show the band frolicking on the lawns outside the mansion. Fairport are seen relaxing, hanging out, getting it together, tuning up, eating cornflakes ... images of sunshine after the storm ... they show just what Fairport did on their holidays.

Quoted extensively in the *Rolling Stone* feature, the 20-year-old Thompson's ambitions are typically unambitious – a tape recorder for his flat, guitar practice four hours a day (to keep up with Swarb), a determination to improve his performance on the football field, and an avowed fondness for Ike and Tina Turner's 'River Deep, Mountain High'.

Regarding Fairport's new direction, Thompson explained: 'Traditional music was doing all right in England until the coming of communications ... then it disappeared entirely, as American music floods over on radio and record. So now there's electric music coming over from America, there's traditional music here, and there's no link at all ... In America, their folk music is a straight line ... white music went over and became bluegrass ... then it got electrified and it's Nashville now. Over here it's nothing. Folk music is still a guy standing with a finger in his ear and a pint in his hand at a folk club.'

Folk music had survived war, plague, pestilence and famine. But in 1969, following Fairport Convention's summer sojourn at Farley Chamberlayne, it was about to receive its biggest shock in centuries.

Richard and Perri Thompson in the garden of their grandmother's home in Scotland, 1949
Photo courtesy Joan Thompson

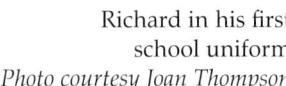

Richard in his first school uniform
Photo courtesy Joan Thompson

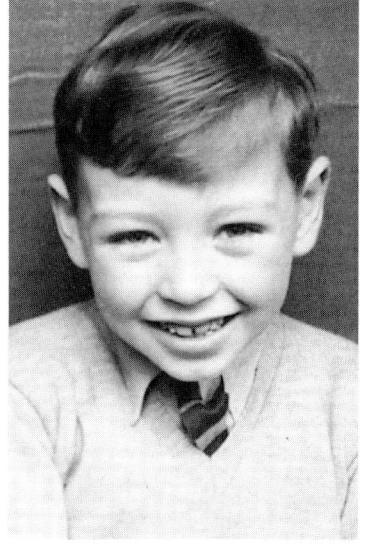

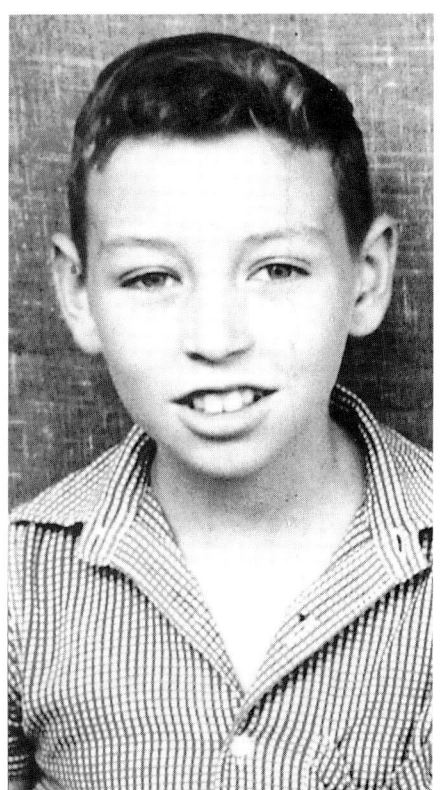

Pre-teen Thompson with regulation fifties short back and sides
Photo courtesy Joan Thompson

Perri, unknown chum and Richard, Christmas 1955
Photo courtesy Joan Thompson

The teenage Thompson, rebelling against (local) authority
Photo courtesy Joan Thompson

Fairport Convention, 1968.
Left to right: Ian Matthews,
Simon Nicol, Ashley Hutchings,
Martin Lamble, Sandy Denny,
and Richard Thompson

Dave Swarbrick, Richard and
Sandy Denny rehearsing for
the *Liege and Lief* sessions
*Photo courtesy Ashley
Hutchings; Edward Haber
Collection*

Fairport Convention,
Philadelphia Folk Festival, August,
1970. Left to right: Dave Pegg,
Dave Mattacks, Richard Thompson,
Dave Swarbrick and Simon Nicol
Photo: Frank Kornelussen

Richard at about the time of
Henry the Human Fly
Photo: Toni Arthur, courtesy Linda
Thompson Kenis/Hannibal
Records—Rykodisc Europe

Left to right: Linda, Sandy Denny, Gerry Conway, and Richard in 1972, performing outside of London
Photo: Frank Kornelussen

Wedding day, Richard and Linda, 1972
Photo: Andy Horvitch, courtesy Linda Thompson Kenis/Hannibal Records—Rykodisc Europe

Early '70s
Photo: Andy Horvitch, courtesy Linda Thompson Kenis/Hannibal Records—Rykodisc Europe

Cambridge Folk Festival, 1975
Photo: Robert Ellis, courtesy Island Records/Jo Lustig Management; Edward Haber Collection

Backstage at the South Yorkshire Folk Festival, mid-'70s
Photo: Andrew Lloyd Rotherham, courtesy Linda Thompson Kenis/Hannibal Records—Rykodisc Europe

High Muslim days, c. 1976
Courtesy Island Records; Edward Haber Collection

Coming out of semi-retirement
First Light photo, 1978
*Photo: Gered Mankowitz,
courtesy of Chrysalis Records;
Edward Haber Collection*

Chapter 7

FOLK SONGS WERE OF THE PEOPLE, by the people, and for the people – a currency which spoke of changing seasons and unchanging ritual. Songs of unconsummated romance and unrealised love.

In the days before widespread literacy and mass communication, minstrels wandered from village to village, singing news of battles lost and of battles won, of regicide or an outlaw's execution.

Folk songs were sung on street corners and at fairs, on market day and at executions – with life held so cheap, there were plenty of executions. In his *Making of the English Working Classes*, E. P. Thompson wrote: 'The procession to Tyburn was a central ceremonial of eighteenth-century London. The condemned in carts – the men in gaudy attire, the women in white with baskets of flowers and oranges which they threw to the crowds – the ballad-singers and hawkers, with their "last speeches" (which were sold even before the victims had given the sign of the dropped handkerchief to the hangman to do his work): all the symbolism of "Tyburn Fair" was the ritual at the heart of London's popular culture.'

The full flowering of the folk song tradition is bordered by the Restoration of Charles II and the Industrial Revolution. In the eighteenth century, increasing literacy and the popularity of the broadside ballads saw them printed and sold for a penny each. The broadsides were the tabloid press of the time – the most popular items being those which dealt with sex, death, murder, royalty and war. Though intricately constructed and historically relevant ballads were sung, these were not popular with the man in the street, who even then preferred the sexy and the scandalous, the ghoulish and the gory.

The popularity of the broadsides, the most immediate form of communication available at the beginning of mass literacy, was reflected in their sales. The account of the 1827 'Murder of Maria Marten and the Red Barn', for example, sold upwards of half a million copies.

Class was at the top, and bottom, of the folk song tradition. Well catered for both spiritually and temporally, the aristocracy had no need to take heed of wandering minstrels. Because of its primitive nature 'folk' was despised by the landed gentry, who believed that the peasants had little to say, and frowned upon by the professional musician who simply couldn't comprehend that an untutored labourer was capable of finesse in performance.

In the late eighteenth century Sir Walter Scott began collecting and collating folk lore and ballads, though not everyone was enamoured of such gentrification: 'They were made for singing and not for reading,' Scott was cautioned by one singer. The collecting and annotating of folk songs got seriously underway during the mid-nineteenth century and collectors became a familiar sight in rural areas from the 1880s onward, although due to their superior dress and tone, they were frequently mistaken for tax inspectors.

The collections which form the basis of what we now know as traditional folk music, are those of two men, both pictured on the inner sleeve of *Liege & Lief*: Francis Child and Cecil Sharp. Fairport certainly took 'Sir Patrick Spens' (on *Full House*) and 'Tam Lin' from Child's collection, while 'The Deserter' and 'Reynardine' are similar to songs which Child collected. Sandy Denny provided basic versions of traditional songs she had learned in the folk clubs, while Ashley Hutchings persevered at Cecil Sharp House to come up with definitive versions of an agreed song.

American-born Francis James Child's definitive five-volume work, *English and Scottish Popular Ballads* which was published between 1882 and 1898, gathered together over 300 ballads. His work forms the foundations of the folk movement in Britain. While Fairport were preparing to record *Liege & Lief*, Simon Nicol remembered 'at least three sets of Child books in the house at any one time'. Child was determined to preserve the rich oral tradition of indigenous folk music. In a time before gramophones and tape recorders, this meant notating the songs wherever and whenever he found them on his travels. It is in the very nature of an oral tradition that variations are found in each isolated community. In some instances, Child found himself dealing with up to 25 different versions of the same song.

When Francis Child died in 1896, the baton passed to Cecil Sharp, whose fascination with folk song began late in the nineteenth century, when he overheard a folk song ('The Seeds Of Love') sung by his gardener, the aptly named John England. Sharp is credited with collecting nearly 5,000 folk tunes during his career. Recognising the impossibility of preserving a definitive version of a song passed down the generations,

Sharp was agreeably surprised to hear a ballad about Robin Hood sung by a traditional singer, matching almost word for word a printed ballad of some 200 years before. Interestingly, Sharp noted that while the singer repeated the lyrics verbatim, he introduced a slight variation in melody every time he sang.

In *Folk Song in England*, folklorist and scholar A.L. Lloyd (who loyally supported Fairport around the time of *Liege & Lief*) wrote: 'By what means do melodies wander? How does it happen that what seem to be variants of a single tune turn up in a Rumanian funeral lament, a Hungarian love song, a Dutch hymn, a Spanish ballad and a highwayman song sung by an elderly couple whom Vaughan Williams met one autumn day when bicycling in Sussex?' Paddy Moloney of the Chieftains once told me that an air he had learned on the tin whistle from his mother in Ireland, he heard repeated almost note perfect in Bulgaria 30 years later.

Lloyd identified the musical conduit as a sea of humanity which ebbed and flowed, carrying shepherds who roamed from Transylvania to the Crimea, over hundreds of thousands of miles, wagon-trains loaded with wine which trawled from the Carpathians to Poland and soldiers, returning from war with songs they picked up on their travels, vagrant scholars, travelling circus folk, merchants, sailors, gypsies . . .

During the golden age of folk-song collecting, a further problem arose over the suitability of certain songs for chaste Victorian ears – songs which were sung originally by rough, ill-educated people, lacking the refined sensibilities of their 'betters'. The themes would be familiar to the mass audiences of today. The language may alter and the technology improve, but the familiar themes of sex, infidelity, cuckoldry, seduction, wantonness, intrigue, prurience, licentiousness, lubricity and carnality endure.

In 1818, the scholar Thomas Bowdler nobly took it upon himself to make Shakespeare suitable for everyone, his *Family Shakespeare* ensuring that 'those words and expressions are omitted which cannot with propriety be read aloud in a family'. Bowdler's technique would be familiar to the gentrifiers of the folk ballads. There was no place for rural earthiness in polite drawing rooms of the Victorian era.

In his introduction to a collection of Somerset folk songs, as late as 1910, Cecil Sharp wrote: 'In a few instances, the sentiment of the song has been softened, because the conventions of our less delicate and more dishonest time demand such treatment.' A few years before, fellow collector Lucy Broadwood had found a rich collection of songs in Horsham, Sussex 'which by their titles promised to be amongst the very oldest ballads'. But she was thwarted, because they too 'were considered ... unfit for ladies' ears'.

The traditional songs which featured in Sharp's collections dealt with the universal themes, of love and death, war and peace, work and rest. And they remind you forcefully of how much depended on the elements – bringing in the sheaves and the harvest festival were not simply the stuff of quaint celebration, they were the very staff of life.

Always hovering over the tradition were the dark clouds of war. The British government did not introduce conscription until 1916, when the unimaginable scale of the losses on the Western Front made it unavoidable. Since Cromwell's formation of the New Model Army nearly 300 years before, Britain had relied on volunteers to fight on the fields of Waterloo, the banks of the Nile, the Crimean coast and the veldt of South Africa ... All these wars and their warriors, commemorated in song. The Army or Navy offered young men a rare opportunity to escape the harshness of life on the land, that their fathers, and their fathers before them, had endured. The recruiting sergeant who plied you with pints of ale didn't dwell on blood, death and mutilation. Volunteers were lured to the colours with tales of duty and honour. Traditional ballads both condoned and condemned those illusions.

Fairport's decision to include 'The Deserter' on *Liege & Lief* reflected this traditional fascination with the military, but in keeping with the times, the band chose a song which sympathised with the individual, rather than dwelling on military glory. 'The Deserter' concludes with the last hope of every soldier about to be shot for desertion – that the reigning monarch will ride up at the very last moment, like a pantomime Good Fairy, and grant clemency.

In England prior to the Industrial Revolution horizons were limited to the next village, or occasionally a nearby county town. Only the services offered any opportunity to travel, and on the whole, village life was hard and static. Life on the land was marked by rituals and festivals, while the changing seasons dictated the shape and substance of life. Entertainment and information came only from itinerant balladeers and holiday rituals around the maypole.

It was only when factories began to spring up in the larger towns, that agricultural workers, tempted by the higher wages, began moving to the smoky and overcrowded cities. 'But migration to the factories had meant loss as well as gain,' wrote G. M. Trevelyan in *English Social History*. 'The beauty of the field and wood and hedge, the immemorial customs of rural life – the village green and its games, the harvest-home, the tithe feast, the May Day rites, the field sports – had supplied a humane background and an age-long tradition to temper poverty. They were not reproduced in mine or factory, or in the rows of mass-produced brick dwellings erected to house the hands.'

At the time of the Industrial Revolution, the population of England numbered approximately nine million of whom a third worked in agriculture. But six million people still lived in the country, so rural and agrarian traditions survived and even flourished. The slow emergence of mass-market newspapers and cinema made no substantial inroads and at the beginning of the twentieth century, Great Britain was still essentially rural and parochial.

All that would change with the outbreak of the First World War in August 1914. The Army recruiting stations could not cope with the millions of young men who flocked to enlist. The whole nation was soon devastated by the inconceivable scale of the slaughter. British losses on the first morning of the Somme, in July 1916, equalled those for the whole of the last European land war, the Crimea, half a century before. The casualties were so severe that entire communities were decimated. The First World War rocked Great Britain to an extent the nation found almost impossible to bear. Today, even the tiniest hamlet in the quietest county, has a war memorial etched with the names of ploughboys and ostlers, gamekeepers and poachers, all from one tiny village.

The impact of the Great War on an England just emerging, blinking, into the twentieth century, was devastating. It robbed the country of a whole generation who lay dead in the mud of Flanders, or appeared as mutilated reminders of the conflict in the irrevocably altered landscape of 1918. This was the time 'when the maypole, which had once been the centre of so many village greens', as the folk singer Shirley Collins wrote, 'was replaced by the memorial stone'.

With the post-War world more receptive to transatlantic influences in the shape of jazz and movies, folk music was abandoned during the 1920s. Perhaps the old songs were too painful reminders of all that had been lost. Or maybe they simply seemed 'old-fashioned', with the growth of cinema as *the* mass entertainment form. In the years leading up to the Second World War, with radio becoming the prime source of home entertainment, British folk music all but disappeared.

Writing of the changes in Europe in the immediate aftermath of the Second World War, A. L. Lloyd noted: 'The young villagers in particular became filled with a sense of purpose that their parents often lacked, passivity was replaced by initiative, apathy by elation, humility by a sense of self-importance. At the same time as new material perspectives came into view, the cultural horizon of the villages widened too, through schools, films, radio and such. The local song tradition proved robust enough to receive all kinds of new nourishment and to digest it satisfactorily. Only a moribund tradition is dominated by the past; a living tradition is constantly sprouting new leaves on old wood and sometimes quite suddenly the bush is ablaze with blossom of a novel shade.'

British folk music was prettified and rarified, placed on the concert stage, rendered unrecognisable in reverent settings by Benjamin Britten. Or trivialised and sweetened for consumption in the classroom, ensuring that whole generations groaned at the prospect of another lengthy ramble out one May morning-o. The lack of interest in folk music came hand in hand with increased consumerism, new technology, travel and a proliferation of leisure opportunities.

As the chief recipient of the overflow of American culture, Britain's growing Americanisation was already marked. When 'The Folk Revival' arrived, it too came from America, and was called Bob Dylan. The one-man-band element of Dylan's music had its own constituency and on his first trip to London in 1963, Dylan absorbed much of the traditional folk music of the British Isles. Dylan was so impressed with Martin Carthy's handling of the traditional 'Lord Franklin', that he hijacked the tune for 'Bob Dylan's Dream'; Paul Simon also owes a debt to Carthy and the familiar Simon and Garfunkel arrangement of 'Scarborough Fair' was widely believed to have come from Carthy.

Even at the height of his mid-60s rock'n'roll turbulence, Dylan saluted the folk tradition to Nat Hentoff: 'There's nobody that's going to kill traditional music. All those songs about roses growing out of people's brains and lovers who are really geese, and swans that turn into angels – they're not going to die.'

Like Paris in the 1920s, London in the early 1960s was a magnet for disaffected American artists. In the wake of Dylan, Richard Farina, Paul Simon, Art Garfunkel, Tom Paxton, Jackson C. Frank and Phil Ochs also came to listen, and to learn.

Purists still held folk sacrosanct. Exceptions were made for the concert platform, but generally the party line was that folk was an oral medium, and that the Child ballads were definitive and not to be tampered with. The International Folk Music Council defined folk music as 'the product of a musical tradition that has been evolved through the process of oral transmission'.

'Oral' was the sticking point. Oral meaning mouth to mouth, kissing down the centuries. The success and motivation of the folk revival of the 1960s was its irreverence and its iconoclasm. Those knights in denim, with acoustic guitars replacing the lances, weren't interested in the purity of unaccompanied balladeering, they were simply responding to the timeless, blood-and-guts tabloid melodrama. They recognised the inherent quality of a song and didn't give a stuff where it came from.

In America, Bob Dylan divided opinion. Seen by many as inheritor of Woody Guthrie's mantle and spokesman of the New Left, purists were outraged when Dylan abandoned the simple guitar and vocals which had fuelled his first four albums, and went for out-and-out rock'n'roll. The boos which greeted Dylan's electric baptism at the 1965 Newport Folk Festival – at which Joe Boyd was a stage manager – were only a harbinger of what was to come. Dylan's subsequent world tour with The Band in 1966 was a rock'n'roll *High Noon*, with Bob as Gary Cooper facing up to audiences who greeted him with blank incomprehension or outright hostility. Guitarist Robbie Robertson told me that they started taping those watershed shows, not for a proposed live album, but to play back in hotel rooms after the gigs: 'We thought, "Jesus, they can't be *that* bad!"'

When Fairport Convention came to record *Liege & Lief* during the late summer of 1969, the traditionalists were still arguing for the inherent purity of folk music – even if nobody heard them over the amplified electric guitars – they didn't want anybody tampering with their music. The attitude of the young turks of the folk revival was summed up by Steeleye Span's Tim Hart, quoted in *The Electric Muse*: 'Most English traditional song is unaccompanied song, and the only argument is – should you or should you not accompany it at all? After that, I'm not interested in any argument as to what degree you can go to. To me, it's equally outrageous to accompany a traditional song on a Spanish guitar or an American instrument as it is to accompany it with an electric guitar.'

Folk music had adapted to changes all down the years. It was there when Mary Queen of Scots sat awaiting execution in Fotheringay and when Francis Drake overheard 'Ladies of Spain' sung by a street singer, prior to setting sail in search of El Dorado; it serenaded Samuel Pepys when he bought a shirt in Westminster Hall to replace the one singed during the Great Fire of London; and it was there in the sea shanties sung on the wooden vessels which took Nelson's navy to Trafalgar.

Songs which knew no composer, credited to 'Trad. Arr.' or 'Anon' had dug deep into the psyche of the nation, whether it was 'Greensleeves' cooed to a fair maiden in the long corridors at Hampton Court, or 'Wash Me In The Water Where You Wash Your Dirty Daughter' sung by long lines of khaki troops as they snaked up the French roads to the trenches of the Western Front.

Folk music was often just a fragment of a song, a half-heard phrase, a vaguely remembered chorus, a distant melody ... But it was capable of being vibrant and alive. Passed through the generations, it rang down the centuries. Now it was time to ring some changes.

Liege & Lief took its title from the homage ('lief') that serfs paid to the Lord or liege of the manor. The title evoked a feudal system which had long disappeared from English society, but whose ramifications persist to this day. The original album's inner sleeve was also a homage to a world long-gone, with illustrations depicting arcane customs such as wren hunting, pace-egging and Morris dancing.

Ashley: 'If you look at the *Liege & Lief* cover, that gives a very good idea of the feeling. There's a lot of magic on that cover ... I think it was blessed. I think all that union was blessed.'

Of Fairport's members, it was group founder Ashley Hutchings who was keenest on the direction the band were taking on *Liege & Lief*. Richard, energised by their guitar/violin interplay, was busy developing his songwriting partnership with Swarbrick, who remains Thompson's longest-serving collaborator. For Ashley though, their achievements at Farley Chamberlayne that summer of 1969 were revolutionary: 'Fairport were ... the first band to make a success of British folk-rock. But I also think that an important contribution to music – folk and rock – is the Fairport way of doing things: loose, relaxed, improvised, risk-taking, fun-loving way of setting about making music ... Of course, we wouldn't have come up with the music if we had been a conventional band. If we had been four guys only, we'd have played a certain type of music in a certain type of venue. We played everything from all over the world at all sorts of venues, and that was what led to *Liege & Lief*. It happened because ... we were willing to take chances.'

Fairport had their equipment permanently set up in the large drawing room overlooking the lawns at Farley Chamberlayne and rehearsed every day. It was hard work, as the band had to marry centuries-old, largely unaccompanied folk songs with electric rock'n'roll instruments. There was also the practical aspect of introducing new members Dave Mattacks and Dave Swarbrick to the existing repertoire.

As well as the traditional songs which Fairport were trying out, Ashley remembers the band 'keeping the thread with Dylan' – his 'Open The Door Homer', 'Down In The Flood' and co-written 'Ballad Of Easy Rider' (which appeared on Richard's *Guitar, Vocal* album) were among those worked out. Richard Farina's 'Quiet Joys Of Brotherhood', a version of which Sandy included on her second solo album was also rehearsed. But the real thrust at Farley Chamberlayne was backwards, as Fairport left behind the hurly-burly of the late 1960s and made a pilgrimage back to the almost-forgotten roots of the people's music.

Ashley: 'It was certainly a very magical period, also a very strange period. It wasn't simply us having a ball all the time, there was a lot of heart-searching going on. It was hard work to actually put those things into the rock format, but it was exhilarating and magical in the profound sense.'

The opening track of *Liege & Lief* was the only Sandy Denny/Ashley Hutchings collaboration: 'Come All Ye' sounds like a rather forced attempt at recasting Fairport as 'rolling minstrels'. But the song effectively sets the scene for what was to follow. 'Reynardine' has its origins in folk tales stretching back to the twelfth century. The 'sly, bold Reynardine' portrayed here is a seducer and Sandy's singing was rarely bettered.

'Matty Groves' has gone on to become a staple of the Fairport repertoire, and remains perhaps the best-loved of all the band's folk-rock fusions. Richard kicks off that irresistible riff, reinforced by Mattacks' drums and the added zest of Swarbrick's jaunty fiddle. 'Matty Groves' is the first opportunity to relish the interplay between Swarbrick and Thompson, a feature which became such a highlight of subsequent live performances. The nineteen verses accumulate to tell their bloody tale of how the sin of Lord Darnell's unfaithful wife is not her infidelity, but rather that she commits it with a social inferior. Order is restored in the final verse, with Lady Darnell buried on top of her lover, 'for she was of noble kin'.

'Farewell, Farewell' closed Side One of the album. A flawless example of what Fairport were capable of at their peak: Sandy's haunting handling of a Richard Thompson ballad, steeped in tragedy and parting, as Swarbrick's fiddle weaves its distant adieu. The lyrics are a taste of what was going through Thompson's mind ('And will you never return to see your bruised and beaten son? Oh I would, I would, if welcome I were, for they loathe me every one ...'). Typical that even in that era of peace and love, Thompson's concern is with parting and loathing.

Thompson took the tune for his song from the traditional 'Willy O'Winsbury', which he knew from a 1968 album by Sweeney's Men. That record – along with Shirley Collins and Davy Graham's 1964 *Folk Roots, New Routes* – was the trailblazer for what Fairport attempted

Richard Thompson

with *Liege & Lief*. Sweeney's Men were an Irish trio of Andy Irvine, Johnny Moynihan (who later formed Planxty) and Terry Woods (later of Steeleye Span and the Pogues). Irvine had found 'Willy O'Winsbury' in the Child ballads, but confused by Child's numbering system he got the wrong tune for the song. As fate would have it, it fitted perfectly, and this is the tune, one of the most haunting of the entire tradition, which Thompson borrowed: 'rotten words, great tune'.

Thompson himself is dismissive of the song: 'It's too personal, the lyrics are too convoluted to understand. I think even then I found it very hard to say I love you.' He does himself a disservice. 'Farewell, Farewell' is a poignant, moving song of parting, and 'the cold North wind' of its refrain can still chill.

'The Deserter' begins on the East End's Ratcliffe Highway – a notorious thieves' paradise in the nineteenth century. It was another traditional song, a typical tale of a soldier pressed into service, who deserts, is captured, undergoes 300 lashes, and deserts again. Following on from the cathartic 'Farewell, Farewell', Fairport's reading is rather pedestrian.

The instrumental medley gave Swarbrick's fiddle an opportunity to shine. Long a firm favourite of Fairport audiences, the memory of Swarbrick, fiddle stuck under his chin and a fag in his mouth, weaving prodigiously fast jigs and reels from his bow remains one of the archetypal, enduring Fairport images. It is as much Ashley Hutchings' underpinning bass as Thompson's guitar which are remarkable on this track.

'Tam Lin' has been attributed to Robert Burns (not the Scottish poet's first contact with rock'n'roll, Bill Haley and the Comets had borrowed 'Rockin' Through The Rye' from his 'Auld Lang Syne'). *Tam Lin* was also the title of a 1971 film starring Ava Gardner, which cited Burns as its source. Fairport's 'Tam Lin' is a rather leaden interpretation of the mystery. From the very beginning, Sandy's delivery suggests she is not looking forward to the subsequent 21 verses. Richard delivers a timid solo and Swarbrick follows suit. The band's handling of 'Tam Lin' lends substance to Thompson's own view of *Liege & Lief*. He told me in 1980: 'I prefer *Unhalfbricking* ... *Liege & Lief* sounds slightly artificial, too claustrophobic, over-arranged. There was a dimension missing – it needed more space in the music.'

The only Thompson-Swarbrick collaboration on *Liege & Lief* came with the album's closing track, 'Crazy Man Michael'. Swarbrick already had the melody and Richard added the lyrics. It's a song steeped in the imagery of roses growing from the breasts of dead lovers. 'Crazy

Man Michael' inadvertently kills his own true love and is forever condemned to wander the earth, shunned by human society, able to communicate only with animals. Like the Wild Huntsman, the Wandering Jew and the Flying Dutchman of fable, 'Crazy Man Michael' must wander for all eternity, knowing no peace.

At the time of the album, Thompson was fascinated by the Scottish ballad tradition, which inspired the structure of 'Crazy Man Michael'. Swarbrick's mournful violin heightens the inherent tragedy of the narrative, and with Sandy's wistful and atmospheric vocals, 'Crazy Man Michael' is a substantial conclusion to the album.

Talking to *Flypaper*'s Frank Kornelussen in 1984, Thompson admitted the song was 'about Jeannie, really. "Crazy Man Michael" is kind of guilt, because in some way I felt responsible for her dying ... There wasn't any way I was, but I just felt that at the time.'

Like so many ground-breaking, classic albums, *Liege & Lief* has not necessarily worn well in the intervening years. There is a timidity to it, a reverence of the text which diminishes the dramatic possibilities of the songs. Uncharacteristically, Joe Boyd's production also seems curiously flat. But back then, *Liege & Lief* was undeniably seen as a landmark, not only in Fairport's career, but in the development of indigenous rock'n'roll.

Richard: 'I think we thought it was an important record – we just didn't know how important – well, it wasn't that important in terms of world music. And in terms of British music, Fairport was always a cult ... folk-rock was always a cult and still is ... it didn't really shake the world but it certainly changed things all over the place – in other countries it changed things as well which was interesting.

'It was conceived as being a project record and then we'd go back to doing what we were doing before. It was a one-off, let's do this traditional record and see what happens. But once we started we obviously had to keep going, there was no going back. It was a contrived record but it had to be ... I don't think it's a great music record – there's good stuff on it but also some stuff that doesn't hang together ... But Fairport definitely made more successful records in terms of music – the one before and the one after were more musical records. "A Sailor's Life" might be a more successful track than almost any track on *Liege & Lief*.'

Liege & Lief was advertised as 'The first (literally) British folk rock LP ever' on its release in December 1969. It went on to become Fairport's best-selling album, with sales of around 100,000 copies, virtually double those of *Unhalfbricking*.

Richard Thompson

The reviews were respectful rather than ecstatic: *Friends* captured the feel of the times: 'Get your favourite elf on the phone ... borrow a record player, take it to the nearest piece of countryside you can find, get your little elf high on Mead and stuff and play *Liege & Lief* ... It doesn't necessarily follow that you're going to dig everything about this album, especially if you preferred "Meet On The Ledge" ...'

Rolling Stone preferred *Unhalfbricking*, calling *Liege & Lief* 'a nice album to put on to accompany sitting by the fireplace or staring vacantly at a candle flame ... Where, essentially, is something to excite those of us who find artiness worthy enough of quiet admiration but a little boring?'

While enlightened members of the folk establishment, like the Watersons and Bert Lloyd, were enchanted by Fairport's new direction, and many others could appreciate the necessity for Fairport to forge a new direction following the crash, fans of the 'old' Fairport were disappointed by the group's wholehearted, uncompromising commitment to electric folk.

Journalist John Platt had followed Fairport from their earliest days at UFO, and retained fond memories of them as an interpretive band: 'I can remember seeing them at that free concert in Hyde Park in 1968, and being very impressed by the way they handled American material like "Reno, Nevada" and "Suzanne" ... I think quite a few of their fans would have preferred a gradual absorption of the traditional material into their set. A lot of people loved the early Fairport.'

A concert at the Royal Festival Hall in September 1969 – where Fairport's opening act was Joni Mitchell – offered an opportunity to see the new Fairport in action. Whatever people's feelings about the band's pillaging of traditional folk in preference to their own songs or imaginative reworkings of American material, there was no denying the sparks which flew onstage.

After months spent rehearsing at Farley Chamberlayne, Fairport were primed and ready. Ashley and Mattacks had meshed as a rhythm section; Simon provided a steady rhythm guitar, keeping the middle covered, allowing plenty of room for Richard and Swarbrick's fiery jousts. Sandy's singing soared above the electric mayhem.

Here was the intensity and dynamism which Fairport had been keen to capture, but which hadn't quite made it onto *Liege & Lief*. But the album was not a stopping point, Fairport saw *Liege & Lief* as a swansong to the 60s, and a signpost for the 70s.

That, at least, was the plan ...

Chapter 8

THE FAIRPORT SPLIT immediately after *Liege & Lief* was the most divisive of the band's history. Though the clash of personalities which led to Fairport's major sundering was clearly inevitable: a six-piece band that was pulling in at least five too many directions.

Richard: 'Sandy, as well as being the greatest singer and the most fun, was also hard work. She took a bit of man management – smoothing the edges down. She was a big personality – she had a big temper, a big laugh, a big everything – so you had to have the old kid gloves on sometimes, but she was great. When she left, it seemed fairly inevitable that she had to do that.'

I only met Sandy Denny once. It was sometime during 1977 and she was doing a spate of interviews to try and whip up some interest in *Rendezvous*, her fourth and as it turned out final, solo album.

Sandy was very nice. Friendly, smoked a lot, had that very throaty sort of laugh smokers have. Except with her it was rather sexy, not phlegmy. And, yes, she was smaller in the flesh than you'd expect from seeing her onstage.

Eventually, as the tape wound on and her nervousness wound down, Sandy did look back to the Fairport split of 1969:

'Well, Swarb and I were always somehow a very fractious couple of people to have in a band all at one go. He's always had a mind of his own, and so have I. Richard is very strong to have in a band. He will always manage to get across what he wants and get it ... So three of us in a band was a fairly volatile group of people, and what with Tyger [Hutchings] as well, who has also got a mind of his own. It was no wonder that somebody had to give eventually, and I was one of them.'

Sandy had been singing folk songs for nearly five years before *Liege & Lief*. She regarded the album as a detour, an opportunity to revisit familiar territory in unfamiliar company. Instead of singing 'The Wagoner's Lad' with only her guitar as accompaniment, Sandy now had Richard's wailing electric Stratocaster behind her, Ashley and Mattacks laying down a rock-solid rhythm and Swarbrick, like a chain-smoking Robin Goodfellow, puckishly sprinting around the stage.

Liege & Lief had broken new ground, crucially within the context of re-interpreting traditional music from the British Isles, rather than second-hand Chuck Berry. There was room for the material Richard was writing, which drew on the well-spring of that same tradition as well as space for Thompson to develop his own playing. With *Liege & Lief*, Fairport had proved that 400 watts enhanced rather than diminished the impact of the material.

For Ashley Hutchings, the man who had raised Fairport from the ashes of the Ethnic Shuffle Orchestra, *Liege & Lief* was the epiphany. The Child ballads and Cecil Sharp House were Ashley's Damascene conversion. This was where the Holy Grail was held, and Ashley was determined that Fairport wholeheartedly pursue the direction begun on *Liege & Lief*.

So it was ironic that Ashley was one of the first to walk soon after the album's release. Ashley was determined to pursue the electric folk path, working with indigenous, traditional material, rather than relying on material generated from within the band. In pursuit of his vision of an electric Albion, he left Fairport and went on immediately to form Steeleye Span. Though with hindsight, Ashley admitted that the stress caused by the crash earlier in 1969 had a lot to do with his decision to quit. He told me once that he didn't feel he was 'in total control' at the time he made his decision to leave Fairport.

Swarbrick, on the other hand, was only too happy to rub the folk fraternity up the wrong way. Of the traditional scene he had recently quit, Swarbrick told Robin Denselow: 'I didn't like seven-eighths of the people involved in it, and it was exceedingly opportune to leave.' He was excited by the possibilities offered by Fairport, while continuing to draw on a tradition of which he was extremely knowledgeable.

Simon was exhilarated by the invigorating reworkings of the folk material, and amiable as ever, was happy to go with the flow.

Dave Mattacks was the new boy, keen to keep his head down, and avoid the inevitable clash, but quietly taking it all in: 'It's very interesting, after the experiment, if you will, of that album. How it polarised Ashley and Sandy. Ashley wanted to go further in that direction; but for Sandy it was just too much deja vu for her. Sandy's reason for going was, "I've done this, I don't want to pursue this traditional thing, what I'm into is writing my own songs . . ." Whereas for Ashley it was a revelation . . . And Richard kind of staying in the middle saying "I like this, and I don't feel that strongly about that, or I don't feel strongly that way or the other", but pursuing the English thing without the flag-waving aspect of it.'

Richard: 'I think the writers wanted to keep the style, but actually to write in the style and make it a contemporary thing – which is what Sandy and I really went on to do anyway, to be contemporary in the tradition. Ashley wanted to bring Andy Irvine and Terry and Gay Woods into the band, to make it an eight piece which was totally impractical – fifteen guitar players or something. Swarb was probably happy to keep going as it was – he was still really excited by playing electric and he wanted to keep doing it.'

Sandy was the first to leave. Fairport were scheduled to appear on Danish TV, performing material from *Liege & Lief*, in November 1969. The driver sent to collect her from the flat she shared with Trevor and take her to the airport reported she wasn't there. The remaining members of Fairport drove to Heathrow Airport and it was during that 40-minute drive that Sandy's unhappiness with the band's future direction became clear to them all. Ashley even suggested Fairport invite 61-year-old Bert Lloyd to join.

In Denmark, Fairport learned that Sandy was flying to join them and honour their commitments, which sparked something off in Ashley's mind and *he* too decided to call it quits.

Joe Boyd: 'They decided that that particular direction which they had been going in – as a kind of English answer to American folk-rock – was what they were going to become. A truly English band concentrating on British material.

'I think this was a combination of Richard's feelings, Sandy's interests and the newly found conversion of Ashley ... Sandy had been involved with the traditional for a long time, but always rather ambivalently. She sang traditional songs as well as her own compositions. She was amused at Ashley's fanaticism, he would come back from Cecil Sharp House and say "I have just discovered this magnificent song" and she would say "Well, I was singing that when I was seventeen!"

'I think that Sandy's career in the folk clubs suffered at the hands of the purists, who always viewed her as a corrupter. She sang with a guitar, she didn't sing unaccompanied, she sang her own compositions, which at that time was considered a little "Not Done"! ... In a way, joining Fairport had been her step away from it all into a different world.

'To suddenly discover that, having gotten into the rock'n'roll business, she was now in the same band as someone who was almost as doctrinaire about British traditional music as those people she had fled from . . . upset her. And also, Ashley's point of view that her songs – or Richard's songs for that matter – were not really to be encouraged. This, I think, alarmed her as well.'

Within weeks of releasing their most triumphant album Fairport were reduced to four men, lacking the visual focus and vocal dexterity of Sandy Denny.

Barely six months after the happy days spent at Farley Chamberlayne preparing *Liege & Lief*, Fairport Convention were no longer a band. The community they tried so hard to create had not lasted a calendar year. As 1970 dawned, Fairport were rapidly forced to re-evaluate their prospects. They knew from previous experience, that if people thought of Fairport at all, they thought of a band fronted by a female singer.

No obvious leader emerged in the wake of Sandy and Ashley's departure, although as the oldest and most experienced, Dave Swarbrick was soon at the helm.

Joe Boyd: 'I was concerned because I was a big fan of both Richard and Sandy's songwriting, and I hated to see that go by the board. I was concerned because I felt that the directions they were going on *Unhalfbricking* would be very successful in America . . . but the abrupt about-turn in events, and their change in style, forced a complete re-think, and made them in some ways less obviously commercial in America.

'I was also concerned with the dynamic . . . between Richard and Swarbrick, in the sense of Richard not being an aggressive person in terms of holding his own, and Swarbrick being a more aggressive person. I was concerned at some times during those sessions of the growing dominance of Swarbrick. People would turn to him because he was the one most experienced in that type of music, and my instinct was always to trust Richard in every possible situation. I would always say to myself that whatever Richard felt or wanted, or what his instincts were about something, were the ones that were apt to be right, and I didn't have the same feeling about Swarbrick's instincts.'

By the beginning of 1970, Fairport had long since shaken off the 'English Jefferson Airplane' tag. Through hard work and a series of increasingly confident albums, they had established themselves as one of the best-loved British bands of the era. Their sales may not have matched those of their Division One contemporaries such as Pink Floyd, and beside newcomers and label mates King Crimson, Fairport may have seemed a tad old-fashioned; but they were held in great affection by the music press and by a fan base spread wide over university campuses.

Fairport

To continue at all, though, Fairport had to get out and get gigging, and for that, they needed a bass player. A singer could wait.

Richard: 'We thought well, we can get a better bass player and women, no more women in the band! ... We thought, the rest of us all get on together, we all like each other, we're all going to have a good time – no problems on the road, we're all going to be good pals – maybe it's better to try a five piece and share the vocals around. Nobody wanted to sing but we'd have a democratic process to decide who sings the songs – and see what happens.'

Dave Pegg came highly recommended by Swarbrick, which had made Richard and Simon wary. They imagined some grizzled folkie veteran of the folk clubs, lugging round a stand-up bass to gigs. They soon found themselves outstripped at audition by Pegg's fluency on the electric bass.

Peggy had undergone the most rigorous pre-Fairport apprenticeship, serving stints with local Birmingham bands the Crawdaddys and the Ugleys during the post-Liverpool Beat boom. Peggy also plugged in with the Exception, one of whose early singles featured Robert Plant on tambourine.

The Led Zeppelin connection was further forged when Peggy moved on to join the Way of Life, featuring John Bonham on drums. It was while pounding away in the Way of Life that Bonham was asked to join Zeppelin. Peggy, meanwhile, went on to join the Ian Campbell Folk Group where he met Swarbrick, Ralph McTell, Harvey Andrews, and others on the burgeoning folk club circuit.

The day of Dave Pegg's 21st birthday, he saw Fairport play a gig at Mother's in Birmingham, and the week after he received a phone call from Swarbrick asking him to audition. He drove down to London for an audition with the Foundations (still getting plenty of work in the wake of 'Baby, Now That I've Found You') in the morning and Fairport in the afternoon.

Richard: 'We just carried on, probably drank a lot, but it was a very comradely band – everybody really got on well with each other, we were all good chums. It doesn't always happen in bands but Fairport was pretty pally all the way through, and at that point with Peggy coming in as a real social catalyst, it all got a lot more relaxed – so we really enjoyed ourselves.'

Richard was still living in the old Brent flat by the North Circular. His childhood enthusiasm for the majesty of steam trains was still evident, and visitors to the flat remember Thompson's predilection for playing records of steam trains rather than the latest album by Ten Years After.

Richard Thompson

Simon: 'He certainly had more than one LP of steam trains. He wasn't an obsessive train spotter, but I think he went through a trainspotting phase ... But we did play all sorts of music too. Richard was a serious fan of John Coltrane. The pre-War, swing jazz stuff was much in evidence along with Satie and Debussy. It was all likely to be played at high volume with all the windows open at 2.30 in the morning.'

With fond memories of the days spent 'getting it together' at Farley Chamberlayne, and with the practical necessity of somewhere cheap to rehearse, Fairport settled on the Angel, an old converted pub in the village of Little Hadham near Bishop's Stortford.

Along with Peggy and his wife Chris and daughter Stephanie, Mattacks, Swarbrick and family, Simon and his girlfriend, Richard moved in to the Angel.

Richard: 'The problem was we weren't really living anywhere. We'd spent the summer at the house in Winchester and we had to get out of there for some reason. Swarb had sold his house in Pembrokeshire and I was living in a flat in Brent with Simon and Ian in the shadow of Brent Cross flyover. There was a phone call from Swarb saying "I'm on my way – I'm in the removal van, where do I go?" So we said "well, we don't know Swarb, we'll call you back!"

'So we ended up living at a house that we had turned down as being totally unfit for human habitation – which was the Angel in Little Hadham – where they now make Hadham water, I understand. If it's anything to do with the stuff we were putting into the ground twenty years ago, I wouldn't drink it. So that was an adventure in itself. The Angel was a shell of a building – a disused public house – for a while we were all in there, with families in some cases, one or two rooms each. The families generally got two rooms – a suite! There was a shared kitchen, one really uncomfortable bathroom. But it was fun, it was probably more fun for me because I didn't have a family.'

Dave Pegg: 'We lived at the Angel for about a year and we all had our separate rooms. Richard had this harmonium ... Everybody had their own hi-fis, and the only music that we had in common was *Music From Big Pink* and the Band's second album. Everybody had those albums and they were always being played. One of the rooms out of the five had one of those records playing all the time more or less, and I was pleased to be able to tell Rick Danko that the other night, he's a big Fairport fan. He's known about Fairport since 1970 when he was introduced to the group by Elton John.

'Communal living hadn't happened to any of us at the time, I don't think anyone had done that student kind of thing. It was like straight from home into a place with twelve people, one toilet and bathroom, a not very efficient hot water system, so if you did want a bath, you had to get up really early in the morning. Everyone had different hours, there were some people who were nocturnal, and others – notably ourselves because we had a young child living there – we had to get up seven o'clock in the morning and go to bed reasonably early.

'You learned an awful lot about the other people living in the house in a very short time, and those kind of character assessments tend to be very true, people never change . . . It was very beneficial to the band I think, we all remained friends. We all got fleas from the TV room, various other diseases used to do the rounds, various people, including my daughter, got ringworm. It wasn't that we were a bunch of dirty people it's just that that's the way that it was in those days.'

Dave Mattacks: 'We went to the Angel in Little Hadham, in Hertfordshire, and that is where the *Full House* line-up lived and worked, and that wasn't great. It would have been great, and probably helped matters, if everyone's living quarters had been self-contained, but there was a shared bathroom and a shared kitchen, so it was less than ideal. You certainly do bond with people in those situations . . . Maybe if we'd been teenagers, but we were all in our early twenties, Chris and Peggy had just had Steph . . .

'There was certainly something to be said for spending time together outside of doing a gig and rehearsal rooms, and it definitely did help. It's a constant source of bemusement to me that I know four or five people from that era better than I know my wife.'

With showbiz fame and glamour still a long way away, Richard Thompson was settled in the Angel, surrounded by his groaning bookshelves, long-playing records of steam trains and his longbow. Simon remembers him, clad in Lincoln green, practising with his bow and arrow on the disused tennis court at the back of the Angel.

Musical direction was a long way from Fairport's collective mind as they prepared for their first performance since the departure of Sandy Denny and Ashley Hutchings. The major concern was for the band to survive, to keep on keeping on. Hampstead's Country Club on 29 January 1970 marked Fairport Convention's return to the world after eight weeks away, a month of which had been spent breaking in their new bass player.

Dave Pegg: 'Nobody was singing. I couldn't sing. I could hardly talk. I had a list of all the numbers, what key they were in . . . but I thought "They can't *all* be instrumentals". They tossed a coin to see who was going to sing, and it was down to Swarb and Richard.'

Richard Thompson

From being the sleepy-eyed figure, lurking at the back of the stage, sheltering beneath his lion's mane of curly hair, Thompson was literally pushed to the front of the stage, and was gaining in confidence with every gig. Over Fairport's short career, Thompson's name had been steadily moving up the masthead. People were now singling him out for his distinctive songs, songs which seemed capable of celebrating, and commemorating, an England which had disappeared beneath the motorway and high-rise.

It was as a guitarist that Thompson was shining through. At that time – 1970 – the 'guitar hero' was in vogue. Eric Clapton had pioneered the trend – the 'Clapton is God' graffiti had first appeared around London in 1966 following former Yardbird's pioneering work with John Mayall's Bluesbreakers.

Towards the end of the 60s, Mayall was a clearing house for all the brightest and the best. Clapton, Peter Green and Mick Taylor had all served time in the ranks of Mayall's guitar army. The formation of Cream in 1966 had elevated Clapton to Olympus. Clapton's old band, the Yardbirds, also proved a finishing school for guitar heroes – Jeff Beck and Jimmy Page followed in Clapton's footsteps.

Then along came Jimi Hendrix who flamboyantly re-wrote the book, and created his own special niche in the pantheon. But by the beginning of 1970, Hendrix was channelling all his energies into consolidating his American success. He had largely turned his back on his adopted homeland, and hadn't performed in the UK in over a year.

Richard Thompson was far too withdrawn and modest to be thought of as a guitar hero. Those who recognised talent when they heard it knew how good a guitarist he was. But his understated style of guitar-playing was contrary to the cock-of-the-walk flashiness of the guitar hero. You couldn't just stand at the back of the stage as Richard did. The fancy fretwork had to be seen to be heard.

Thompson always eschewed the trappings of guitar heroics; head down, he just let everything shine through his playing. There was never any real opportunity for him to go through the guitar hero motions, Fairport weren't that sort of band. His playing was undeniably fluid and mesmerising, but Fairport's strength was as a band, the glory spread among the hydra-headed Fairport. A Thompson solo would swiftly be followed by a Swarbrick tour-de-force. For Richard Thompson though, the word was out, and opportunity was waiting to knock.

With Swarbrick on board, and with no discernible focal point since the departure of Sandy Denny, Thompson slowly began emerging from his shell. Undeniable sparks flew between Thompson and Swarbrick onstage. All the violinist's enthusiasm for playing in front of an electric band to rock'n'roll audiences was matched by the guitarist's willingness to try and match Swarbrick's unfeasibly fast fiddle-work.

The Fairport set of the *Full House* era allowed plenty of room for instrumental virtuosity. Clinton Heylin's exhaustive set lists of the period reveal that Fairport relied heavily on the twin-pronged attack of Swarbrick and Thompson – 'Jigs and Reels', 'Dirty Linen', 'Toss The Feathers', 'Battle Of The Somme', 'Mason's Apron', 'Sir B. McKenzie', 'Flatback Caper' . . . all were largely 'Trad. Arr. Fairport', and were also instrumentals.

Even the vocal performances were chosen essentially as platforms for alarming instrumental displays: 'Tam Lin', 'Bonny Bunch Of Roses', 'Sir Patrick Spens', 'Matty Groves' and 'Sloth' were all effectively instrumental set-pieces, with only the odd intrusion from vocal ensemble. But the sheer volume of gigs the band were now undertaking, meant that the vocals did begin to improve.

Joe Boyd: 'I think that Richard had the confidence, and I think that Swarbrick actually helped that way a lot. He helped convince Richard, as I had, that he could be a lead singer – and I think Swarbrick wanted to sing more as well.'

Richard had already visited America in the tragic aftermath of the crash in the summer of 1969, but Fairport Convention finally made their American debut as a band in April 1970 at San Francisco's Winterland, supporting the hugely popular Crosby, Stills, Nash and Young. Quite what the denim-clad, patchouli-wearing audience made of the five scruffy herberts singing about 'Henry Tomkins' wife' and a jolly hangman goes sadly unrecorded.

Further slots supporting Island labelmates Jethro Tull and Traffic brought Fairport to wider American audiences, but it was toe-in-the-water time, and the band's real contact with America would come later in the year.

I spoke to Steve Winwood in 1986 about Richard Thompson and Fairport, and asked him if Traffic were aware of Fairport? 'Oh very much so, yeah. They were a great influence on Traffic. The same record label as well, which seemed so important at that time, that family atmosphere . . . I'd always been a great lover of traditional music, because when I started with Spencer Davis, he and I used to do gigs, just the two of us, in folk clubs around Birmingham, which is actually where I met Swarbrick and knew Dave Pegg . . .

'We did a lot of tours with Fairport just after Traffic started, and Richard was showing a lot of talent, as did the band. Richard always intrigued me the way he managed to combine American music with

Richard Thompson

English traditional music, and I still find that fascinating. I guess I'm a bit of a frustrated musicologist – I don't have that collector's mind of names, record labels and family trees, but I do find that musical anthropology very interesting. And Richard, you can hear, has a great knowledge of it.'

One of Thompson's own fondest memories of Fairport's first American tour was the band's only American recording session, in Los Angeles: 'It was spotted in the A&M vaults on eight-track a while back. It was the *Full House* line-up, we did "Staines Morris", "Bonny Bunch Of Roses" – maybe three or four things – it sounded great – I don't know if we were so hyped up because it was Goldstar which was where Phil Spector used to record – but we imagined it would sound great before we went in – it was just one of those great sounding rooms, stuff was coming off the tape and just jumping at you. I think it really did sound good. But when it was time to make the next record I think we probably felt that we'd gone past that material.'

Back in Blighty, Fairport had some prestige gigs lined up – Hornsey Town Hall; supporting the Incredible String Band at the London Palladium; the St Cecilia's Church Organ Fund benefit, Little Hadham, where Miss Caroline Shillacker walked the ankle competition! But Fairport's big one was their appearance on the Saturday afternoon of the Bath Festival of Blues and Progressive Music. Still buoyant from the 1969 clan-gatherings at Woodstock and the Isle of Wight, Bath (26–28 June 1970) was the first big UK festival of the year.

For 25 shillings you could hear bands of such calibre as the Byrds, John Mayall and Frank Zappa, names who were such a feature of the preceding years. And then there were those who would come to dominate the global music scene during the new decade – Led Zeppelin and Pink Floyd. Bath proved to be a landmark show for both bands. 'All times subject to possible change' the programme noted. The Floyd were scheduled on at 10.15 on the Saturday night, eventually appearing at around 4 a.m. on the Sunday. But it was worth the wait, as the piece the band chose to premiere was 'Atom Heart Mother'. Zeppelin were scheduled to appear below Sunday night headliners Jefferson Airplane, so that the band could take advantage of the Sunday evening sunset.

Fairport were on the Saturday afternoon, squeezed in between the Keef Hartley Band and Jon Hiseman's Colosseum. It was a bright, gloriously sunny afternoon – wasn't it always a bright, gloriously sunny afternoon back then – when Fairport took to the stage.

Their set, if memory serves, drew heavily on the instrumentals, the jigs and reels which everyone delighted in. Of course it was all to do with length back then – How long can you sustain your tremolo? How long can you extend your solo? But there was already a weariness afoot over the likes of Hot Tuna's blues jamming, and Maynard Ferguson's piping, sub-Blood, Sweat and Tears jazz-rock fusions.

Fairport's blisteringly fast instrumentals seemed ideally suited to the festival spirit that Saturday afternoon. Bath came at a time when cohesion and unity were still on everyone's mind – we all knew about the Woodstock vibe, or had at least read the *Rolling Stone* report of the festival, and knew that chanting could stop the rain.

The sort of music Fairport sent spinning out over the Shepton Mallet showground that Saturday afternoon was drawn from a well-spring of tradition. The band's folk-based set fitted in perfectly with the prevailing convivial spirit and desire to return to rurality. To camp out on the land and set your soul free was just the thing to do after a greasy hamburger and five pints of cider on a sunny Saturday afternoon.

The siting of the festival at Bath (well, quite near Bath) had a lot to do with the half-remembered myths and legends which were so abundant in the lush Somerset fields. It was a time of Tolkien and Narnia, a time of mead and memories of maypoles. Fairport Convention were the house band of the madding crowd.

The festival site at Shepton Mallet was just a joss-stick's throw from Glastonbury Tor, arguably the most mystical place in the whole hippie ethos. Glastonbury was widely believed to have been the location to which Joseph of Arimathaea brought the Holy Grail – the chalice from which Christ drank at the Last Supper, and the most revered artefact of the Christian church. It was around the legend of the Grail that King Arthur built a courtly code of knightly chivalry and purity. Glastonbury was long-held to have been the burial place of King Arthur.

All in all, the Bath Festival of Blues and Progressive Music had found its perfect location. And all that hippie-dippie stuff seemed perfectly in keeping with the set that Fairport played that Saturday afternoon.

Although electric, the frenetic melodies and essential buoyancy of the music seemed to hark back to those Elysian times. It was a feeling which was confirmed when, soon after witnessing Fairport's set, I duly went out and bought their current album. It was their first post-Sandy effort, *Full House*.

Chapter 9

FROM THE OUTSIDE of course, you weren't aware of any problems: that Richard and producer Joe Boyd were at loggerheads; that the group were flipping coins in the studio to see who would sing; that it would prove to be Richard's last album with Fairport ... All you knew at the time was that *Full House* was the new album by Fairport Convention.

There they are on the gatefold, looking very earnest in some leafy rural idyll. There too is that little flying witch on a broomstick, familiar from other Witchseason records. And here, on the pink Island label, it says that the songs, which sound like they are as old as the myths of Glastonbury, were actually fashioned by 'Thompson/Swarbrick'.

There is a rather contrived rurality about the project – the front cover is weak and Thompson's sleeve notes sound like he's been sipping too much mead. But all doubts are vanquished when you get to the actual songs.

Richard: 'We'd driven ourselves in the *Liege & Lief* direction and having done it, we wanted to keep going. It was just a reflection of what we were listening to at the time, we were listening to a lot of that stuff like field recordings of Fred Jordan and others. We were discovering stuff all the time. Like let's make a new tune; let's take one line of this reel and slow it down and move it up a minor third and see what that does to it; let's take one line of this ballad and make a whole song out of it, chopping up the tradition to find new things to do ... like a collage.'

Confounding all critics and overriding all expectations, *Full House* is actually a far better record than either Fairport or Fairport fans had any right to expect. While the singing is still as weak as watered-down beer, in harmony, the vocal deficiencies were ably disguised.

'Walk Awhile' is a perfect statement of intent, an opening salvo which struts and swaggers with all the panache of a displaying peacock. Belying such a jaunty opening, Thompson's hand can be discerned in the reference to 'undertakers' bowing their heads.

Instrumentals and 'Walk Awhile' aside, the abiding air of *Full House* is melancholic. The remaining Thompson/Swarbrick collaborations – 'Sloth' and 'Doctor Of Physick' – and the mournful, concluding 'Flowers Of The Forest' – are as sombre as any compositions Thompson has lent his name to.

'Sloth' exists in a dislocated world where 'the right thing's the wrong thing', and while it was frequently used live as a platform from which Fairport spun off lengthy improvisations, on record the song has a haunting, wistful quality, which resolves with the concluding 'Just a roll, just a roll . . .' Dave Pegg remembers Thompson and Swarbrick fashioning an answer song called 'Fath' at the Angel, but not getting much further than the title.

'Sir Patrick Spens' had been tried out while Sandy was still in the band. The song was considered by experts 'the finest thing in Scottish balladry', and certainly Fairport's driving riff reinforces the bold dramatic drive. Winding down, 'Doctor Of Physick' is shot through with menace; Swarbrick's fiddle flays the mournful melody, while Thompson's guitar cracks and lashes like a whip. The descending refrain, 'Doctor Monk unpacks his trunk tonight' suggests a Pandora's Box, packed full of evil. The overall atmosphere of the song is of shadows edging further into darkness.

Long held to be traditional, 'The Flowers Of The Forest' actually comes from an eighteenth-century poem by Jane Elliott. It is perhaps the most beguiling lament ever written, a tune which hints at the sweetness of melancholy and was played at the funerals of both Sandy Denny and Phil Ochs.

The Scottish half of Richard Thompson wallows in the pibroch and the lament which echo across the Scottish Borders – it can be found in his own work and in his handling of traditional Scottish ballads. But of them all perhaps, 'The Flowers Of The Forest' exercises the strongest pull; it plucks at the heart strings, even if you have never been nearer to Scotland than a late-night viewing of *Brigadoon*.

In a press release around the time of *Full House*, Thompson is singled out for 'His unkempt individualism and affection for Coltrane and Debussy, [which] led the others to look to him for wisdom and new material, which, after some hesitation, he now supplies in ample doses.'

The Swarbrick collaboration remains the best-known and most fondly remembered of all Thompson's songwriting partnerships. Although they created only a handful of songs together, these shaped two crucial Fairport albums. The songs which Thompson and Swarbrick produced in that brief burst are probably the finest originals in Fairport's history.

Richard Thompson

Richard: 'Swarb and I'd sit at the Angel, in front of the fire late at night and get the guitar out and he'd say "I've got this tune I've had for a long time, see if you can do anything with this" and so he'd play "Sloth" or something and I'd say leave it with me. So we'd figure out melody first and then I'd go away and try and do the lyrics. It's hard to do lyrics to order while you're sitting there – I find it's usually deserving of some reflection. I think we wrote some really good songs like that. "Crazy Man Michael" I wrote to a different tune – "The Bonnie Hoos Of Airlie" – which it scans better to, but Swarb came up with a really good tune so we tried to shoehorn it into Swarb's tune and that's the one we used on the record.'

Simon: 'There was a generational gap. Although Swarb is only seven years older than Richard, that's a big difference when you look back on how old Richard was at the time ... Swarb had been married three times, he was a parent. He'd got all these records out under his own name. They were the guys who had the creative baton that they were prepared to pass between each other ...'

Two Thompson/Swarbrick songs, 'Sickness And Diseases' and 'The Journeyman's Grace', were written and rehearsed while Thompson was still with Fairport but not recorded until he had left the band, appearing on *Angel Delight*, the first post-Thompson Fairport album. The songs come from living at the Angel and reflect Thompson's fascination with all things rural, littered with references to 'dowsers', 'hawkers', 'rovers' and 'circles made of stone'.

'Now Be Thankful' was a 1970 single, best remembered for its B-side, an instrumental, the name in its title coming from Fairport's fondness for Barry Humphries' Barry McKenzie cartoon strip in *Private Eye*: 'Sir B. McKenzie's Daughter's Lament For The 77th Mounted Lancers Retreat From The Straits Of Loch Knombe In The Year Of Our Lord 1727 On The Occasion Of The Announcement Of Her Marriage To The Laird Of Kinleakie'. It was only ever intended for *The Guinness Book of Records* – and made it – as the song with the longest title.

The one abiding masterpiece of the Thompson/Swarbrick partnership is 'Poor Will And The Jolly Hangman'. A near-relative of the Incredible String Band's *Hangman's Beautiful Daughter*, Thompson's lyrics draw on all manner of sources; a random jotting down of notes ... the fee given to the Tyburn hangman for the rope; noblemen were expected to pay their executioner between £7 and £10 for the privilege; Judge Jeffreys ('The Hanging Judge') and the Bloody Assizes of 1685; John 'Babbacombe' Lee ('The Man They Couldn't Hang').

There is a world-weariness in Thompson's voice as he sings 'No purse for a champion; No true love come over the stile . . .' 'Poor Will And The Jolly Hangman' has all the Fairport hallmarks of greatness, suggesting age-old wisdom allied with contemporary vigour, a song which heralds a life for the band without Sandy Denny. But as ever with Fairport, nothing was quite that simple.

'Poor Will And The Jolly Hangman' was intended for *Full House*, but Thompson dug his heels in, causing further friction in the Fairport camp: 'I really didn't like the vocals – I thought that was the real problem, none of us could really sing it and it sounded like it. I think that was the reason, but it probably should have been on the record.'

Joe Boyd: 'I felt the album [*Full House*] was short . . . with "Poor Will And The Jolly Hangman" it was going to be twenty, twenty-one minutes a side. I just felt that in terms of balance, it was part of the mood of the album. It always seemed to me that it belonged on that album, I thought it would fit perfectly, with those brilliant minor notes . . .

'Richard was seemingly becoming more and more perverse in the studio. We had a lot of arguments over *Full House* . . . He was very fussy about things, and whenever I would say "I like that solo, let's keep it . . ." he would say "no, erase it, I want to do another one". And whenever I said "no, I don't like that, let's do another one", he would say, "no, I like that, let's keep it . . ." We had a big argument over "Poor Will And The Jolly Hangman" . . . He thought the song was flawed and insisted on taking it off the album.'

Even without 'Poor Will And The Jolly Hangman', *Full House* garnered respectful reviews. The critics seemed surprised that not only had Fairport survived the shock of Sandy Denny's departure, but had managed to come up with a strong new album to boot.

Chris Welch got into the swing of things in his *Melody Maker* review: 'Aye, gather round me bully boys – once there was a time when Fairport Convention albums were as hard to obtain as a Grope O'Shanter at Michaelmas . . .' before going on to call *Full House* perhaps 'their best yet', a view shared by *NME*. *Record Mirror* felt that Fairport: 'have done for British folk music what bands such as the Flying Burrito Brothers, the Byrds and even Bob Dylan have done for American country music'.

In *Rolling Stone*, Ed Ward developed the idea with a comparison which delighted the British band: 'The music shows that England has finally gotten her very own equivalent to The Band . . . By calling Fairport an English equivalent to The Band, I meant that they have soaked up enough of the tradition of their countryfolk that it begins to show all over, while they maintain their roots in rock.'

Richard Thompson

In strictly commercial terms, *Full House* got rather overlooked in the slew of releases during 1970, the year which saw the release of *Bridge Over Troubled Water, Led Zeppelin III, Let It Be, All Things Must Pass, Cosmo's Factory, Atom Heart Mother, Plastic Ono Band, After the Gold Rush, Sweet Baby James, Live at Leeds, Deep Purple in Rock* and the soundtrack to *Paint Your Wagon*.

Life at the Angel proceeded along in an amiable haze from which Fairport ventured onto the football pitch, the pub, or to gigs. Dave Pegg remembers they were still keen to play whenever they could: 'When we lived at the Angel, we had a little group called the Purple Flange, we just played acoustic instruments at the local folk club ... It was an excuse to get out and go along and do the folk clubs.'

At this stage in his career 21-year-old Thompson couldn't envisage a life outside Fairport. Ashley Hutchings' dogmatism over traditional material had been bypassed, so there was a ready home for any songs Thompson felt like contributing. The five men all got along together, though the non-writers respected Thompson's pre-eminence in the group and allowed him space, for his zen and archery, his astrology and outside sessions.

Dave Pegg: 'In that particular line up there were never any High Noon scenarios, it was a very happy bunch of people, and there was no real drama with the *Full House* line-up at all, we'd had great times together. Richard – this was before he was a Muslim – was one of the chaps, he would never get out of it, like some of the rest of us would, but he did partake of the odd glass of whisky ...'

Richard: 'It was all wild and crazy. The Fairport/Steeleye football match – it was very hard to play football after you'd been spiked with cannabis and stuff.

'The legendary 5 November fireworks party was almost a national disaster. Our road manager had a friend at Gamages in the firework department who used to slip him all this good display stuff – naval military display mortars and stuff – it was about £400 worth of fireworks which was a fortune in those days, more like £4,000 these days. A huge amount of fireworks, things you buried in the ground and this was in the middle of a quiet little village in Hertfordshire – and all these people turned up because they heard there was a good party going on – a lot of Peggy's nefarious friends from Birmingham – the Cozy Powells and John Bonhams and people – all turned up dancing on the tables, there was a lot of people and you couldn't see for smoke – it was just ridiculous. At one point, about two in the morning, these two uniformed figures came through the mist like a Charlie Chan film and asked us to stop as they'd had hundreds of complaints.'

It was adolescence prolonged into adulthood. Living together at the

Angel made Fairport into (slightly) grown-up versions of William and the Outlaws. Richard's life at the time was inextricably bound up with that of Fairport. They had been together, men and boys, for five years and they had survived a tragic crash together. Professionally, they had established themselves, and with *Liege & Lief* had made a real breakthrough. Fairport provided Richard with an umbrella, under which he could write in tandem with Swarbrick and indulge in lengthy guitar improvisations, knowing that the band was there to support him.

There was little of real adult concern to bother Fairport: Joe Boyd and Anthea Joseph at Witchseason looked after the business side of their life; gigs were plentiful, and record royalties ensured that, by the band's modest standards, they could enjoy a relatively comfortable standard of living at the Angel.

By the middle of 1970, Thompson and Fairport were resigned to life as a popular, top of the Second Division, English rock'n'roll band. As time passed, the *Liege & Lief* experiment seemed more of a diversion than a foundation for a career. While Fairport continued to incorporate traditional elements into their music, it was done with little of the scholastic and experimental approach which had been so characteristic of *Liege & Lief*. Now, the traditional element was grafted on, either as crowd-pleasing instrumentals, or with the covers of traditional songs sitting alongside the burgeoning Thompson/Swarbrick catalogue.

It was a nice enough life – what would later come to be known as a lifestyle. In his room at the Angel, cluttered with a long bow and quivers full of arrows, with shelves groaning under books, Thompson began writing songs which he naturally intended for Fairport, even if he couldn't really imagine them fitting the band's style.

By their second visit to the States, in September 1970, Fairport were as tight as at any time during their career. Swarbrick and Thompson were still sparking off each other, Mattacks was firmly installed on the drum stool and Pegg on the bass was proving to be an undeniable asset. And with Richard happy to parade his virtuosity on guitar, Simon was developing in confidence as a vocalist.

Richard: 'I think we did two tours, which was great fun. It was strange stuff, some of it severely under-attended, there was some cow palace in Minneapolis where everybody cancelled – Ike and Tina Turner had cancelled and all the others, so we were about the last ones left on the bill who actually turned up to play in this huge auditorium with only about two hundred people.' Fairport also played the Philadelphia Folk Festival and filled in with dates based on Joe Boyd's contacts in and around the Boston area.

Richard Thompson

Dave Pegg: 'We didn't have any money. Our budget was $10 a day. If you were careful you could manage. We'd spotted this bar in Ann Arbor, and it looked like a perfect place to play music . . . We said can we play here, and the guy who ran it said you'll have to audition, so we said we're not fucking auditioning, but Simon said "I'll audition!" He was so desperate to get the free drink so he went in on his own and passed his audition, so we all played there on a Monday night, to about forty people. By the end of the week we'd got about four hundred people in. One night Dave Mattacks threw a wobbler because there wasn't room for his kit to be set up, so Richard played drums. We got paid in beer, drank them out of draught Bass by the end of the week.'

It wasn't an arduous schedule. The band's first full American tour didn't stretch Fairport and would probably have remained unremarkable had not someone – in typical Fairport fashion, no one is quite certain who, how or why – decided to record the band's residency at Los Angeles' prestigious Troubadour club in the first week of September 1970.

Richard: 'The LA Troubadour was fun. Everyone who played there had to sign to do three or four engagements . . . and of course you wanted to play there the first time, but a lot of people got famous in the meantime and had to go back to the Troubadour to fulfil this terrible obligation. But it was quite a place, it was a great hang-out for folkies – we met a lot of the Los Angeles folk fraternity there.'

Linda Ronstadt, a regular with fond memories of the Troubadour, told Marc Shapiro: 'We all used to sit in a corner and dream. The Troubadour was like café society. It was where everyone met, where everyone got to hear everyone else's act. It was where I made all my musical contacts, and found people who were sympathetic to the musical styles I wanted to explore.'

Another regular was Loudon Wainwright III who remembers seeing Fairport that year: 'The first time I laid eyes on Richard was when he was playing with Fairport, who were playing at the Troubadour . . . In fact, I remember him drunk, with his head down on the table at the bar at the Troubadour, the only time in my life I've ever seen him drunk . . .

'At that time it was the happening room. Then it was, in American showbiz terms, the showcase room. I remember seeing James Taylor play, the first time after his record came out, Carole King on piano – I remember getting *very* drunk that night, realising how big this guy was gonna be – Irish coffees as I recall.

'I played there when my records came out. It was the West Coast version of the Bottom Line . . . and it was full of songwriters and musicians, you could see Phil Ochs there. Roger Miller used to hang out there. Roger McGuinn would come in and out. Bobby Neuwirth, the Band who were all living out in Malibu then, and it wouldn't be unusual to see Richard Manuel or Rick Danko just hanging out there, just drinking.'

Fairport were booked in at the Troubadour supporting Rick Nelson and the Stone Canyon Band. Nelson having dropped the 'y' from Ricky was, at the grand old rock'n'roll age of 30, in the process of beginning again. Richard remembers being really impressed by Nelson's band, and by Rick himself: 'He was a really nice bloke, very nice to us, despite what we must have looked like to him'.

Peggy's abiding memory was not the music, but the bar tab. Apparently Fairport were paid $500 for their Troubadour residency, and ended up owing the Troubadour $1,500 for the band's alcohol consumption.

For an unknown band from Britain, Fairport attracted quite a few famous faces. Odetta came to watch, as did Linda Ronstadt, who was enchanted by what she saw. When asked up to help Fairport out, Ronstadt called out that she didn't know any English songs, to be stymied by Simon replying 'Don't worry, we know all yours.' Reluctantly, Ronstadt joined the scruffbags onstage. With her back to the band, Linda took a nervous deep breath and sang the first two lines acapella, before Fairport joined in with a note-perfect backing of her version of 'Silver Threads And Golden Needles'.

Joe Boyd: 'Richard took this sort of chicken-pickin' Nashville guitar solo, that was an imitation of every Carl Perkins solo, and every steel guitar solo, and everything combined into two choruses, which staggered her.'

Ronstadt is a recurring thread in the Fairport/Richard Thompson tapestry and later in the Richard and Linda story. Ronstadt had brought together in her backing band Don Henley, Glenn Frey and Bernie Leadon who were later to quit and form the Eagles. The intriguing prospect of north Londoner Richard Thompson joining that quintessentially Californian group is one of rock'n'roll's great 'What ifs ...?' 'Welcome to the Hotel Finchley.'

Richard: 'The Stone Poneys was the original band that Linda was in, and then Linda's backing band was what became the Eagles. Don Henley says that I was asked to join but I don't remember being asked, I wasn't asked directly, but I might have been asked through management or something. But I was supposed to have been asked to join Traffic as well and I don't remember that either. I would have hated it – I'd have hated being on the road with four or five miserable Americans – they always seem miserable. And if you see them now, they still look miserable on stage – like they don't want to be there and they don't like each other. I like them as people, I know Bernie Leadon a bit and I used to know Glenn Frey a bit and they're nice enough people but being on the road with an American band would have driven me up the wall.'

Marc Ellington, who had sung backing vocals on *Unhalfbricking* and later became one of Richard's closest friends, understood Richard's appeal to American musicians: 'There were natural parallels between what was happening with Fairport and what was happening with Gram Parsons . . . and later on, the Eagles were certainly keen to get Richard involved. There have always been a group of serious musicians in America who have been aware of Richard and how talented and important he was . . . the first thing that all these people want to know is what Richard Thompson's up to.'

Dave Pegg: 'American musicians were very taken by Richard, all the guys that subsequently went on to become the Eagles used to hang out at that bar, and we'd be doing two or three sets a night. Linda Ronstadt would get up and sing, and Richard could play that country-rock thing. He had a very open mind and he was probably as good as any of those cats. For someone who'd come from London roots, the way that he played the guitar was up there with all those Californian guys . . . He could play all the country licks, the rock'n'roll thing . . . if you listen to some of the stuff he did with the GPs, devastatingly great guitar playing.

'It's something that's just inside him, it's not what he does, but he has great command of all these various guitar styles. It didn't go unnoticed by the Californian Mafia. In fact subsequently, I think the Eagles did ask him to join them. As did the Band. When I was talking to Rick Danko the other night, he was saying when Robbie Robertson left, he wanted Richard to join the Band but some of the other guys didn't. So I said "Well, it's a good job Richard didn't because he was already so far advanced in his own career." Richard was a big Band fan. The Band with Richard would have been fantastic.'

The presence of an eight-track mobile, the release of *Live at the LA Troubadour* in 1977 and its subsequent reworking as *House Full* in 1986, ensured that Fairport's stint at the Troubadour was well documented. It's possible to hear just how good and fluent and flexible and fast they were. Richard lets rip some achingly eloquent solos and Swarbrick's playing is out to break records (Richard: 'All the tempos were very up – I think Swarb was still on his slimming pill phase – where all the tempos were unbelievably fast!'). Simon's dulcimer playing, particularly on 'Battle Of The Somme' is atmospheric and poignant, while Peggy and Mattacks prove themselves the Wyman and Watts of the folk-rock fraternity.

The Fairport sense of humour, all too frequently overlooked in the gloomy tradition of Thompson/Swarbrick songs and the bloody murder ballads, is represented by the inclusion of the old music hall chestnut 'Yellow Bird'.

Sadly, the live albums are prevented from being a wholly representative souvenir of Fairport's stint at the Troubadour by the absence of 'The Birmingham Water Buffalo Club'. Peggy's old mates from Birmingham were also in LA at the time Fairport were playing at the Troubadour – though accommodated at the fractionally larger Forum. On the night of 4 September 1970, Led Zeppelin gave what is widely believed to be one of their finest shows and afterwards made their way to the Troubadour. Fairport were in the habit of playing two sets a night, one either side of Rick Nelson, with the second set lasting for as long as the band could stand.

Simon Nicol: 'Zeppelin came down, and it was all Peggy and Bonzo, Old Firm Night ... Neither Mattacks nor I spent much time on stage once they got down, we were supernumaries. I do remember Mattacks' silver sparkle Gretsch bass drum, which had been immaculately positioned and totally solid for the whole preceding seven or eight sessions, jumping forward three or four inches on Bonzo's first strike.'

Dave Pegg: 'I was the drinks monitor that night. Richard played really well, and it was fantastic, with Planty and Jimmy Page who was slightly disadvantaged because he was playing Simon Nicol's Gibson L5 which had a wound third string and very heavy gauge strings, so Jimmy couldn't really get into his stride. Richard was playing his gold-top Les Paul which was subsequently bought by John Martyn.

'It was a great night. "Hey Joe" was done, it was things everybody knew. There may have been some Presley-type things, but I can't remember, I was a bit out of it.'

Picture the scene: it's three o'clock in the morning, a bleary-eyed crowd of around 50 punters have been drawn to the Troubadour to hear esteemed folk-rock fusionists Fairport Convention. Instead, they get to see a whole lotta Led, the biggest rock'n'roll band on the planet, jamming the night away with Fairport.

Jamming was the order of the day. It allowed superstar musicians like Page, Clapton and Hendrix to let their hair down and play away from the spotlight. There is an astonishing camaraderie between musicians – R&B guitarists are best friends with MOR drummers; jazz trumpeters spend whole evenings not coming to blows with rock pianists; while proto-Heavy Metal meisters enjoy strutting their stuff with English folk-rock wizards.

The tapes were rolling throughout the jam, but in characteristic style Zeppelin's late manager Peter Grant removed the tapes of his boys and Fairport right after the gig. Piecing together the frail memories through a haze of booze and time long-gone, the two bands are known to have jammed on 'Hey Joe', 'Morning Dew', 'Banks Of Sweet Primroses' and a couple of Presley rockers, probably 'Mystery Train', and maybe 'That's Alright Mama'. Joe Boyd also has an abiding memory of 'Jimmy Page trying to keep up with Richard at jigs and reels'.

For the record, the Fairport/Led Zeppelin connection in full: Thompson was one of the featured guitarists on Al Stewart's 1970 *Love Chronicles* album, along with Jimmy Page; Sandy Denny duetted with Robert Plant on 'Battle of Evermore' on the fourth Zep album; Fairport supported Zeppelin at the 1979 Knebworth shows, which proved to be Zeppelin's final UK shows; Robert Plant guested at Fairport's Cropredy reunions in 1986, 1992 and 1993; Richard Thompson played on 'Come Into My Life' on Plant's 1993 *Fate Of Nations* album.

Richard: ' "Hey Joe" was definitely one of the selections and there were others but I can't remember what else, it's a bit hazy to me that period. I know Peggy was involved in some serious drinking contest with Bonham and Janis Joplin – it was three sided – which started at Barney's Beanerie down the road – and ended up when they found Bonham two days later stark naked by the swimming pool and the rest of the band had gone to Hawaii. They'd gone to do some gigs but they couldn't find him, I think he missed two gigs. I think Peggy won. Peggy was a profound drinker in those days, he used to keep playing and down a pint at the same time, hammering on with the left hand. That used to go down very well!'

Their brief brush with superstardom over, Fairport returned to the Angel and began limping round the familiar UK college and club gig circuit to reactivate interest in *Full House*. The band's set drew on their recent album, sprinkled with some *Liege & Lief* era material and some as yet unreleased Thompson/Swarbrick songs, 'Journeyman's Grace' and 'Poor Will And The Jolly Hangman'. And so it went on, setting off from the Angel, to Sheffield, back to Little Hadham, then out to Cardiff. A short break home, then away to Newcastle, Glasgow, Leicester, Oxford . . .

Full House was Joe Boyd's last album with Fairport. He had found Thompson's dogmatism in the studio untenable, but other factors contributed to his decision to return to the States and take up a staff job with Warner Brothers: 'Richard and I were having a lot of clashes, so that wasn't very rewarding. Nick Drake had decided that his next album was going to be with no arrangements whatsoever, just him and a guitar ... Mike Heron was becoming very involved in Scientology, and so our communication was a little bit strained ... Sandy was difficult at that point, she was in Fotheringay, and I was having a lot of financial arguments with her ... Sandy and Nick and Richard and Mike were the four that were my main concern in life. It seemed to me that they weren't too interested in listening to my advice, and I was finding it more and more difficult to work with all of them, and so when the offer came along from Warner Brothers ...'

For Thompson, albeit unknowingly, the links were being severed. Like a galleon, linked to land by ropes from the quay, Thompson was unwittingly letting each one go. Solitary by nature, even in the hectic camaraderie of the Angel, Thompson was still being very much his own man and there was something about his solitary and withdrawn nature which some found intimidating. It seems to be a Thompson characteristic that however outwardly friendly, he gives the feeling that what you're getting is only the tip of the iceberg.

The Richard Thompson who occupied a room at the Angel towards the end of 1970 was happy enough to go trucking round the country with Fairport, but niggling at him was the thought that there must be more than this and in retrospect he admits: 'I was probably at that point starting to write stuff for *Henry the Human Fly* [Thompson's first solo album] ..., or at least stuff that I didn't know where it had a home.'

A revealing insight into Thompson's state of mind at the time came in a lengthy interview with *Disc & Music Echo*. Roy Shipston tracked Fairport down and observed Thompson on his home turf. Spread over two pages of the issue dated 22 August 1970, with a photo of Richard looking like one of Robin Hood's Merrie Men, the interview is a fascinating all-purpose, 'alternative lifestyle', hippie-dippie feature, with Thompson coming over as a cross between Neil out of *The Young Ones* and Molesworth's chum Fotherington-Thomas: 'Hello flowers, hello trees'.

In fairness to Richard, the music press of the time was full of this sort of guff. It was all part of the post-Dylan legacy: musicians being perceived as leaders, expected to have 'the answer'. Sifting through back issues of any of the four weekly music papers of the time (*Melody Maker, NME, Disc, Record Mirror*) there are similar rambling discourses, just waiting to come back and haunt both journalist and subject in later years.

Richard Thompson

Diving in at the deep end, Roy Shipston informs *Disc* readers that: 'Richard is very clearly involved in astrology. It is the most important thing to him after music. "I'm really going to get down to it for the next ten years, I intend to get a diploma in astrology . . . I think that lots of things are related to discoveries in astrology." As an example, he explained that Al Capone and the general underground movement occurred as a result of the discovery of Pluto . . .'

Like a hoover, Thompson sucks up every alternative aspect around – Indian tea ('there's definitely a time and place for herb tea'); family ('I really enjoy being a stranger to my relations'); reincarnation ('I think it takes a few years to get into your next life, to adjust to it. I have the standard belief of the Karmic Laws . . .'

Taking a deep breath, Thompson then shares his views on archery: 'I wouldn't kill anybody, I just shoot at targets. But if there is anything left after a nuclear war, they would be very useful'; ambition: 'I want to be the best guitarist in the world, the best songwriter, the champion archer and the world's best astrologer'; religion: 'I don't pray regularly . . . but I pray because sometimes it really works, a concentration of mental powers that you throw out in one direction'; songwriting: 'I find it very hard, but if I didn't write songs I'd go potty'; and, finally, Fairport Convention: 'Things will change, and the style will change, but it will be gradual. I've never noticed things changing. I've always thought it was pretty constant – but it has changed a lot. It is surprising how many musical styles we have been through and how many people have been in the band. But at the time it has always struck me as being very stable.'

Within six months, Thompson had served his notice to quit. He was finding a career in Fairport restricting: 'It goes back to what I felt about *Liege & Lief*, I felt there was a dimension missing . . . The music just wasn't right; I was writing stuff that just wasn't right for the band, stuff which ended up on *Henry* . . . and *Bright Lights*. In a sense, it broke my heart, but it was a gut instinct. Fairport's approach was limited . . . I think they, and 'folk-rock' got pigeonholed . . .'

Thompson broke the news to Fairport at the Angel one day late in January 1971. The band were gobsmacked.

Dave Pegg: 'When Richard left, I thought it's all over now Richard's gone. Although he was never a pushy character, everyone in the band respected him so much, because of his musical ability and the way that he was. He would come up with great ideas and lyrics, and he was always the leader of that bunch of people, and if Richard chipped his oar in, everyone would pay great attention to what he was saying.'

Simon Nicol: 'He just stopped getting into the van. We carried on doing the gigs, because it was the easiest option and there wasn't time to get anything else organised ... He carried on living at the Angel, still paid his share towards the cornflakes.'

Richard: 'I was feeling hemmed in for some reason. I think I was feeling that this wasn't the way I wanted to go somehow ... I felt I needed to get away and make some mistakes of my own and not have to be responsible for writing stuff for a band – I could just write something for myself for a while.

'It was really not planned ahead because I had no idea what I was going to do and I didn't move out of the Angel – I was still living there. So it was "I'm really sorry lads but I've got to leave the band, I know it's a shock but I'll go and make some tea and perhaps you'd like to have a chat about it!" So I went off and made the tea and they stayed as friends which was nice, and they still are.'

Part 2
Richard and Linda

Chapter 10

LINDA: 'My first definite memory of Richard was meeting him in a Chinese restaurant in the Kings Road sometime in 1969, more or less opposite Sound Techniques ... They'd just put "Crazy Man Michael" down, I'd been at the same studio, recording a jingle for Kellogg's Cornflakes and went in to see Sandy.

'I was *potty* about Joe Boyd, but he sat at one end of the table, and I got stuck at the other end with this vegetarian person while I was stuffing the sweet and sour pork down ... I said "Why aren't you eating meat?" and he said "When you eat meat, you eat the bad vibes from the slaughterhouse". I remember he was very nice but he didn't talk very much, and I was ogling the top of the table ... Richard was as white as death, terribly thin, like a sheet of A4 paper.'

Linda Peters was born in Hackney, east London in 1948, but her family were Scottish and she spent her teenage years in Scotland. She returned to London after A-Levels, to study acting at the London Academy of Music and Dramatic Arts (LAMDA). Linda loved acting, but found auditions intimidating and by 1969, she was working the folk circuit of Bunjies, Cousins and the Troubadour.

It was through her friend Sandy Denny that Linda met Joe Boyd and his nascent Witchseason ensemble: 'Witchseason was one big dysfunctional family. I suppose I got into it through Sandy, who was going out with Joe. I met him at the Troubadour, where everyone met up. I'd met Sandy in the folk clubs, where I was singing a bit myself. I knew the Incredible String Band, loved them, because they were Scottish. I'd known John Martyn since we were thirteen or fourteen – he used to deliver papers to my house.'

Linda's main income came from demo-ing pop songs of the period and breezy commercials. In partnership with guitarist Paul McNeill, she released a single in 1968, lifted from the Basement Tape source which Fairport had also plundered for material, the song was Bob Dylan's 'You Ain't Goin' Nowhere', which accurately described the single's chart progress.

Richard Thompson

Linda's bread and butter was commercial work and sessions: 'I remember when I did the session with Elton John (to try and interest other artists in the Witchseason roster of songwriters) he was very nice and very pro, but not the sort of musician that we worked with ... He was "Elton" then. I called him Elton, although some of the studio people called him Reg. Arrogant fools that we were, we were very sniffy about him ... He was just this pop singer ... Sandy would do the odd advert, and say "Don't tell Richard I did this will you?" It's so funny now because it's the exact opposite. When I was working in California, some guy came in from another studio and said we need somebody to sing a Wrigley's commercial, and people like James Burton, who were there, said "Oh Linda, you've got to do it, it's a commercial!"'

Such snobbery was very much part of the late 60s music scene. There was a distinct division between 'us' and 'them' – the serious underground musicians, and the pap cluttering up the frivolous pop charts.

Linda: 'They had to have that. If you don't have record sales you have to have that. They genuinely believed they were way above all that. And they were right. They were certainly very arrogant about that. They just felt they were better than "pop" singers.'

After a few years flogging round the folk circuit, Linda happily sacrificed artistic ambitions and devoted herself to commercials: 'I really liked doing them. "Ski, the full of fitness food", cornflakes, and "flour so fine it flows and flows." They were incredibly well paid, and left you a lot of time free.'

Linda was also first call for songwriter Tony Macauley, and remembers providing vocals on his hit song for Pickettywitch, 'That Same Old Feeling' and demo-ing Edison Lighthouse's 'Love Grows (Where My Rosemary Goes)'. Linda was now close to the whole Witchseason circle and particularly Sandy: 'Sandy had this manic depressive side, but she was capable of having a really good time. What kept me out of that spiral was simply sheer lack of talent ... I did write later on, but that was one of the drawbacks of being around Sandy and Richard, they were so good ... When Sandy joined Fairport, she was on about ten quid a week. None of them had any money, and I was doing these Kellogg's commercials, and earning a fortune.'

Linda's relationship with Joe Boyd meant she saw quite a lot of Richard long before they went out together, she remembers him at the Angel: 'He was a big drinker, but he was never really drunk much, he had a fantastic capacity for booze. I don't remember him drinking beer, but I think spirits and wine. He used to do horoscopes and he would do people's birth chart and charge a bottle of wine.'

Richard and Linda

The idea that Witchseason was one big happy family is given the lie by Linda: 'As far as writing goes, there was certainly competition between Richard and Sandy ... I think there was a certain lack of generosity amongst all those people. But they were young, and slightly competitive. I know that when Richard played guitar for Nick [Drake], they didn't talk. I'm sure they saw each other as rivals. Joe was "daddy", kind of thing. There was Nick and there was Richard and they were the two golden boys. Sandy was his golden girl. He did all the String Band things, but in retrospect, I think those three were the most important.

'Richard and Sandy, Nick, John Martyn, these are all great talents, but nobody walking past in the street has any idea who they are. It's a pure cult thing. When I was working with Richard and we were making albums, people asked me what I did, I used to say I was an interior designer, because I couldn't bear saying to people I'm a singer, and they'd say "Oh, what do you sing?" It's much easier if you're Sonia and you can say: "I was in the Eurovision Song Contest!" '

Linda became engaged to Joe Boyd and spent most of 1971 with him in America. Boyd was persevering with Warner Brothers where his work included spells on the soundtracks of *A Clockwork Orange* and *Deliverance*, and putting together a documentary feature on the life of Jimi Hendrix.

Following the collapse of Fotheringay so soon after splitting from Fairport, and reluctant to get involved with another group so soon, Sandy Denny enlisted musicians she already knew and respected, for a date at the Lincoln Festival in July 1971. The Happy Blunderers comprised Sandy, Richard Thompson, Dave Pegg and Fotheringay's Gerry Conway. The set was drawn from Sandy's forthcoming solo debut, *The North Star Grassman and the Ravens*. Thompson stayed on for a short American tour and that autumn undertook a UK college tour to promote her album.

It was quite something at the time, Sandy had after all, been the winner of 1970's prestigious *Melody Maker* poll as 'Best Female Singer' and Thompson's kudos was still intact following his split from Fairport. Though still living at the Angel, Richard was commuting to London, where he undertook a staggering amount of session work.

Richard: 'Being a head-in-the-clouds kind of chap, I was rather bad on the long-term planning – I still am. So I left Fairport as a gut reaction and didn't really know what I was doing, except writing. I was writing stuff and it seemed interesting and I thought it would be fun to make a record. And at the same time – 70–71 – I was doing a lot session work

Richard Thompson

as a way of avoiding any serious ideas about a career. It was also partly a financial consideration, if you did a session, you could get £12 plus £1 porterage.'

Credibility intact and his stature enhanced by the Fairport years, Thompson was an in-demand gun for hire on the session circuit during 1971. While offering anonymity session work took the pressure off having to create anything original himself, he was also well paid for relatively little effort.

Some sessions were simply returning that which was owed – Nick Drake, Mike Heron and John Martyn were all Witchseason and Island colleagues. The Fairport link with Ian Matthews was continued when Richard appeared on Matthews Southern Comfort's debut album, and Matthews' solo debut, *If You Saw Thru' My Eyes*. Al Stewart and Fairport had shared many a concert platform and now Thompson appeared on Stewart's *Love Chronicles* thinly disguised as 'Marvyn Prestwick': 'Marvyn' (*sic*) in homage to the Shadows' lead guitarist Hank B. Marvin and 'Prestwick' after the Scottish airport Elvis Presley landed at on his way back to America from Army service in Germany in 1960 – the only time the King ever set foot in the United Kingdom.

John Kirkpatrick: 'I was in the middle of making my own first record (1972's *Jump at the Sun*) and Richard and Ashley played on one song: Ashley was "Humphrey d'Etchingham" and Richard was "Agnes Mirren", because he'd done so many sessions he just wanted to be called something else.'

Linda: 'I remember being at the Nick Drake session, and that was difficult, because Nick didn't talk and Richard didn't talk. I think Richard felt that his work was very perfunctory on it ... There was definitely a bit of rivalry there too, because Nick was Joe's darling ... Richard did quite a lot of sessions for the Seekers, he was very friendly with Bruce (Woodley). I think they were drinking buddies. They were ever such nice guys, and Richard would play on the records but say "Just don't put my name on it."

'I came back from America in 1971, very fed up, and just started ringing everyone I knew, including Richard ... And we just got together around then. When I came back from America, he was working in Sandy's band, and doing sessions by the score. Always with Pat Donaldson and Dave Mattacks. Richard would turn up with his guitar, one day he went along to do a session with one of those folkie lady singers – and there were Pat and DM. They all cracked. Richard smashed his amp and said "Right! No more sessions!"'

Though still living at the Angel, Thompson was in London on the night in February 1971 when a Dutch lorry driver, late for the ferry at Harwich, lost control at the top of the hill and smashed his lorry straight into Swarbrick's bedroom. The driver was killed, but Swarbrick was unharmed.

Dave Pegg: 'None of us had any money as such, we did have bank accounts, but Richard didn't have a bank account, ever. Richard had left the band, but all his stuff was in his room, which was the room above the one the lorry went in. It completely demolished the front wall of the house, so all of Richard's stuff was hanging out – his bed, his hi-fi – so we had to try and salvage it before the elements came in ... We found a whole load of cheques he'd accumulated from sessions which he'd never bothered to put in the bank.'

Linda: 'Richard was no good with money or business. When I first met him, he always had cheques in his pocket that were fifteen months old, so they were out of date, he never cashed cheques. He didn't care. He was *so* un-materialistic.'

Linda's first recorded collaboration with Richard came in January 1972 when she sang on *The Bunch*, an album of rock'n'roll favourites recorded by Fairport alumni at Virgin's Oxfordshire studios, The Manor. It was a cheap project to underwrite, Virgin's Richard Branson was looking for a band to try out the studio and residential facilities of his new investment prior to opening it to paying clients.

The project was put together by Sandy's partner, Trevor Lucas. The two had kept a low profile following the collapse of Fotheringay, and Trevor saw *The Bunch* project as an opportunity to escape the spotlight and work with some mates on songs they had all grown up with.

Released in April 1972, *The Bunch* surprised a few people. A sense of humour was not necessarily expected in rock'n'roll at the time. The concept of a group of serious, intense musicians rocking out to old Chuck Berry songs was unsettling to say the least.

Thompson enjoyed the recording ('fun, but terribly self-indulgent') but had problems with the artificiality of the project: 'It was a bit of a throw-away in a sense. Conceptually Ashley and Fairport and myself and Sandy – we were developing this fairly fragile style of music that no-one else was particularly interested in, it was this British Folk Rock thing – that had a logical development to it and that was the path we were going down and *The Bunch* was rather a retro-step. It wasn't really what we should have been doing at the time, *Morris On* was the kind of record we should have been doing – *The Bunch* was just a bunch of folkies doing old rock'n'roll songs, so what.

'It would have been more valid to do Led Zeppelin arrangements of

Richard Thompson

"Sally Racket" or to do a rockabilly version of "Blue Bonnets Over The Border". It's just a not particularly valid record. It's a little self-indulgent in terms of arrangement. It was the kind of thing that was fun to do – but then so what, what's fun got to do with anything?'

The basic rhythm section was that of Fotheringay drummer Gerry Conway and bassist Pat Donaldson who remembers *The Bunch* as being 'just thrown together: let's have a good time for a week, stay at the Manor, and record some old rock'n'roll songs with a bunch of people. I think it was Trevor who got some money off Island. There wasn't really any pressure, there was no ego flying around about "my song", it was just old pop songs. People were pigeonholed as a "folk singer", then up comes Sandy singing an old Everly Brothers song ... It was the first time I heard Richard play rock'n'roll for any length of time, instead of just for one song. That's a whole other side of the man, his knowledge of music is enormous. He just never stops. It astounds me ...'

The Bunch was a good opportunity for Thompson to display his playing favourites: Jerry Lee Lewis' 'Crazy Arms', Dion's 'My Girl In The Month Of May', Hank Williams' 'Jambalaya', Chuck Berry's 'Sweet Little Rock'n'Roller' and a clutch of Buddy Holly. Today, when tribute albums and albums comprising cover versions are as central to an artist's CV as Greatest Hits and Live albums, *The Bunch* retains its ramshackle integrity.

Arguments about the nature of 'folk' and 'pop' and 'rock'n'roll' raged in pages of *Melody Maker* at the time. What matters today is the impact of the music they made at the Manor back then. Whatever you choose to call it, popular music has rarely produced a more heart-stopping moment of fragile beauty than Sandy Denny and Linda Peters' version of the Everly Brothers' 'When Will I Be Loved?'

Thompson, Denny and Hutchings went on to try and develop a particularly English type of rock'n'roll but would never deny their original influences. Hutchings was probably the most partisan – in *The Electric Muse*, Robin Denselow recounted Hutchings literally pulling the plugs on Thompson at an Albion Country Band gig when the guitarist tore into a Chuck Berry song. But by 1995, Hutchings was happy to participate playing Bruce Springsteen's 'No Surrender' at his 50th birthday bash.

The Bunch gave Thompson a chance to break cover without showing the world what he'd been creating since quitting Fairport a year before. That would wait until he was ready. One record to which Thompson contributed more than paid guitar, was Shirley Collins' *No Roses*. This album marked the debut of Ashley Hutchings' post-Fairport, post-Steeleye Span outfit, the Albion Country Band. The convoluted history of the early Albions makes Fairport Convention look like something that isn't convoluted at all.

Ashley was still pursuing his vision of indigenously English music, played with electric instruments and Thompson was beguiled by the prospect of making rock'n'roll which sprang from British soil but nevertheless acknowledged its American roots.

No Roses featured many familiar names from the English folk-rock fraternity – as well as Thompson and Ashley, Dave Mattacks, Simon Nicol, Lal and Mike Waterson and the Young Tradition's Royston Wood. There was also a new chum for them all to play with, accordionist John Kirkpatrick. The tall, amiable and engaging Kirkpatrick has worked consistently with Thompson since 1971, both on record and on the road. He was a good man for Thompson to meet at that time, with a knowledge of traditional folk music, particularly morris tunes, which was unequalled.

John Kirkpatrick: 'I started morris dancing when I was twelve. Then I began playing for it as a teenager. It had been my life really; instead of beating up old ladies and squeezing my spots all day, I was doing morris dancing and learning how to play my accordion.

'I used to sing in the church choir, and the morris team was an offshoot of the church originally. I had no interest in pop music in my early teens. I was dancing, and loved it to bits, and tried to find out everything I could about it. I was totally involved in the folk-dance world, and there was lots going on in London at that time, the mid-60s.'

The *No Roses* sessions had been smooth. None of the frictions which had marred the *Liege & Lief* era were evident and Thompson was emerging from his session jag of 1971, so when Ashley suggested another attempt to realise what they had tried with Fairport barely two years before, Thompson was happy to get involved. He was increasingly interested in playing traditional music on electric instruments, he had indulged himself with *The Bunch* and had some money from his session frenzy, so working with Ashley and Kirkpatrick, whose knowledge of traditional folk far outstripped his own, was a tempting prospect.

The nearest Thompson got to a description of what he wanted to do was 'English rock'n'roll' – that was the ghost at the feast of *Henry the Human Fly*. But that didn't mean simply electrifying Morris tunes, rather he saw himself as an alchemist carefully blending the English traditional with the vigour of American rock. Thompson envisaged brass more redolent of Methodist hymns than R&B; he was looking as much toward East Grinstead as Memphis for inspiration. He heard rhythms sounding more like 'the old Sally Army' than the Bar-Kays.

Richard Thompson

Dave Mattacks: 'Richard's music after *Liege & Lief* is English rock'n'roll, not in a Kinks way, in a very idiosyncratic way in the direction of English folk music, but without the finger in the ear, ye olde nonny-no stuff . . .'

John Kirkpatrick: 'I first met Richard when Ashley got the group together to rehearse *Morris On*, in fact the very first rehearsal was in my front room in Tottenham . . . We also did a short tour with Shirley Collins – Ashley, Richard and myself, and Royston Wood was driving the bus, so he sang a couple of songs as well. It was only ever three gigs in the south west of England. Shirley was married to Ashley at the time. It was after she'd made *No Roses*, so we did some things from that, we played a couple of tunes, everyone did a little bit. It was a bit shambolic, but great fun. Short and sweet . . . I just loved playing with Richard, and being in his presence. He's so mesmeric, and so mysterious.'

Morris On, released in April 1972, consisted of Morris dance tunes recorded by Hutchings, Thompson, Kirkpatrick, with fiddler Barry Dransfield and Dave Mattacks on board to swell the ranks. There is a widespread opinion that morris dancing was invented specifically to annoy people drinking beer in the open air, but it can actually be traced back to the fifteenth century, with links to pagan rituals, freemasonry and mummers plays. One theory has its origins in Spain, morris being a corruption of Moorish. The popularity of the dance and its accompanying seasonal rituals owe much to its flamboyant energy. The birth of spring was always cause for celebration and communities which had survived a freezing winter, gave thanks to God and prayed for their crops to survive and flourish.

Morris dancing offered an opportunity for musicians to play their fiddles, home-made pipes and to make welcome the spring. Dancing around the maypole, the bright and colourful morris teams delighted in all manner of disguises, dressing up as women ('The Moll'), or blacking their faces in the style of the Moors. Other characters included Bavian the Fool, a dragon (familiar from Saint George's battle) and Malkin the Clown.

John Kirkpatrick: 'I wish I'd kept the letter where Ashley outlined the idea for *Morris On*. I remember he said he'd done Fairport and done Steeleye, and was talking to Royston Wood at the time about having a specifically English band, which after *Morris On* became the Albion Country Band. He just said he was interested in doing a folk-rock album, using morris music, a folk-rock rhythm section . . . He'd obviously been talking to Barry (Dransfield) before, and Mattacks and Richard,

Richard and Linda

and would I be interested? When *Morris On* came along I thought it was fantastic to be able to play with these people. I'd loved *Liege & Lief* and Steeleye, but I thought what's the point in making a morris record, everyone knows about morris music, because everyone I knew was into morris dancing. I thought what a stupid idea!'

The album was fuelled by Kirkpatrick's life-long enthusiasm for morris dancing and the unique style of music which accompanied it. Thompson's role is simply that of a session man, he features on none of the solo vocals, and his playing is muted throughout. It is an ensemble piece, with Hutchings' resonant bass guitar and Kirkpatrick's jaunty vocals and multi-instrumental abilities shining through. For Thompson, morris music was another strand to be added to his bow. For all its undeniable enthusiasm, *Morris On* rings false. The artifice extends to cod 'rural' accents and a wishful-thinking, rose-tinted view of Eden before The Fall, which *Liege & Lief* had managed to avoid.

John Kirkpatrick: 'We recorded *Morris On* at the end of 1971. Because it had worked so well, Ashley and Royston suggested having a band which was basically *Morris On* on wheels ... They asked me just before Christmas 1971 if I was interested in being in the Albion Country Band, which they'd concocted for Shirley's record – it wasn't an existing band – it was just a bunch of people who'd played on *No Roses*. We had one day's rehearsal in Cecil Sharp House. The band was: Simon Nicol on drums, Richard, Ashley on bass, Royston singing, Sue Draheim on fiddle and myself ... It was very nice, but Sue [Harris], to whom I was then married, had just packed up her full-time job so we could work as a duo just after Christmas 1971. So the timing was appalling. I was committed to working with Sue, so I said no ...'

With his wave of session work and the diversions of *The Bunch* and *Morris On* behind him, Thompson's energies were now directed towards his crucial solo debut. By now Richard and Linda were living together and to help Ashley out in the Albion Country Band, Richard and Linda agreed to come on board as last minute substitutes.

John Kirkpatrick: 'Ashley asked Sue Harris and me if we'd both join the Albion Country Band with Martin Carthy. But there was going to be a couple of months' gap, so they formed the caretaker Albion Band with Richard and Linda. Which lasted for two months, no longer, just a few dates to fulfil the gigs the band had.'

Aside from honouring those gigs, Thompson's main contribution to the Albion Country Band was providing two songs for the album which became *The Battle of the Field*. 'The New St George' was written for, and appeared on, *Henry the Human Fly*, but was ideally suited to the

Richard Thompson

idyll of Hutchings' new band, particularly the resounding chorus: 'Leave the factory, leave the forge/And dance to the New St George'. The song's vision of an Albion plundered by the greedy, preying on the needy, an Eden poisoned by 'the backroom boys', was a prescient warning of environmental devastation, but charged with the forceful mysticism of William Blake.

Thompson wrote 'Albion Sunrise' to order, specifically to marshal the morris dancing troupes. As the opening track on *Battle of the Field*, it fits the bill perfectly – vocals by Simon Nicol and Ashley Hutchings make it almost a Fairport reunion – and promises 'the faded flower of England will rise and bloom again'.

John Kirkpatrick: 'The Albion Country Band that made *Battle of the Field* got together at the beginning of 1973, and recorded in the summer. At the same time, we recorded *The Compleat Dancing Master*, which was the follow-up to *Morris On*, and the Albion Country Band fell apart about August 1973. Because the band didn't exist any more, the record was postponed until 1976.'

When the principal songwriter of a band splits, interest always focuses on the first solo album. It can be postponed. It can be disguised. It can be complicated. But there comes a time when it has to be made. And then inevitably, there comes a time when it has to be released.

Chapter 11

OVER THE YEARS Richard Thompson has been particularly disparaging about the qualities of *Henry the Human Fly*, insisting that the poor quality of the vocals let it down, and that he will one day go back and re-record them; just like Bruce Springsteen, who has been threatening to do the same for *Darkness on the Edge of Town* for twenty years now.

Richard: 'What I'd like to do is to go back and re-do the vocals. If Wordsworth could go back and cross out the exclamation points, surely I can go back and re-do the vocals.'

John Kirkpatrick: 'Right after *Morris On*, Richard was about to make *Henry the Human Fly*, we got on well and he asked me on it . . . It was fairly early days for me as a session musician. I'd played on a few folk records, but my experience was limited to playing tunes and going "oompah oompah".

'That record was the first time I had to do anything else. There were some specific tunes, like the strathspey on "Nobody's Wedding". It goes straight into a very straight Scottish strathspey, no problem about that, some folkie melodies, very much like traditional tunes. So that was fine. Then on "The Angels Took My Racehorse Away", he said "Well, there's this riff, it goes like this, and then just play anything". And no one had ever said that to me before!'

Pat Donaldson: 'Just to be asked to do the *Henry* sessions was a treat. We'd sit down and learn a song in the studio, get the chords right, then we'd go in with Richard and cut it live . . . The songs were ready to go; there is some wickedly good stuff on that album . . . My memories are that the basic tracks were done in under two weeks. There wasn't all that fuss and bother about putting every instrument under the microscope. It was a question of listening to the whole thing played back, and if it all sounded good together . . . That was a philosophy of Joe Boyd's, which I'm sure Richard picked up. As far as Joe's concerned, recording is actually making a record of what happened at the time . . .

Richard Thompson

As long as there weren't glaring mistakes, but of course the technology wasn't there to be doing that, spending hours and hours and hours, taking this piece from there and putting it there, we were working on sixteen-track machines. You had to cut tape if you wanted to do that, you couldn't do it with the push of a digital button.'

Richard: 'The songs were interesting. To me it seems like an eccentric record – I suppose I was an eccentric. There's a lot of different influences. I suppose that 'Roll Over Vaughn [sic] Williams' is the sort of overture – the statement of intent – this is what it's going to be like. It's the dilemma of being a British musician who wants to represent British tradition in some way. If you want to be contemporary you can't ignore America and if you want to be true to your roots then you have to take that on board as well. It was having to fuse two cultures together – consciously or unconsciously. It wasn't clinical. I'm not sure how much I was really thinking about all that stuff at that point. If I'd had more of an overview of it then I wouldn't have done it that way and I'd have made a better record. It was just songs that came up – I wasn't particularly thinking of the style or anything – it just happened.

'It's a strangely acoustic record – there's not much electric guitar playing on it because I hadn't really figured it in – I'd forgotten that was something I should be doing on record. I really just wanted to make a record of songs. And I wanted to see what they sounded like all together on a record. I don't think Island Records were probably very happy about that – I mean if they had any interest in me at all it was probably as a guitar player.'

As a statement of intent, the opening track on *Henry the Human Fly* serves well. 'Roll Over Vaughn Williams' is refreshingly ambiguous, acknowledging both the quintessentially English composer Ralph Vaughan Williams, whose work drew on Tudor choral music and traditional folk melodies, and Chuck Berry. 'Roll Over Beethoven' was Berry's 1956 American hit, the sort of song which earned him his reputation of the first poet of the juke-box. The Beatles also included the song on their second album, advising the besotted youth of America to 'roll over ... and tell Tchaikovsky the news'.

'Roll Over Vaughn Williams' was a salvo aimed at complacency. 'Run for cover, things are bad/But now they're getting worse ...' chides Thompson, before the song's 'chorus': 'Live in fear, live in fear/Live in fear, live in fear', and following that with a beautiful, menacing, gut-tightening solo.

The song is a broadside nailed to the maypole. Fear, terror and menace stalk the song. A baleful missive to Thompson's muse ('Don't expect the words to ring too sweetly in your ear ...'), there is also the element of betrayal ('Fool your friends and fool yourself/The choice is crystal clear ...'), before concluding with a jibe at the folk establishment ('Do you laugh or do you stick/Your finger in your ear?'). And all the while, the comfort which should be drawn from the lapping chorus, warns instead: 'Live in fear, live in fear/Live in fear, live in fear'.

The whole album is shot through with mistrust and menace. Thompson's vocals, which he insisted on losing way down in the mix, are ghostly and other-worldly, wafting onto the finished record like a wraith. And while some of the playing is plodding and the production a mite wayward... *Henry the Human Fly* is a magnificent record, quite unlike anything else around at the time, or since.

Thompson is toying with the traditional form, with half-remembered names and phrases floating like flotsam in the songs – the Lanark Silver Bell is the oldest horse race held in the country, and the name which inspired Thompson to write 'The Angels Took My Racehorse Away'; Jimmy Shand tunes 'Highland Wedding' and 'Mairi's Wedding' litter Thompson's own 'Nobody's Wedding'.

Henry the Human Fly is Richard Thompson revisiting the present. 'The Poor Ditching Boy' sounds like it could have been sung by the navvies who dug deep on the Victorian railways, but it's also quintessential Richard Thompson, from the very first words of the dour scene-setting opening verse:

> Was there ever a winter so cold and so sad
> The river too weary to flood;
> The storming wind cut through to my skin,
> But she cut through to my blood.

Best of all is 'The Old Changing Way', an age-old 'traditional' song, written by a 23-year-old. Dwelling on the travelling tale of two gypsy brothers, riven by poverty and neglect, Thompson fashions an accurate and acute account of travelling people in a song born of the recent past – 'tinkers', 'spikes' and 'tin' were familiar words 40 years before, when George Orwell was down and out and on the bum.

Along with 'Pictures Of Lily', 'Painted Ladies' is one of *the* rock'n'roll odes to masturbation. It also boasts a great Thompson opening: 'It's a grey, grey morning, the rain it do fall/I'm feeling hungry and low ...' Whether self-abuse or idolatry, 'Painted Ladies' is one of a long line of Thompson songs – 'Mingus Eyes' and 'From Galway To Graceland' are two others – which chafe against false idols. Here it is artifice and superficiality (the 'film stars and beauties') which Thompson rails against, in a voice over-weary from worship. Albeit clumsy, the line 'they can't hold a candle to something that trembles' contains a deeper truth. And the concluding lines are as damning and affecting as any Thompson has penned:

> God help the children playing their game
> The end of the game is goodbye
> They pass through your vision like thoughts in a dream,
> Your good times are slipping away
> It's time to move on, or go down with the ship . . .

'Wheely Down' is a cartographer's delight. In this song the lay of the land becomes a sinuous delight. Again, Thompson uses his deft ability at evoking a past which comes from an appreciation of life, rather than a Crabtree and Evelyn catalogue:

> All things must change within the earth . . .
> For the worms will rot the miller's wheel
> And the rats will eat the grain . . .
> And the kestrel turns in the empty skies
> On high over Wheely Down . . .

It's not all grey, grey mornings though. 'The Angels Took My Racehorse Away' has sentiments worthy of the most maudlin country and western song, Thompson milks the heart-tugging subject matter (favourite horse, gone before its time; angels inform owner, owner heartbroken, but comforted by thought of favourite nag in Horse Heaven) while unleashing a solo of ferocious intent following the first chorus.

Linda: 'When I was doing a record in LA, and I played the album to James Burton, I said "There's a track I love on this record, 'The Angels Have Taken My Racehorse Away'" . . . After it had been on for a while, James Burton turned to me and said "What language is this?" I assured him it was English. He listened a bit more, then said, very politely, "I think you're playing it at the wrong speed". . .'

The wilfully obscure 'Shaky Nancy' was dedicated to Richard's first guitar tutor, Richard Roberts-Miller. Where he strives to be deliberately quirky ('Cold Feet', 'Mary And Joseph', 'Twisted') Thompson sometimes falters, but otherwise *Henry the Human Fly* remains one of the most underrated albums of the era. Even at the time, it was an album to be seen with. Like appreciating Nick Drake's *Bryter Layter*, or Gram Parsons' *GP*, while the artists were still alive, *Henry the Human Fly* was an oddball album, and remains an essential selection for oddballs everywhere.

Richard and Linda

While Thompson may have had his own doubts about the album's long-term commercial potential, he was nonetheless stunned by the ferocity of the critical response. Linda remembers his shock: 'He was very young, and it was his first solo album, and it got slated. I remember we went for a walk on Hampstead Heath one Thursday morning, and he got *Melody Maker*, and he sat down and read it, and couldn't believe it. Because, you know, he thought it was good ... It's a wonderful record. Okay, the vocals could have been mixed further forward, but it's terrific. Anyway, when you're that age, and it's your first record, and everybody says it's absolute garbage, except for Sandy and Trevor and me ... He went into a severe decline ... I don't think he was ever going to make another record.'

That *MM* review which so upset Thompson was pretty swingeing. Andrew Means' piece ran in part: 'Some of Richard Thompson's ideas sound great – which is really the saving grace of this album, because most of the music doesn't. The tragedy is that Thompson's "British rock music" is such an unconvincing concoction ... Even the songs that do integrate rock and traditional styles of electric guitar rhythms and accordion and fiddle decoration – and also include explicit, meaningful lyrics are marred by bottle-up vocals, uninspiring guitar phrases and a general lack of conviction in performance.'

It wasn't hubris on Thompson's part. He knew just how damaging a bad review in *Melody Maker* could be at that time. The *NME* was still to make any real impact on the 'progressive' market, *Sounds*, *Disc* and *Record Mirror* helped, but it was the *Melody Maker* that really mattered. And the first named release in two years by the former guitarist of Fairport Convention wasn't exactly a high priority. At the time of Thompson's debut solo release, the record industry still reeling from the break-up of the Beatles was bracing itself for Ziggy-mania.

The criticisms levelled at *Henry the Human Fly* have as much to do with the overall sound of the album as its content. Following George Martin's work with the Beatles, records were expected to sound crisp and clean. Today *Henry the Human Fly* sounds like it was recorded with Richard in the next room; but in 1972, with David Bowie and Slade and Marc Bolan and Roxy Music teetering towards pop immortality in their stack-heels, satin and tat, Richard Thompson's *Henry* ... seemed a universe away.

This was the era of Gary Glitter not 'The Poor Ditching Boy'. The weekly UK music press could appreciate American authenticity, the music of the Band, the Eagles and Little Feat was venerated for its rootsy purity. But there was precious little time for *Henry* ... With the 'coloured girls going "doo-do-doo..."' and beside the stylised cool of Steely Dan, there wasn't much space for an album with some bloke dressed as an insect on the cover.

Thompson's sleeve note began: ' "Bugger" said God, "raining again..."' Ambrose Bierce's *Devil's Dictionary*, which was also quoted, was a required text in the early 70s, along with *Gormenghast* and *Catch-22*. Bierce's cynical aphorisms ('Applause: the echo of a platitude') found currency and favour among those with grey-spined Penguin Modern Classics stuck ostentatiously in the back pocket of their jeans.

Richard: 'The cover's just so tackily done – really badly executed. We had this idea – wouldn't it be great if – and then they said here's the budget £14 6s 9d so the whole thing didn't quite have the panache. It was supposed to be a really great costume and they turned up with this pathetic little thing, so it went downhill all the way from there really. Even the typeface was bad.'

Warner Brothers had a reciprocal deal with Island, which gave them first option on any Island releases for North America. To everyone's amazement, Warner's offshoot Reprise, picked up *Henry the Human Fly*, and the USA braced itself for an outbreak of Thompson-mania. The press release which went out to record stores with such headings as: 'Top Gear Guitar', 'Familiar Folks', 'Well Wrought Words', implied that while the bulk of American record-buyers would prefer Chicago, Neil Young, or America, this was Thompson's 'first time out front, and a base must be established'. It continues, 'The lyrics like many good things must be studied to be appreciated: it may take a listening or two before the greater part comes through.'

In fact, *Henry the Human Fly* remains, unequivocally, the lowest-selling record to be released by any arm of the mighty Warner Brothers empire. Today, nearly a quarter of a century on, it seems a matter of secret pride to Thompson, but back then it was heartbreaking.

Richard: 'That's what it said in the Warner Brothers in-house magazine – which I never saw. I can imagine in the States it'd be lucky to sell a couple of thousand at that point, but I think it's done incredibly well since – it's probably sold about fifteen thousand world sales.'

In fact *Henry the Human Fly* sold less copies than John Cale's baroque masterpiece *Paris 1919*; less than David Ackles *Subway to the Country*; less even than Graham Nash's *Songs For Beginners*... Quality can never be judged by sales, but God help us, surely *Henry the Human Fly* must have sold more than the second album by Tiny Tim?

The drubbing accorded *Henry*... certainly made Thompson nervous about touring America. He needed to go there on the back of an album

Richard and Linda

which had picked up strong reviews and good regional sales. In the event, Thompson didn't perform in America for nearly a decade, which was more to do with his religious faith than any sour grapes. But as the plaudits flooded in for *Shoot Out the Lights* ten years on, Thompson must have wryly reflected on the calumny heaped on *Henry* . . . all those years before.

Perri: 'He seemed pretty lost – a sort of wandering minstrel – until Linda married him and put his feet on the ground.'

Joan: 'Well I think I met Linda, more or less, on the wedding day – it was 30 October 1972 – which was my birthday, the day I moved and the day my son was married. All three things on one day and it went like clockwork!

'Well it was the most strange wedding and yet it was a wonderful wedding. We knew nothing about it – I had a cousin whose daughter had met Richard and Richard said "Oh I'm getting married tomorrow or the next day" – something quite close – so my cousin said "Did you know Richard was getting married" – it was the first I'd ever heard of it. So of course we got in touch with Richard and arranged to be at the wedding. It was a very quiet wedding – only Linda's parents, and my husband and I – just a very small wedding party at an Italian restaurant in Hampstead – and it was really lovely. Richard looked an absolute sight – I really could have disowned him because he looked so awful – with the hair and everything.'

Chapter 12

Professionally, it was lonely in the middle.

Linda was beginning to make her mark, particularly after her stunning take on 'When Will I Be Loved?' from *The Bunch* and her association with Richard. But in the wake of the perceived failure of *Henry the Human Fly*, being known simply as 'ex-Fairport Convention' did about as much for Richard's public image as being one of Elizabeth Taylor's ex-husbands.

So following the release of *Henry ...*, and with Linda at his side, Richard did the ostrich thing, and buried his head in the folk clubs. The press and punters were surprised that a 'star' such as Thompson should shun the bright lights and return to his roots.

Linda: 'He worked with Sandy, then did an about face. Because he'd never worked acoustically – although people think of him as a folk-orientated artist, or whatever, he certainly never was. He started off playing electric guitar. He'd never played acoustic guitar. He's a rock'n'roll musician. That's all there is to it.'

Certainly Richard's teenage meanderings around the London music scene in the mid-60s had made him a familiar face at folk clubs and *Liege & Lief* was undeniably a folk-rock fusion. But the songs Richard had written for *Henry the Human Fly*, while drawing on the folk tradition, had little direct link with the folk community.

John Kirkpatrick: 'A lot of those he wrote in those earlier times, you hear in every folk club you go to, people are singing Richard Thompson songs, but they're all the earlier ones, "New St George", "Poor Ditching Boy", "Down Where The Drunkards Roll", "We Sing Hallelujah". A lot of those were presumably written to sound like folk songs, and they worked, because a lot of folkie people have taken them up ... You do hear some of the later ones, like the motorbike one ... There's always one folkie thing on each record.'

Thompson enjoyed upping the ante in the folk clubs. Besides the obviously 'folk' material drawn from the Fairport repertoire or written

Richard and Linda

for the still-to-be-recorded *I Want to See the Bright Lights Tonight*, Thompson enjoyed slipping in such defiantly un-folk covers as John D. Loudermilk's 'Break My Mind', Buck Owens' 'Together Again', Cab Calloway's 'Minnie The Moocher', Hank Thompson's 'Wild Side Of Life', Hank Locklin's 'Please Help Me, I'm Falling'.

Thompson found the competitiveness and narrow-mindedness of the folk world stultifying, but with his tail between his legs following the poor response to *Henry the Human Fly*, folk clubs offered a welcome sanctuary. The couple could play a regular circuit which didn't involve journeying far from their Hampstead flat and the songs Thompson had written recently seemed to lend themselves to that embalmed world.

During the folk revival of the mid-60s, every club featured a Dylan wannabee perched on a stool, an old coat-hanger for a harmonica holder, clunking through an interminable rendition of 'A Hard Rain's A-Gonna Fall'; or a piercing 'Stepford Wife' Joan Baez, hair ironed straight and long, delicately promising that: 'There but for fortune go you or I, mm, mm, mm...' Dylan's 'defection' to rock'n'roll in 1965 however was taken as a personal insult and by the early 70s, there was something other-worldly about the folk scene which existed in its own universe, untainted by commercial pressures.

The tradition of music passed on by word of mouth, generation to generation, like a verbal baton, is enticing. To think that a folk song like 'Barbara Allen', which Samuel Pepys found such a 'perfect pleasure' in 1666, was also one of the highlights of Bob Dylan's 1991 *Bootleg Series* box set. That is the folk tradition in action. By the beginning of the 1970s, however, 'folk' was lapping idly in a backwater. When Bob Dylan had taken 'folk' out of the clubs and into the charts, the fair weather friends followed and the late 60s development of progressive rock had taken potential folk club audiences further away still.

Fairport's folk-rock synthesis was specifically aimed at a rock audience, there were problems anyway – physical and philosophical – about getting a six-piece rock'n'roll band into a folk club, which was frequently just a small room above a pub. Fairport and the myriad Fairport families (Steeleye Span, Fotheringay, Matthews Southern Comfort) were all aimed squarely at rock audiences, in rock venues. So the fact that by the end of 1972, Richard Thompson was back playing the folk clubs was considered 'a big deal'.

With Linda there to share the stage and take the lion's share of the vocals, some of the weight was off Thompson's shoulders. You couldn't help but be drawn to Linda. She was undeniably a cynosure. She was extrovert and outgoing, radically at odds with her nervous, bumbling partner. She even made an effort at 'performance', something generally frowned upon in the rarified atmosphere of folk clubs. There was something sensuous and comely about Linda onstage; beneath the sexiness a sense of humour, a trace of ribaldry.

The contrast between the two of them on stage was what made it work. Thompson playing the serious folkie musician, doodling with his range of foot-operated bass-pedals, while Linda connected with the crowd. Thompson could stun from 50 paces with a frenzy of unfeasibly nimble fret-work, while Linda, singing a song like 'Has He Got A Friend For Me?', was capable of sending a sliver of ice into your heart.

Moonlighting from Fairport, Simon Nicol helped Richard and Linda out as they scaled the folk club depths: 'Before there was an effort to make it into an electric band, we did the folk clubs as a trio . . . It was just after they got married, and it was lovely. I look back on that period with great affection . . . It was really powerful. You could hear a pin drop at most of those gigs. Rapt attention. Two acoustic guitars, and the bass pedals went through a little backline combo amp, we'd use house microphones . . . It was stuff from *Bright Lights . . .*, and *Hokey Pokey*, in the process of creation, Hank Williams' songs . . .'

Happily married, Richard and Linda muddled along, playing tiny clubs, and with a record label who thought that 'promotion' was what you got in the Army. But although he did interviews and attempted to play the game, there was something wilfully off-kilter about Thompson at the time.

Linda: 'Richard was very madly eccentric when he was young. He only ate cheese sandwiches, nothing else. He used to do interviews with an alarm clock on the table, and when it went off, the interview was over. Because he never ate anything but cheese sandwiches, you could see his veins through his face, which was pure white. He was a vegan and a vegetarian before anybody had ever heard of these things.'

The 1970s are a foreign country, they did things differently back then. There wasn't this whole myth coiling around Thompson's head. Between Fairport and *Bright Lights . . .* was an impressive CV of sessions and a poorly received solo album. The world was no longer waiting breathless for Richard Thompson to deliver.

Even if his sales figures were negligible, Linda remembers Richard's standing in the musical community of the time was considerable: 'I think that's always been his reward, and his cross in a way. "Esteemed by your peers" is a euphemism for sales figures through a magnifying glass. He always did have that, and critical acclaim.'

Linda: 'I remember when *Tubular Bells* came out, and Mike Oldfield called him up and said "Will you do the follow-up record with me? Maybe you could do the lyrics." I said "You've got to, you've just got to. Because if that last one sold . . ." And he did try, but he said "I just can't. You have to believe me, if I could do it, I would, but I just can't do it." '

As the 70s drew breath, rock'n'roll was facing the same complacency which had made the breakthrough of the Beatles in 1963 such a welcome necessity. Suffocated by the progressive pomposity of rock bands circa 1973, a torpor settled over the whole scene and hung there, like dry ice at a Rick Wakeman concert.

Tales From Topographic Oceans and *Tubular Bells* were hailed as major works. Then pop pounced on what Tony Curtis called 'da classics'. The Nice, Emerson, Lake and Palmer, Procol Harum, the Moody Blues – even Deep Purple – all dabbled in clumsy classic-rock synergy. During the early 1970s, much-needed light relief was provided by the pantomime good humour of Elton John, who at his peak, accounted for an astonishing two per cent of *all* record sales throughout the world.

Bob Dylan was in hibernation; the Rolling Stones had become tax exiles; and any group that had more than two consecutive Top Twenty hits were 'the new Beatles'. Bowie was teasing the media with the death of Ziggy and the birth of Aladdin Sane. Lennon and McCartney were using the letters pages of *Melody Maker* to conduct a bitter, bile-filled correspondence. The word was out on the brightest of the new Dylans, Bruce Springsteen. Mike Oldfield was Mozart with a Revox. But in all the quest for new sounds and new sensations, there still wasn't much interest in the work of Richard and Linda Thompson.

The couple had some friends at court. John Peel always found room for a session to promote any current product. Music journalists like Colin Irwin, Jerry Gilbert, Geoff Brown and *The Guardian*'s Robin Denselow, all regularly sang Thompson's praises. But in their heart of hearts, everyone knew that nothing more than cult status was likely to be afforded a man who spent a sizable portion of a Radio One session performing songs such as 'The Neasden Hornpipe' and 'The Avebury Particle Accelerator'.

There was only really one manager who handled acts the like of Richard and Linda Thompson. He was born and bred in New York – an end of an era, Big Apple showbiz manager; and if anyone was born to deliver the line 'Kid, I'm gonna make you a star', it was Jo Lustig. Brooklyn-born Lustig came to London in 1960, looking after a Nat 'King' Cole concert tour of the UK, and stayed.

Jo Lustig: 'I did PR here, for the Carlton Tower Hotel, the Playboy

Richard Thompson

Club. And I did publicity for a lot of the folk tours coming over here – Dylan, Peter, Paul and Mary, Judy Collins. I decided to give a party for Peter, Paul and Mary, and I invited a lot of English folk artists, the ones I didn't know I got through the Folk Guide in *Melody Maker*. And one of the first people who came was Julie Felix, who I then managed . . .

'I took the producer of the *Eamonn Andrews Show* down to Cousins. If I'd staged it, it couldn't have been better – Saturday night, there was a queue outside, Cousins only held thirty people, and the queue was twenty people, but we had to fight our way through into this little club. And it was like a Paris basement, all dark, and Julie, this sultry girl there, singing "Masters Of War". He booked her for the Saturday night, and the following week. I got her on at the Albert Hall in 1966, that was a big show, she then went on to do *The Frost Report*. Nico I also looked after; she did *Ready Steady Go* the same time Julie had her first television series.

'Because of Julie, Bert Jansch came to me, and said he and John Renbourn wanted to form this group, and that Nat Joseph at Transatlantic wouldn't back them. The actual Pentangle contract just said Bert and John "and three musicians", and Pentangle exploded. So all of a sudden, I was the Jewish guru of the folk scene.

'Richard, Linda and Simon Nicol came to me and I signed them as "Hokey Pokey", but then Richard and Linda went off to make the *Bright Lights* . . . album . . . It sold, but I think Richard's sales have stayed on the same level all these years. Not chart sales, but enough . . . because a record company doesn't have to spend a massive amount on Richard. There wasn't any need for tour support, it was a good touring scene then. Folk was where comedy is today. Comedy has replaced folk as a club scene . . . there was a good club in every city.'

Thompson was writing songs for his first album with Linda. Perhaps the knowledge that there was someone to help carry the vocals made the material for *I Want to See the Bright Lights Tonight* stronger and less quirky than that on *Henry the Human Fly*. By spring 1973, a year on since the release of *Henry* . . . and its ritualistic slaughter in the music press, Thompson was keen to get in and record.

Richard Williams had joined Chris Blackwell's Island Records as head of A&R (Artists and Repertoire), following his departure from *Melody Maker*, where he was deputy editor: 'Muff Winwood had been doing A&R, but was more interested in production . . . I had a conversation with Muff as soon as I got there, and he said there are a few hangovers, some outstanding problems. And one of them was Richard Thompson. He said there's this album we gave him the money to make

Richard and Linda

– which was *I Want to See the Bright Lights Tonight* – and nobody's very interested in it. *Henry the Human Fly* must have been a bit of a commercial disappointment, and although Island was altruistic and independent, and known for only recording good stuff, success was important ... Either a record had to do well, or somebody had to believe in it a lot. And it seemed as if neither of these things were true at that point of Richard.

'Island was very much into not just releasing stuff. There had to be a dynamic behind something ... One of the first things I did was to order up the master copies of *Bright Lights* ..., it was sequenced and everything. I remember it clearly: it was in two tape boxes, labelled side A and side B ... As soon as I put it on I thought this was fantastic, it had everything I wanted from Richard – the John Coltrane of the guitar, and the folk poet of the rainy streets. Linda brightened it, made it more commercial, and I thought that "Bright Lights" itself seemed a really commercial song.

'So I went to David Betteridge, who was Island's managing director, and said I think this is a really good record, and he really liked it. We sat around this big round table and played Richard and Linda's album and everyone liked it. As soon as they heard "Bright Lights" itself, they all said "single"!'

Richard: 'It did sit on the shelf for a long time. I know Island were really not very happy with it. I think it was Muff Winwood at the time who was our A&R man, who I haven't spoken to to this day – I don't know what they were looking for. If they wanted us to go back and re-record it, we weren't very keen to do that. We thought it was a good record but I think it took almost a year to come out.'

With Linda as wife and musical partner, Richard Williams his champion at Island, and with *Bright Lights* ... in the can, Thompson had every reason to believe that this could be the breakthrough year. But, as at every stage of Richard's professional career, a gremlin was loose in the works.

Richard Williams: 'I rang up and spoke to Richard, and he was just on the point of signing with Jo Lustig. He had a manager, he had an interested A&R man, so it seemed as though there was something worth doing.

' "Bright Lights" did come out as a single, but in those days it was hard to get stuff like that played on the radio, unless it was something instant – Sparks or Roxy Music. We put something like "Bright Lights" out as a trailer for the album, with the hope it might turn out to be a freak hit ... There had been precedents, you think of "Whiskey In The Jar", or that Fiddler's Dram song, or "Si Tu Dois Partir".'

Richard Thompson

Island's Chris Blackwell was devoting his considerable energies to the label's marketing of music from his birthplace of Jamaica. Blackwell was convinced that Bob Marley and the Wailers could be major players on a world stage, if he could break them out of the ghetto of ska, which was how reggae was widely perceived back then. Marley's 1973 *Catch a Fire* album was a breakthrough, described as 'reggae's *Sgt Pepper* . . .' and would consume much of Island's energies during the year, but Richard and Linda Thompson weren't relegated out of sight.

Richard Williams: 'The English company were keen to establish that they could support things and see them through as well . . . Betteridge was keen that Island should be a fully functioning independent record company, not just a vehicle for Chris' enthusiasm, like Marley and traffic, good as they were. . . . When it came to a record like *Bright Lights* . . ., you weren't talking about Roxy Music's second album, but pretty much everything that came out on Island had a certain cachet with the *Zig Zag* readers, the John Peel listeners. . . .'

The sessions for the album had begun in May 1973, with an eye to a September release, but it wasn't finally released until April 1974. Conspiracy theorists delight in the delay of *I Want to See the Bright Lights Tonight*, believing that Thompson was being deliberately squeezed out of the limelight. What is certain is that Island sat on *Bright Lights* . . . and didn't immediately recognise its inherent brilliance.

I Want to See the Bright Lights Tonight was as much a victim of Prime Minister Edward Heath's three-day week as it was of record company chicanery. Determined to break what he perceived as their increasing stranglehold on UK industry, Heath's confrontation with the trade unions led to draconian restrictions on work and leisure activity, and eventually to a three-day week for industry and no television after 10.30 p.m. The oil crisis and consequent shortage of vinyl on which to press records was yet another factor. So if there was a conspiracy over the release of *I Want to See the Bright Lights Tonight*, it was a labyrinthine one worthy of Oliver Stone, involving Prime Minister Edward Heath, Sheikh Yamani of OPEC and Muff Winwood of Island ecords.

ichard: 'It was just whatever songs had been written in the last year or so – I don't think there was a particular philosophy. I wanted to go in and use Pat Donaldson and Timi Donald who were also in Sandy's band, or had been – we thought we had a tight rhythm section and so we should just go in and smash it down as fast as possible. It was an incredibly cheap record to make, I think it cost about £2,500. I think we did rhythm tracks in about two to three days. I think it is a good record – it stands up quite well. It's probably what *Henry* . . . should have been – the singing's better and the arrangements are a bit more coherent. And it was interesting to try out some stuff – I was a big silver band fan at one point and I'd been dying to try something along those lines.'

I Want to See the Bright Lights Tonight is now recognised as a classic album. In 1987 *Rolling Stone* voted it the 86th best album of the past twenty years ('doomy, foreboding songs that sound as if they could have emerged from the mists of the British Isles any time during the past several centuries'). *Bright Lights* ('Total US Sales: 15,000') appeared between Michael Jackson's *Thriller* ('Total US Sales: 20.5 million') and Sly and The Family Stone's *Stand!* ('Total US Sales: 1.5 million'). In 1995, *Mojo* magazine placed *Bright Lights* at no. 70 in its century of the Greatest Albums Ever Made (this time squeezed between Stevie Wonder's *Talking Book* and Elvis Costello's *This Year's Model*).

Contemporary reviews were not so enthusiastic, although undeniably better than those which had greeted *Henry* . . . in 1972. Long-time Thompson admirer Bob Woffinden in the *NME* was typical: 'The exuberant title track is quite untypical of the material surrounding it, and helps to alleviate the prevailing atmosphere of world-weariness. Which shows there's more to Thompson than sour grapes. Some of these songs are minor classics, and will be remembered for a long time. . . . So while I wish Richard Thompson would forget that he has "only sad stories to tell to the town", this album is a solid reminder that whatever comes out of the West Coast, British is best. Something as good as this is not easily emulated.'

The album has entered music business mythology as a classic which took only a week and £2,500 to make. Thompson has never dithered in the studio; the songs came fully formed, he'll play them to the musicians he's selected, then record the songs as live as possible. Even by his standards though, *I Want to See the Bright Lights Tonight* was quick off the blocks.

The basic tracks were laid down in a week at Thompson's familiar stomping ground of Sound Techniques in Chelsea. John Wood, who had engineered all the Fairport albums, was owner of the studio and co-produced *Bright Lights* . . . with Richard. Thompson's turbulence with Joe Boyd over the *Full House* album had subsided, but Boyd was still busy with Warner Brothers in Los Angeles and was never seriously considered as producer.

I Want to See the Bright Lights Tonight can lay strong claim to being Thompson's masterpiece. The wilful quirkiness of *Henry* . . . is buried, the maturity of the writing evident, the songs have an enduring strength. And Linda's handling of the material should not be overlooked either; it is her singing which gives the songs life.

With the scope of the music embraced on *Bright Lights* . . ., Richard Thompson came as close as anyone to creating a uniquely pre-punk, English rock'n'roll. Thompson's traditional bent is evident on folk club favourites 'When I Get To The Border', 'Down Where The Drunkards Roll' and 'Withered And Died'; while the title track proved that Thompson could turn his hand to an astutely commercial song as easily as something moody and unclassifiable like 'Calvary Cross'. 'The End Of The Rainbow' seemed to confirm the widespread suspicion that Thompson's ability to plumb the depths of human despair indicated someone who dwelt on the dark side.

Linda's handling of 'Withered And Died' and 'Has He Got A Friend For Me?' is especially elevating. On the latter, she conveys the eternal teenage lament of being lonely on a Saturday night while Thompson's wit shafts in with the rhyme: 'Your boyfriend's good-looking, he's got it all there/He looks like God made him with something to spare . . .' But what lifts the song another notch is the fleeting, descriptive: 'He's got the haunt of the sea in his eyes . . .'

Richard: 'I think she was a great singer. Her voice was best in the early days, I think on *Bright Lights* she had much better voice quality and control and then it slowly deteriorated, which was a shame. But I can enjoy the good stuff – a record is a record, a performance is a performance – talent is talent.'

'Withered And Died' has that wispy huskiness, which was characteristic of Linda's very best singing, weaving itself around a familiar Thompson lyric, where dreams are not golden and redolent of pleasure, but rather 'Withered And Died'. The tug of the moon on the tide is here, a Thompson hallmark later employed to great effect on 'Dimming Of The Day'.

Thompson's use of a silver band on the title track is no mere sound colouring, he had been keen for some time to work with 'the English equivalent – as near as you can get – of an American horn section . . . something like the Salvation Army or that sort of sound'.

Nick Hornby's novel *High Fidelity* deals among other crucial issues with the use of brass in pop. Here the hero gently guides his girlfriend towards a better understanding:

> 'See, this is the sort of moment where men just want to give up. Can you really not see the difference between "Bright Eyes" and [Solomon Burke's] "Got To Get You Off My Mind"?'

'Yes, of course. One's about rabbits and the other has a brass band playing on it.'

'A brass band! A brass band! It's a horn section! Fucking hell.'

The more elementary girlfriend lessons had already included Hornby's hero explaining about our hero:

> 'Richard Thompson,' Anna repeats in a voice which suggests that over the last few days she has had to absorb a lot of information very quickly. 'Now which one was he?'
>
> 'He's a folk/rock singer and England's finest electric guitarist...'

Aside from the novelty of hearing a brass band on a 'pop' record, there is something resolutely, resonantly English about their use on 'I Want To See The Bright Lights Tonight'. Silver bands, brass bands, colliery bands and marching bands, all are a uniquely redolent aspect of English music, which too often fall beside the popular mainstream. The trades union movement used the resounding sense of community evoked by brass bands as a focal point for ceremonies and banner-waving days. The massed brass giving silver volume to a communal voice.

On 'Bright Lights . . .' too, the sound pours down like silver. Rich and florid: cornets, trumpets, tubas and euphoniums, all pealing proudly in unison. The CWS (Manchester) Silver Band, while adding a rich and unforgettable texture to the song, is also a homage to a dying tradition. Thompson scored the brass arrangement himself, and it is the unlikely instrumentation of the brass punctuation and Thompson's jagged electric guitar which gives 'I Want To See The Bright Lights Tonight' its musical edge. The song remains inimitable in the list of Thompson compositions, for its plain, undiluted optimism: a song about looking forward to the weekend, with no strings attached.

'Down Where The Drunkards Roll' (*Bright Lights* . . . is a very bibulous record) has Linda's vocal hauntingly shadowed by Trevor Lucas' rich bass voice. Thompson's affinity with the folk tradition is fully realised on 'When I Get To The Border', but rings false on 'We Sing Hallelujah' – as on 'Albion Sunrise' around the same period, Thompson's determination to pursue the English rock'n'roll route falters. The same false note is struck by 'The Little Beggar Girl', the knee-jerk, rich-versus-poor tale not helped by the melody or Linda's mannered vocal.

The album concludes with 'The Great Valerio', a stark and unsatisfactory end. The song is one-dimensional, Linda's vocal steely and unbending, while the lyric is dragged down by its cumbersome circus imagery.

I Want to See the Bright Lights Tonight showcased Linda Thompson as a vocalist of distinction, and fully confirmed Richard as a writer of individual and idiosyncratic purpose. For many though, the outstanding track on *I Want to See the Bright Lights Tonight* is the penultimate 'The End Of The Rainbow'. In a body of work hallmarked by a certain bleakness, 'The End Of The Rainbow' is in a mausoleum all of its own.

Brewer's Dictionary of Phrase and Fable explains the rainbow legend thus: 'If one reaches the spot where a rainbow touches the earth and digs there, one will be sure to find a pot of gold. Hence visionaries, wool-gatherers, day-dreamers etc are sometimes called "rainbow chasers", because of their habit of hoping for impossible things.' Thompson's cleverness lies in inverting the anticipation of a pot of gold at the rainbow's end.

Linda: ' "The End Of The Rainbow" is very bleak. It was written after the birth of Muna – I keep telling her not to take it personally! Richard has a very bleak side. In fact, he's probably less bleak now, he's always smiling, and it always looks really wrong to me ... He is a serious person.'

Muna: ' "The End Of The Rainbow" is supposed to be about me ... I listened to that when I was about sixteen for the first time, and I remember just crying and thinking, you know, "Great!" '

Richard: 'It's a bleak song. But I don't find bleak songs particularly depressing. You have to go to that point sometimes, you have to write that dark song – you have to feel that dark mood – you have to express it and then ... I'm not tackling the joy of childbirth, I'm not talking about my own kid – I'm writing a story – it's a fictional episode – I think it's really written in character to tell you the truth.'

Linda: 'I think that pessimism is irrefutable. Underlined by the fact that the best songs are those pessimistic ones, they're the true ones. The jolly ones – some of them are good, I like "Tear-Stained Letter", that's a good rollicking one – but for the most part, the jolly ones, like 'Bright Lights', they weren't about anything. They weren't about anything at all. And the bleak ones were the best.'

Quite the bleakest and most harrowing of all Thompson's compositions, 'The End Of The Rainbow' has a black and bitter refrain that begins comfortingly:

Life seems so rosy in the cradle ...

but is soon betrayed by the stark:

> But I'll be your friend, I'll tell you what's in store.
> There's nothing at the end of the rainbow,
> There's nothing to grow up for any more.

Even more despondent is the composer's conclusion that 'every loving handshake is just another man to beat'.

'The End Of The Rainbow' travels into the heart of darkness, and beyond. Thompson's resigned and bitter vocal; the darts of electric guitar which pepper the song like falling tears, the knowledge that this was written immediately following the birth of his first child ... Though undeniably a wonderfully constructed song, the fact that Thompson finds such fault in a world which lies just beyond the nursery door, makes the song chilling. The unavoidable image of a baby lying in its cradle, symbolising innocence and hope, compounds the song's nihilism.

Richard: 'It's probably the bleakest song I've written. I suppose if you didn't know me and know what a jolly chap I am, you might actually think that's a pretty unremittingly bleak song, without any mitigating levity to it ... When I do it in concert, I do it as a request usually and it has an effect on the audience, that's for sure. Elvis Costello told me that when he did it for a while, people used to cry out "No, no, it's not true, don't worry Elvis, it's all right".'

Twenty years later, Richard wrote another song for his eldest daughter: *Mirror Blue*'s 'The King Of Bohemia', with the poignant refrain:

> Did your dreams die young?
> Were they too hard won?
> Did you reach too high and fall?
> And there is no rest
> For the ones God blessed
> And he blessed you best of all.

Muna: ' "King of Bohemia", that was written for me, which I love, it's such a beautiful song. But he never says anything. I was at an interview with him, and they asked him "was that written about someone?" ... and he kind of looked at me ... he hates bringing any meaning to his songs. He's always said to me he wants people to come to their own conclusions about a song, if there's a picture story already there it can sometimes ruin it.'

I Want to See the Bright Lights Tonight sat in Island's vaults for nearly a year before Richard Williams plucked it out of oblivion and arranged for its release in April 1974. While they waited for their album

Richard Thompson

to be released, Richard and Linda and Simon Nicol toured briefly as a trio Hokey Pokey, which soon expanded into a group Sour Grapes, who supported Traffic on a sixteen-date UK tour that spring. The Thompsons enjoyed the opportunity to work with a decent PA and reach wider audiences courtesy of Steve Winwood's band, but Sour Grapes was not the happiest group of musicians ('The bass player only joined us about four hours before the first gig in Dundee,' Thompson told *Zig Zag*).

Touring, good reviews and record royalties were low on Richard Thompson's list of priorities by this time. The emptiness inside – which had seeped into 'The End Of The Rainbow' – was brought into sharper focus when a chance conversation with pianist Ian Whiteman, some impressive Islamic literature and a meeting on the Euston Road combined to lead Thompson towards the Sufi faith.

Richard: 'When I was about sixteen I started to get interested in life, you know, in Zen – I think that was the first thing, finding a book on Zen in a bookshop and thinking, "wow, this is just great". So I was a sort of weekend spiritual person for some considerable time – I suppose I read my way through the Stuart Watkins philosophical bookshop. A for Anthroposophist all the way to Z for Zen and I thought gosh, these Sufis sound really cool, this is really where it's at, this is just great. That was about 1973, and it was like whatever you were thinking inside suddenly appears on the outside. That strange thing that happens in life where even if you don't know it, you're being a magnet for something.

'Suddenly while I'm thinking all this sort of pseudo-spiritual stuff about how great the Sufis are, suddenly the real ones turn up and I thought, "Wow, what's going on here?" It was one of those things that actually has a lot of discipline and that was real, so all the rubbish had to go out of the window and I had to start doing the real stuff.'

Chapter 13

RICHARD: 'I just thought, Oh, this is actually who I've always been.'

During his first 24 years, Richard Thompson had immersed himself in music, train-spotting, astrology, archery, reading; dabbled in painting, stained glass, drinking, and investigated alternative beliefs A to Z. Thompson seemed to have a magpie interest in everything. But he had yet to find faith in anything.

Recently married and a first-time father, Thompson still felt a gap in his life, a vacuum where the belief should be.

Richard: 'I thought these people (Sufis) have a really great quality and I thought with a bit of work I'm actually like these people – I'm the same as them. There's nothing I have to do. There's no conversion really, you just accept this is who I've always been – that's really what I felt. At the time when I might have thought I was a Christian or I was something else, you know, it was just the same – it's labels you stick on it – nothing really changed.'

Perri: 'I think that spirituality he gets a lot from mother – she's a very spiritual person – a truly good person and always does think on another dimension spiritually.

'It was a bit of a shock when he converted, but at the time everyone was into everything – I mean I was into Buddhism and I was interested in Hindu temples. It was part of that whole scene. People were all floating about and trying different things, trying different religions and ways of living, growing vegetables and living in communes.'

Fans of Richard and Linda at the time assumed that the Islamic conversion coincided with the making of the *Pour Down Like Silver* album in 1975, on the sleeve of which the couple appear in Muslim headgear. In fact, Richard first became interested around the time of the recording of the *Bright Lights* ... album in 1973.

Linda was initially the more reluctant of the two to get involved in the religion, but she was not surprised by the extent of her husband's interest at the time: 'Ever since he was in Fairport, he was the airy-fairy one: never ate meat, never wore leather. He read Gurdjieff and Madame Blavatsky while everybody else was reading the *Beano*. I always thought when he was forty he'd live on a mountain; I didn't think it would happen as young as it did. I thought, oh we'll have to trek off to the Outer Hebrides, because I knew that he did get very uncomfortable in the world sometimes.'

The catalyst for Thompson's interest in Islam came from his contact with Ian Whiteman, who had been session pianist on *The Bunch* album early in 1972. Whiteman and other members of the late 60s band Mighty Baby had left to form Habibiyya, who recorded the Sufi-influenced album *If Man But Knew* in 1972. The Sufi faith seemed to offer Thompson the certainties which he felt were lacking in his life.

Linda: 'I was quite enamoured of it myself. At first when I went into it I was quite strong, I would say "Why are the women and the men separate?" And I'd question everything. But I got sort of beaten down by it. Before Richard and I became Muslims, I was certainly the dominant – not to say domineering – partner. I actually wasn't too keen on that trait in myself and men are very much supposed to be the dominant force in Islam, and I thought it was good for Richard, it made him come out of himself a bit, a lot actually. So I thought, well it won't do me any harm to play a subservient role – in fact I think it did.'

Immediately following their conversions, the Thompsons kept a foot in either camp. They still performed and made records, but Richard particularly was drawn further and further into the Sufi faith. It provided him with answers where before there had only been questions.

Linda: 'When Muna was a few months old, Richard and I converted to Islam and left the flat in Hampstead for the commune soon after. I had the good sense to hang on to the flat although Richard gave all the furniture away. I would have sold it, he gave it away.'

With their base at Thurlow Road in Hampstead gone, the Thompsons moved to an Islamic commune based around a number of squats in Bristol Gardens and Formosa Street in Maida Vale.

Joan: 'They had a lovely flat in Hampstead – a beautiful home and then they gave it all away. As parents we couldn't do anything about it – Linda seemed to go along with it and as far as I could see she was quite happy. I think that if she'd said no way, maybe Richard wouldn't have gone. They chose to do it but it wasn't a very good idea really, it was a bad idea.'

The Sufi strand of Islam which attracted Thompson was founded in the eighth century, and took its name from the Arabic 'suf', a rough woollen robe, which was taken as an indication of the believers' strong ascetic strain. For Thompson, Islam offered a profound certainty. Until he studied the writings of the Prophet, Thompson felt adrift and cut off, ill at ease in a world of crumbling values and increasing materialism. In the Koran, whose 114 chapters contain the fundamental beliefs of Islam, Thompson found at last a purity of purpose.

He embraced the faith and all that it entailed. 'Islam' itself is Arabic for 'submission', submission to the will of Allah. Islam has many parallels with Christianity and the teachings of Christ (the fall from Grace, the Day of Judgment) and is often perceived as the purest of religions. It centres on the oneness of God, His omnipotence and munificence.

Marc Ellington: 'I don't think Richard changed after "the conversion". Where he was heading and where he is as a person wed very comfortably with what he found in Islam ... Islam is probably closer in many ways to Christianity than anyone would be willing to accept. I would be very concerned if Richard were a Mormon, or a Jehovah's Witness, because those are probably much further away from the teachings of Christ than Islam ... I can't see anything in his coming to Islam which has created peculiarities ... He's very relaxed within himself.

'Also you have to remember that all these kids in Fairport were terribly spoiled in many ways. Joe Boyd kept them very much in a cocoon ... they never really had to get out there and suffer much. Things were – if not laid on a plate – things were taken care of ... I think when Richard decided that he was moving away from that, he had to pick up an awful lot of pieces and become very self sufficient. He grew up in front of us.'

Islamic belief insists upon the Five Pillars of Faith, which are binding to all male believers: profession of the faith; praying five times a day towards the holy city of Mecca; almsgiving; fasting from dawn until dusk during Ramadan and making a pilgrimage to Mecca once during your lifetime.

One of the problems of Islam for people brought up with twentieth-century Western sensibilities, is the position of women in Islamic society. Certainly life was tough for Linda in the Maida Vale commune: 'I think the women did have a hard time. Someone who came to the commune said that all the men – they all had turbans and everything – looked like they'd stepped out of *Lawrence of Arabia* and the women – we all had babies and weren't allowed to have prams – looked like something in a Kurosawa movie. I think it really was a way of quelling women.'

For Thompson, Islam and the teachings of the Prophet were a light shone into a dark corner of his soul. He feels that the faith itself is not biased against women, but that traditional Arabic prejudices have to some extent corrupted it. Talking to Justine Picardie of the *Independent on Sunday* in 1995, Thompson denied that women should be kept in purdah: 'A lot of that is really Arab tradition. Very little of that is Islam, very little indeed. Islam came as a liberation for women when it arrived 1,400 years ago. Women were way below horses and camels in the Arab world – seriously, they were well down in the league table – and it elevated women at the time.'

Despite her salutary experiences, Linda acknowledges the truth of this: 'Theoretically women are not supposed to play a subservient role: Islam was the first religion to say that women have to have their own money. But like everything else it got very bastardised over the years, especially in countries like Saudi Arabia . . . it did get twisted around.'

Perri: 'Mother and I went to see them in this ghastly place in Maida Vale – and Richard appeared in these white robes and he looked amazing – we went along with it, mother sat on the floor – men in one room and women in another room. Linda had Adam [their son] on the floor with no electricity, no nothing – she was a really brave person – I liked Linda a lot. She really went along with that whole thing. But then we all did, we all went along with these daft ideas but we were all trying different ways, new ways of living.'

Bernard Doherty: 'I went to Maida Vale a couple of times. It was like going into something very different. All the women – they weren't kept in a room – but they were all together, and Linda was amongst the girls. We'd go to gigs, and they'd pray in the dressing room, while DM and Simon would go down to the bar . . . The beard was the transformation. It wasn't until *Pour Down Like Silver* that it really came out. There were talks at the time: was he going to be called something else? Were we going to change the name on the album? Was he going to be Richard Thompson or the name they gave him?'

Ironically, given the asceticism of the Sufis, or perhaps appropriately, given the enlightenment Thompson gained from Islam, *Hokey Pokey*, the record the Thompsons were making at the time of their conversion remains one of the brightest in their catalogue.

Richard: 'A bit of everything, you get the bossa-nova and what have you. I think its quite a music-hall-influenced record – so was *Bright Lights* . . . and so was *Henry* . . . actually – I was a big fan of George Formby and Harry Lauder and Gracie Fields.'

Track for track, *Hokey Pokey* probably has more 'up' songs than any other Thompson album. There were songs in which Thompson's world-weariness was evident, 'I'll Regret It All In the Morning', 'The Sun Never Shines On The Poor' and 'Old Man Inside A Young Man' for example, but whereas only the title track of *Bright Lights* . . . displayed real sunshine, *Hokey Pokey* came brimming with chirpiness. For once the Thompson regime of cut-and-run recording had faltered. *Hokey Pokey* was recorded over a twelve-week period. Thompson's voice was particularly weak, and Linda was suffering from the first signs of dysphonia, the vocal malady which would shadow the remainder of her singing career.

The album title came from the cry of street vendors, selling a cheap form of ice-cream, popular until the 1920s. As the bulk of ice-cream salesmen were Italian, it's believed to be a corruption of 'Ecce, ecce' ('Look, look'). Talking to Geoff Brown in *Melody Maker* prior to the album's release, Thompson said he'd like to call the album ' "Mitzpah" . . . It was a thing in the First World War. When the fiancé was at the front, he'd have a ring with "Mitzpah" written on it, which just means "The Good Lord watch between us when we are apart". That's a nice idea.'

'Hokey Pokey' itself is full of double-entendres. Whether deliberate or not, the song's details of cross-dressing ('Fellas in the alley all look like girls . . .') are a reflection of the sexual ambiguity of the early 70s Glam scene. Otherwise, Thompson has a field day with the song's 'fnar-fnar' humour. Having established it's a song about ice-cream, Linda titillates, singing lines like: 'Feels so good when you put it in your mouth/Sends a shiver all down your spine.'

Thompson the guitarist lets fly with some truly wicked playing, particularly the burst following the second verse, and again, as the song winds down on its long journey from Carry On Pokeying. An acoustic version of 'Hokey Pokey' appears on the 1975 *Over the Rainbow* album, recorded at the much-loved north London venue's final night. Richard and Linda appear alongside Procol Harum, John Martyn and Kevin Coyne. DJ John Peel introduces them, citing *Bright Lights* . . . as his favourite album of 1974.

'I'll Regret It All In The Morning' is a magnificently weary, morning-after song. Its bitter, bile-filled lyrics are filled with all the stale disgust of a one-night stand, fuelled by unwanted whisky and desultory lust. Thompson bitterly resented the song, telling Rob Mackie in the late-lamented *Street Life* magazine: 'I really don't like the sentiments of that song, and it's the worst bit of singing on the record . . . I've just become very disillusioned with the song: it was me a couple of years ago, but it's not me now.' Thompson typically does himself a disservice, the song

Richard Thompson

may be flawed, but its atmosphere is finely caught in the couplet: 'I'm so drunk I couldn't care/If that's a wig or your own hair . . .'

'Smiffy's Glass Eye', leaves no pun unturned in Thompson's account of the optically challenged Smiffy, based on someone the Thompsons knew from Sound Techniques. English playground tactics are employed by the eponymous hero – conkers, marbles – until Thompson's punnery climaxes with a blind eye turned to the Cyclopian hero's demise. 'It's about cruelty and how people destroy each other through being very superficial', Thompson told *NME*'s Bob Woffinden. 'The kids hate him and pick on him and destroy him. It's terrible when someone is disliked because of his appearance; you should only see what is in someone's heart . . . So the song's about cruelty, which it puts over in a jokey way. It's an amalgamation of childhood memories and various playground horrors.'

Thompson has described 'The Egypt Room' variously as 'halfway between the Coasters "Little Egypt" and George Formby' and as 'Dickens meets Patricia Highsmith'. The imagery though is distinctively Thompsonian:

> The man with the cane and Italian shoes
> Creeps like a lion looking
> For a lonely Christian . . .

'Never Again' was written in the immediate aftermath of the Fairport crash which killed Thompson's girlfriend, Jeannie Franklyn. Thompson told Geoff Brown of the genesis of the song in 1969: 'Used to frighten me a bit this song. It's very weird. Eventually I convinced myself that I ought to write a third verse, and I did and now I like it . . . but funnily enough it still expresses the same emotion . . . It's strange, I don't really think I wrote it. It just came from somewhere.'

The breezy 'Georgie on a Spree' was inexplicably chosen four years later as theme song for a long-forgotten BBC TV drama *Kiss the Girls and Make Them Cry*.

'Old Man Inside A Young Man' is another of Thompson's living on the edge songs – 'The only kiss for me is the kiss of a knife . . .' 'I'd rather be dead on my feet than dead down in the ground . . .' Its impact is reduced, though, by a lacklustre vocal and dawdling melody.

'The Sun Never Shines On The Poor' is the one song that sounds like the *Hokey Pokey* cover. The scene-setting is as inimitable as 'Waterloo Sunset':

> The urchins are writhing around in the mud,
> Like eels playing tag in a barrel

Richard and Linda

> The old Sally Army sound mournful and sweet
> As they play an old Christmassy carol . . .

The song's second verse is a catalogue of woe which could have come straight from the pages of the classic socialist novel *The Ragged-Trousered Philanthropist*. Though considering the freshness of his Islamic conversion, perhaps the song's final lines give a better indication of the state of Thompson's mind at the time, those that are 'poor in the heart', he sings, are 'the worst kind of poor'.

Classical harpist Sidonie Goossens ushers in 'A Heart Needs A Home', one of Thompson's most haunting compositions. Linda's tremulous vocal reinforces the song's aching sense of loneliness. It is a stabbing picture of the desolation of a world where 'eyes cry rivers . . . when you're on your own'. In the end, Thompson seems to be saying, the home that the heart will find is the bourn to which we gratefully return. Better still is the version of the song on *Guitar, Vocal*, with Linda's double-tracked vocals and Thompson's stabbing electric guitar lending further poignancy to the already aching song.

'Mole In A Hole' is the album's only non-original composition, and indeed, the only contemporary cover version Thompson has ever included on an album. It was Richard and Linda's favourite song by Mike Waterson, and one they used to feature regularly onstage. On record, the novelty soon palls. Knowing the circumstances of the recording of the album, the temptation is to speculate that the reason for its inclusion is in the anti-Christian third verse 'My friend got so friendly with friend Jesus, Friend Jesus took my only friend away . . .' But that doesn't explain the album's final lines, disproving the idea that heart-felt religion is the panacea: 'My friend he was so wise he got religion, that's why I'm alive today and he is dead.'

Despite it all, *Hokey Pokey* remains a joyous album, which is perhaps why it features so low down the list of Richard and Linda 'faves'. Fans like their Richard straight from a hard day's gloom-digging, not chirpy and cheerful.

The reviews reflected how unsatisfying some critics found that chirpiness. In *Melody Maker*, Steve Lake spent much of his review blokishly bemoaning the increasing utilisation of wives in contemporary rock'n'roll. Mind you, he may have had a point. At the time Kris Kristofferson and Rita Coolidge, Paul Kantner and Grace Slick, James Taylor and Carly Simon, Paul and Linda McCartney, John and Yoko . . . were all taking up column inches.

Lake struck a solitary note, claiming that Thompson had been

Richard Thompson

'quietly sacrificing his originality ever since the inception of Fairport Convention, but clearly seems to have hit rock bottom with this hopelessly twee and banal bunch of tunes'.

In *Sounds*, Jerry Gilbert put his finger on an important point: 'The songs aren't necessarily any better than on *Henry the Human Fly*, which either makes that an underrated album or this an overrated one judging from the huge differential in media assessment...'

Phil Hardy, writing in *Let It Rock*, got right behind the record. It is a particularly astute review recognising that Thompson wasn't just another 'ex-Fairport' act: 'Thompson may be soaked in the folk tradition, but he makes no attempts to synthesise "folk" and "rock", as do, say, Steeleye Span... The realities of Thompson's world are neither moon and June nor the teenage wasteland... In short, the Thompsons don't sing about the insulated worlds one retreats into in one's headphones, but about the world that one meets out on the street, about a world that too much rock sweeps under the carpet. The overall result is a gloomy – but realistically so – album that ain't exactly going to chase your blues away, though the odd songs like "Hokey Pokey"... and the achingly beautiful "A Heart Needs A Home" are guaranteed to give the listener a lift. No, *Hokey Pokey* isn't an album to retreat into your fantasies with, rather it's one to shatter them. Buy it – and when you've worn it out, get another copy.'

Bernard Doherty: 'The cover was done by Shirt Sleeve Studio, a place off Tottenham Court Road. They were students of Peter Blake's [*Sgt Pepper* cover artist]. I think Jo had some deal with them, they'd just done *Commoners' Crown*, the Steeleye Span cover, really lavish. They built the model for that, and they created that sort of trade union banner for the *Hokey Pokey* sleeve.'

Richard Williams: 'By the time of *Hokey Pokey*, Jo was pretty much directing Richard's career, and A&R didn't have a lot to do with it. Richard went off with John Wood and made his records himself, he didn't bring his demos in. I was always keener on the Coltrane than the folk side of things; I liked the swirling guitar, the real heavy doom... So *Hokey Pokey* to me was more sunny. But the company liked it, I think they thought the album was more in the direction of one day having a hit single.'

Business-wise, the Thompsons were making a living. Their income was bolstered by Linda's wages from session work and commercials. Sporadic royalties came their way, and as Richard Williams recalls, there was still the odd session: 'Richard didn't come into the office much, a bit more than Nick Drake... We got on fine, he knew I liked his music. I got him on a John Cale track, on *Fear*. There's about a thousand slide guitar players on it, Phil Manzanera, Bryn Haworth, who I signed to Island, and Richard.'

Until their absence between 1975 and 1978, Richard and Linda Thompson received healthy notices for each album and every major concert appearance guaranteed a usually favourable review in the weekly music press. The kudos was largely shovelled in Richard's direction, as songwriter and guitarist. His was the head on which the hosannas were heaped, although by the time of their second album together, Linda was being singled out as a vocalist of distinction. By 1975 though, Richard and Linda Thompson were still very much a cult act.

Linda: 'I would never say to people I was a singer. I was mortified to be twenty-eight, or whatever, and nobody had ever heard of me. I used to make things up that were much more glamorous, I'd say I was an interior designer or something. I liked the critical kudos, and I liked the fact that other musicians liked what we did. But I would have loved commercial success. Richard would have loved it even more, but you know, he managed to not say that very much.'

Manager Jo Lustig was the unlikely balance at the other end of the see-saw. Richard could afford to remain wilfully un-showbiz as long as he knew there was someone like Jo Lustig taking care of business. Over his ten-year association with Thompson, Jo Lustig also looked after Jethro Tull, Ralph McTell, Richard Digance, Mary O'Hara and Steeleye Span, during their phenomenal 'All Around My Hat' success.

Jo Lustig: 'What can you say to an artist like Richard Thompson? "You've got to be more commercial"? You handle him on his level, or not at all ... Linda gives the impression of being the stronger partner, but Richard was still in control ... Linda was always more outspoken, more outgoing, but it was Richard.'

Linda: 'I don't know that it was so odd that we were managed by Jo Lustig. We were wimpy about business things, it was actually better to have this person we could blame everything on – "Oh we would have done your hay-gathering ceremony in the middle of the night for £2 10s, but Jo won't let us ..."'

Thompson was still involved with music, but he wasn't concentrating any longer. One of the competing interests was an antiques business run with fellow Islamic followers: 'I had a couple of shops – one in Crawford Street, in London, Leopold Antiques – we inherited the name and one in Church Street market off Edgware Road. I was far too soft to ever be an antique dealer – I just felt sorry for the old ladies, it was horrible, trying to get their really nice Welsh dressers out of them for forty quid and then try and sell it for as much money as possible. I tended to be far too kind to the old ladies and far too soft on the potential purchasers.'

In performance prior to their almost total withdrawal from the music scene between 1975 and 1978, the Thompson shows were stripped down, ascetic affairs. Thompson would only play acoustic guitar, seated, while Linda – who by her own admission had 'the stage presence of a totem pole' – was left centre-stage and isolated.

At this point, early on in the conversion, and prior to their complete withdrawal, Thompson was still keen on making records. Jo Lustig, who was now managing an ever-increasing number of folk acts, recruited a keen young assistant to help out.

Bernard Doherty: 'I was infatuated with the music business. I was running a record shop in Kilburn High Road when Fairport's *Babbacombe Lee* came out, and I phoned Island Records desperate to get a display window, I had this big noose in the window. I'm sure it was the only window devoted to a Fairport album anywhere in the world.

'Out of the blue, someone called me and said "Do you know a bloke called Jo Lustig?" I said I'd seen his name on the back of a Nico album, doesn't he manage Roy Harper? He was looking for someone to work for him, this would be early 1975. He had this funny little office off Exhibition Road. I imagined rock managers to be cigar-chomping, loud music, but there was this rather austere, library feel to his office.

'Jo brought the Chieftains in to do the Albert Hall on St Patrick's Day. They'd played some Arts Theatre in Covent Garden and sold it out in a day and Jo got wind of it. When I arrived in the office, Jo was talking to Claddagh Records. They were all postmen, Paddy Moloney was the only professional musician, the rest all had day jobs. When I arrived, he was busy courting them.'

The Chieftains may have been keen to give up their day jobs, but Richard Thompson had been working hard in the music business since his school days and new interests were now to the fore. He'd simply lost interest in pushing himself and his music further.

Richard: 'The regrets I would have would be career stuff, I was too flaccid in the 1970s, I just wasn't thinking tightly enough to make a difference. Especially the later 70s, where I made really indifferent records, I just didn't have my mind on the job.'

Chapter 14

LINDA: 'If that was a career strategy, it should be in the textbooks as how to bury yourself up to your head in sand.'

Throughout the 1970s, Thompson's career just seemed to drift. Thompson was still doing the business, it's just that not many record-buyers were paying attention. Richard and Linda were rock's best-kept secret.

The career direction of Richard and Linda Thompson sometimes reads like an Ealing script, they appear as Henry and Min Bannister, shuffling into Sound Techniques to record an album they know no-one will buy, or into Broadcasting House for an increasingly infrequent Radio 1 session and then disappearing again.

Bernard Doherty: 'Within two weeks of arriving at Jo Lustig's office, it was obvious that Richard and Linda didn't seem to have any cohesion as far as tour dates. They seemed to do dates when the Bron Agency rang up every couple of weeks to say "I've got a gig for Richard". It would be the Shakespeare Arms, or the Malden Festival in Essex. And when the money was right, Jo would say yes. And when it was not he'd say no, even though it was quite a good gig or quite a good career move.

'My job was to make sure that they got paid. That the gig went alright. That the PA we'd booked – which was usually with some tinpot PA company – was there. Linda would sing, Richard would play acoustic guitar, but he'd also play this bass pedal, which got a Hammond Organ effect through his amp.

'It was like Viv Stanshall, very English eccentric. He'd introduce songs in that way and he'd refer to "rock" and pop music from the past. He'd do a duet and say "This is our tribute to Paul and Paula". He'd do a country song, one of those answer songs – "you've been cheating", "no I haven't", "yes you have".

'It was all very much on a shoestring. They were going out for about £200 a gig. But John Curd, from Straight Music wanted to book him for the Roundhouse and Bron gave him a figure of £1,500, we couldn't believe it when they accepted.'

Despite Jo Lustig's efforts to ensure a wider audience, Richard and Linda were destined to remain a minority cult. The idea of aggressive marketing by record companies was in its infancy, and it's not surprising given Thompson's natural reticence, his burgeoning interest in Islam and the very nature of his music, that any marketing budget Island had would go to more obviously commercial acts.

Bernard Doherty: 'Island sort of liked Richard. But Richard never said "Right, I'll do a week of interviews". They didn't really know where he was or what he was doing.

'We would go on the road. I would take Jo Lustig's Volvo Estate and collect Richard and Linda. I'd book rehearsal rooms, book the musicians. Because they all loved Richard so much, you could tell Dave Mattacks or John Kirkpatrick and they'd drop everything to come. There were always money problems. They weren't selling more than 15–20,000 with any album. But it was amazing how many people seemed to have them.'

A contemporary account records the 'Bright Lights' single shifting around 25,000 copies, but Thompson was resigned: 'Ex-Fairports have a long history of records that get to about number thirty-one,' he told Rob Mackie. As Dylan sang in 1975: 'It's a strange way to make a living . . .'

Richard and Linda were on the periphery of pop. Despite the inherent quality of his songs, Thompson couldn't crack the crossover. All it needed was one hit (the following year, 'Year Of The Cat' took Al Stewart from bedsitter bard to the American charts) or one cover version, to effectively translate Richard Thompson into something substantial.

Jo Lustig: 'I used to send Richard's songs all over the place, I had a lot of friends, they'd all say "wonderful, wonderful". But the folkies wanted their own material, except for the ones who wanted to do Dylan . . . I think it would have made a lot of difference to them if, say, a country singer had had a hit with a song of Richard's, because if someone has a hit with a certain writer, then other people want the material.'

By their standards, 1975 was an active year for Richard and Linda Thompson. They were gigging regularly, but while the music press heaped praise where it was due, one national sniffily found that 'the content of their material far outweighs their shambling stage act'. The Thompsons seemed to exist in some limbo, a festival bill from August

1975, found them billed below Wishbone Ash, Lou Reed, the Mahavishnu Orchestra, Soft Machine and Caravan, but above the Heavy Metal Kids, Babe Ruth and the Climax Blues Band. But Thompson still had friends in all the right places. The results of the 1975 Zig Zag British Guitarist Poll had Thompson placed second only to Eric Clapton. Behind him in third position was Jimmy Page followed by Paul Kossoff with Keith Richard ranking fifth.

However, such a placing gave a distorted picture. Since his conversion, Thompson had eschewed the electric guitar, relying on acoustic for live work.

Bernard Doherty: 'At that time the big question was: would he ever pick up the electric guitar again? The Stratocaster had definitely been left at home.'

Jo Lustig: 'Richard came to me and said "look, my Mullah doesn't want me to play electric guitar. I don't know what I'm going to do about my career. Do you still want to handle me, because I'm not going to be working?" I said "Richard, I'll be here for you." There wasn't a lot to do after they went off to live in the commune in Norfolk ...'

Richard Williams: 'Richard not being able to play electric guitar seemed rather like not just chopping off one of his hands, but both of them.'

Bernard Doherty: 'The crunch date was the Queen Elizabeth Hall when suddenly Richard said he would play electric. That was probably the first time I saw him stretch out on electric ... There was all this mystique about whether he would play "Calvary Cross", because it had all these religious overtones. Everyone wanted him to play it. And he did, it was so great. He went back to plugging in.

'All the band had enormous grins after the Q.E.H. show. They were all such a homely bunch, happy to play with him. It was a sort of unwritten law that Richard was the virtuoso, not only as a guitarist, but the bastard could write songs as well. There was that feeling that he was the governor – they always called him "Henry" – but in a sort of "he is the boss" way.'

The Thompsons had paid their dues around the folk clubs a few years before, but taking what gigs they could get, Richard and Linda agreed to appear at the 1975 Cambridge Folk Festival. Such an appearance would have been unthinkable a few years before, but now folk and rock fraternities were the best of friends again.

Bernard Doherty remembers Richard and Linda's appearance at Cambridge: 'There was a certain sort of arrogance towards the audience. I remember the shock on Peggy's face when they struck up

Richard Thompson

"Together Again"... They were playing a Fats Domino lick to a Country song, and Richard obviously introduced it as a traditional American folk song. That was great, to hear this heavy riff on a Buck Owens song in this sweaty tent, Richard plugged in at last. That feeling "Oh fuck, Richard's got his guitar, hurray", he's doing his feedback tricks.'

It was at that gig that a young teacher-trainee called Clive Gregson had his first close encounter: 'The first time I saw Richard I was at college, and we went to the Cambridge Folk Festival... I was totally blown away by Richard and Linda, *Hokey Pokey* was the current record. I thought the songs were good, but I'd never seen anybody play guitar like that. So from then I got into it wholesale, got the records, bought the Fairport stuff. So it was the guitar, then the songs, and Linda as a singer... The songs were awesome, so unusual, very English, with Scottish overtones... Something other-worldly, a spooky element in those songs.

'There was an accessibility, at a time when shows were like Yes, total pretentious crap, and pop music was pretty stale, the rag end of the Glam Rock thing. There was an intimacy to Richard and Linda's stuff... There was something about the shows that was very uplifting, even though a lot of the material was quite miserable... but it's actually a lot more interesting to listen to that, it makes your brain work a bit more, than listen to the Beach Boys singing "It's very sunny, let's go surfing"...'

In November 1975, to promote their third album together, *Pour Down Like Silver*, Richard and Linda set off on a fourteen-date UK tour. Accompanied by Dave Pegg, Dave Mattacks and John Kirkpatrick, the tour has loomed large in the Thompson legend, as three tracks were taped live at the Oxford Polytechnic, two of which ('Night Comes In' and 'Calvary Cross') proved to be the talking point of Thompson's *Guitar, Vocal* compilation, the first time Thompson stretched out on guitar, on record.

John Kirkpatrick: 'When I first played with them, it was Richard and Linda, bass, drums and me, so there was plenty of room for me. The later it got, the bigger the band, the harder it was. It was great to establish my role in Richard's music in those smaller bands, I was like a rhythm guitar, a keyboard, even an accordion sometimes... definitely the most widening thing I've done. You listen to the live "Calvary Cross" on *Guitar, Vocal*. Wonderful experience, the space to do it... I listen to them and think "Blimey, is that me doing that? Morris dance music one minute, out there in space the next."'

Dave Pegg kept in touch with Thompson after he quit Fairport in 1971, and had worked sporadically with him on tour and in the studio:

Richard and Linda

'You would hardly have known that Richard had become a Muslim, apart from the fact that on the tour, we had twelve curries in eleven days. It didn't bother me. What did bother me was later on when I saw him play Birmingham Town Hall when he had the all-Muslim band, and that was pretty unnerving because musically it was a complete disaster, although they were all great musicians in their own right, or had been ... It didn't make any difference to us that Richard had become a Muslim, it just meant he didn't drink and was more choosy about what he was eating. He didn't suddenly go strange and try to convince everybody they should join him, he was just very much the same down-to-earth normal person that he always seemed to be. We were quite scared at the time, we thought "oh dear, the prayer mat's gonna come out".'

Simon: 'When we did that tour supporting Traffic, it was obvious that they were making compromises, that they were beginning to draw away ... from infidel society, and my feelings of being a trio with a rhythm section started to move towards a rhythm section accompanying a couple ... I think they were spending more time with people who read the Koran than with those that didn't. And there were more musicians who didn't read the Koran than those who did.'

John Kirkpatrick: 'I remember at a break in one session on one of Richard's albums, Simon (Nicol) was literally crying into his beer. He couldn't believe the change that had come over Richard. He'd known him all his life, and now it was like somebody else you had to start getting to know all over again. The most spectacular thing was that every couple of hours, he'd get out his prayer mat and dive down. After a take, he'd be on his knees, and you didn't know quite what to do. You know, we'd look at each other and say "Are we supposed to join in?" ... They would both do it. It was very public to begin with ... Linda was certainly into it as well. But gradually that aspect of it became much more discreet. He would just disappear, then re-appear ... He was still just as funny and witty and playing just as well, so I don't think it affected his work.'

Pat Donaldson: 'I didn't notice anything ... maybe he'd grown a beard, but then people do that anyway. It's not the great revelation ... The accidents, the deaths in Fairport, that can't have been an easy thing to go through, because I think – I didn't know those people – but I was always under the impression that they were a friendly bunch of people, they lived together in these houses ... Young, a close-knit group of people doing something and enjoying themselves, it becomes more than friends, it's like family. And when that accident happens, you're there on the spot, that must have an extraordinary effect on you ... So who knows what led him ...'

Not everyone was so sanguine about Thompson's conversion. Dave Mattacks: 'Let's just say I had a bit of difficulty relating to him during that Sufi period.'

The more Thompson discovered about Islam, the less interested he became in music. In retrospect, Linda can discern the positive elements of her conversion, but at the time she found it hard and unremitting: 'We were in the commune, but out and performing, then at one point our Sheikh forbade Richard to do music ... On the other hand, he always encouraged me, "you have a voice and you've got to sing", which was very peculiar. He was an amazing man, Sheikh Abdul Q'adir. I remember him giving talks in the 70s, and when he'd veer off from religious things, he'd say, "You know, the terrible thing is, that man who is head of the CIA is going to be President". This was twenty years before Bush became President!'

Bernard Doherty had begun working for the Thompsons' manager, Jo Lustig, just as the couple were finishing recording *Hokey Pokey*. Within a few weeks, Doherty was the main conduit between Thompson and Lustig, spending a lot of time with Richard, in the car on the way to gigs, backstage at concerts, in rehearsal rooms, at Lustig's office ... But he wasn't surprised by Thompson's religious convictions: 'It wasn't really a shock, because we were moving in circles where things like that happened ... it was only when people explained to me what it entailed: that you had to pray four times a day, all the things about cutting peoples hands off. To me it was something he did, and I wanted the real Richard to come back. But that's what everyone wanted ... Simon Nicol must be his best mate, and he was totally puzzled by it. I think of all the people, Simon was the most bemused by it all.'

Jo Lustig: 'The performances before they went away were very subdued, with Linda wearing her scarf, and Richard seated and playing the guitar. But I liked them both very much, and I thought well I'll keep managing them, he might change his mind ... My criterion for managing somebody is "can I listen to them every night for a three-week tour?" Do you know how soul destroying it can be when you hear some bands, night after night? But Richard and Linda were wonderful.'

It wasn't long before the Thompsons decided to put the music business and London completely behind them. With daughter Muna and baby Abu Dharr (later Anglicised to Adam and now known as Teddy) who had been born at Bristol Gardens in 1976, they moved to an Islamic commune at Hoxne near Diss, on the Norfolk–Suffolk border.

Richard and Linda

Perri: 'I didn't go to Suffolk, my mother and Aunt Evelyn went. I gather it was super but fairly basic ... from the female point of view pretty tough going. But Richard gave extremely good reasons, it was a structure in a time when everyone was looking for some kind of answers and some sort of structure.'

Linda: 'It was a fairly ascetic life. We definitely both tried to get rid of a lot of horrible Western traits ... No phone, no television, no record player, no electric light, no hot water ... You didn't buy anything store bought, so the women would make bread in the morning and cakes. You were always cooking and there were no washing machines or anything, so it really was a full-time job ... Drudgery really.'

Richard: 'Linda hated it. I mean, I did get a lot from it, but there's a lot of stuff I didn't get from it and a lot of stuff I hated when I was there. But it was the 70s ... it was a thing that you did in the 70s, popped off to your alternative lifestyle in the country. It was fine idealism, but in reality it's very hard to unplug from the system. You probably have to go a lot further to go than Norfolk ... But that was the 70s and that was the thing people were doing. In terms of everyday life it was probably quite hard; it was hard on women and children.'

Joan: 'Well I was quite interested in it – I'm always interested in different religions – and I like to try and understand them and I see the good in some of them – in fact most of them. And I thought well he doesn't smoke and he doesn't drink and he looked absolutely wonderful – normal with the beard and everything, so I wasn't all that distressed ... They went down to Suffolk – it was a lovely old house and they seemed happy enough. It was separate, the men had the downstairs and the women upstairs with the kitchen – big kitchen and a big stove – they all seemed very happy and there were chickens clucking all over the place.

'My husband didn't go along with any of this at all – the only thing that pleased him was when Richard was successful and normal ... and then he did everything for Richard – looked after his house, decorated the house – did everything for Richard – he was extremely proud.'

Richard: 'For a few years I just found it difficult frankly, to deal with my family – you just do – if you're going to embrace something radical like that and you take the whole philosophy on board, you really ask yourself a lot of questions and it's confusing. I was basically confused and I also probably believed that the good guys were the good guys and the bad guys were the bad guys, which I certainly don't any more. Sometimes the good guys are the bad guys and sometimes the bad guys are the good guys – so I try to judge people as I meet them these days,

Richard Thompson

rather than saying: "well if you don't belong to my club, you can't be any good". I did a lot of that in the 70s, which is a very bad thing.'

Muna: 'What I remember about the commune is my brother fell out of a window and my mother making dates with marzipan in ... I remember there being a lot of people, but I thought that was completely normal.'

I remember interviewing Thompson for the NME in 1977. It was my first major piece for the paper. I tended to concentrate on folkie-type things, but on the NME in 1977, even Eater were perceived to have more relevance than Richard Thompson, who had been out of the public eye since the low-key release of *Pour Down Like Silver* in 1975.

Thompson had requested copy approval. This was laughed out of court. The interview went ahead anyhow. It was in Island's offices at St Peter's Square. Dressed in a turban and autumnal brown, Thompson was reserved and subdued, but smiled a lot, and was friendly and outgoing. He was off-hand about the albums which fans treasured, denying that *Pour Down Like Silver* was wilfully ascetic ('I just couldn't find the musicians, they weren't available . . .') and still managing to convey an enthusiasm about the direction his music was taking: 'I'm very enthusiastic about music at the moment. I don't feel addicted to music – I used to, it used to be a drug to me – but now I play because it's enjoyable.'

Looking back, I suppose Thompson was promoting the tour he was planning with all Islamic musicians, or perhaps *Guitar, Vocal*, but I was too awestruck to notice. I also failed to notice that he had largely turned his back on all the lyrical trivia I concentrated on from *Henry the Human Fly*, but he was too polite to tell me.

Thompson was accompanied at Island Records by a man I can only assume was his Sheikh. He didn't say anything, while Richard was very forthcoming, but occasionally Thompson would glance in his direction, and receive a nod or infinitesimal shake of the head.

Thompson was keen to distance himself from what had once been, telling me: 'It's nice that people are interested in the music, but it's something I would try and be detached from. The danger is that people's interest is in you, rather than what comes out of you.'

Thompson dislikes the interview process to this day, but back in 1977, he found it acutely painful discussing a sea-change in his life, and his music, to a bunch of journalists from papers more concerned with the wisdom proffered by Generation X.

Richard: 'It's confusing when you take on board a whole philosophy of life and you're not sure what to do about the old one ... it's very confusing and very overwhelming and I think I probably treated some people very, very badly at that point – chucked them out of my life, you know, thinking they were worthless – I think because you get so enthusiastic when you find something that's good for you, you think everybody else deserves it as well, but other people are probably quite happy without you shouting about it, so it was probably a confusing time.'

Bernard Doherty: 'Linda in all this, I couldn't understand. Linda liked the normal things that someone of around thirty years old who'd been in the music business liked. She liked nice clothes. I remember her finding clothes that matched the Muslim thing, but were designer. She'd go off to South Molton Street and find something . . . There were these rules, but she hung on to her silk and perfume . . . I remember on tour, during the Muslim time, she was obviously wrenched apart with her love for him.'

Looking back, Linda admits she was unhappy at the commitment which the faith required and the changes which she perceived in her husband: 'The men would go off and have coffee, and talks and seminars and lectures . . . I don't know how it worked, but they got more spiritual or something, eventually Richard got a green turban – which was the epitome – and when he got that, I ran away and went to stay with my mother . . .

'My father was ill, so I thought "fuck this", and split. I was away for about six weeks, and eventually came back. I was pregnant with my son at the time and all the women would come to me and beg me to go back, never Richard, because he wasn't supposed to do that . . . They'd say "You've got to come back, he's got a green turban". I said "I don't care if he's got a green willy, I'm not going back". But I did eventually go back, because, pregnant, you're a bit vulnerable . . . but it was quite tough.'

Chapter 15

THE LAST THE WORLD heard from Richard and Linda Thompson between 1975 and 1978 was their *Pour Down Like Silver* album, which Island released in November 1975. Even before a note had been heard, I remember being arrested by the cover. Life-size heads of Richard and Linda, staring ... Richard vaguely into the middle distance; Linda hard at you.

Of course, there had been rumours, but this was the first proof that the jaunty yeoman of *Liege & Lief* and *Morris On* was truly dead and buried. Something had certainly changed with that record: the turbans, the Arabic writing, the songs which – even by Richard Thompson's mordant standards – were stark and ascetic ... All combined to convey that what had once been, was now no more.

Richard: 'It was a stark record, but I think it was by accident in a sense – we were intending to have Simon [Nicol] come and play rhythm guitar and he wasn't available so everything ended up sounding very stark and I was always going to overdub rhythm guitar and stuff, but we thought we'll just leave it, what the hell ... so everything sounds extremely empty. A stark kind of record.'

Linda: '*Pour Down Like Silver* was when Sheikh Abdul Q'adir said we could make music, as long as it was to God ... the picture for the cover was taken very early in the morning in the flat in Thurlow Road. "Dimming Of The Day", "Beat The Retreat", "Night Comes In", they're all about God, and considering they're all about God, some of them aren't bad.'

For all its Islamic overtones and undercurrents, much of *Pour Down Like Silver* could only have been written by the shy, retiring, English middle-class Richard Thompson. The record is peppered with Thompson references both overt and covert.

'Beat the Retreat' is a ceremony performed by the English army: drums, fifes and pipes marshal in an impressive marching display. In 'Streets Of Paradise' the references include 'The Sash My Father Wore',

Richard and Linda

a popular Irish Loyalist ballad; 'a bullet I can chew' comes from the soldier's habit of removing the paper round a bullet by chewing it off; one of Ewan MacColl's best known songs was 'Dirty Old Town', to which Thompson refers in the third verse. 'Jet Plane In A Rocking Chair' . . . includes a reference to a 'dancing bear', a popular sight in Shakespeare's day.

'Night Comes In' was already featured in Thompson's stage set as an opportunity to stretch out on electric guitar. A devotional song to the Prophet, 'Night Comes In' conveys some of the frenzy which the fourteenth century Islamic monks ('dervishes' of the Mevlevi sect) achieved ('Dancing till my feet don't touch the ground/Lose my mind and dance forever . . .').

'Dargai', the slow instrumental which concludes the album, is a Scottish strathspey, composed by James Scott Skinner. 'Dimming Of The Day', which precedes the instrumental, has Thompson at his most lyrically Scottish, notably on the line 'now all the bonny birds have wheeled away . . .'

'Dimming Of The Day' remains one of Thompson's most reflective and acutely touching songs. There is a sense of real intimacy when Richard joins Linda half way through the first verse, for the line: 'You pulled me like the moon pulls on the tide . . . .' 'Dimming Of The Day' is Linda Thompson's own favourite song of her ex-husband's, and a perfect conclusion to an album so much of its time and place.

Clive Gregson: ' "Dimming Of The Day" was a song I'd played in the folk clubs, so it went on the second Any Trouble album, *Wheels in Motion*. It is still my favourite Richard song. It's just a massive, incredible expression of personal longing. It's very unusual in that it kicks off in one key and goes to the first bridge. It's an unusual structure in that it's not really a chorus, it has a hook at the end of each verse. It goes verse, middle-eight, verse, middle-eight, verse, extra line, stop. It flows perfectly, and it changes key for each section, it's musically quite complex, and yet doesn't sound it . . . It's totally effortless, and yet very sophisticated.'

Pour Down Like Silver is a deceptively simple album with a haiku-like style to the songs, a stark and multi-textured quality. With the benefit of hindsight the record has a feel of finality to it. Thompson only lets rip on electric briefly during 'Hard Luck Stories', otherwise, his mood is serene and beatific. Weary and resigned, his voice sounds like he is going through the motions before he quits living in the material world.

It may be a difficult record to like, but there is much to admire in it:

the restraint of the performances, the subdued nature of the songs, the spartan production and instrumentation. All were at odds with the flamboyance of the rest of the rock'n'roll circus at the time, but then Richard Thompson had never been a willing participant at the bear garden.

Pour Down Like Silver was a suitable valediction, a coda to Richard and Linda Thompson's Island years. From their position as relatively successful performers, they bid the music business adieu without any real pangs of regret.

On stage, Linda had been the focal point since the beginning of their partnership, even though she was clearly unhappy with her role as front person.

Bernard Doherty: 'They had just come back from supporting Traffic, and Linda had taken quite a pasting from the Glasgow audience – "Sing up girl". It wasn't very much of a "show". It was a folk show. Richard would be sitting to play. Linda was very irritating in that . . . her body language said "I'm nervous". She was always in awe of him, because she would always say in the car "Well it's alright for you, you've got a guitar round your neck". She was always very shy, just holding the mike, looking down.

'She lacked stagecraft. She needed to just stand there and pierce the audience between the eyes. Look, look in the way that Sinead O'Connor, or whoever. Sure, they're nervous, but they would take the audience on. Linda would never take the audience on. A little shout from the audience and she'd go "What? Pardon?" She'd ask them.'

When it came to recording, Linda was there as the voice to bring Richard's songs eloquently to life. But Pat Donaldson, who played with Richard and Linda on a clear run right through from *Henry the Human Fly* to *Pour Down Like Silver*, felt that Linda suffered from always being compared to Sandy.

Pat Donaldson: 'Linda, rightly or wrongly, lived under the shadow of Sandy. The two of them were friends, Sandy was up on this pedestal as a singer-songwriter, and Linda was her friend who happened to be a singer. But I think more from the producer's chair, and maybe the engineer's chair too – but certainly not from Richard, definitely not from Richard – she was certainly given short-shrift from the other side of the glass, and not given the time and consideration that Richard was necessarily given . . . I think she felt some insecurity as well, felt that she wasn't as good as Sandy. Whether she'd been led to believe that by constant talk from Witchseason people, that's something I can't answer, but that's certainly my impression ... It seems to me she had a lot of pressure on her from the wrong people.'

Out of the public eye for three years between 1975 and 1978, the Thompsons still had a loyal and devoted following, but Richard was now more interested in other things.

Bernard Doherty: 'Richard was always busy. He was always painting. He'd arrive at the office covered in white paint. He always had music going on in the car – gospel music, Al Bowlly. So I don't think he ever lost his interest in music per se; I think he just lost interest in that horrible thing, the star-making machinery.'

For Linda, the family's time in the Maida Vale squat was at least made tolerable by its London location. When the commune moved to East Anglia, her memories of the period darkened: 'Things actually got worse when we went to Hoxne. At least when we were squatting in the commune, we all squatted in separate houses, so we had our own spaces. But when we went to Norfolk we were all living together. Like a lot of people who live in communes, who have that way of life, there wasn't a lot of cleanliness and I got really sick.

'My parents would say "Oh the spark's gone out of you", and of course they were absolutely right. I think they were very sad, but on the other hand I didn't, and absolutely couldn't, have cut off contact the way Richard did with his family. Even if I lied about it, I would still see my family.'

Bernard Doherty: 'He disappeared to Norfolk. We didn't phone him up. Dee [Lustig] would try and find out where to send a cheque ... We didn't get many calls asking where he was. If you're not pushing somebody ... and there were so many acts out there. I moved into their flat in Hampstead with Suzanne, who later went on to marry Bruce Thomas from the Attractions. She worked at Stiff Records. It was amazing coming back to find the Damned all over Richard Thompson's old flat.'

Over the years, Richard's commitment to Islam has never wavered, although he has lightened up considerably and now wears his undoubted faith more lightly. He can even enjoy winding up credible journalists who question his faith, relishing a telephone conversation with a *News of the World* hack: 'Oh yeah: chop off the hands of unbelievers. I told him I was married – with five wives!'

Linda, who was with Richard during the first zealous years of his conversion, now looks back over twenty years and is keen to stress the positive aspects, but she hasn't forgotten the problems she felt at the time: 'Of course, in a very real sense, that *should* be more important, your living alone and dying alone; your quest to better yourself and make yourself a better person. That should be more important. But on the other hand, that's only given to really rare individuals. It's like being able to play the guitar really fabulously at eighteen: it's not given to everybody. Not everybody is meant to shed the world in that way.

'It was very drudging, the life then. There was some sweetness there, between us. There's a lot to be said for trying to better yourself, be it financially or spiritually . . . But it wasn't a normal kind of family life, and if you're a Westerner, it's very difficult.

'We both made a pilgrimage, *hajj* to Mecca, not together, we went in separate years . . . That was an amazing time, I'm very glad I did that. I see now there were things I learnt then that were invaluable lessons. But it was tough. If I examine it now . . . I wouldn't like to do it again, but when you were busy and you had a lot of kids and you were washing and cooking, you're not as neurotic.'

Richard: 'It was extraordinary. I suppose the nutshell description of it is – you go all that way and it's just a journey to yourself – when you get there, there's nothing there. But you're very intensely aware of yourself and your own shortcomings and your own blessings, whatever you've got, you're very aware of it. It's a difficult journey, a very difficult journey, but you arrive at your own heart, I suppose.

'It's like looking in a mirror. But in Mecca when you look in the mirror you see absolutely what's there – you can't hide – that's the strange thing about the place. It's very intense and you can't hide from who you are. If you're a saint and there's nothing of *you* there, then what you see in the mirror is just beauty – what you see in the mirror is God – because there's nothing of you there.

'It's extraordinary. But it's hard to actually describe, because all you do when you go there is geometry – you go round this black stone thing and you run between these two points, which is where the wife of Abraham was searching for water and ran between these two points and then the well opened up. So you run between these two points – circle, straight line and then a point – you stand on the plain of Arafat which is supposed to be the final gathering place of humanity – at the end of the world that's where everyone will end up – they'll be driven to this point – so they say. So all you're doing is geometry but something happens to you, something profound is going on without you having to think about it. If you do it, it happens. You just have to go there and do it and things happen.'

During the years away, between 1975 and 1978, Thompson did break cover sporadically. Notably, he played on the sessions for what was to

Richard and Linda

be Sandy Denny's final album *Rendezvous*. Sandy told me delightedly: ' "Candle In The Wind" . . . Richard Thompson plays guitar on that, which is great, because he hasn't played on anything, you know what he's been like. But he only did that a few weeks ago and he really was incredibly into it. I think he was relieved to get back on the electric guitar and start wailing away.'

Joe Boyd: 'I didn't see a lot of Richard at that time. There was a little sensitivity just because I'd been engaged to Linda, she had lived with me in California . . . But in the end I had gone over to their house to have dinner, and it was all quite friendly. Then about six or eight months before *First Light*, Richard was kind of groping what to do for his next record . . . Richard, John and I met and talked about the three of us working together. John and I would co-produce it. He wanted to work with the Islamic band . . . So we went into the studio, to Island at Basing Street, where we spent two days putting down tracks, and it was a disaster.

'It was really, I felt, very poor. I didn't have much confidence in the musicians that he was working with. The atmosphere was strange and it just didn't seem to work . . .'

There was also an ill-conceived short UK tour during 1977, with musicians who were chosen not for their musical abilities, but because they shared Thompson's Islamic beliefs.

That was the summer that Punk finally broke out of the bin-liners and into the charts. For the first time in a decade, music had come from the street. Punk had not been sanctioned by the music press or talked up by the record industry. The initial impetus came from a generation who were tired of the hoary old prog-rock clichés and for whom Bob Dylan and the Beatles were bankrupt forces.

It was the year that Elvis Presley died ('good fucking riddance' opined Johnny Rotten) and the year that saw the Sex Pistols tear to no. 1 during the week of Her Majesty's Silver Jubilee with 'God Save the Queen'. It was the year of the safety pin and the blitzkrieg bop. It was emphatically not the year for a turban and prayers five times a day.

I saw a show at Stevenage's Gordon Craig Theatre, a municipal auditorium with no atmosphere, onstage or off. The audience was curious, and even by the Thompsons' low-key standards, the presentation was minimal. The lighting was muted and anyone expecting a run through familiar territory was in for a disappointment. The bulk of the songs were versions of material written for the Thompsons' next two albums (*First Light* and *Sunnyvista*) which nobody had yet heard.

The mood and the music was leaden. As a show, it simply didn't happen. Such was Thompson's determination to deny his glittering career, that he concentrated almost entirely on new music. Even allowing for the notorious British intolerance of anything 'odd' or overtly religious, the Thompsons that night – and that tour – fell on stony ground. There was an enormous groundswell of curiosity and affection for them, and unfamiliar as they were with Islam, if the music had conveyed the couple's joy and enlightenment, those audiences would have responded in kind.

Thompson deliberately eschewed any guitar-hero pyrotechnics and the whole experience was desultory and unsatisfactory. The following year, Thompson would himself concede that the 1977 tour had been 'a miscalculation'.

Bernard Doherty: 'They had that Sufi band, all those congas, I call it his Santana period. It was awful. "In God's Garden" was this track that went on and on . . . I went down to rehearsal, and as I went up the stairs I could hear them all, banging away, and I thought this isn't Richard, this is a bongo band.'

The band was drawn from Muslim musicians with whom Richard had kept in touch ('amateurs' recalled Linda, 'all amateurs'). By all accounts, the band was basically Mighty Baby, but with new Islamic names Haj Jamin (Mick Evans), bass; Haj Abdul Jabbar (Roger Powell), percussion; Haj Abdul Lateef (Ian Whiteman), keyboards. Plus Haj Yahya and Ragayya, backing vocals. The only non-Muslim was session drummer Preston Hayman.

A set list which has survived runs:

'The Flute Song' ('The Flute Tells A Story')
'Madness Of Love'
'King Of Love'
'Strange Affair'
'The Bird In God's Garden'
'Rescue Me'
'Take Me To My Own Country
('The Fire In The Garden')
'Layla'
'Majmun'
'When I Get To The Border'
'Night Comes In'

Only 'When I Get To The Border' and 'Night Comes In' were concessions to pre-conversion Thompson. 'Strange Affair' and 'Layla' appeared on subsequent Thompson albums, while 'The Bird In God's Garden' was dusted down for a French, Frith, Kaiser, Thompson collaboration.

Richard and Linda

Bernard Doherty: 'Between *Pour Down Like Silver* and *First Light*, they did tour, that was with the Sufi band. Richard would wear all white. I thought I was on the road with Mahavishnu. Richard was very cynical about other musicians who'd drifted that way. I remember him taking the piss out of Mahavishnu and all the jazz musicians. He'd talk about religion a bit. I was such a thicko – Essex boy, raised a Catholic. He was very aware of the guilt and the fear. He always felt you didn't suffer any fear being a Muslim. There wasn't a fear of death.'

Richard and Linda were effectively off the scene for three years following the release of *Pour Down Like Silver* in 1975. All that broke the silence was the 1976 compilation *Guitar, Vocal*. To all intents and purposes, the Thompsons had moved away from the realms of their career and into a different world.

From a distance, Richard Thompson viewed the music scene with distaste. Immersing themselves in the world of Islam, the Thompsons forbore material trappings. ('Do you listen to your old records?' I once asked Linda. 'Difficult,' she replied. 'We don't own a record player').

During his three-year isolation, Thompson re-acquainted himself with the joy of working with his hands. Even now, he feels that music is a transient thing and finds real pleasure in physically creating something. At the time of his conversion, his zeal was such that, under instruction from his Sheikh, he gave up playing guitar altogether. Linda: 'He wasn't making any music, but he was making arrows.'

Thompson still inspired loyalty in the press. In *Zig Zag* Paul Kendall put together a celebratory five-page Reelin' In The Years tribute to Thompson ('To mark the tenth year of Mr Richard Thompson's illustrious career as a purveyor of fine music to the public at large ...'). That May 1977 issue had Thompson staring moodily from its cover and was the magazine's lowest-selling issue ever. The next month, Johnny Rotten was on the cover, and the magazine recorded its highest-ever sales. The writing was on the stalls.

During the Thompsons' exile in the fenlands, Jo Lustig negotiated a new contract for them, this time with Chrysalis Records. This left Island a free hand to delve into their archives, and rather than release a dubiously titled Greatest Hits or Best Of ... compilation, Richard Williams sat down with Thompson and long-time associate John Wood to put together the neatly titled double album *Guitar, Vocal*, which was released by Island in June 1976.

In retrospect, *Guitar, Vocal* is effectively one of the first 'box sets', a comprehensive, chronological overview of an artist's career, which collected together rare and unreleased material. Standard record industry practice at the time was to cobble together a compilation of previously released material, or put out a live album of sure-fire studio favourites, punctuated by a lot of people going 'whoo'.

It is to Thompson's credit, that he was willing to have his dirty linen hung in public. *Guitar, Vocal* is actually as sustained a package as Thompson's official box set, 1993's *Watching the Dark*.

Richard Williams was still at Island, and *Guitar, Vocal* was one of his final projects for the label: 'I'm sure *Guitar, Vocal* was my idea, and that I went to Lustig and said why don't we do something like this to make people appreciate Richard in a different way ... I talked to John [Wood] who approached Richard, and I think Richard took an interest. I'm sure that "Throwaway Street Puzzle", "Mr Lacey" and "Poor Will and the Jolly Hangman" were his idea. Simon was around a lot at the time, and I think "Ballad Of Easy Rider" and "Sweet Little Rock'n'Roller" were his ideas.

' "Night Comes In" and "Calvary Cross" were definitely mine, because I'd taped those at the Oxford Poly. We'd sent the Island Mobile to do that, and I can't for the life of me remember why. It might have been for a live album, or it might just have been let's get it down. It was only about £500 a day to do that, and the engineers all liked Richard.

'I thought those two long things were the best he'd ever done. He just tore the guts out of them. I loved the songs, and that – to me – was the way they were meant to be done. The other two things that were definitely my choices were "A Heart Needs A Home" and "Dark End Of The Street", which was one of my favourite songs, whether done by James Carr or Ry Cooder or Richard and Linda, it's a sort of infallible song. I think "A Heart Needs A Home", if I could keep one thing of Richard's. I can't understand why it's never been a hit for anyone.

'Now I can't remember whether he said he'd go and do those two short recordings ['Flee As A Bird', 'The Pitfall/The Excursion'] or whether he just went and did them. Maybe he felt that to do them was to represent his present self. That he knew those big electric things were part of him and that they had to be there. But perhaps the two recent things were a symbolic presence.

'I'd been through my Sufi period in 1969, so I wasn't very impressed with Sufism when I heard Richard was ... I remember he didn't look very well whenever he did come into the building ... Jo was very guarded about it.

'He did do a second and third album for us, and sometime after *Hokey Pokey* it became apparent that he wasn't going to be a pop star, either by his inclination or the public's ... The record company subconsciously filed him away as someone to be proud of.'

Richard and Linda

Guitar, Vocal marks the real beginning of the Richard Thompson cult. Few living artists had been celebrated in such a way, and Thompson's career 1967–1977, certainly merited such an overview. The collection panned from his days with Fairport Convention, back in the hazy sunlight of 1967, through the summer of Punk, to Thompson's espousal of Islam and his rejection of the record industry.

Concerned with new and more important journeys, Thompson was happy to let someone else do the looking back for him, and Richard Williams' selections for *Guitar, Vocal* did full credit to the scope of his career to date.

With the benefit of hindsight and knowing what other Fairport gems were available from the BBC Radio One sessions, I would quibble with the choice of 'Mr Lacey', but it was a treat to have 'Poor Will And The Jolly Hangman' made widely available. 'Sweet Little Rock'n'Roller' from the LA Troubadour was reckless and riotous, lacking the primness of Thompson's reading on *The Bunch*.

The most intriguing addition to the Fairport canon was 'The Ballad Of Easy Rider', significant inasmuch as it was recorded at the *Liege & Lief* sessions, during which Fairport were deliberately altering the direction of English rock'n'roll. The inclusion of such a steadfastly American song was revealing. Although credited to the Byrds' Roger McGuinn, Bob Dylan is known to have had a hand in the song's creation. Obviously inspired by Dennis Hopper's *Easy Rider, the* cult film at the time Fairport were recording their seminal album, Sandy Denny handles 'The Ballad . . .' with her familiar aplomb, and Thompson's solo is typified by his restraint.

Linda injects an ache into one of rock and soul music's most aching songs. Her vocal on 'Dark End Of The Street' is elemental and enriching. Thompson's sombre, acoustic playing only underlines the song's darkness.

All that darkness is kicked into touch by a seat-slashing version of the Cliff Richard hit 'It'll Be Me' which follows. Originally recorded by Jerry Lee Lewis, Cliff had the British hit. 'The British Elvis', was a firm favourite in the Thompson household during the late 50s. Richard's sister Perri was at school with the daughter of Cliff's producer, and was present at the original 1959 recording session for Cliff's debut album, recorded 'live' at EMI's Abbey Road Studios. On the second *Doom & Gloom* collection, Thompson was to include a live cover of Cliff's 'Move It', widely hailed as the first authentic British rock'n'roll record.

Hokey Pokey contributor David Thomas identified 'Flee As A Bird' as a Clog Dance from Kerr's *Second Collection of Merry Melodies for the Violin*! An interesting choice for Thompson, given that it was recorded in the middle of his reclusive period when clog dancing was rarely a feature of the Thompson household.

It was for the two lengthy guitar, vocal workouts that the record was remarkable. Guitar solos by guitar heroes were traditionally flamboyant exercises, guitar solos were for showing off. But here, Thompson lets his solos build organically, growing and developing – particularly on 'Night Comes In' – to a terrifying, shrieking conclusion. Thompson's singing has gained in confidence and there is a strength, a sureness to his vocals here. The power of Thompson's playing is undeniable, but what lends the songs structure and muscle is the foundation laid by Dave Pegg's bass, and particularly, Dave Mattacks' ferocious drumming. Throughout, John Kirkpatrick's accordion playing adds spectral atmosphere and ghostly colouring to the composition.

Thompson saved the best until last: 'Calvary Cross' is a breathtaking reading. Thompson's singing is possessed, he sounds like he's truly lost in music, immersed in his muse as certainly as any Dervish trance. John Kirkpatrick shadows Thompson's guitar, and Pegg's bass soars to unimagined flights of fancy as Thompson reaches further and further toward the precipice.

The reviews accorded *Guitar, Vocal* were the first intimation that Thompson was finally being recognised as some sort of buried treasure of British rock. The care which had gone into its compilation, the quality of the writing and the blazing intensity of his playing couldn't fail to entice the critics.

It was ironic that they came too late to Thompson. At the time of *Guitar, Vocal*, Thompson seemed determined to give up on music. It was doubly ironic that his talent should finally be appreciated at a time when the UK music scene was convulsed by the first tremors of Punk.

Many wrote of the excellence of *Guitar, Vocal*, few as eloquently as Angus MacKinnon in *Street Life*: ' "Calvary Cross" is unrelenting, Thompson's song to his Muse ... A cluster of guitar harmonics before Thompson drains every last reverb echo from the song's stately chords. The painful, dignified climb to Golgotha. Two verses with chorus preceding another instrumental stretch. Kirkpatrick trails Thompson's every step as he breaks away from layered rhythms into a frantic coda. More harmonics, silence, applause quickly faded. Catharsis.'

Chapter 16

LINDA: 'I DON'T KNOW what the catalyst was, but Richard suddenly seemed to be open to leaving [the commune] not to stop being a Muslim. He said "But we have nowhere to live" and I said, "Yes we have, because I held on to the flat without your knowledge", so we came back down to London. It was tough, he didn't really have a life, then when he got out into the world again, I think he'd really just wasted his twenties and thought, I'm going to do something in my thirties.'

Thompson allowed himself to be led back into the jaws of the monster. But first, he did some tentative toe-dipping. He was back 'wailing away' on Sandy Denny's *Rendezvous* during 1977, while he and Linda contributed backing vocals to the country-blues sea-shanty 'Poor Old Horse' on the Albion Band's triumphant 1978 album, *Rise Up Like the Sun*.

Rise Up Like the Sun was produced by Joe Boyd, back in harness for the first time since he quit to join Warner Brothers in America at the outset of the decade. The Fairport fusion was furthered by Ashley Hutchings, Dave Mattacks and Simon Nicol joining together nearly ten years on, to recreate the *Liege & Lief* rhythm section.

Talking to Colin Irwin in *Melody Maker*, at the time, Thompson spoke of Fairport and folk-rock: 'I think it's become increasingly uninteresting. I haven't heard anything interesting in that direction . . . apart from the Albion Band, who are sort of an eccentric version of it. What they're doing is very interesting, but then Ashley's always exploring . . . Folk-rock became a very blinkered thing. It went up this alley, and couldn't get out. It seemed rather absurd, it had one particular approach and in the end it never varied.

'It became so cliché-ridden, and they weren't even good clichés . . . It didn't move. The way it should have moved was for the pendulum to have swung back a bit towards what everyone was doing before they entered folk-rock. Be it a simpler way of playing traditional music or a more straightforward rock'n'roll music, and blowing up the influences a little bit more. It went up a cul-de-sac, which wasn't to my taste and I didn't enjoy listening to it.'

The song that concluded the original vinyl version of *Rise Up Like the Sun* was the marathon 'Gresford Disaster', an account of a 1934 colliery tragedy. John Tobler and David Suff's sleeve notes for 1992's CD release of the album, reveal that one early version incorporated brass band arrangements with John Tams and Thompson trading alternate verses. It was revealing that on one of his first post-*Pour Down Like Silver* recordings, Thompson not only returned to the markedly English tradition of the Albion Band, but worked on a song about a specifically English incident which evoked the rich brass sound he had used so effectively on 'I Want To See The Bright Lights Tonight'.

Over the years, John Tams has spoken with something approaching reverence of Thompson's abilities. No mean tunesmith himself, Tams was for many years a member of the Albion Band and the moving force behind the Home Service. As musical director on a number of National Theatre productions during the 1980s, Tams was always keen to incorporate Thompson's songs ('Night Comes In' featured in *Dispatches*; 'We Sing Hallelujah' and 'Calvary Cross' in *The Mysteries*).

Speaking to Ken Hunt for *Swing 51*, Tams paid Thompson the ultimate compliment: 'He's the greatest all-rounder. He's the Ian Botham of the music business as far as I'm concerned ... I regard him more highly as a writer than anyone else in the kingdom ... "Poor Ditching Boy" ... draws directly from the tradition so marvellously. And yet, it can be easily wrought either way, depending on whether it's sung by an unaccompanied group, when you wouldn't know it from a traditional song, or done with an electric rhythm section, when it will move somewhere else ...

'I understand a bit of [the guitar] – I know where to plug it in and turn it on – but after that, he goes somewhere else, and I don't understand how he can continue to develop so massively in all his skills, as a writer, singer and guitarist. He's quite the finest we've ever developed. I'm only glad that he comes from here. I've spent so much of my time idolising great American bands and musicians that it's really good to be able to stay at home and idolise somebody from the home country.'

From a discarded 1972 Thompson demo tape, Albion Band mastermind Ashley Hutchings had selected two songs for the *Rise Up Like the Sun* sessions: 'Rainbow Over The Hill' and 'Time To Ring Some Changes', a masterly composition which Thompson himself did not release until the live *Small Town Romance* in 1984, although he went on to re-record the song for 1990's *Hard Cash* collection. The song is worth studying in some detail as it encapsulates a number of perennial Thompson themes. As well as his cleverness in harnessing unpalatable truths to a stirring melody, 'Time To Ring Some Changes' also evinces Thompson's black humour. While written from the heart, his tongue is firmly in his cheek as the song piles up its impact in triplet.

The vocal pairing of John Tams and Simon Nicol is masterly. 'Time To Ring Some Changes' is quintessential Thompson. Opening with the image of a crumbling old house and its apathetic landlord, Thompson uses the building as a symbol of a decaying England. The song is one of the few in which Thompson wears his outrage on his sleeve and although written in 1972, the song still had resonance during the post-Punk year of 1978. The picture is of a world where nobody and nothing can be trusted, where there is no value in anything:

Oh the politicians they look so smug,
You say 'tell the truth' and they give you a shrug,
You might find the truth swept under the rug ...

Even before his conversion to Islam, Thompson had been wary of superficial glitz:

So you fall in love with the girl you've seen,
Diamond-studded on a TV screen;
The change in your pocket won't buy you a dream ...

The song offers some hope, but the composer cannot resist a sting in the tail of the concluding line:

But everything you do leaves you empty inside.

'Rainbow Over The Hill' from the same 1972 Thompson demo, was recorded at the *Rise Up Like the Sun* sessions with Linda Thompson on vocals. Intended as a 1978 Albion Band single, it remained unreleased only appearing in 1992 as a bonus track on the CD reissue of *Rise Up Like the Sun*. Featuring some striking guitar from the Albions' Graeme Taylor (one of the few guitarists who can muster Thompson's intensity and sustaining emotion on electric guitar), 'Rainbow Over The Hill' is largely unremarkable, save for its refrain:

Rainbow over the hill,
Rainbow over the hill.
Rain clouds lifting,
Just when you think they never will ...

Richard Thompson

The idea that rain clouds should lift rather than pour in a Richard Thompson song makes this a noteworthy addition to the canon.

Another project which occupied Thompson during 1978 in the lead-up to his official comeback album, was Julie Covington's debut solo album. Covington had reached no. 1 the previous year with the first single taken off Andrew Lloyd Webber and Tim Rice's long-overdue follow-up to *Jesus Christ Superstar*. *Evita* was the most eagerly anticipated theatrical event of the decade, and got off to a flying start with Covington's 'Don't Cry For Me Argentina'.

Julie Covington – popular largely thanks to the TV series *Rock Follies* – landed the title role for the record of *Evita* in the face of massive competition, but shock waves were felt all along Shaftesbury Avenue when, to her eternal credit, Covington declined to play the role in the stage production though it would certainly have established her as a major player on both sides of the Atlantic.

Joe Boyd: 'I met Julie Covington, and she asked me to do her single, the A-side was "Only Women Bleed", and the B-side was "Easy To Slip", a Lowell George song which I knew Richard knew. So I got Simon and Mattacks and Pegg, and we went to Olympic, and supposedly this was the first time Richard had played electric guitar for X number of years. Simon was almost in tears, so moved by the experience of hearing Richard play – because he was playing brilliantly. I remember Simon saying "I just can't believe that this guy is going to give this up".

'Julie is a wonderful singer, and she had this gigantic, worldwide hit. She then turned down the opportunity to play Evita in the West End, to go on tour with the Ragged Trouser Theatre Company ... one of those left-wing theatre companies. Richard Branson, on the strength of *Evita* ... signed her up. Then she started to agonise about what she should do. She had Branson and Simon Draper suggesting all sorts of things; they had in mind that she would do show tunes and theatre songs.

'The truth was that her private collection was the McGarrigles, Sandy Denny. Then it just so happened that I was going out with Diana Quick, an actress who was a friend of hers, and we went out for dinner with Julie, and she basically said will you produce a record? I was a bit dubious about the whole thing, but agreed to do the single, which worked okay, and was a hit ...'

Julie Covington, the album, is a Richard Thompson/Fairport Convention record by extension. Produced by Joe Boyd, with Thompson as the featured guitarist and a roundup of the usual suspects including John

Richard and Linda

Kirkpatrick, Simon Nicol, Ian Matthews and Trevor Lucas. Besides 'I Want To See The Bright Lights Tonight' which was the album's opening track and single, Covington included John Lennon's 'How', Kate Bush's 'The Kick Inside', Sandy Denny's 'By The Time It Gets Dark' (which Sandy had not herself released) and Anna McGarrigle's 'Dead Weight'. It remains a remarkable record though inexplicably unavailable on CD.

Joe Boyd: 'We got involved in Julie's album, and decided to bring over an American rhythm section of Andy Newmark and Willie Weeks and a keyboard player, Neil Larson, and I asked Richard if he would play guitar. And the first day, these three Americans had no idea who this guy was, he was just some funny looking, very schtumm English guy. By the end of the first day, the three Americans were open-mouthed at Richard. I remember Andy Newmark came in and said: "This guy is unbelievable, who is he? Where's he been? What does he do?"

'At that point, I rang up Jo Lustig, and I said: "Listen, if you have any sense at all, you will seize this opportunity. I've got these guys over here, you'll get a good deal with them. We've got two or three off days in the middle of Julie's sessions and then they can stay on until the end, there's time available at Britannia Row." This was after the experience with Ian Whiteman, and I said if you're ever going to get a record out of Richard now, this is the time to do it. The material is there and these guys love Richard, they're gonna kill to play with him. It would be great.'

The release of *Guitar, Vocal* had reminded people of the scope and depth of Thompson's music, although his records still weren't selling outside of a small circle of fans. Bernard Doherty, who was still working for Thompson's manager Jo Lustig, felt that Thompson's songs deserved to reach a much wider audience: 'Jo really tried to push Richard's songs. "Never Again". We thought that was a must for a Joni Mitchell-y, Julie Felix-type, and I used to spend hours looking up managers, get an address to send them a song. Jo really tried to get Richard's songwriting away, to try and get some royalties coming in.'

Jo Lustig: 'The thing with Richard was, his albums weren't expensive to make, there weren't any parties or promotions, he didn't need tour support. He was a good act to have. Same with Capitol now, if he sells a couple of hundred thousand, they're happy.'

Following a decade with Island Records (beginning with Fairport back in 1968), Thompson had switched teams in 1978, when Jo Lustig negotiated a new deal for Richard and Linda with Chrysalis Records.

Richard Thompson

Chrysalis was started as a booking agency in the late 60s by Chris Wright and Terry Ellis. Jethro Tull and Ten Years After were the label's original strengths and Chrysalis became pioneers of the Prog scene, signing Procol Harum, Gentle Giant and Blodwyn Pig. The mid-70s saw a run of hits with Steeleye Span and Leo Sayer, but it was the astute snapping up of Blondie in 1977 that gave Chrysalis their crack at the title. Blondie was one of the most successful of the bands thrown up by the Punk boom, with five UK chart toppers in under two years.

Jo Lustig had already landed deals with Chrysalis for his clients Steeleye Span, Mary O'Hara and singer-songwriter Richard Digance, so the label seemed a safe haven for the Thompsons. 'Richard and Linda Thompson occupy a unique place in contemporary British music', ran the opening lines of the Chrysalis press release which accompanied the release of *First Light* in October 1978.

Emerging from three years self-imposed exile to make a new album for a new record company, Richard Thompson found rock'n'roll had transmogrified into Rock Music, and was now officially Big Business. Rock was now out there pitching in a multi-media, global marketplace. Pink Floyd – Fairport's fellow travellers on the London Underground of the late 60s – were now capable of selling out any stadium anywhere in the world; their 1973 album *Dark Side of the Moon* had become one of the top-selling titles of all time.

It was no longer a question of shuffling into the studio, bashing out a dozen tunes, releasing an album, and hoping no one would notice. The 1970s were the decade that rock'n'roll grew up and entered the marketplace.

Punk had kick-started rock'n'roll again, but it was not a global phenomenon, and relied on the buzz-saw enthusiasm of teenagers who were capable of swiftly changing allegiances. In short, Punk didn't sell. What the record companies were looking for was another Elton John, a self-contained singer-songwriter. Someone who could sell to the teenagers who had grown up with the Beatles and were now entering their sedate thirties. The 1970s was the decade which polarised pop: caught between the brazen single salvos of the Sweet, T Rex and Mud and the introspective bedsit bardery of James Taylor, Carole King and Don McLean. Into this unfamiliar territory Richard and Linda Thompson nervously crept. Chrysalis were treating *First Light* as a high-profile project and reluctantly Thompson agreed to promote the project to the best of his ability.

Talking to Colin Irwin in *Melody Maker* immediately following the release of *First Light* Thompson explained his years away from the cut and thrust of the music biz ('Quite honestly, I just got cheesed off') and spoke frankly about what had been and what was to come:

'It's very hard to live your life according to music, I refuse to do it. I think music has to be a hobby for someone like me. Do something else, and music is the thing you do at the dance on Saturday night . . .' Later on, Thompson opined: 'It's very strong stuff, music. Very powerful. It can have a variety of effects depending on its quality. It can have a physical effect, it can drive people mad, it can give people courage, it can make people terrified, it can put people to sleep, wake people up, put people into trances, it can kill . . .'

The impetus for *First Light* came from Thompson's immersion not only in the religion of Islam, but also its culture. Much of the material on the record was directly inspired by the Prophet Mohammed ('Sweet Surrender', 'Layla' and 'First Light' were all devotional compositions, thinly disguised as love songs). 'Strange Affair' and 'First Light' were translations of existing Arabic texts, while 'Layla' was inspired by a 'an ecstatic song of yearning' which Richard learned from an Algerian teacher.

The other 'Layla' was familiar to millions of rock fans as the first release by Eric Clapton's alter-ego outfit Derek and the Dominoes, and has been a hit for Clapton at precisely ten yearly intervals since its initial success in 1972 (in 1982 as a straight re-release and in 1992 the *Unplugged* version). Clapton's 'Layla' was an intense, pleading love song to his true love Pattie Boyd, then inconveniently married to Clapton's best friend George Harrison. Clapton had been inspired by a Sufi friend Ian Dallas, who had lent the guitarist Nizami's book *The Story of Layla and Majnun* ('Layl' is Arabic for night).

'The Choice Wife', an Irish jig popularised by piper Willie Clancy which both Planxty and the Chieftains had recorded, led into Thompson's own composition, 'Died For Love', the most authentic 'traditional' song he had ever tackled. Ironic that an album which characterised Thompson at his most Islamic, should also feature a song so close to the subject and structure of traditional English folk balladry.

Bert Lloyd called the traditional 'Died For Love' 'one of the best-known English love songs'. For the sake of completism, he identified an 'obscure connection' between the song and 'A Sailor's Life' which, of course, had been the starting point for Fairport Convention's long journey, ten years before.

'Don't Let A Thief Steal Into Your Heart' is the Thompsons' unconvincing stab at the prevalent disco trend. Richard contributes some piercing guitar, but the song is best remembered as the one that got away. ('The Pointer Sisters covered it on an album,' said Linda. 'The only album of theirs not to go platinum, typical.')

'Strange Affair' is one of the couple's most haunting songs. Thompson translated it from the Arabic poem 'Song and Praise of the Shaykh' by Si Fadul al-Huwari, but only the first two verses of the song are included here, the third 'missing' verse can be found on the demo version, included on 1985's *Flypaper* compilation, *Doom & Gloom From the Tomb*. Linda has never sung with such quiet fervour as here and Richard's vocal, echoing his wife's, lends the performance a ghostly aspect.

The album's most secular song is one of only two joint compositions in the couple's six-album career (the other was 'Did She Jump Or Was She Pushed?'); 'Pavanne' was a lyric of Linda's, which came to her almost entirely in a dream, with Richard merely tinkering with the structure. The song was 'inspired' by the activities of the Baader-Meinhof terrorists, who were violently active in West Germany at the time. The title comes from a sixteenth-century Spanish dance (the 'slow, courtly dance' of the song's final verse). Perhaps the most cinematic of all Thompson songs, it switches scenes with a sure touch, from casino to presidential palace. And all the while, the assassin (born with a silver spoon in her mouth like Ulrike Meinhof), stalks her prey. Linda's chilling vocals match the woman 'with eyes cold as the barrel of a gun'.

'House Of Cards' took its cue from the tumbling cards in *Alice in Wonderland*, but harks back to the crumbling house in 'Time To Ring Some Changes', another metaphor for a decaying and corrupt political system. It is worth recalling that the bankrupt government the Punks railed against and which dissatisfied Thompson at the time was the last Labour administration; Jim Callaghan's government collapsed in 1979, paving the way for Margaret Thatcher and seventeen years of Conservative rule.

The album closes with 'First Light', Thompson's devotion to the Prophet Mohammed, 'my only hero' he said at the time.

Of his new songs, Thompson told Colin Irwin: 'Arabic's a very strong language, a very powerful language, an extraordinary language. There's this ... vast stock ... and in Arab countries it's still sung as pop music. There's all this twelfth- or thirteenth-century Egyptian ... very ecstatic poetry, and it's still sung on Egyptian radio with strings, electric guitar, drums. It's as well known as Shakespeare or the Beatles.'

Looking back, Thompson is particularly scathing about the albums recorded during his period at Chrysalis: 'Maybe those records should have had more thought put into them – a bit more of an overall philosophy. I just think they're kind of slipshod records where there wasn't enough thought and enough planning in the songs or in the overall idea of what it's supposed to be. *First Light* sounds like it's trying to be commercial in a really kind of pathetic way, without understanding what that really means. Commercial not being something that we were particularly good at, except on our own terms. It was leaving our own terms and trying to be something else. It was trying to be something to please other people, which I'm very bad at doing.'

John Kirkpatrick: '*First Light*, I remember Andy Newmark, Willie Weeks and Neil Larson had all come in to play on a George Harrison record. They hung around to do a record for Julie Covington as well. Richard's record was done in the same studio around the same time. It was a really big, meaty sound ... It was a very different approach. I don't remember him being any different himself ... I'd say Richard has changed much more since he's been in America than he did over that period.'

Drummer Andy Newmark and bassist Willie Weeks were a rock'n'roll Sly and Robbie, *the* rhythm section for hire. By the time they came to record *First Light*, they had already worked with Sly and the Family Stone, the Doobie Brothers, Steve Winwood, Donny Hathaway, Roxy Music and George Harrison, while ahead lay John Lennon's final sessions.

Richard: 'Probably the record I like the least is *First Light*, I really don't like it ... They were all great musicians, but it was probably just stylistically a wrong call ... To me the record sounds kind of wrong and I'm not mad about the songs. It's a half-baked record. I really didn't think enough about the material.'

At the time Colin Irwin was typically effusive in his *Melody Maker* review, calling *First Light* a 'formidably outstanding work'. He also put readers' minds at rest assuring them that *First Light* doesn't plough the same thankless furrow as the bleak and thankless Islamic tour of the previous year.

In the *NME*, Graham Lock was less enthusiastic, but reluctant to dismiss the album: 'I want to see the bright lights again. *First Light* is too distanced, too subdued. A cold, heavy elegance.'

Back on the road with John Kirkpatrick, Sue Harris, Dave Pegg and drummer Dave Sheene, Richard and Linda played a dozen gigs to promote *First Light*. The set obviously drew heavily from their current album, but dipped back to Fairport days to include 'Genesis Hall' and tipped its hat to Phil Spector with 'Then He Kissed Me'.

Chrysalis were happy rather than ecstatic at the sales of *First Light*.

Richard Thompson

Thompson had played the game by record company rules: he had toured to promote current product, undertaken press interviews to whip up interest in the album and had pitched 'Don't Let A Thief Steal Into Your Heart' as a single to generate further interest in his latest waxing. But the sales of *First Light* were unremarkable. Despite being Thompson's best-produced record to date, he still couldn't crack the 20,000 barrier in Britain. To have written and sung a song such as 'Strange Affair', and have it so widely ignored, was an understandable source of frustration to both Richard and Linda.

A year passed, then the Thompsons were back on the road again to promote their second Chrysalis album. *Sunnyvista* was probably the weakest album the Thompsons ever lent their name to. Richard was intrigued by the possibilities of the Roland guitar synthesiser, an expensive guitar-triggered keyboard which he had first employed on *First Light*. This new toy together with Thompson's Islamic beliefs, probably explain the lack of distinctive guitar on both his Chrysalis albums. *Sunnyvista* is the more overtly political of the two, which may go some way to explaining its fundamental weakness. The cover track portrays a smiling future, which owes more to Aldous Huxley's *Brave New World* than the bleak Orwellian *1984*. But the satire is heavy-handed, and there is a weary feeling that it has all been done before.

The same sense of tired political comment is apparent on the record's opening track 'Civilisation', a butterfly-breaking wheel of a song. For all the compassion taught by Islam, Thompson is at his most cursory and dismissive here: pre-packaged food, television, nine-to-five working routine, car worship, fantasy sex ... all the tired old targets incur Thompson's indignation. Where once we may have expected compassion for life on the treadmill endured by the majority of working people, now there is only scorn: ('You're a vegetable, with a heartache').

Sunnyvista is a testament to Thompson's Islamic muse, while the Dylan-esque 'You're Going To Need Somebody' and 'Why Do You Turn Your Back?' also testify to Thompson's beliefs. However the 'Allah, Allah' refrain of the top-heavy 'Justice In The Streets' offers little in the way of hope or encouragement for the rest of us.

The atmosphere is lightened by the cajun-style 'Saturday Rolling Around' with Kirkpatrick's swaggering accordion well to the fore, and by the traditional folk elements apparent on 'Borrowed Time'. Weak and one-dimensional as *Sunnyvista* is, Thompson is too canny a musician not to understand the need to leaven the bread. So space is also found on *Sunnyvista* for some of Thompson's best ballads ('Lonely

Hearts', 'Sisters', 'Traces Of My Love') – songs which allow Linda full reign of her astonishing vocal range.

'Lonely Hearts' is everything the title track isn't. Shot through with compassion and care, it evokes the desolation and isolation of big city living. Here is the world of lonely hearts columns, and the enforced, transient solitariness of living in a capital city where you daren't take the chain off the door and your only companion is a blank TV screen. That honest and heartfelt sympathy is the song's strength, and what makes it all the more outstanding is its inclusion on an album which reeks of heartlessness. *Sunnyvista* is both uncomfortable and smug. A caption in a bottle, thrown by the chattering classes to the unredeemed and the underprivileged. The writer seems to have little sympathy for those who are opiated by television, who survive on junk food and have no ambition beyond a win on the weekly football pools.

Like so much of *Sunnyvista*, the cover was an ill-conceived stab at satire. The Camden housing estate pictured on the sleeve later went on to win an architectural award. Talking to Linda just after the album's release, she told me: 'The cover was a mistake. But then all our covers are mistakes. I don't know how we do it, but we seem to have the worst record covers in the universe.'

Richard: 'I don't think it's a great record. We had a lot of trouble with rhythm sections on that record – we tried a lot of different things – stuff didn't work. I think it's the last record we used Timi Donald on – Timi had a kind of a style which suited the seventies but as we were getting out of the seventies, he was probably too on-the-back-of-the-beat to really make it happen.'

Bernard Doherty's memories of the album are more specific: 'I remember being in the office and being sued by Thomson Holidays, because some bright spark at Chrysalis wanted to "get attention" ... We used their logo, and we got a nasty letter. I don't think it was ever taken off the shelves. They threatened litigation, but I don't think they ever sued.'

Among the cast of thousands credited on *Sunnyvista* are Squeeze's Glen Tilbrook, Thompson's old chum Marc Ellington, Kate and Anna McGarrigle, and someone who would soon play a more significant role in Richard and Linda Thompson's professional career.

Chapter 17

GERRY RAFFERTY FIRST STAKED his claim in partnership with Billy Connolly. The Humblebums assiduously worked the folk clubs of the late 60s, but Connolly's between-songs patter soon began taking priority over Rafferty's more melodic material.

Rafferty's debut solo album, 1971's *Can I Have My Money Back?*, united him with fellow Scot Joe Egan, and the pair went on to form Stealer's Wheel, who though massively popular in the mid-70s, were stalked by bad luck and unreliable management. While the Wheel are best known today for 'Stuck In The Middle With You' (recently used in *Reservoir Dogs*) their first two albums were characterised by Rafferty's folk-influenced pop songs.

Post-Stealer's Wheel, Rafferty's career continued to be dogged by management problems and he looked set to remain a footnote in the pop encyclopedias, until a song lifted from his 1978 *City to City* album took him stratospheric. 'Baker Street' remains one of those pop songs, which once heard are never forgotten. Whether as another map reference in the pop lexicon of London, or a companion piece on any one of a hundred compilations; 'Baker Street' established Gerry Rafferty as a major player and is remembered for the best known saxophone in popular music.

Rafferty was an admirer of Richard Thompson's work and having guested as a backing vocalist on *Sunnyvista*'s 'Lonely Hearts', Rafferty returned the favour by employing Thompson as a session guitarist on *Night Owl*, the album which followed the worldwide success of 'Baker Street'. A further link in the chain was forged by one of Rafferty's band, the multi-instrumentalist Pete Zorn who later became an occasional, but essential, member of the Thompson inner circle. Zorn was born in America, but settled in the UK working as a session musician in the early 70s. The first meeting with his future boss was in strange circumstances: 'Richard came with Bernard Doherty to probably the least likely gig I had ever played: I was backing Dana ... We met up backstage and I thought "Oh God, what's he going to think". He was fine, because he does go to a bewildering variety of gigs, but even for Richard...!'

Gerry Rafferty took Richard and Linda out as his 'special guests' on the 1980 UK tour to promote *Night Owl*.

Bernard Doherty: 'They were well looked after on the Rafferty tour. It was just after "Baker Street", so there were good crowds. He was being very nice to us; he was obviously a fan. We could use their PA, their roadies would set everything up for us. We just had to turn up.'

However the Rafferty tour didn't do much to help the flagging *Sunnyvista* and Chrysalis passed on the option to renew the couple's contract. So while Jo Lustig did the rounds to secure the Thompsons a deal, the couple went into Dave Pegg's Woodworm Studios in Oxfordshire during June 1980 to record some demos for their next album. Richard and Linda re-worked 'For Shame Of Doing Wrong' (from *Pour Down Like Silver*) and covered Sandy Denny's 'I'm A Dreamer'. Linda was keen for Richard to record more of Sandy's songs. 'Richard does not like recording other people's songs,' Linda told Ken Hunt in *Swing 51* at the time of the release of *Shoot Out the Lights*. 'I suppose maybe especially Sandy's. I'd like to record Sandy's and Nick's [Drake], but he'd never hear of it. Maybe it would bring back memories for him which he doesn't want to dredge up again.'

That Thompson relented and recorded 'For Shame Of Doing Wrong' and 'I'm A Dreamer' was due to Sandy featuring them on what proved to be her final album, *Rendezvous*. Sandy's premature death in 1978 was caused by tumbling down a flight of stairs; she died a few days later of a brain haemorrhage. Her death had a profound effect on all those who knew her, and elements of 'Did She Jump Or Was She Pushed' were taken to refer to Sandy's demise.

Thompson denied the song was specifically about Sandy's death and in 1981 he told me: 'I don't think of [the songs] as being gloomy. I think of them as being serious, about serious subjects. Most of them are, in fact, optimistic. But Shakespeare wrote a lot of tragedies, and you don't go and stick your head in the gas oven after you've seen *Hamlet*. "Did She Jump Or Was She Pushed" is like a cinematic song, a journalistic song. You're not making judgments, you're recording events, recording someone's path through something – which path people choose to take.'

As well as half a dozen songs which found a place on *Shoot Out the Lights* when it was finally released in 1982, Thompson also recorded demos of the lolloping, cajun 'Lucky In Life', as well as the male chauvinist anthem 'Modern Woman' ('you'll never see the wind blow the

Richard Thompson

style out of her hair/She's cool as a snake, and some say it doesn't end there . . .'), complete with hallmark, gutsy Thompson solo. Thompson also demo-ed the priceless 'How Many Times Do You Have to Fall (Before You End Up Walking?)', which was memorably rescued by Simon Nicol for inclusion on Fairport Convention's *Gladys' Leap* album. Thompson's own version has only surfaced on the (now deleted) CD *Small Town Romance*.

'Speechless Child' was also recorded at these demo sessions. I can remember seeing Richard and Linda during a series of shows which Ashley Hutchings had overseen at Joan Littlewood's old Theatre Royal in Stratford East during 1979, with each night emphasising a different strand of the Albion Band. Richard and Linda were special guests one night, and this was one of the songs they performed. The response was astonishing, that tiny Victorian music hall rang to the rafters, the audience mesmerised by the subdued power of their performance. Ashley came on and explained away the lack of encore by saying something like: 'There are very good reasons why Richard and Linda are here, and very good reasons why they can't do an encore.'

Even by the standards of a man for whom bleakness had become a byword, 'Speechless Child' is beyond bleak. Linda sings of an autistic child, 'in a place where no one can reach you, a better place than this cruel one'. With Richard's delicate guitar and Linda's heartfelt vocal, 'Speechless Child' is both stark and immensely moving.

Badly burned by management himself over the years, Gerry Rafferty shared Thompson's wariness of record company politics, so while Jo Lustig was pursuing major labels, during the early autumn of 1980, Rafferty stepped in and offered his services. The plan was that Rafferty and his long-time partner and co-producer Hugh Murphy, would underwrite the cost of the next Richard and Linda Thompson record. Rafferty would then tout the tapes of the finished album around the record companies, the highest bidder getting a 'Gerry ("Baker Street") Rafferty Presents Richard and Linda Thompson' album.

It was too good an opportunity to miss. Even Thompson could see the commercial potential of the carrot dangled before his eyes. A smooth, Gerry Rafferty-produced album could act as his entrée to the lucrative American market. 'Baker Street' had reached no. 2 in the States during 1978, and while he couldn't cut his music to such commercial cloth, Thompson appreciated that Rafferty knew what would constitute a successful, radio-friendly album in America. Lustig was keen to capitalise on Rafferty's success following 'Baker Street' and Rafferty was keen to work more closely with the great Richard Thompson.

Richard and Linda

Rafferty block-booked Chipping Norton Studios in Oxfordshire during September and October of 1980. Among the musicians involved were Rafferty's rhythm section of bassist Pete Zorn and drummer Liam Genockey, and on keyboards and backing vocals Hugh Murphy's wife Betsy Cook – with whom Linda went on to work following the Thompsons' divorce. There were also the familiar faces of John Kirkpatrick, Simon Nicol and former Albion Band medieval multi-instrumentalist, Phil Pickett.

Pete Zorn: 'Rafferty was very much a fan of theirs, I think the songwriting was what attracted him ... Richard and Linda were without a deal, so Rafferty and Hugh [Murphy] put up the money to record an album, which they would then shop around. Apparently, they made the mistake of shopping it round to everyone at once, and everyone knew that it was being shopped around, and everyone turned it down. So they lost a packet on it. The last estimate I heard for it was £40,000.'

I interviewed Linda in 1980, at the time the Thompsons were recording with Gerry Rafferty, and it was all sunshine and light. She was convinced that following the poor sales of their two Chrysalis records, this was going to be the one to put them back on the map: 'It's good to have a musician at the helm. The new material is different; Gerry has been selective about the material. He has a great feel for continuity, whereas the last record was terribly disjointed, and a lot of the songs didn't go together ... It would be nice to sell records, not to the *Rumours* stage because there's nowhere you can go but down. But it would be nice to do 150,000, that would be great ... Gerry's more of a perfectionist than we are, and he's made us work a bit harder.'

At that time, the plan was to finish the album, hawk it round the record companies, and have it out during the first half of 1981. Proceedings were to be kicked off with the release of the album's first single, 'Just The Motion', which had just been completed when I spoke to Linda.

Thompson himself was equally sanguine about the project near the beginning. Talking to him in 1981, two years since *Sunnyvista* and a full year before the eventual release of *Shoot Out the Lights*, I asked why the Rafferty album had still not seen the light of day. 'We weren't able to sell it. It was recorded at what I suppose is average album cost these days, about twenty-five grand. And at the time it wasn't a good time to ask record companies for advances. I thought the Gerry Rafferty way was a way of approaching it, fairly lavish. I suppose I was attracted to the idea of doing it with Gerry because it was a way we'd never done it before. To go in and make an album which was viable for the American market.'

Richard Thompson

That the Rafferty-produced album never made it into the shops was also to do with the clash between artist and producer. The seeds of the problem lay in Rafferty's perfectionism, which jarred with Thompson's more spontaneous approach to recording. In the past, while recording, Thompson had tried to recreate a live sound as much as possible: lay down basic tracks, then the familiar guitar, vocal. Any overdubs were crisply and quickly undertaken, occasionally a guitar fill or some instrumental colouring. Backing vocals were grafted on, and you'd be out in the time it took Peter Gabriel to come up with an album title that wasn't 'Peter Gabriel'.

Richard: 'He wanted to finance a record and it seemed like a good idea at the time, but I found Gerry very hard to work with, I must say. Painstaking and fanatical on certain small details, which is irritating for other people. As a producer he wasn't a good communicator and he really wanted to do everything himself. I think that was the main problem as a producer, that he was more like the artist. He really wanted control over absolutely everything. When he got to the mixing, I just didn't bother turning up for the mix because if I said something it was totally ignored and I thought "hey, whose record is this anyway?" – and that was the last time I spoke to Gerry Rafferty.

'He wasn't able to place it anywhere – it wasn't a great record, it just sounded like our record with layers of Gerry Rafferty over the top. It sounded really kind of muddy, like a lot of his records did, but without the sort of panache of "Baker Street" which is a great record.'

Gerry Rafferty preferred a fuller sound; as a producer he believed in overdubbing repeatedly until he achieved the desired lush effect. Takes were recorded over and over again, until one matched his precise producer's ear. In record-producing terms, Gerry Rafferty was Phil Spector, while Richard Thompson was Nick Lowe.

Pete Zorn: 'The main difference and the design flaw between the Rafferty version and the released *Shoot Out the Lights*, was that Rafferty only knows one way to make records: lay down a good, solid rhythm track, overdub all the solos, overdub all the vocals. Richard is not at his best under those conditions. Most of the live vocals and guitar survived. We did "Don't Renege On Our Love" for a day and a half, and this is a six-and-half-minute track. We'd do the long fade, we'd sit there, and people would be talking for ten or fifteen minutes in the control room, not a word to anyone in the studio. Simon Nicol was playing in a corridor downstairs and occasionally you'd hear him say "Is everyone still there?" It was a terrible strain on everybody that way of working. Why not say "We're not sure, let's go straight to another one".

'It was sounding very clean, very polished, it didn't have any of the raw edge the songs warrant. It was neither fish nor fowl, and I'm not surprised that people passed on it.'

The two albums contained exactly the same material ('song for song' confirms Zorn). No alternate arrangements or unreleased tracks emerged from the Rafferty-produced Chipping Norton sessions. The fundamental difference was in the production. Talking to Ken Hunt in *Swing 51* in 1982, Linda admitted: 'I liked it [the Rafferty album]. I thought it was good. Richard hated it . . . But then I like slick stuff. I thought it was alright. I didn't see what was wrong with it at all.'

Pete Zorn came away from the Chipping Norton sessions buzzing with the strength of the songs: ' "Wall Of Death" was one of the ones I went away with, unable to get it out of my mind. It had that Byrds-revival type of thing, a very solid song. The first song since "Bright Lights" that sounded as though it was on the radio already.'

Although Thompson wasn't speaking to Rafferty by the end of the sessions, at least Rafferty and Hugh Murphy had a finished Richard and Linda Thompson album to shop around. The trouble was, nobody was biting. Every label to which the album was offered, including Virgin, Stiff, Charisma – even Rafferty's own label, United Artists – all passed.

Following the lengthy sessions at Chipping Norton, Thompson grew increasingly disillusioned with the mixes Rafferty was touting around during the early part of 1981. Even putting aside the manifest differences in recording strategy, Thompson felt that Rafferty had softened the sound of his songs and diluted the essence of his work, grafting on unnecessary sweetness where wormwood was required.

John Kirkpatrick: 'I suppose the Gerry Rafferty version of *Shoot Out the Lights* could be classed as "easy listening". If that had come out, their career might have gone in a different direction, because Gerry Rafferty had such a big hit around that time, and that sound was very acceptable to people.'

It was all academic, as the Thompsons remained without a deal and the finished album just lay dormant. Frustrated at the delays surrounding the couple's album and to while away the time, Thompson recorded his first solo album in a decade. 1981's *Strict Tempo* was Thompson's first record without Linda since *Henry the Human Fly*, and to date his only instrumental album.

Richard: 'I think we didn't have a deal at that point, it was hard to get a deal. Yeah, two records for Chrysalis, we weren't thrilled with Chrysalis, and I'm sure they weren't thrilled with us. So, I wasn't really sure what to do at that point, and so I think that the reason we did

Richard Thompson

Strict Tempo was as a kind of a sideways step – to make a record that wouldn't be seen as anything in terms of career, but it would just be product. It would be something to do, something to get on the shelves – or not! – without affecting a potential record deal of some kind. So that's what we did. As you know it was a remarkably cheap record – about £800 or something – I think we recouped it within hours of release. I think we'd actually driven round to HMV in Oxford Street and recouped! Delivered our own records!'

Bernard Doherty: 'I think John Martyn had just done a live mail-order thing, and he'd made a lot of money doing it, and Richard went ahead with *Strict Tempo*. That was the Richard Thompson album I wanted, I'd grown up with him sitting on stage playing guitar.'

Aside from Thompson on acoustic and electric guitar, bass, harmonium, mandolin, banjo, mandocello, dobro, hammer dulcimer and penny whistle, the only other featured player was Dave Mattacks (drums, percussion and piano): '*Strict Tempo*, that was great fun. A little eight-track in north London somewhere, the guy in the studio obviously didn't know Richard from a hole in the ground . . . we just went in and did it. If I recall, it was done with him playing rhythm guitar, me playing drums and he overdubbed. I'm very proud of that record. I think he owes me a large Remy for that, the number of times it's been re-released.'

The album's twelve tracks were simply some of Richard's 'favourite tunes, and I hope they may appeal to you too'. Nine were traditional, one was Moroccan, one was original ('The Knife-Edge') and one was a cover of Duke Ellington's 'Rockin' In Rhythm', which Thompson remembered from a 78 his father owned. The music which swirls around *Strict Tempo* sounds like being trapped inside a Harlem ballroom run by a jazz-loving Moor from the Scottish Highlands. *Strict Tempo* is the music of Thompson's pre-pop recollection, filtered through the miasma of childhood memory – of holidays spent in Aberdeenshire, and of trying to emulate the swirl and skirl of the bagpipes on the electric guitar.

Strict Tempo is an opportunity to relish Thompson's fluency on the guitar, electric or acoustic. The only overdubs he allowed himself were when he proved unable to play more than one instrument at a time! It was all a welcome relief from the elaborate Gerry Rafferty sessions of the previous autumn. *Strict Tempo* is the sound of Thompson having fun, like getting to impersonate the entire Duke Ellington Orchestra on two mandolins, mandocello and two acoustic guitars.

Thompson told me in 1982 that the album had shifted around 7,000 copies by mail order alone, and that 'the reason I did *Strict Tempo* was simply because I didn't have anything else to do'. *Strict Tempo* was the sole release on the Elixir label, which Thompson 'founded' and ran from Jo Lustig's office. But any plans to be a record company mogul were soon thwarted when Joe Boyd approached Thompson and asked him to inaugurate his Hannibal Records label.

Another one-off project which held Thompson's attention for six gigs during the summer of 1981 was the GPs, a short-lived supergroup featuring himself, Ralph McTell, Dave Pegg and Dave Mattacks.

Dave Mattacks: 'The Pope had just got shot, and my name for the group was the Grazed Pontiffs. The only thing on the book were a few dates in Ireland, during which we tried to keep the group name's origins quiet . . .'

I saw the band play at a warm-up gig at Putney's Half Moon the week before their official live debut. The Half Moon is a footnote to any Fairport/Richard Thompson history. Situated just down the road from where the Rolling Stones started out, the Moon began life as a jazz pub, before switching to R&B and folk. It is still going strong. Fairport often used it as a rehearsal space prior to Cropredy, and it was only just round the corner from Ralph McTell's home. So when the GPs were launched, the venue was obvious.

The music at the Half Moon took place in a dark, smoky room at the rear of the pub with the stage at the right hand corner at the back. It was always sweatier than a Mogul's turban in that back room, but that August night in 1981 when the GPs took to the stage, there was hot work afoot at the Moon.

The GPs were an opportunity for the principals to let what was left of their hair down. Thompson could stretch out on his favourite Hank Williams' Country tunes, rock out on covers of Eddie Cochran or Jerry Lee Lewis songs without having to worry about 'balancing' a Richard Thompson show. In the GPs, Thompson was just the guitarist and shared the vocal duties with Ralph McTell. He didn't have to concern himself with tempering the rock'n'roll with pensive, introspective self-written acoustic material. The GPs tore through their short career with the tenacity of terriers.

It offered Thompson the time and the place to indulge in his heartfelt, but little known, appreciation of Tamla Motown. One of the undeniable highlights of Cropredy 1995 was Richard's 'I Heard It Through The Grapevine', accompanied by Roy Wood's brass section. The GPs version of the 1964 'Baby Don't You Do It' owed more to the Band than Marvin Gaye's original. The band also featured Smokey Robinson's 'I'm The One You Need' in their brief lifetime.

Thompson also savaged 'Going, Going Gone', a frequently overlooked

Richard Thompson

highlight of Dylan's *Planet Waves* album. Thompson tackled the song with all the inconsolable tragedy of a penitent. But that was a rarely glimpsed side of the GPs – during most of their time together, the GPs were simply one of the best pub bands ever.

Dave Pegg: 'The GPs came about because Ralph McTell *always* wanted to be in a band, and he's not cut out to be in a band. It's like Martin Carthy when he bought his Telecaster and then hated it. Two of the world's best acoustic guitar players, and they both want Telecasters, the low strap, and to sing rock'n'roll songs.

'Richard didn't have anything to do at the time, and we were looking for somebody to headline the *Friday night at Cropredy*, and you think well, Ralph wants to play in a band, DM and I both love Richard's and Ralph's songs ... They both have such good taste. If you wanted to put a throwaway band together to go down the pub, what would you do? ... We only did half a dozen gigs, but we rehearsed for weeks in Putney at Ralph's house, it was just great happening music. You'd get Richard doing "Going Going Gone", which is much better than Bob's version.'

Richard: 'I thought the GPs was kind of irrelevant.

'It was supposed to be a pub band. It was to try and do something that would be a good platform for Ralph [McTell] especially, and Peggy and DM love playing covers and they get the chance to do it. Ralph's in a funny position where his audience is either blue-rinsed "Streets Of London" or it's *Animal Alphabet* under-eights, and he's this really great singer-songwriter but he's lost his audience because of a couple of career accidents, and the people who should be listening to Ralph have all gone. So I think Ralph's frustrated and he really just wanted to be in a band and get up with the lads and have a go. But I'm not sure it was actually a good concept and I didn't feel really happy playing covers – I don't really like doing covers to that degree, unless it's as a joke.

'I think they only did three gigs. If you only do three gigs it's always "legendary". But it wasn't what I wanted to do for more than three gigs.'

Succumbing to public pressure, Dave Pegg put out a fifteen-track CD of the GPs in 1991. It was recorded at the 1981 Fairport reunion which – for one year only – was held at Broughton Castle, the other side of Banbury from Fairport's traditional site at Cropredy. Dave Mattacks admits: 'I don't like my playing on that record, I think I was going through my pseudo-heavy metal phase at the time.'

The highlight of the 1981 Fairport reunion had been Thompson's cajun-styled 'Woman Or A Man', similar to his earlier triplet-structured 'Time To Ring Some Changes', and lyrically very much in the 'is-she-or-isn't-he?' style of the Kinks' 'Lola':

Richard and Linda

> She was the kind of woman that a man could crave,
> From her high-heeled shoes to her permanent wave,
> 'Cept maybe she was needing a shave ...

'Woman Or A Man' had originally been intended for *Sunnyvista*, but 'it was a bit lightweight,' Thompson told Ken Hunt. 'You know our records are very gloomy and depressing, so you can't possibly have a track like that on it!'

That 1981 reunion had also seen Judy Dyble emerge from parenthood and retirement to be coerced back on stage to sing a selection of songs she hadn't sung in fifteen years, then disappear back to a life outside Fairport again.

In his mini biography for the 1981 Reunion programme, Thompson has some fun and deftly re-invented himself as the only son of musical parents: 'Remember Bob and Betty Thompson and the Swing-Airs?' It is as a saxophonist that the other Richard Thompson shines: 'However, after Haberdashers and Sandhurst, a military career seemed inevitable.' Then, by chance, Richard chances upon 90-year-old Wally Swinburn ('the last of the "Anglian Crosscut" players') and his life is never the same again: 'Thompson's first four albums in the Swinburn style (*Anglian Heritage, A Swinburn Garland, Crosscuttin'* and *I Remember Wally Swinburn*) were all classics of their kind, but sold miserably. In desperation, he took up guitar, and filled in time playing with Fairport Convention, a popular group of the seventies ... Since leaving the band, Thompson has been working on a biography of his mentor and studying the Czab, the Bulgarian instrument which he claims is the missing link between "Anglian Crosscut" and the late forties dance band music of the style of Bob and Betty and the Swing-Airs.' Or maybe all that Richard wrote in the programme is true, and everything else is a lie ...

Two years after *Sunnyvista*, and still without a record deal, Thompson decided to resuscitate *Shoot Out the Lights*.

Richard: 'Joe Boyd appeared on the scene at some point and said "well, how about doing a record. We'll have to make it cheap because it's Hannibal Records – can we do a record for twelve thousand quid or something?" It seemed like a good philosophy at the time. Just strip back and make a quartet record with myself and Nicol and DM and a couple of bass players, Dave Pegg and Pete Zorn – and just keep it really simple. We salvaged some of the material from the Rafferty epic – and that's what we did.'

Chapter 18

JOE BOYD: 'I was then in a wonderful position. They were getting really anxious because they hadn't had a record out in quite some time, and there was another point at issue that Jo and I had argued about. When we talked about a deal, I had made a big point about touring America and Jo had said "Oh no, no, no ... We don't want to do little club tours. We want proper, major label release in America, and once the record's been a success, we'll go play Carnegie Hall." That was his way of approaching America, and I said "I think you're crazy. You've got to get Richard over there, playing, opening for somebody, playing the smallest club in town, it doesn't matter, just get him over there."

'So when they came back to me I said, "okay, here's the deal: we do the record in four days, and we'll take the money we would have spent on more elaborate production, and we'll put it into the air fares for the group to go to America." Richard said fine, Jo was muttering. But that's what happened. The catch was, it took more than four days to do Linda's vocals – she was pregnant, she had trouble breathing ... But it was clear the record was terrific from the minute we recorded it.'

Linda's pregnancy with the couple's third child, resulted in some of the more obvious differences between Rafferty's version of *Shoot Out the Lights* and the familiar released version. Voice problems necessitated swapping some of the song's vocals around – 'Wall Of Death' was originally conceived as a duet, but ended up with Richard taking the most prominent vocal role. 'Don't Renege On Our Love' was originally sung by Linda, but Richard took the finished vocal on record.

Diving into Barnes' Olympic Studios, Thompson undertook a cut-and-run version of *Shoot Out the Lights*. With Joe Boyd back behind the board, the eight-track album was finished in a matter of weeks, with Boyd capturing Thompson's preferred method of working – guitar, vocal cut live and as few overdubs as humanly possible. It was a record cut in direct response to Gerry Rafferty's *Shoot Out the Lights*, the antithesis of his multi-layered production.

Richard: '*Shoot Out the Lights* is just like a stage performance, you've got a stereo set up like a stage and it's basically live. All the records are basically live, to varying degrees, there's varying degrees of stuff added, or vocals re-done or whatever. Just about all the guitar playing's live all the way through – I very rarely overdub on guitar – solo anyway. If guitar bits get overdubbed, it's little bits of doubling or rhythm.'

Playing the Rafferty bootleg back to back with Boyd's officially sanctioned version, the differences are much less striking than you might expect. True, Rafferty's is lusher, but it's not a hanging offence. Whether the official *Shoot Out the Lights* is a better record than the one Gerry Rafferty slaved over is ultimately a matter of taste. But as the man with his name on the cover, Richard Thompson was surely entitled to his Director's Cut.

With his band Any Trouble in difficulties, Clive Gregson was delighted to be asked in to help out with the Joe Boyd version of the record: 'I was approached to do *Shoot Out the Lights*, I've no idea why. At the time of making the record, Linda was very heavily pregnant, and I think she was physically feeling a bit ropy, and they just felt it would be nice having a couple of people propping up the croaking . . . I don't know whether they couldn't get a deal with the Rafferty album or Richard scuppered it because he wasn't wild about the record . . . [Rafferty's] is actually a better sounding record than *Shoot Out the Lights* became . . .'

In fact, the Rafferty versions of the *Shoot Out the Lights* songs aren't as saccharine as Thompson believed at the time. Listening to the Rafferty record again after a ten-year gap, Richard was pleasantly surprised by how good some of the songs actually sounded, and sanctioned the inclusion of three tracks from the Chipping Norton sessions on the *Watching the Dark* box set.

Thompson's original judgment was certainly right on the Rafferty version of 'Walking On A Wire', the official version has a bite and menace the earlier one lacks. Thompson also shakes off his bitterness like black rain in a solo of sustained brilliance, shot through with venom.

Because of the events that took place soon after the 1982 release of *Shoot Out the Lights*, the album is frequently taken as the 'great autobiographical marriage break-up' record. It is worth remembering that these songs were first recorded in autumn 1980, well before either

Richard Thompson

Richard or Linda realised they had a problem with their marriage. Following the couple's separation and divorce soon after the release of the record, Thompson quickly tired of questions which treated *Shoot Out the Lights* as purely autobiographical.

Richard: 'The songs were already written, the album was already recorded and it wasn't really until we took it on the road that the marriage stopped happening. Whether it was remarkably prophetic songwriting or what, I don't know, or perhaps it's just a bunch of songs that I write anyway and maybe the songs fitted the interpretation. If you also figure that originally, I would sing a song of Linda's and she would sing a song of mine and then the keys got switched around, the vocals got switched round, it all adds to the confusion.'

Despite the writer's protestations and the time-scale which suggests that any autobiographical content must come down to subconscious premonition, there is something spooky about hearing a song like 'A Man In Need', or listening to Linda singing the first two lines of her husband's song 'Walking On The Wire':

I hand you my ball and chain,
You just hand me that same old refrain . . .

Even the cover suggested all was not well: Richard sitting grinning while his wife stared inscrutably down from a photo on the wall. In fact, Linda was pregnant at the time of the photo shoot and insisted on having a head-and-shoulders shot. But there was surely something, even from the outside, that suggested all was not well.

The title track was Thompson's response to Russia's 1979 invasion of Afghanistan. As a follower of Islam, Thompson supported the Muslim government, which had been overthrown by Brezhnev's invading armies. From the very beginning, the invading Russians were harried by Muslim freedom fighters, The Mujaheddin. The Russians occupied the country for the next ten years, and found themselves trying to combat a wide-ranging guerrilla war, bogged down just as the Americans had been in Vietnam.

Although inspired by the Russian invasion, there is a phrase in 'Shoot Out the Lights' which offers an insight into that very English, middle-class wish to repress anything approaching real emotion. It is typical Thompson:

Keep the blind down on the window,
Keep the pain on the inside . . .

Talking to Tom Russell in *Omaha Rainbow* in 1983, Thompson was asked about his background, and stated, emphatically: 'Middle class.

Totally. Suburban middle class. In the middle class you don't have the social stigma, but you do have this thing called extreme boredom. Which forces you to do something. You have to get out of the suburbs. The suburbs are death.'

In those stultifying middle-class suburbs, life goes on quietly, not in front of the children, and behind carefully drawn curtains. Nothing is revealed, much is unspoken. A characteristic of the English middle classes is their distaste for anything close to real emotion.

Shoot Out the Lights contains one of Thompson's best-loved songs, 'Wall Of Death'. As cut by Rafferty with Linda singing and overlaid with banks of Betsy Cook's keyboards, the original did diminish the song's dark impact. Even re-recorded, the composer is typically disparaging about the song's impact: 'The cheapest of all rock songs. Someone I worked with who does a lot of sessions, said every album he ever plays on there's either the circus song, or the fairground song, or the one about the clowns . . . It's just wanting to drive yourself to the edge – it's geeing yourself up to have the courage to live on the edge, it's like a sort of a mantra.'

'Wall of Death' is quintessential Thompson: it's living life on the edge, teetering on the brink. It is the best articulated of his tightrope-walking, high-wire balancing material:

Let me ride on the wall of death one more time,
You can waste your time on the other rides,
But this is the nearest to being alive . . .

No stranger to the circus and its place in the rock'n'roll repertoire (the Everly Brothers 'Ferris Wheel', the Beatles 'For The Benefit Of Mr Kite', his own 'Great Valerio' . . .), Thompson had no hesitation in utilising as many circus sideshows as he could envisage on the song. Thompson told me in 1981: 'I like fairground songs, and fairground imagery's great, because you can use it for anything. You can use all the rides as these real deep symbols for ongoing, living situations.'

Thompson has fond memories of seeing the 'Wall Of Death' as a child at Hampstead fair, with a motor cyclist riding around the inside walls of a giant cylinder, defying gravity, held up simply by speed and nerves of steel. It's a breath-taking image, and one which is wholly appropriate to Richard Thompson.

It's all there: the traditional English fairground imagery, the roller-coaster of emotions, the element of danger, the belief that life is at its most illuminating staring down the barrel of a loaded gun. 'Wall Of Death' is testament to Russian Roulette as the only game in town.

Richard Thompson

On its release, *Shoot Out the Lights* was greeted by the usual fulsome reviews accorded all Richard and Linda Thompson products. Angus MacKinnon in *Time Out* typically summed it up: 'All in all, another cornerstone from a master builder.' Gratifying as the reviews from the English press were, it was the American response to *Shoot Out the Lights* which took everyone by surprise.

Bernard Doherty had quit Jo Lustig's employ, and gone on to work with Joe Boyd to get Hannibal Records up and running: 'My abiding memory is of each day Joe coming back with a new mix, which we'd play on the ghetto-blaster in the office, and each one sounded wonderful. I think they knew they were onto something. And then all those amazing reviews started coming in – *Rolling Stone*, *Time* . . . We could not believe that this album was getting all that attention.'

Shoot Out the Lights cemented itself in favour in America. *Rolling Stone* particularly championed the record, voting it the ninth best album of the 1980s, and the 24th best record released during the magazine's twenty-year history. Thompson was chuffed at the response, and told the magazine: 'I think *Shoot Out the Lights* was a strong collection of songs. I'm flattered the critics think well of it. I wish it had sold a few more.'

Someone who knew what he was talking about when it came to guitars, Lou Reed commented in *Musician* magazine: 'I thought the guitar on *Shoot Out the Lights* was really, really good. I was absolutely stunned when I first heard it. I didn't believe anyone could do that anymore.'

Joe Boyd: 'I'd been led into the bonus track trap on CDs, and had put "Living In Luxury" on *Shoot Out the Lights*. I'd just forgotten completely that I'd done it and I was listening to it, and there it was, and I thought what the hell is this doing on here? I hate this song. I rang Richard up and I said we're redoing the package of the CD . . . let's take this opportunity to take "Living In Luxury" off the CD, and we can advertise "New! Improved! *Shoot Out the Lights* – without bonus track!" Which he thought was fine.'

Thompson had originally envisaged *Shoot Out the Lights* as the album to establish a foothold in America, which is why he had gone along with Gerry Rafferty in the first place. Now it seemed he had managed it on his own terms. Thompson hadn't been to play in America in a decade; he had never toured the States with Linda. His only USA shows had been with Fairport back in 1970, and briefly playing back-up to Sandy Denny during 1972.

Richard: 'I suppose in terms of myself and Linda as an act, we never went to the States, probably because of the family, having young kids. With three kids, it was always hard to plan an American tour – there never seemed to be time to go over and do it. I think Jo could have been a bit more instrumental in broadening our horizons. But I'm not sure we were really supplying him with the ideal material.'

Bernard Doherty: 'Jo was responsible for *not* sending him to America. When the money wasn't there, Jo didn't really try very hard ... Richard was sort of this thing on the shelf that was good for the cred of the company. Jo would fight tooth and nail for Richard. All that negotiating for record contracts, the big stuff that a manager would do, I had nothing to do with. I did a budget, if we managed to string five dates together – a folkie club here, a festival there – that was a tour.

'Richard was a bit lazy and wouldn't really push it. He would never come in the office and go "I want to go to America! There's flights on Virgin, this new airline, and you can get there cheap ..." If I had a complaint against Jo, bless him, he didn't really push Richard hard enough to go to America. There was a time he could have gone out there and carved a niche.'

Richard Williams: 'I don't remember any serious talk about whether Richard should go to America at that time ... It would be completely unrealistic to expect a million people to have a Richard Thompson album, and to put it on between Billy Joel and Paul Simon ... Richard always got great reviews, but the trouble is that each album gets the same review, more or less, and you were selling to exactly the same people.'

As soon as those American reviews began to appear, it was evident that a Richard and Linda Thompson tour of the States was essential. However, buoyed by the experience of recording *Strict Tempo*, and bored with the delays surrounding *Shoot Out the Lights*, Thompson was up for working without Linda, who was still experiencing difficulties with her third pregnancy. A handful of solo American shows was agreed for late 1981.

Jo Lustig ensured that Richard Thompson was the first act to headline at the City of London's prestigious Barbican Centre. Thompson appeared with John Kirkpatrick, Pete Zorn and Dave Mattacks at the first of the Barbican Preview Concerts on 24 November 1981.

A fortnight later he was appearing solo at a club called McCabe's in San Francisco. It was run by a 33-year-old native of California and folk-music enthusiast called Nancy Covey.

For those debut American solo shows, Thompson drew on a wealth of his own material, stretching back over fifteen years ('Genesis Hall',

Richard Thompson

'Beat The Retreat', 'I Want To See The Bright Lights Tonight', 'Never Again', 'Meet On The Ledge'), sprinkled with a familiar hybrid of covers ('Honky-Tonk Blues', 'Break My Mind', 'Dark End Of The Street', 'It'll Be Me'). Occupying the stage alone, with shows stretching up to two hours, Thompson was captivating. America was enchanted. Profiling him for *Rolling Stone*, Kurt Loder's piece was headlined 'Richard Thompson: Rock's Best-Kept Secret'. Reviews of Thompson's debut at McCabe's bandied around adjectives like 'flawless', 'staggering' and you-couldn't-buy-it hyperbole: 'Thompson ... proceeded to blow the capacity crowd away.'

Thompson returned to the States solo, early in 1982, paving the way for a full band tour to promote *Shoot Out the Lights*, which had been recorded in haste at the tail end of 1981. It was those January shows in New York which were recorded and later released as *Small Town Romance*.

At the end of one of his first New York shows at the Bottom Line, Thompson nervously asked 'Any requests?' Starved of his talent for ten years, he was met with a barrage of titles, which showered the stage like the English archers' arrows at Agincourt. One American fan even requested 'Throwaway Street Puzzle', the B-side to Fairport Convention's second single, 'Meet On The Ledge' back in 1968. Thompson declined, and delivered instead the unreleased 'How Many Times'. 'Anything anyone wants to hear?' he asked again. More shouts, then a snappy career summation from way at the back: 'Everything you've ever done!'

Pleased at last to have an album he was happy with available, the next problem was meeting the demand. Enthusiastic as it undeniably was, Hannibal remained a small, independent outfit, struggling to supply retailers with copies of the album. A major label would have been able to put more muscle behind *Shoot Out the Lights*, and more importantly, meet the distribution demands.

Bernard Doherty: 'Hannibal Records was financing so many different things, we had DeFunkt, Joe "King" Carrasco, Kate and Anna McGarrigle. Joe was mortgaging off everything, he'd sold the rights to his Jimi Hendrix movie. It was really the petty cash tin ... Joe was a really good producer, but when it came to the next project, if the money was there, he'd spent it. We had terrible financial problems. I think *Shoot Out the Lights* sold a helluva lot more copies than what Richard Thompson got royalties for. I think if it had been with a major, with the backing of a Warner Brothers, it might well have done all right.'

With the *Shoot Out the Lights* reviews flooding in to Hannibal's tiny

London office (*Time*: 'It is a record that has no contemporary equal ...'), and following the enthusiasm which had greeted Thompson's solo shows, it became imperative for Richard and Linda to quickly capitalise on that American interest.

Joe Boyd and Jo Lustig were agreed that America was finally ready for Richard and Linda Thompson. The problem was, that after a decade together, Richard and Linda Thompson were no longer ready for each other.

Chapter 19

RICHARD: 'I'M PROBABLY a bad communicator, so whatever I was feeling, maybe for a long time, probably didn't get communicated. And sometimes with relationships, you're not aware of how badly you're communicating or how depressed you are or how kind of lifeless your marriage is until you meet somebody else. Unfortunately that's the way it works usually. So you meet somebody else and go "Whoaaa, Crikey, where have I been for the last ten years?"

'So I think I was completely the instigator and the mover in breaking the marriage up. It was a terrible time to do it – we had a young baby . . . It's not something you want to do, it's just like you get hit by a truck I suppose. And you want to break up with your wife but it's the kids who suffer, it's always the same problem. It's very difficult – but it's like there's nothing you can do about it. There was no point in sticking together – having a terrible marriage for the sake of the kids or something – I really don't think that works – this is what our parents did and I'm not sure it was any better. So, it was a difficult time for everybody, it was a time to just grit your teeth and get on with it.'

Nancy Covey: 'The way it happened . . . I was staying with some friends in the north of England, and I'd seen a leaflet for the Fairport Festival, this was the year I'd turned down Cambridge, so on a lark, I took the train down to Castle Broughton. And I really liked it, the difference between that and Cambridge . . . I thought, this is interesting.

'I wasn't actually aware that Richard was playing, but that night, when we were all staying at the hotel, someone said there's Richard Thompson, and I thought well that's somebody I need to meet.

'He was sitting drinking coffee, everyone else was having a drink at the bar. So I went over and introduced myself, told him about McCabe's and had he heard from his manager that I wanted to book him. He said he'd wanted to go there for a long time. He said "Why don't you set something up, I'd be happy to go over". He gave me his home phone number and said "book something and let me know".

Richard and Linda

'I do remember meeting Richard at a folk club in Hampstead, I thought it was at a Brass Monkey gig, this was on a previous trip. I was sitting with Martin Carthy, I think, and I was introduced to Richard and Linda, I'm sure. But it was a thirty-seconds, "Hi, how are you?"'

Linda: 'I got pregnant, and I was very sick with Kammy. I remember Richard had to do a few things on his own, and he did one folk club up in Hampstead. I was going to go with him to see Bob Davenport, but I didn't feel very well, so he went up on his own. The club wasn't far from our home ... and that was the night that he met Nancy. Nothing happened that night, but then at Cropredy, when I was a bit more pregnant, they started up something. And that continued throughout my pregnancy, and then I guess he waited until the baby was born, and when the baby was about four days old, he left.

'He said "I've got to go and do some music in Florida" and he actually went off and had a holiday with Nancy. Then he came back and told me, and I remember him saying "I've got somebody else", and I said "Can she sing?" ...

'He told me she was thirty-four, the same age. So I thought that's good, at least she's not nineteen. That would be terrible for me. I'd just had a baby, you are out of your mind anyway when you've just had a baby, so it was very, very hard. Very difficult.'

Nancy: 'The irony of the whole thing is that Richard is a very moral person. We met, but the timing sucked ... It's one of those things, you're thrown together when you work together. When I met him at the club that had nothing to do with it, and even when I met him in Cropredy, it was business, I was trying to get him over to McCabe's.

'But then when I set up a solo tour for him in order to get him to play McCabe's, we spent a lot of time together, you know, at gigs and interviews. That's when we met each other properly and we spent a lot of time together – Jo Lustig was there too – things didn't happen then but ... it was interesting.'

Aside from the moral, marital and parental obligations, the Thompsons were committed to undertake a tour of the States to promote *Shoot Out the Lights*, their sixth and as it turned out, final album together. It was an important tour, Richard hadn't performed in America since the early 70s, and the couple had never appeared together there in concert.

The band comprised Richard Thompson (guitar, vocal), Linda Thompson (vocal), Dave Mattacks (drums), Pete Zorn (bass, sax) and Simon Nicol (rhythm guitar, backing vocals). They were committed to two dozen American shows. To all concerned, the experience became 'The Tour From Hell'. It was May 1982.

Richard Thompson

Richard: 'It was a really stupid idea to go on tour – I suppose Jo Lustig said, "Well, if you don't do this tour you'll never work in America again" or something. Perhaps it wasn't quite that strong, but I suppose we thought we should try and get through this for the sake of both of our careers.

'We should try and get through this tour, if we cancel it will look very bad to the punters because of the short notice. So we did it, it was a big mistake – relations were not very good – occasional violence, you know. It must have been very hard on the musicians – on Pete Zorn and DM and Simon – really tough on the lads.'

Linda: 'Richard didn't want me to go on the American tour. Jo Lustig thought I shouldn't go, but then said "maybe you should" – he was actually very good. And you know I'd always had these vocal problems, but as so often happens when somebody hits you on the head with a mallet, you forget about the pain in your foot. And as it happens – although it was The Tour From Hell, definitely – I sang very well. I'm sure I didn't really enjoy it, but in retrospect, it was great, because it completely freed my throat.

'We were committed to this tour, which was the first time we'd toured America together. Because we'd been Muslims and we hadn't been allowed to work for a long time, we'd never got round to touring America or Australia, or any of those places that wanted us to go . . .

'I think musically, it was a very successful tour. I mean, I was very wild. We did this club in New Jersey and I was trashing the dressing room, and they said "Jesus, the Sex Pistols weren't this bad". And I thought "That is so fantastic. I'm worse than the Sex Pistols"!

'Oh, I stole a car in Canada. In spite of all the pain, there were lots of liberating things. I was that kind of person anyway, but I'd really kept it in . . . so it was like Mount Vesuvius . . . and the singing was fabulous.'

There were enthusiastic audiences in Washington, Baltimore. Boston, Chicago . . . Everywhere the Thompsons played, the crowds lapped it up. *Shoot Out the Lights* had brought a new crowd, to join the old Fairport faithfuls, and those who had grown enamoured of Linda's singing back in 1974.

Richard: 'The marriage was basically over and going on tour with someone you've just broken up with and you are not getting on with terribly well, was a disastrous idea. I don't know how we got through it. I think we got to Santa Cruz and Linda bailed – I think she just didn't turn up for that one, so that one and I think San Francisco she wasn't there. I think we did well to get that far – it was just stupid. There were apparently some extremely highly charged performances – so I'm told!'

Richard and Linda

Linda: 'I used to trip him when he was going by onstage. I belted him onstage at one point. And of course, the audience loved it more than the music. People would say "I know you're splitting up, but you should go on working together". Which I actually would have done, but I know Richard wouldn't have entertained the idea.

'In New York, we were doing two shows a night, and I'd meet these mad people, like David Blue and Eric Andersen, after the first show, and wouldn't show up for the second show. When Linda Ronstadt came to the show in LA, and all the other musicians, I really felt good for the first time – people would say to me, without knowing what was going on with Richard – "My God, that was your show". So, stupid as it might sound, that was a big help. Because really I hadn't performed well for a long time ... So it was quite good to go out on a high.'

Joe Boyd, with both his record producer and label owner's hats on, was determined to get a souvenir of the tour.

Joe Boyd: 'The tour was a fantastic success. Linda sang like an angel, all that nervousness just went. It was clear from early on that it was a fantastic show – Linda's singing, Richard's playing, the whole thing was so intense. It became clear to me because of what was happening, that I had to record it ...

'The only place there were two shows close together was in the Bay Area, at Santa Cruz and the Great American Music Hall. I got a good deal for a mobile truck to record the shows. They were the last two shows of the tour, which I thought was good, because they'll be really honed, and before those dates was Los Angeles, which was the big emotional date of the tour, because Linda had lived in Los Angeles with me, she knew Linda Ronstadt, Carly Simon, all these people were friends from her time in LA ... It was also Nancy's home town, so it was like going to the heart of enemy country.

'She gave the performance of her life. The show at the Roxy was unbelievable, just an amazing show. Afterwards, Linda Ronstadt was there, and she enveloped Linda. She knew everything was going wrong, and she said "You're coming with me, we're getting you out of that crappy motel". There were two days before the next show at Santa Cruz, so Linda whisked her away to Brentwood. It was breakfast with Jerry Brown, a workout massage at Jane Fonda's Health Club, the whole bit. Linda just kind of collapsed, all the built-up tension, all the intensity there had been – she'd gone to Los Angeles, she'd done it, and it just poured out of her ...

'She had this wonderful, idyllic day and a half in Brentwood, with celebrities, being pampered and looked after ... Linda Ronstadt rang me and said "look, that's a ridiculously early plane to Santa Cruz, I'll get her on a later plane". So I thought great, she won't see the sound truck, because when I had said I wanted to record a show, she told me not to let her know when I was recording because she was so nervous.

'So I went to the airport to meet the later plane, and she wasn't on it. She apologised and said she just couldn't do it, but she'd be there for the last date in San Francisco ... They recorded the show without her. I met her in San Francisco, but for that show, it was as if the catharsis had taken place; the edge had completely gone, and her nervous tic was back, her pitch was bad ...'

The shows were electric. Linda had never sung better and Richard was playing with a subdued fire. As well as all of *Shoot Out the Lights*, Linda welcomed the opportunity to sing the songs her late friend Sandy Denny had made her own with Fairport, 'Genesis Hall' and 'I'll Keep It With Mine'. Richard also essayed 'Sloth', with ample opportunity for florid guitar work.

Loudon Wainwright III had first met Richard and Linda during the mid-70s, and had got to know them well as a couple. During that 1982 tour, he went along to watch a couple of shows from out front: 'He would stand in a corner of the stage, stoic is the only word ... She was falling all over the place. I think she was quite out of it, the two times I saw it. I don't know if she admits that now, but from having not had a drink for ten or eleven years, or a drug, being a good Muslim wife, Linda found out who she was: which is a tough chick from Glasgow. And that's what she became. She was out of control. And it was very exciting.

'I always felt Linda was a great singer, but onstage she was stiff. She would just stand there, and be all over the stage, and coming up to him, and singing at him, and he would be doing this aloof thing. Cold, cold ... It was great to see, because in the meantime, he would be firing off these great riffs and licks ... So the whole thing was terrific to watch. And if you went backstage, tears ... I thought it was a wonderful thing, from a musical point of view. But she was obviously in real pain.'

Obviously it was a traumatic time for everyone concerned. Committed to dates, locked together in a tour bus with the knowledge that the two principal players were in the throes of a separation, but that the show had to go on. It was particularly hard for old friends.

Dave Mattacks: 'Suffice to say the atmosphere on the whole tour was ... tense. Simon, myself and Pete Zorn, took to running away. There was some great stuff onstage, but it was not a pleasant tour ... They were communicating, when she wasn't kicking him ... I don't blame her. I don't blame her, I don't blame him. If I was in her position, I couldn't have got up there and sang "A Heart Needs A Home" . . .

'I don't remember the *Shoot Out the Lights* sessions being particularly stressful, but the American tour was very tough . . . When I say it was hard work, it was nothing compared to what either of them was going through, it wasn't easy being around them. In that position when you're touring with friends, the last thing you want to do is to be seen to side, so you're trying to play this middle ground, and deliver as a musician, and do the arm-round-the-shoulder bit to both of them.'

For Simon Nicol and Dave Mattacks, it was a particularly difficult time. Nicol was probably Richard's oldest friend but had known Linda for over ten years. Mattacks went right back to the Fairport days. Pete Zorn had come to it fresh, playing on both the *Shoot Out the Lights* sessions and could add a perspective to the whole eventful period.

Pete Zorn: 'Coming in to it at that stage, it was very difficult for me to figure out. Everyone seemed tense when Linda was around, which I thought was the norm. It was the first time I'd recorded with them . . . I couldn't work out if it was between those two, or the conditions he was working under. I think it was easier recording than it was on the road because they didn't travel well . . .

'Richard had certainly told Linda [that the marriage was over], he also told her, "by the way, we have a four-week tour of the States to do". Jo Lustig, to his credit, lied to her and told her it was a two-week tour. So two weeks into the tour, already nail-biting, I was sitting next to her in the bus at the back, she's looking through her purse for her plane tickets, and said "Wait a minute, this isn't right". I said "What's the matter?" "Well, I'm supposed to be going home tomorrow . . ." And everyone's going "What are you talking about? We've got another two weeks to do!" She went hysterical, literally. We were holding her down. By that time, there had been four major incidents, one in an airport.

'Richard was stoic throughout . . . We each let them know if they wanted to talk, we were there, but neither of them did, so from that point, we had our own tour, because it was the only way you could stay sane. In the end, you're all in that seven-passenger Chevy van the next day.

'Dave and I maintained that Richard would make out all the set lists for everyone and pass them out, and all you had to do was look at the first five numbers, and it was like "Man In Need", "Walking On The Wire", and you'd go "Oh nooo . . ." There was no pussyfooting around with it.

Richard Thompson

'Richard just left Jo to do what he does best, whatever that is. Jo just grew up with everyone who's important now ... He was never an organised entrepreneur. That was the "You're Not Dave Pegg" tour, because Jo had printed all the posters before he asked if Dave was available. I was second call, so I was nobody for that entire tour. At the end of every gig, somebody would always lurk up and say "You're Not Dave Pegg".

'It was the best of times, it was the worst of times. Onstage, it was fantastic. Linda was fantastic. Some of the things she would do as occasional one-offs, like "Pavanne", you'd just never forget. Even now, people in the States will come up and say, "I've got an old tape of one of those shows ..." and it really is stunning.

'It was, with a few memorable exceptions, the only neutral area. There were times when she kicked him in between numbers, things like that. Richard would do a "But seriously folks" kind of thing ... There was a place on Rhode Island, a pit of a gig, the dressing room was under the dance floor, and the promoter had to pull Linda off Richard. And always it was Richard trying to get to the other side of the room.'

Linda: 'I came back here after the tour. Richard stayed on in Los Angeles with Nancy. I stayed with Linda Ronstadt. She and Jerry Brown nursed me to health. It was hysterical. She was making me chicken soup ... She was fantastic. When we were doing the Roxy, I think she literally found me drunk in the gutter on Sunset Boulevard after the show and picked me up and took me to her house and I stayed there quite a while.'

As the word got out about the tangible onstage tension, *Shoot Out the Lights* came under closer scrutiny. Critics viewed it as the great autobiographical statement, believing Thompson had announced to the world it was all over via eight songs on a long-playing record.

The world got all the gory details from *Time* magazine on 30 August 1982: 'Each song has the clenched power and pitiless clarity of a Francis Bacon painting ... Their appearances become events. They are rites of passage for novitiates, acts of communion for initiates. The Thompsons put on shows of acetylene brilliance, but these events for them are something else entirely. They are an ending. The marriage has run aground. Further collaborations are uncertain. *Shoot Out the Lights* may have to stand as the summing up of one of the most extraordinary creative partnerships in rock. There is between the partners now the usual portion of blame and bitterness and confusion ...'

Talking to Tom Russell in *Omaha Rainbow*, Thompson called the the *Time* piece 'baloney. *National Inquirer* standard'. Reacting to the magazine headline: 'The Thompsons Create A Powerful LP Out Of A Broken Marriage', Thompson did go on to concede: 'What's disturbing to me is the fact that the songs are very relevant to that but were written two years ago. If it was true, then it was subconscious ... seeing something ahead. I was never aware of that possibility. It was all subconscious ... It's kind of worrying ...'

Nancy: 'It was unfortunate timing and I was not interested in being with a married man. He wasn't interested in fooling around on his wife. But people fall in love when they do, at inconvenient times. I had no desire to have a guy leave his family and I know that when we were first together, it never occurred to me that that would happen ... But I think it was a bolt of lightning for him too. He tried to make a go of it but he's not a guy that can lie very well.

'Linda had said, you know, if you go on the road, guys do what they do, I don't want to know. She probably shouldn't have said that ... It was a very horrible period. Richard will always feel bad, but you can't change what happened.

'I can't put words in her mouth, but it seemed to me like ... a catalyst for something that looked like it needed to happen. She's been married ten years, we've been married ten years ... I just wish that they had figured it out before me.'

Weaving through the Cropredy crowd during the blisteringly hot August of 1995, her lively 3-year-old son Jack in her arms, her eyes searching for the banner under which her American visitors are gathered, half an eye on the stage which is about to welcome her husband, Nancy Covey literally has her hands full.

Both wilting in the sunshine, we exchange greetings. Aside from the immediate concerns of finding her Festival tourists and getting Jack to sanctuary, Nancy clearly has something on her mind. She knows that our first interview left some unanswered questions. She feels that, in the public eye, Linda will always be Richard's wife, and that Nancy will always be typecast as 'The Other Woman', the second Mrs Thompson.

Nancy is concerned to put the record straight about the chronology of the split. We agree to try and find time in a schedule which includes her accompanying Richard on live dates in Belgium, Norway and Guildford.

After Guildford, the Thompson family decamp to their home in California for the rest of the year. There are all the worries of dividing your time between two homes, remembering you've left Fraser's *Golden Bough* in London, or The Band box set in California. With her husband not being the most ... worldly of men, Nancy knows she's looking at re-defining the word 'hectic'.

Richard Thompson

Just before she quits stage right at Cropredy, Nancy makes any further meetings redundant, as she encapsulates that whole tortuous and troubled period of a dozen years before. 'What can you say?' she asks, shielding her eyes from the bright sunshine. 'You fall in love with the right man, at the wrong time . . .'

Part 3
Solo

Chapter 20

NANCY: 'PEOPLE USED to write that Richard Thompson is now based in America. And we'd read it sitting in our horrible flat in Crouch End, with no heating ... He walked out with nothing; a guitar, a suitcase, no car.'

In Hampstead in 1995, Nancy Covey – now Richard's wife of ten years standing – looked back on those first difficult days together, thirteen years before. The Rubicon had been crossed, the die cast. Linda was left with the couple's three children, their second daughter Kamila having been born just before the couple split. Richard established a new home for himself and Nancy in north London, while Nancy who was still working at McCabe's, tried for a while to be on two continents at once.

Nancy: 'After the end of the *Shoot Out the Lights* Tour, Richard stayed on in the States. He didn't play any dates. They had broken up, which is why it was "The Tour From Hell". She said "why don't you stay with Nancy and see how it goes". She probably didn't think it would stick. But it did.

'I was at McCabe's, so I was in the States and he was here. I would come over. He would come over for tours. He had the kids, and it really tore him apart. It was very hard. We were actually trying to be based here, which was why I left McCabe's, because I couldn't commute over here.'

Nancy Covey was born in Los Angeles in 1948: 'My father went to Hollywood High School – where James Dean went in *Rebel Without a Cause*.

'My mother was very different from Richard's. She was a modern woman in the wrong era, the 50s. We listened to this folk music programme, which played Leadbelly and Odetta, while she was cleaning the house on Saturday morning. My sister was into Bob Dylan. I took guitar classes with my mom when I was twelve, playing folk songs. But I had long finger nails, I was not a guitar player. But I liked folk music and we'd see Sonny Terry and Brownie McGhee at the Ash Grove.'

Richard Thompson

Drifting through school in LA during the mid-60s, Nancy caught the wanderlust which bit so many of her generation: 'When I was twenty, I did the back-packing, hitch-hiking round Europe, staying in youth hostels for two years. I went to the Blind Faith concert in Hyde Park and Richard said he was there. He thought Fairport played, but he couldn't remember. I was there. All I could see was feet, but just think, if I'd gone up there and met Richard then, just think of all the grief we would have saved.'

Nancy returned to the United States during 1970, soon after four American students were shot dead by the National Guard during an anti-war protest at Kent State. It was an experience which left her bitterly disillusioned with the nation and its government under President Richard Nixon.

Nancy: 'So then I went through my rural hippie phase, I went to college in Oregon. I was studying to become a teacher, but – and do remember these were the hippie days – I also took courses in kayaking and Red Man's consciousness. I was drawn to this college because I'd read in an alternative college guide that the teacher lived in a tree house!'

Returning to Los Angeles with a couple of degrees, instead of working as a teacher, Nancy found herself: 'putting up posters for a Doc Watson concert at McCabe's, in Santa Barbara. The next thing is, I'm a partner with two other people and putting on a six-concert Doc Watson tour. I stood to make fifteen per cent of the profits, but they didn't tell me I would also lose fifteen per cent of the loss, which is what we did. Anyway, I was hooked.'

Nancy stayed at McCabe's for a decade eventually booking acts for the prestigious club which doubled as a guitar shop. It was liaising with Richard during his debut solo American dates late in 1981 which drew the couple close together. Immediately following the 1982 'Tour From Hell', Richard left Linda and began living with Nancy.

To his great discomfort, Richard Thompson found his life outside music public property. His career had always been conducted away from the headlines, except when his conversion to Islam in the 1970s attracted some media attention. The split with his wife and singing partner coincided with the release of their most acclaimed album together and re-stoked the furnace of interest. Despite fifteen years in the public eye, Thompson was still essentially a private man who squirmed as every interview and feature dissected *Shoot Out the Lights* for possible insights into the marriage break-up.

The coals were raked over and over, and Thompson just shut down the blind and pulled up the drawbridge at his tiny Crouch End home. Nancy – resigned to being forever seen as 'the other woman' in Richard's life – still had her job at McCabe's and her life in Los Angeles to escape to.

Nancy: 'I ran the concerts at McCabe's for ten years. Looking back, if there was a name for what I was doing, it would be "Unplugged World Music". But of course it wasn't fashionable then. I'd ask people down, get them to play without their band. I'd try to pay the musicians really well, I'd pay more than the Roxy and they didn't have to bring their band. McCabe's was a guitar shop; the concerts didn't make money on their own. Bobby Kimmel started the concerts and he was the bass player in the Stone Poneys, so he knew Linda [Ronstadt] and Jackson Browne used to come down and I took over from there in the early 70s.

'One of Loudon Wainwright's records was done at McCabe's, but we weren't allowed to sell drinks. So we did it like a private party, we gave away free champagne, it was like being on the airlines. Loudon wanted them to be a little bit loose. The difference in the audience was so amazing, I'd always had a sober crowd before and now they were laughing at every joke and it was a great night.

'Steve Goodman was someone I really wanted and it took me years chipping away at his manager ... When I had Flaco Jiminez on, this young band called up and said they'd play for free if they could open for Flaco. They said they were Los Lobos d'el Este de Los Angeles.

'The most exciting show was what I called "The Anniversary Show". It was my tenth anniversary and I'd decided to leave, so I just called everybody I knew. Officially, it was Jennifer Warnes, Richard, Van Dyke Parks and T-Bone Burnett on the bill. But then T-Bone brought Elvis [Costello] down and Warren Zevon and Jackson Browne were there. And when Elvis walked in, I remember the gasps.'

It was in the summer of 1984 that Nancy finally left McCabe's and moved to be with Richard full-time. Thompson was enchanted by his new companion, 'her surname is the collective for quails,' he boasted to the London *Evening Standard* at the time. With the most difficult decisions behind him, Thompson was again able to put all his energies into recording. With *Hand of Kindness* he left the darkness behind him and walked out into the light.

Nancy: '*Shoot Out the Lights* was written before they broke up ... By the time of *Hand of Kindness*, I think he was happier.'

Pete Zorn: '*Hand of Kindness* was a lot of fun. Three days for the basic tracks with everyone. One rehearsal, so everything was fresh ...

Richard Thompson

As ever, there was little or no tinkering with the songs once they arrived in the studio. Thompson is not one for amending lyrics or arrangements in the studio. Like Alfred Hitchcock, who could see every scene in a film in his head prior to shooting, and then found the actual filming to be a chore, Thompson has all the songs for an album mapped out before entering the studio, and once there, goes for a quick and untampered recording.

Clive Gregson: 'I got a call from Boyd to do *Hand of Kindness*. I heard the tracks and thought they were absolutely colossal. In losing Linda as a singer, Richard had not figured out what he wanted vocally. I think on that record he was a little bit stuck as to how to work it. So you basically have him, me and Pete Zorn, and it didn't really work, because we all have the same range, we all sound very similar ... He should have got another woman in to sing, but that really would have been nightmare city, eventually that's what happened with Chris [Collister] and I, but I think it needed a bit of distance.'

With the multi-instrumental Pete Zorn utilising saxophone as a counterpoint to John Kirkpatrick's roistering accordion, with Clive Gregson on board, and Christine Collister waiting in the wings, Thompson had the template for a long-term working unit. It was a framework which he would build on and use, on record and in live performance, for much of the next five years.

Joe Boyd: 'I enjoyed making *Hand of Kindness*, the sessions were great. The most memorable track for me was the take on "Devonside", which I think is one of the great live performances Richard has ever given. That was definitely a hair standing up on the back of your neck moment. It was pretty much all there, there are a couple of overdubbed backing vocals or something, but I think we used his live vocal and live lead guitar. He wanted to re-do the vocal, but I kept it.'

'Devonside' is one of those marvellously agile Thompson songs, which come from an accumulated knowledge of the folk tradition. It sounds like it was sung by George III's soldiers returning from the Battle of Lexington. But Thompson supplies a chill edge to the song, with the refrain of 'the shiver in her eyes'.

Hand of Kindness is a step away from the sombreness which dominated *Shoot Out the Lights*. The album retains its fair share of Thompsonian melancholy, but also brims over with the energy of 'Tear-Stained Letter', 'Both Ends Burning' and 'Two Left Feet'.

Shoot Out the Lights is still perceived as *the* album about Thompson's dissolving marriage, but if you're looking for clues, they abound on *Hand of Kindness*. A year in gestation following Thompson's decision to separate from Linda, songs such as 'A Poisoned Heart And A Twisted Memory', 'Where The Wind Don't Whine' and 'The Wrong Heartbeat' are all shot through with a weary reflection on love gone wrong. They may not be autobiographical in the strictest sense, but there can be little doubt about the events and the feelings which inspired Thompson to write them.

The most moving song on the record is the keening 'How I Wanted To', Thompson's most aching vocal in an age, set to a tune which weeps melancholic descending chords. There may be other elements to the song, but it still reads as an adieu to Linda, a song to say sorry for the heartache.

John Kirkpatrick: 'I really enjoyed *Hand of Kindness* ... When he played through "How I Wanted To", I wanted to go up and cuddle him because it was such a moving gesture ... I took it he was singing about Linda, all the things he wasn't able to say to her, kind of owning up, as himself ...'

It was producer Joe Boyd's idea to use Pete Thomas and Pete Zorn's saxophones on the track, to emulate the effect of Van Morrison's sublime 'Into The Mystic'. Although the saxes never made it onto the finished track, they did wind up on the lion's share of the record and there is no denying that they beefed up Thompson's 'sound'. With the textures John Kirkpatrick could produce on his accordion, there was an altogether richer strand developing.

Concentrating on the battle of the saxes, Thompson deliberately pushed his music away from the softer, 'folkier' sound with which he had been associated. Even before their personal problems, Linda's vocal difficulties had been forcing the couple toward a gentler sound, but with Linda out of the frame, Thompson could indulge in punchier rockers such as 'Two Left Feet' and particularly 'Tear-Stained Letter', which remains a perennial stage favourite.

Thompson's singing on *Hand of Kindness* had certainly inched up a notch. He sounded more confident, almost swaggering through some of the record's beefier songs. Talking to Ken Hunt just prior to the album's release, Thompson again denied any autobiographical element in the material: 'I wouldn't ever write a real blatant song ... I wouldn't do a Joni Mitchell, because that's not the kind of song that I like anyway ... I think ambiguity in music is a good thing ...'

Due to the perennial financial problems which threatened Hannibal Records, label-owner and album producer Joe Boyd remembers turning his hand to cover photography: 'My most vivid memory is of traipsing down to the riverfront ... In those days, Hannibal was even more broke than ever, and I ended up taking the cover picture.' The *Hand of Kindness* cover was shot only a few hundred yards from Richard's old stamping ground, Sound Techniques Studios, and coincidentally, a stone's throw from where his sister Perri now lives.

The *Hand of Kindness* reviews were uniformly excellent. Writing in *Time Out*, Geoff Brown was taken as much by Thompson's playing as his songwriting: 'The construction of the second solo in the rampant, rocking version of "Tear-Stained Letter" ... is breathtaking, opening further down the scale than Duane Eddy ever ventured and progressing upwards in a series of skittering runs. The sad, tender ballad "How I Wanted To" essays a solo of totally opposite import, each delicate note ringing rich and true.'

The Times found *Hand of Kindness* 'something of a triumph'. While in *The Guardian*, Robin Denselow preferred it to *Shoot Out the Lights*, and again singled out Thompson's playing as one of the album's enduring highlights.

Colin Irwin, writing in *Melody Maker*, called the album 'the most satisfying thing Richard Thompson has done since he strolled into a recording studio with Linda nearly a decade ago and knocked out the legendary *I Want to See the Bright Lights Tonight*. And, I shouldn't wonder, the best British album we're likely to hear all year.'

Thompson was consolidating his future and forged a close working relationship with long-time fan Clive Gregson. When I was working at *Melody Maker* during the early 80s, the Hannibal offices were just round the corner in Covent Garden. I remember Clive coming into the *MM* local the Oporto, after singing backing vocals on *Shoot Out the Lights*, as happy as a kid who'd got locked overnight in the sweetshop.

Clive's group Any Trouble, who the *Maker* had called 'The most exciting group since the Pretenders' had been dropped by Stiff Records after a couple of albums. To everyone, but chiefly, Clive's surprise, Any Trouble were picked up by EMI. It was on their final EMI record, 1984's double *Wrong End of the Race*, that Thompson contributed blistering guitar to 'Open Fire', as well as some sinuous picking on 'Lucky Day' and exuberant backing vocals to the cover of the Foundations' no. 1 'Baby, Now That I've Found You'. The latter song was written by Tony Macauley, for whom Linda used to sing demos back in the 60s, and just to further that Fairport connection, the Foundations were the group Dave Pegg tried out for in the morning, prior to his successful afternoon audition for Fairport Convention.

Even if he was still with a tiny UK independent label, Thompson's standing was at odds with his record sales. He was in demand and held

Solo

in awe. If a session interested him enough, he'd do it, cash was not the motivation. Between *Hand of Kindness* which was released in 1983, and *Across a Crowded Room* (1985), as well as helping Clive Gregson out with his floundering Any Trouble, Thompson appeared on albums by T-Bone Burnett, David Thomas and the Pedestrians, Dave Swarbrick, Loudon Wainwright III, J. J. Cale, the Golden Palominos and Swedish group Folk Och Rackare.

Loudon Wainwright III: 'I was making *Fame & Wealth*, and somehow got wind of the fact that Richard was in New York. I was producing the album, and hired Richard as guitar player. After a couple of over-produced records, *Fame & Wealth* was a voice-and-guitar record. Richard played on two tracks, a great afternoon. Spending some time with him, it struck me that he had lightened up considerably.'

Thompson also took to the road with a vengeance in that period between leaving Hannibal and signing with Polydor. The Richard Thompson Big Band comprised Simon Nicol (rhythm guitar, vocals); Pat Donaldson (bass); Pete Thomas and Pete Zorn (saxophones); John Kirkpatrick (accordion), Clive Gregson (guitar, keyboard. backing vocals) and Christine Collister (vocals).

The 'fun' switch was firmly on during that time. Ensuring that the horn section had plenty to keep them occupied onstage, Glenn Miller's 'Pennsylvania 6-5000' was a regular fixture. And among the familiar covers ('Together Again', 'Honky Tonk Blues', 'Great Balls Of Fire') Thompson set out to singlehandedly cause a Lord Rockingham's XI revival, with roity-toity covers of 'Hoots Mon' and his lordship's revved-up 'Loch Lomond'. On a good night, Thompson could also be persuaded to loosen up on 'Danny Boy'. But this was not the misty-eyed, Erin's green shore 'Danny Boy', Thompson took his cue from Conway Twitty's four-on-the-floor rockabilly re-working.

The 1984 release of the 'live/solo in New York' record, *Small Town Romance*, was as much a celebration of Thompson's independence as it was a musical statement. Thompson fans were fragmented, there were those who felt the need to cry 'Judas' every time he picked up an electric guitar, while others stifled a yawn when he went acoustic during the quiet bits of his amp-threatening big band gigs.

Small Town Romance is the only opportunity to hear Thompson's own versions of 'Time To Ring Some Changes', 'Woman Or A Man', 'How Many Times Do You Have To Fall?' as well as the otherwise unobtainable title track and the unremarkable 'Love Is Bad For Business'. 'Small Town Romance' is Thompson's scornful take on the withering effects of living in a pinched community. A place where

Richard Thompson

blinds twitch, inhabited by 'old flames with bad memories'. The album proved to be Thompson's swansong for Hannibal.

Joe Boyd: 'Richard is the best kind of combination: compromising and ambitious. After *Hand of Kindness*, Hannibal had an option, but in order to exercise that option, I would have had to pay him an advance greater than I could have afforded. I knew also that Hannibal had less money, less marketing clout than before, and that Richard would be better off taking such a good offer ... I worked out a deal where I agreed not to exercise the option and we would put out *Small Town Romance*.'

Small Town Romance was intended as a souvenir of the New York shows in 1982. It is a curio in the Thompson catalogue, such a curio that as part of a later settlement with Hannibal, he insisted on its deletion. Over the years Thompson has vowed to replace it with a live solo, acoustic record more to his liking. We are still waiting.

Richard: 'Touring solo is easy, I just go out with my tour manager Simon [Tassano], sometimes with Danny [Thompson] and it's great. We make it into a human schedule so we don't get wiped out, we're not working too hard or driving too hard. I mean how much money do you have to make, how rich do you have to be? On band tours you have to be a lot richer, but on solo tours it's economical and hopefully, with the band stuff, we can get to the point where that's economical as well.

'I don't think we've ever had anybody famous turn up backstage! There's always ones where someone says Bob's in the audience ... We had the Mayor of Milwaukee or something and there's the odd famous bank manager and mayors, because we're now that generation where our contemporaries are starting to run things. The odd White House aide, but no saxophone playing presidents – yet!'

Chapter 21

RICHARD THOMPSON MARRIED Nancy Covey at a small ceremony in Los Angeles on 6 January 1985. In attendance were fellow musicians Jerry Donahue, David Lindley and Albert Lee. The groom looked smooth and svelte in a bow tie and cummerbund. The couple honeymooned in Mexico. Music for the guests was provided by a popular local singing group, Los Lobos.

Further changes in Thompson's life included a new manager, Gary Stamler, who helped land him a deal with Polygram (for the USA) and its European arm Polydor during 1984. The deal resulted in what Thompson assured *Q*'s David Hepworth was the largest cheque he'd ever received ('It just about paid off my alimony'). Thompson's UK affairs for much of the decade were handled by Clive Gregson's manager, John Martin.

Richard: 'It seemed like a good place to go at the time. The vice president of A&R signed me, but he left the label almost immediately, so I was a little high and dry there for a couple of years without the support you need to get anywhere ... It can be really political. Sometimes if they get rid of somebody, they get rid of all that person's acts as well. And sometimes it's not for logical reasons. It's industrial rivalry.'

During Thompson's time with Hannibal, the recording industry had changed again. Punk had not made its predicted mark on record sales so the industry cast around for something that would sell. Enter the New Romantics, who flounced through the early 80s, strutting like peacocks and poking Punk's provocative ugliness in the eye. Glamour and superficial pop frippery were the order of the day. Adam Ant became the 80s first legitimate pop icon, followed by the synthesised *Smash Hits* pop appeal of Duran Duran, Haircut 100, ABC, Wham!, Eurythmics, Human League, the Thompson Twins and Culture Club. It was the success of those synth'n'style bands which paved the way for a second 'British Invasion' of the USA.

Richard Thompson

The release of Michael Jackson's *Thriller* late in 1982 had changed everything. Aside from going on to become the biggest-selling record ever (with sales of 48 million, and still rising), *Thriller* redefined the way the record industry marketed music. It was the first album to be exhaustively mined for hit singles – no less than seven of the album's nine tracks were lifted as singles for the American market – each accompanied by a lavish video. It marked the promo video's coming of age as a marketing strategy.

In the wake of *Thriller*, albums were seen as little more than supertanker vessels, bulk carriers of potential hit singles. And every single was a potential hit if it was accompanied by a video, because Michael had proved it could be done. Consequently, acts profoundly unsuited for the video age found themselves merely extras in their own movie. If the act was simply stylistically challenged, bright young directors, using pop promos as their passport to Hollywood, could usually fix things. But if the hairline was just too far gone for MTV, or the song didn't lend itself to the video treatment, record companies soon lost interest.

Thompson arrived at the tail-end of the video explosion. Polydor envisaged him as a prestige signing, a hallmarked ornament they could display on their corporate mantelpiece, and say 'Hey, we're not in this simply to make money. We also have quality artists like Richard Thompson'. By 1985, when Polydor released *Across a Crowded Room*, Richard Thompson's debut for the label and his first for a major since *Sunnyvista* in 1979, the marketplace was much more tolerant of established acts.

Punk had been a wilful gob in the face of the rock establishment. Shoving aside such dinosaurs as Yes, Genesis and Rod Stewart, the Punks went out of their way to trash any sense of rock history. Few would acknowledge anything before the Sex Pistols. 'No Elvis, Beatles or Stones in 1977' sang the Clash. But with Punk gone the way of all flesh, by the mid-80s, the new generation of bands were only too keen to wear their influences on their sleeve.

REM and the Smiths were only two of the new 'roots' bands who acclaimed the jingle-jangle, twelve-string guitar sound of the Byrds, as well as delighting in the arcane world of Nick Drake albums or Twinkle B-sides. The Pogues, Jason and the Scorchers and Los Lobos were only too happy to name-drop the Dubliners or Gram Parsons to anyone who cared to listen.

Ashley Hutchings had seen the future, and the future was the Pogues. Talking to him for a *Melody Maker* profile around 1980, I asked how he viewed the contemporary folk scene. Pausing over his

Cranks lunch, the founder of Fairport Convention, Steeleye Span and the Albion Band replied: 'I think it badly needs an injection of new blood, of enthusiasm ... We have tackled folk music from a knowledgeable, caring, academic standpoint. Maybe now it's time to tackle folk music without any preconceived ideas or knowledge, to play it as "garage" music'.

Barely months afterwards, garage folkies the Pogues were followed by The Men They Couldn't Hang, Billy Bragg, the Oyster Band and the 'rogue folk' of the English Country Blues Band. They were soon at the throat of the dance-obsessed, image-conscious music industry, with a couldn't-give-a-flying-one attitude.

A generation removed from the new bands of the roots revival, Thompson at least allowed them house room. Playing a gig at London's Dominion Theatre in April 1985 to promote *Across a Crowded Room*, Thompson had the Pogues and the Boothill Foot-Tappers as support.

It was an ... interesting night. The Boothills appealed to Richard Thompson fans with their infectious, good-time, banjo-led ceilidh music, even if it was more suited to the Town and Country Club than the intimate Dominion. But the Pogues were a different thing altogether.

Prior to Thompson's headlining appearance, large elements of the audience kept themselves amused with the football-style chant 'Richard Thompson, Richard Thompson, who the fucking hell are you?' At the end of the Pogues' set, their fans quit the auditorium, leaving Richard and his band to face their own familiar and politely appreciative crowd.

Richard: 'I felt stabbed in the back actually, I asked to have them on the show because I'd heard them and thought this is a great idea – this is the logical thing – punk-folk – so let's have them and the Boothills and make a whole evening of it.

'The Pogues were really rude and horrible and in some cases insulting – and their audience was totally, single-mindedly, only interested in the Pogues and they all left at half time – I should have anticipated something like that but I didn't. So I went from being a Pogues fan for five years to actually not liking them very much ... I still think that they were a good idea, but in practice, it didn't really serve the cause of Irish music to have another drunken Brendan Behan-style person falling all over the stage, because that had all been done, all that falling over bit, it was too much of a cliché.

'He [Shane MacGowan] is an excellent writer – but in terms of stage persona and in terms of style, it was almost the Irish equivalent of Jimmy Shand – the tritest of Irish music being recycled – perhaps that was the idea but it wasn't the best of ideas. I mean, do we really need another version of "The Wild Rover", even if it is the ninety second version?'

Thompson now found himself on the same label as the Style Council, Shakatak and Level 42. Polydor's approach to marketing Thompson during his two-album stretch with them was to emphasise his cult status: 'You may not know this and he certainly won't admit it but, in his own quiet way, Richard Thompson is a living legend' ran the label's inaugural press release to accompany the release of *Across a Crowded Room.*

In the time-honoured tradition of trying to titillate journalists' jaded palates, particularly those who perceived Thompson as some sort of 60s relic, the press release dropped lots of famous names.

REM's Peter Buck was quoted as saying: 'I've been listening to Richard Thompson since I was a kid and he's probably the best songwriter of the past fifteen years. I'm pissed off he never comes to Georgia to play. He reaches to the heart without being maudlin or excessive. What the hell, he's fuckin' great.'

The Smiths' Johnny Marr: 'When I was able to start putting chords together, I was turned on to Bert Jansch, Pentangle and Richard Thompson . . .' The press release concluded: 'Richard Thompson is the quiet legend. If you don't believe the critics, ask Elvis Costello, ask REM, ask Mark Knopfler. They know.'

Compact Disc had not yet established itself as the next big format, so to entice fans to buy both vinyl and CD, and therefore ensure a higher chart position, Polydor added a bonus track to the CD of *Across a Crowded Room*, 'Shine On Love'. A single ('You Don't Say') – with the additional incentive of a live version of 'When The Spell Is Broken' – was also released as a taster.

Cringe as he might at having to enter the market place in such a blatant manner, Thompson knew what he was undertaking when he signed to a major label. And Polydor's marketing strategy obviously paid off: *Across a Crowded Room* became the first album featuring Richard Thompson to achieve a UK chart placing since *Full House* in 1970. On its release in 1985, *Across a Crowded Room* got to no. 80 on the UK LP charts and remained there for a fortnight.

Joe Boyd: 'He asked me to produce *Across a Crowded Room*, which was not a condition of his leaving Hannibal, Richard just asked me to do it . . . I thought he had written a very commercial bunch of songs and I thought we'd made a very commercial record. I was very disappointed in the cover. It was very, very unfortunate from the point of view of trying to make it a good-selling record.

'Polygram were initially very enthusiastic about the record, but the fact is, it didn't really sell much more than *Hand of Kindness*. But then again, none of his records have sold much more than *Hand of Kindness*, which sold, worldwide, in the first five years, something like 60–70,000 copies, about half of what *Shoot Out the Lights* did . . .'

Richard: 'I've probably leaned too much on Joe Boyd who's a kind of naturalistic producer, which is fine up to a point. There are people who are very good at building in the studio, like Brian Wilson, taking it in bits and adding to it. It's quite hard to do that – it takes a certain kind of talent to be able to be totally committed and into it and emotionally attuned when the red light comes on.

'I find that, generally, what I do better is the stuff that is live, and so I try to make a virtue of what I do in the studio. Mitchell [Froom] has ways of making it sound a little more like a record and less like a performance. Which is something I've always wanted to do, I've always wanted to make something that was – not slicker – but that had the right "attitude" in the studio.'

To promote *Across a Crowded Room*, Thompson sat in Polydor's West End offices while a stream of journalists trooped through and asked him if the record was about the breakup of his marriage to Linda. Thompson was happy to talk to sympathetic writers and *Across a Crowded Room* is one of his most talked-up records.

Thompson regularly featured 'When The Spell Is Broken' acoustically. But this full band version is remorseless, with Clive Gregson and Christine Collister acting as a Greek chorus, offering little in the way of comfort ('Can't cry if you don't know how').

'I got interested in Elizabethan poetry,' Thompson told Colin Irwin in *Melody Maker*, talking about 'You Don't Say', 'and that song's expressing Elizabethan ideas. The Elizabethans struck me as being the last people who had a holistic view of existence. Pre-Descartes. Pre-Darwin. Pre-science really . . .'

In the second verse of 'I Ain't Gonna Drag My Feet No More', Thompson sings 'Where I come from, feeling is a crime'. It's more of that shutting out of emotion which informed 'Shoot Out the Lights'. 'It's sort of neo-Caledonian, pseudo 50s gospel. It's about not pursuing something as fervently as one should,' he told *Flypaper*.

'Love In A Faithless Country' is certainly one of the most chilling songs Thompson has ever recorded. His vocal too is icy, like a cadaver dangling from a meat-hook. There is something intense and Teutonic about the song, so it is no surprise to learn that the refrain was a translation of lines by Rainer Maria Rilke, 'Put out my eyes and I can see you still'. Thompson was inspired to write the song by the early 60s Moors Murders committed by Ian Brady and Myra Hindley: 'They murdered without the usual kind of motive, like jealousy or money, just for the fun of it' (*Flypaper*).

Swaggering and boisterous 'Fire In The Engine Room' is another of those seemingly effortless variations on 'Wall of Death'. Interesting that on his first record release since his marriage to Nancy, Thompson should choose to describe a wedding ring as 'a rattlesnake wrapped around your finger'.

A vehement, political piece, 'Walking Through A Wasted Land' tips its hat in equal measure to T. S. Eliot's 'The Waste Land' and Ewan MacColl's 'Dirty Old Town'. To Ken Hunt in *Swing 51*, Thompson revealed: 'It's a song . . . about the brutality of government . . . Regardless of governmental policies, I just feel that the way in which they were enacted, and have been over the last five years, are very inhuman. It doesn't take into account people or people's feelings. I think that a lot of the changes that have happened in Britain over the last five years have been inevitable regardless of who'd have been in power. It was always going to involve a lot of unemployed people, but it could have been tempered considerably, and I don't think there was enough effort made to do that. I just dislike greatly the attitude of this government.'

By the time 'Walking Through A Wasted Land' was released, Thatcherism had really begun to bite. In 1982, unemployment topped three million for the first time since the Great Depression of the 1930s. The inner cities had been devastated by riots during 1981. A second Thatcher victory in 1983 followed the Falklands war. And by 1984 Thatcher had turned her attention to 'the enemy within', the Miners' Strike highlighting the two-nation state of Britain during the mid-80s.

Richard: 'I've never felt the need to champion any particular British political party – I've thought they were all severely faulted, so it's easier to just criticise and ham and spoof and that sort of stuff. I think a lot of the kind of personal songs can be considered political and vice versa. Politics starts with two people – so, often, rather than writing a political song, I've written a sort of political metaphor. Political songs sometimes have a short shelf life. I think there's a time and place for them absolutely, but I think other people probably do it better.

'There's absolutely the time to stand up and be counted – there's a time to write the overt political songs that says, you know, kick out the tyrants or throw off your chains – you are many, they are few. Absolutely a time for that. I'd like to write more political songs. I probably will.'

'Little Blue Number' is rock's most unashamedly fashion unconscious song since Dylan's 'Leopard Skin Pill-Box Hat'. To Ken Hunt in *Swing 51*, Thompson revealed: 'It's . . . fun to write those kind of songs where you talk about something like clothes, you just list stuff. Again, I think it goes back to someone like Chuck Berry, who was great at writing about cars, because he'd burst into these lists of chrome this and supercharged that.'

Thompson commented that 'She Twists The Knife Again' 'reminds me of the Zombies, there's a kind of mid-60s structure to it' (*Flypaper*). Live, Thompson would disconcertingly introduce the song as 'She Knifes The Twit Again'.

In *Musician* magazine, Bill Flanagan drew comparisons between the imagery on 'Ghosts In The Wind' and 'Dimming Of The Day' a decade before. Thompson responded: ' "Dimming Of The Day" is a pretty straightforward love song. It's a different house. Well, it's the same house, I suppose. It's always the same house. It's always the same damn song. It's a different part of the same house.'

For the first time since *Henry the Human Fly*, a Richard Thompson record did not receive ecstatic reviews in the UK. Maybe it was the songs. Or maybe it was the fact that *Across a Crowded Room* was for a major label and a sort of inverted snobbery put the critics' backs up. It was the time of the Indie boom, small independent labels seen as Davids battling the industry's Goliaths. The Smiths and Aztec Camera were venerated on Rough Trade, Frankie Goes to Hollywood on ZTT, the Cocteau Twins and This Mortal Coil on 4AD.

But all the indies did was offer the illusion of independence, the majority were distributed by major labels, who sported them like trophies displayed in corporate boardrooms. Confined to the convenient and critic-proof ghetto of Hannibal, Thompson was safe; signed to a major, he was fair game.

Typical of the reviews was that from long-time admirer Colin Irwin in *Melody Maker*: 'The upsurge of the new folk boot-boys, from the Pogues to William Bragg, may do much to focus attention on one of the true, enduring heroes of the genre . . . This, simply, is the most powerful, single-minded rock album he's ever made. Not, necessarily, the best . . .'

While in *Rolling Stone*, Kurt Loder wrote: 'longtime Thompson listeners may find that, compared to much of his past work . . . *Across a Crowded Room* is faintly disappointing. Such are the burdens of inveterate brilliance. For his cautious re-entry into the commercial big leagues, Thompson . . . apparently decided to accentuate the more

Richard Thompson

accessible rock'n'roll aspects of his art ... Those unfamiliar with Thompson's work are invited to dismiss all of this as purist nit-picking. *Across a Crowded Room* remains a compendium of expertly constructed songs, played and sung with real heart and recorded with an exciting, live-in-the-studio crackle. Rare is the artist from whom such excellence can come to seem a letdown.'

Clive Gregson: '*Across a Crowded Room* is the first record Chris [Collister] and I did together, and we got drafted into the band ... I met Chris in the death throes of Any Trouble. I'd seen her sing in a folk club in Manchester and originally I was just going to write some songs, produce some demos for her. I did a solo record just for the crack. Chris sang on some of that, so we slowly got together ...

'Again, Boyd rang me up and said "Richard's doing another record, do you want to sing on it?" I said at that point that I think we need to look at it a different way. And I said "I've met this girl who's brilliant, why don't we give her a shot?" We were originally booked to do two songs, but we got in there and it was great so we did the whole record.'

Christine Collister was born on the Isle of Man. After a stint as a Butlin's Redcoat, she landed the prestigious 2–6 a.m. slot on Manchester's Piccadilly Radio. For eighteen months, Christine repeatedly sang 'Fire and Rain', 'Desperado', 'American Pie' and 'Killing Me Softly'. She first saw Thompson at a folk club in Poynton in 1984 ('somebody said there was a good guitarist on'). Six months later, she was singing on *Across a Crowded Room*.

Clive Gregson: 'Chris didn't do any lead vocals, we were very much the backing vocalists, so I don't think there were any immediate comparisons with Linda ... I think that he had consciously put that distance. He'd done a few tours, he'd done at least one record without Linda, so people had realised it was a different ball game.

'The original sessions for the album were cancelled because DM put his back out ... It was his first album for Polydor and in some ways Richard was very conscious to maintain his independence. I remember talking to him and he was saying he wouldn't take tour support from them because this meant that you were in their pocket ... So it was very much held together with glue and string on the road ...'

To promote the album Thompson undertook a six-week American tour, with a band featuring Clive Gregson and Christine Collister. The newcomers were Ruari MacFarlane on bass (who worked at the company which had distributed Hannibal Records) and drummer Gerry Conway who was a Witchseason stalwart, notably in Fotheringay with Sandy.

Clive Gregson: 'Six people, bangin' round in a van. It was very much a cult thing, playing clubs, it's interesting to see how it's got bigger . . . The first time we played Minneapolis, we played the First Avenue, Prince's club. That'd be a thousand people and then there'd be the Iron Horse, which was eighty-four people, and it was packed!

'The first gig I ever played with Richard was in 1985, at a theatre in Philadelphia opening for Jean-Luc Ponty which was a bloody nightmare . . . This was the first time with this band. We'd only rehearsed a couple of days, but I knew most of the stuff anyway. So he goes "Right I'll stand off on the left hand side and you can stand in the middle". We did the gig and it was completely bizarre. I had to say to him "Look, I don't think this is such a great idea. You should stand in the middle, because it's your group, and we'll stand either side of you." But it was almost like if he could have got away with it, he'd have played offstage.'

In February 1985, just prior to the American leg of the *Across a Crowded Room* tour, Richard Thompson undertook some low-key dates in Britain.

John Kirkpatrick: 'Richard and I did a world tour, of Benfleet! There were about ten dates. It was very strange, he was living in this one-room flat in Chalk Farm with Nancy. We rehearsed in this room. Folk club people asked if they could book Richard and I as a duo. I thought probably not, but I asked and he was up for it.'

In a year which saw him touring both with an electric band and as a solo, acoustic act, Thompson was only too keen to play some dates with the pressure off. Prestige dates with Kirkpatrick included Benfleet's Runnymede Hall ('adjacent to Castle Point Council offices on A13'), Yesterday's Folk Club in Bristol and the Rockingham Arms in Wentworth, south Yorkshire.

Thompson had called in the Electric Bluebirds' accordionist Alan Dunn for *Across a Crowded Room*, as Kirkpatrick was already committed to American dates with his and Martin Carthy's group Brass Monkey. With the record complete and Kirkpatrick back in Britain, Thompson was keen for them to work together again.

John Kirkpatrick: 'We did a lot of his songs that I knew, "Streets Of Paradise", "Two Left Feet", things where the accordion had a fairly prominent role on the record. I think he was just about to do "Ghosts in the Wind", I really enjoyed playing that one. We did a few of my songs, some traditional tunes, bits off *Morris On*. After that, I was back in the fold again . . .'

With Thompson's first album for Polydor released around the same time as Linda's solo debut for Warner Bros, this was just too good an opportunity for the press to resist: contrast and compare.

Richard Thompson

By her own admission, Linda was uncertain what to do with her life and career, though she accepted that comparisons would inevitably be made: 'I came back, I'd been living on vodka and anti-depressants. I threw away the anti-depressants on the plane because I thought "I'm going back to the children now. I've had my Lost Weekend". I cut down on the drinking. I didn't stop, I think I drank too much for about a year after that. I'd never drunk before. Even before I became a Muslim I wasn't a drinker, my whole family was teetotal ...

'John Tams was fantastic. I met him in a coffee bar, told him what happened, and he said how about you start Monday at the National Theatre? He had a lot to put up with from me. I was a nightmare. Then started a very nice period of being at the National for about a year, with Bill Bryden and Tams on *The Mysteries* and *Don Quixote* with Paul Scofield.

'People asked me to do an album. But the reason I signed the record deal with Mo Ostin and Warners was that Richard had left and we were both looking for a record deal, and Warner Brothers had turned him down, and they said they would take me. And that was the only reason I did it.'

Linda's only solo record, *One Clear Moment*, was released almost concurrently with *Across a Crowded Room* and, in a head-to-head confrontation, came out better than many critics had expected. *One Clear Moment* suffers from a lack of focus and is very much a record of its time, with the vocals coasting on a wash of synthesised keyboards, but Linda's singing is as forceful and distinctive as ever.

Linda: 'In the end, it was eminently forgettable. What I should have done was get together a coterie of musicians that I was used to working with and done it that way ... I phoned Elvis Costello and Kate Bush and all these people I'd like to have worked with, and of course to my immense surprise, they all called me back. Then, when they called me back, I didn't know what to say.

'I went to see Elvis Costello, he was a big drinker and he'd just gone on the wagon at that time. We were in this pub and I was drinking, slurring and promising to call him back. It was just awful, embarrassing ... I went to the studio and listened to the song he was recording at the time, "Shipbuilding". I think I was just obnoxious, I don't remember. But years later, somebody said "What did you ever do to Elvis Costello? He just thinks you're awful".'

One Clear Moment was produced by Hugh Murphy, Gerry Rafferty's producer who Linda had met while working on the aborted *Shoot Out the Lights*. Linda co-wrote the majority of the songs with Hugh's wife Betsy Cook, who was born in Kentucky but came to England to do

Solo

sessions with Gerry Rafferty, Squeeze and Frankie Goes to Hollywood. 'Take Me On The Subway', which has Linda sounding like a muezzin calling the faithful to prayer, was written by Betsy alone.

One Clear Moment has its share of ebullient 80s pop. 'Can't Stop The Girl' would have sat happily amongst the current chart-toppers and should, by rights, have been a hit. The record was particularly well received in America; *Cashbox* called it 'one of the most accessible and moving albums of the year ... The results, however, may prove to be one of the *major* albums of 1985'. While *Time* wrote that 'as records, neither Lauper's nor Madonna's ... get into the depth and irony explored by Linda Thompson on the just-released *One Clear Moment*.'

The record's best-known song turned out to be 'Telling Me Lies' which Dolly Parton, Linda Ronstadt and Emmylou Harris recorded on their 1987 *Trio* album. Linda's lyrics left few people in any doubt as to their source:

> Don't put your life in the hands of a man,
> With a face for every season;
> Don't waste your time in the arms of a man
> Who's no stranger to treason.

Linda's 'evening job' during this period was contributing to the National Theatre's production of the medieval Mystery plays. The musical director was John Tams, with the all too short-lived Home Service as musicians. Linda can be heard in fine voice on the 1984 album of *The Mysteries*.

The reviews accorded Linda Thompson's *One Clear Moment* had been better than she dared hope, and in some cases, even better than those Richard received for *Across a Crowded Room*. Although relations had been strained immediately following the separation, Linda was sanguine about her husband's re-marriage in 1985, and on 21 September, the same year, she married Steve Kenis, an American businessman.

Linda: 'I started to date Joe [Boyd] again. I went to a baseball match or something at Ed Victor's house, he's a big publishing guy. I went with Joe, and met Steve there and we all went to Joe Allen's for dinner and I left with Steve ... So I started seeing him then, when the baby was very young. Kammy was just months old, so I was very blessed that I was taken out of that mad frame of mind I was in. But I don't think that phase was all that self-destructive except to my liver. I think the going mad and having boyfriends was probably a good thing to do. I'd been so held down for so long, it was good just to let rip. But it's not something one would have wanted to go on doing indefinitely ...

Richard Thompson

'Steve was a bon viveur and well-off, in the movie business. He was loud and American and great fun. The day after I met him, he phoned up and said "I'm going to Paris on Friday, you want to come?" That kind of American thing. Steve would say "we'll go to Egypt this weekend, go up the Nile on a felucca". And I'd think "This is better than Rotherham and Barnsley".'

Linda began recording a second solo album in Nashville. Among the featured players were James Burton, Bruce Hornsby and Jennifer Warnes. But the dysphonia, which had plagued her for over a decade, came back while she was recording ('I could barely talk, let alone sing'). Following her re-marriage, Linda gave up all thoughts of a singing career, although she has been consulting with Rykodisc over a comprehensive, retrospective career CD, which would include rare and unreleased material.

Linda: 'It's a shame, but up until that last tour, I never really loved being on stage. I lost my voice completely some time after that. I wasn't having too many problems on the solo record and I did that thing about John Lennon with Bernard Hill for the BBC. But my throat got worse. I would have enjoyed going on doing little bits, but this dysphonia came back with a real vengeance. And by the time I was making a record in America for CBS, I couldn't sing at all. I could only manage a syllable at a time. It was a nightmare. So after that, I thought it was best to hit it on the head.

'The only thing I ever hear myself singing on the radio is "Telling Me Lies", which Betsy [Cook] and I wrote, which is lovely. Even if I heard Richard and my stuff on the radio now, I don't think it would haunt me, now I'd think "Ooh, royalties".'

For many people, Linda Kenis will always remain Linda Thompson. On record, she is bound irrevocably to her first husband and still occupies a place of great affection in the hearts of those who know her through her singing. Over six albums, Linda gave voice to the songs Richard fashioned in their flat in Hampstead. Loudon Wainwright III spoke for many when he told me: 'She was a great interpreter of his songs really. The best. I've never heard anybody do them better.'

The dysphonia finally robbed Linda of the ability to sing, but her willingness had been sapped long before. Perhaps the real tragedy of her professional career as a singer is that she only really began to enjoy performing when it was too late. It is sad that her fondest memories onstage are from the traumatic *Shoot Out the Lights* tour of 1982.

All that is a long way removed from the elegant woman sitting opposite me in the Belgravia town house she shares with her second husband. The house is rarely empty of Linda's three children from her marriage to Richard. Trying to pin Linda down to talk is like trying to catch the wind, her husband's work takes her across the world – on location with Tom Cruise in New Orleans for *Interview With The Vampire*, or entertaining Al Pacino over dinner. For relaxation, it's skiing in Aspen – far removed from Islamic communes in the Fenlands of East Anglia. Hard to believe this is the same nervous, but powerfully poignant singer who accompanied her first husband around smoky folk clubs in the suburbs of Greater London twenty years before.

Linda: 'It is a very different lifestyle. But the easiest thing in the world to get used to. You get used to it *so* quickly. The first time Steve and I went to Los Angeles, we travelled first class and I was a bit overwhelmed. I'd never travelled first class. We went to the Beverly Wilshire in the limo and I was thinking this is just amazing. Three days later, I was standing in the breezeway of the hotel saying to Steve: "The fucking limo's LATE!"'

Chapter 22

JOE BOYD: 'After *Across a Crowded Room* didn't do the business ... I had a very frank conversation with Richard – I think he may already have decided and I may have pre-empted him. I said "Look, I'd love to do the next record with you, but I can't tell you, or Polygram, that I'm going to do anything radically different.

' "I was very proud of *Across a Crowded Room*, I think it was the best-sounding, produced record of yours that I've ever been involved in. It had better production values than *Shoot Out the Lights*, every little detail was really good. But if that doesn't sell, and doesn't reach the market place ... I don't know what to say. Maybe you're better off trying with someone else." '

Mitchell Froom had already produced the Del Fuegos, and worked with T-Bone Burnett, Peter Case, Los Lobos and Elvis Costello when he was approached to work with Richard Thompson. The suggestion came from Thompson's manager Gary Stamler, who also managed Mitchell Froom.

Richard: 'I think Joni Mitchell described producers as the interior decorators – do you get the decorators in on this one? Do you use your own taste or do you get someone else to tell you what wallpaper you want. It's really important to feel comfortable in the studio – or at least feel uncomfortable for a reason. If you're going to have somebody shout at you then at least figure that there's some end to it that you can tangibly taste or feel at the end of the road.

'I probably tend to be too conservative in terms of producers and I probably haven't thought it's very important – or I haven't thought it was important enough. I've been stuck to think of people.

'I like working with Mitchell because it's inspiring. He really thinks quite radically about what his job is and, what music is, and what a record is. He's always throwing things at you, it's very stimulating and it's very exciting. I really feel excited going into the studio with Mitchell and not knowing really what's going to happen to some extent.'

Solo

Clive Gregson: 'They were trying to get Mark Knopfler to produce the next record [*Daring Adventures*] at one point, and Richard just fought it all the way down the line... The record was mixed by Neil Dorfsman, who'd done *Brothers in Arms*, and I think that was the compromise Richard made.

'*Daring Adventures* was a real shift in the way Richard made records. It was the first Mitchell Froom record. The 1986 band was one of the best bands Richard's ever had – it was Gerry, Ruari, John Kirkpatrick, me, Chris. We could do the rock'n'roll, the jazz, the acoustic. We could do the English stuff. It was a great band to play in. I thought we just really covered the waterfront.'

Thompson recorded *Daring Adventures* with a studio band of hand-picked American musicians but toured with another, more familiar, ensemble. The cost of taking the likes of Jim Keltner and Jerry Scheff from Los Angeles to the Half Moon in Putney would have been prohibitive.

Daring Adventures was the record which finally marked 'The Americanisation Of Richard Thompson'. It should have come as no surprise: Richard was married to an American, his manager was American, his tour promoter (Elizabeth Rush) was American, his producer was American. America offered him a sanctuary, and a market which took him at face value rather than always harking back to the past, he wasn't 'folkie Richard Thompson' or 'ex-Fairport Convention Richard Thompson'.

Thompson felt it was time for a change and *Daring Adventures* marked that change. It remains one of his most distinctive albums to date. The familiar sound colourings are there, with John Kirkpatrick's accordion, the Fairey Engineering Band and Phil Pickett's shawms. But the record derives an American sound from Mitchell Froom's spacious production, as well as his use of the Hammond organ and theremin (an early synthesizer used on the Beach Boys' 'Good Vibrations'). It is there on the precision of the drumming and the plucked bass figures.

From the moment the sessions began in Los Angeles, Thompson was particularly enchanted with Jerry Scheff's tales of playing bass for Elvis Presley in his touring band and Keltner's tales of playing with... everyone. That Thompson should switch his allegiance from the stable folk-rock rhythm section of Daves Pegg and Mattacks, and ignore Gerry Conway and Pat Donaldson, was taken by some as indicative of 'defection'.

Richard: 'I think I'm basically a performer and that's the pivot of what I do – so it's a dilemma in the studio – do I just go in and perform

Richard Thompson

and make records that sound like a performance or do I try and contrive ways to make it sound like a better performance – to make it sound like a record – do I try and get some craft into it? Which I suppose has been the great thing about working with Mitchell Froom – he's devised ways of making a performance sound more like a record just by tweaking stuff and distorting stuff and throwing stuff in. Which makes it sound like it has more of an attitude than just being a fairly bland version of a stage performance.'

Despite the pressure to come up with a 'hit' album, the *Daring Adventures* sessions were as relaxed and affable as any for Thompson's previous records. He and Mitchell Froom forged an immediate bond, and Thompson brought in a notebook full of some of his best songs to date.

Thompson was mindful that he was up against it with this record. *Across a Crowded Room* had failed to do the business, in a business where the moguls only rated you as good as your last album. While Thompson was a good name for Polygram to boast, his supporters had largely gone in a series of boardroom shuffles, leaving him alone and isolated in the corporate jungle. The new executives were more concerned with the latest twelve-inch dance mixes, than with a balanced selection of delicately written and brilliantly played songs by an expatriate Muslim with a receding hair line.

Daring Adventures could have been a disaster. Thompson was undeniably under pressure. But with the knowledge that the heat was on, he had turned in some of his most commercial songs. 'Valerie', 'Nearly In Love' and 'Baby Talk' were obviously intended as hit singles, and matched that remit.

Post-*Thriller*, the model for a successful record was Dire Straits' *Brothers in Arms*. A successful pub band, who incongruously found favour at the height of Punk with the delightfully 'old fashioned' 'Sultans of Swing', Mark Knopfler had progressed with each album to a place near the top of Division Two. *Brothers in Arms* put Dire Straits on the world stage.

The album arrived on the crest of the Compact Disc boom. CDs were the new format record companies had been praying for: a platinum opportunity to sell the fans all their old records *again*! Ditch those scratched old vinyl albums. Chuck away those unplayed-in-a-decade eight-track cartridges. Demote the cassettes to in-car entertainment. Compact Discs were the future.

The sound of the switch to the Compact 1980s was Dire Straits' *Brothers in Arms*. To reap some more of that whirlwind, record labels were out to try and replicate the sound and feel of Knopfler's songs and Neil Dorfsman's production.

Thompson was certainly not unaware of what was required. 'Valerie', in particular, has the same compelling, easy-going charm of Knopfler's 'Walk Of Life'. Of course there were those who felt that the process had worked the other way around, that Mark Knopfler's guitar style owed more than a nod to Thompson's. But then, rock'n'roll has always been about having the talent, the opportunity, and the timing to plug a gap. *Daring Adventures* is the one album on which Thompson seemed prepared to follow the dictates of a record label, to try and give them what they wanted, on the assumption that they knew what they were doing.

The success of *Brothers in Arms* had to do with the quality of its songs and production. It wasn't anything to do with the marketing of the principal songwriter and guitarist: as a sex symbol and pin-up, Mark Knopfler wouldn't give Richard Thompson any sleepless nights, or vice versa. Teenage girls didn't go to bed dreaming of Mark Knopfler.

There was something in Dire Straits which appealed to a lot of boys who'd never grown up. A timeless quality to their music, which transcended Punk, Dance, New Wave, New Age . . . For a generation who'd grown up too late for the guitar hero worship of Eric Clapton or Jimmy Page, Knopfler arrived fully formed, with his cherry red Strat and fluent ability to send solos spinning off into the night, almost making you choke on their sweetness.

Dire Straits were a band for all seasons, fronted by someone who was plainly uncomfortable at being a frontman, but was blessed with a God-given ability to play guitar like an angel's breath and write songs which could sell. Hell, reasoned industry veterans, if Mark Knopfler can do it . . .

Daring Adventures proved not to be in quite the same league as *Brothers in Arms*, tailing off at around 19,750,000 copies less worldwide. For Thompson though, the record was a watershed. It saw him cast his nets out to a wider audience, acquiesce to the need for commercial acceptance, and embrace the type of production and song structure which Mitchell Froom suggested. It is a partnership which has endured for over ten years now, longer than any other in Thompson's studio history.

Richard: 'There's more thought that goes in to them before hand – and there's more thought about sound. We think about the sounds of instruments much more: what guitar sound, which guitar, how is this going to jump out of the speakers, what kind of drums – let's not allow the drummer more than two drums, what kind of bass, what kind of accordion? Just thinking about basic sound and then get the sound set up – which can take six or eight hours sometimes – and then record very quickly in one or two takes. They're all quick, compared to other people's, ridiculously quick. They all take four or five weeks at most and it has been as little as a week or ten days.'

There was a growing suspicion that even with Polygram's backing, Thompson was never going to crack the mainstream. Reviewing a 1986 Los Angeles concert in the trade publication *Cashbox*, Brian Kassan wrote: 'With songs that have been wrought from Thompson's own hardships, his themes are often cynical and depressing, which probably would be too challenging or even frightening for American mainstream tastes.' A comment like that might have warmed the cockles of Thompson's heart, but must have sent shivers down Polygram's corporate spine.

Richard: 'It's become an industry. I try to sit on the edge, I really try not to be in it and I don't feel a part of it. I have to interact with it and I try to find painless ways of doing that, ways where I'm not being exploited by it and where I get as much advantage out of it as it gets out of me, which isn't easy. It's always a collision of interest – business and music are really not the same. Far from it, so the interaction point is variable and sometimes there's friction.

'I think stylistically I'm also on the edge of popular music. So I have my own set of problems ... in so far as what's in it for the record company to market me and what do I need from the record company, how does the record company find my audience? Do they know where my audience is – do they know the age group of the audience, do they know the taste of the audience? Generally, no!'

Daring Adventures is one of the unheralded gems lying snug in the Richard Thompson safe-deposit box. It runs the gamut from the exuberant out-and-out rock'n'roll of 'Valerie' to the pensive, folk-inclined 'How Will I Ever Be Simple Again?' Here is something for everyone. From the knowing pop reference ('her boyfriend plays in Scritti Politti') to knockabout fun ('if you don't get over this eating jag/they're going to take you home in a body bag'), all on the same record as the wistful atmospherics of the moonlit 'Missie How You Let Me Down'.

'Dead Man's Handle' is a song tailor-made by Thompson, set to that rolling 'Wall of Death'-style rhythm, and symbolism to die for. (Brewer: 'A handle on the controls of an electric train, so designed that it cuts off the current and applies the brakes if the driver releases his pressure from illness or some other cause ...' Regrettably the entry continues: 'it is now officially called a driver's safety device, a term with less distressing associations').

Richard: 'I got a letter from the son of the inventor of the dead man's handle – he thought it was great – he said in case you didn't know, here's a few facts. It was nice, some nice little pictures and newspaper articles about it, I was rather touched.'

'A Bone Through Her Nose' is one of those cracking a walnut with a sledgehammer songs. For all the calm Islam brought him, Thompson is still capable of working up a full head of steam about what he sees as the diminishing of values, the trivialising of tradition, the erosion of quality. He sees sound-bite culture and ephemeral fast food values in the ascendant.

For Thompson, talking to Bill Flanagan in *Musician*, the song was 'about a certain breed of English girl who comes from a fairly good family, gets out of school at about eighteen and has a couple of years of token rebellion. She becomes a social sort of anarchistic animal, extremely fashion-conscious in the most downbeat possible way. Then, at about twenty-two or twenty-three, it's time to get married. So she marries Henry, who has a very nice house in Smith Square and a charming manor house in Berkshire. They've got dogs and a couple of horses. It's frightfully good. Yet in their rebellious time some of these sorts become quite serious media figures and spokespersons for their generation and stuff. And it's all a total sham.'

'Cash Down Never Never' (hire purchase is colloquially known as the 'never never') is another withering condemnation of contemporary values ('back streets, real scum about'). As with 'Back Street Slide', there is no room for doubt and scant understanding that not everyone may share the composer's value judgments, or aspire to the same high moral ground. While there is little to be said for a life bordered by *The Sun* and *Blind Date*, it is the lot of a large percentage of the population of the UK. To be so dismissive of their circumstances seems jarringly at odds with the compassion Thompson is so eloquently capable of displaying, both in person and in his songs.

John Kirkpatrick: 'One thing about songwriting is that it's good therapy for yourself. You can get feelings out, and then you've dealt with very difficult things ... Some of his more recent songs, considering he's sustained by this very profoundly held faith, I'm surprised at the bitterness and anger and dislike of people that is often very harshly expressed ...'

'Missie How You Let Me Down' features more of that vivid impressionistic writing ('the shape of you is still in the bed next to me') and another addition to Thompson's stockpile of repressed-emotion metaphors ('I could stew in here, like a pressure cooker, and screw down the lid').

If truly effective rock'n'roll love songs today tend to be bittersweet, Thompson's err more towards bitter with a dash of bile. Just a random sweep through *Daring Adventures* finds love 'sold for fool's gold' ('Lovers' Lane'); the memory of love is not to 'send flowers to remember', but 'send thorns instead' ('Long Dead Love'); the object of love is 'the closest to my heart, bar none/Except for my wallet and my gun' ('Nearly In Love').

'Long Dead Love', digs up every available symbol for a love which has withered and died. Beginning with a grave, through to the Edgar Allen Poe image of being buried alive in the second verse, culminating with the calling up of the nineteenth century's most infamous grave robbers Burke and Hare. The song is so mordant that you sense Thompson laughing out of the side of his mouth.

'Valerie' remains a personal favourite, the sort of good time rock'n'roll you hear Thompson crash into onstage and feel all the better for hearing. The lyrics are pithy and persuasive, the rhyming outrageous and addictive. Even the put-downs are affectionate rather than vitriolic. 'Valerie' is a minor Thompson masterpiece.

Daring Adventures winds down with the plaintive 'How Will I Ever Be Simple Again?' Like 'Devonside' on *Hand of Kindness*, this is a walk through a land wasted by warfare. Told by Thompson in his most affecting and direct folk narrative style. Stark and solo, Thompson tries to evoke an Eden before the Fall, but knows that once the apple is bitten, there's no going back.

Talking of 'How Will I Ever Be Simple Again?' to Bill Flanagan, Thompson described it as 'a song of contrast – it's about the confusion in a man's mind between his life and the terrible experiences life shows him, and what he sees in this girl – a real pastoral simplicity. She's a figure from Christopher Marlowe or something – she's out of the past. He's confused by her innocence and her reality. He's very complicated but he yearns for her simplicity.'

Instrumentally and thematically, the song links into 'Al Bowlly's In Heaven'. Albert Alick Bowlly was born in Mozambique in 1899 and made his first recordings with various jazz groups in Berlin between 1927 and 1928. Bowlly went on to become, in the eyes and ears of many critics, the best British popular singer of the 1930s. Al Bowlly was killed in 1941 during the Blitz when a Nazi bomb exploded outside his flat.

Thompson told me he had no particular fondness for Bowlly's singing, preferring him as a convenient symbol: 'It's a classic example I suppose of what happens in many countries, that once you cease to be of use to your country, wilfully or otherwise, you get forgotten. Another government comes, or three governments later they're looking for ways to save money, and they don't remember you being a hero or being of any particular use. So you're just a statistic.

'It's bad jazz though, it's supposed to be bad jazz. It's more Sid Phillips than Benny Goodman – it's more British dance hall swing than anything serious. I think it works well. I think it works better on stage these days than it does on record. I think my parents actually saw Al Bowlly sing at Hammersmith Palais during the war. Yes, he was a kind of symbol, I'm not a huge Al Bowlly fan, I quite like him but I don't think he was Bing Crosby or anything. He was the Great British Hope, but what else did we have, and he died – that's always useful. Perhaps he was the 40s' Nick Drake.

'It's a contemporary song – people say your songs are so nostalgic – but it's not nostalgic, it's now. The guy's having a terrible time now and this is all the baggage that he's brought with him up to this point, this is his luggage. It's the past impinging on the present – which is basically what fiction is. It's what luggage you drag along to this point and how it affects what you do now.'

'Al Bowlly's In Heaven' is one of Thompson's most enduring and haunting songs. It quite effortlessly juxtaposes the glamour of Al Bowlly up on the bandstand, with the huddled lines of unemployed, snaking along the rain-drenched streets. Golden memories of youth:

> I can see me now, back there on the dance floor
> With a blonde on me arm, red-head to spare,
> Spit on my shoes and shine in me hair . . .

Recollected amidst the contemporary reality of: 'Hard times . . ./Hostels and missions and dossers' soup lines . . .'

And hanging over it all is the waste of a war, which led only to betrayal and poverty. Like Elvis Costello's 'Shipbuilding', the scope and sweep of 'Al Bowlly's In Heaven' is breathtaking. As a writer, Thompson has rarely sounded more assured and in control. The jazz style and scat playing slip around the song as comfortably as a pair of much-loved spats. The deftness of 'Al Bowlly's In Heaven' is in understanding nostalgia while avoiding queasy sentimentality.

One of my fondest memories of seeing Thompson perform was with the Big Band at Hammersmith Palais in 1986. 'Al Bowlly' wasn't that

Richard Thompson

familiar then, and hearing it played, while above our heads the shiny silver mirror ball spun out its reflected glory, was like being thrown back in time. Back to a time when Richard's parents came down the Shepherds Bush Road and danced, while outside, the Nazi bombs and rockets fell.

Daring Adventures was Richard Thompson customised for the CD age. Those shiny CDs were able to accommodate twice as much music as the old-fashioned long-playing vinyl records. It clocked in at 47 minutes, nearly ten minutes longer than its predecessor. It happens to be a better and more satisfying record and not just because of the extra value for money.

Clive Gregson: 'I knew that this was a real sea-change when he used the LA session men to cut the record and we just did bits of overdubs. It seemed then that there was a real divergence between what he was going to do on the road – it's a very Nashville thing, they make the records one way, then they take another band on the road to play it. That's pretty much what Richard has done ever since. There's very rarely a correlation between the records and what goes on onstage.'

Thompson was also busy consolidating his reputation on the other side of the board.

Loudon Wainwright III: 'When it came time to make *I'm Alright* – 1984 or something like that – I was living over here. Richard was quite surprised when I asked him to co-produce because I don't think he'd done it before ... I had very small budgets and the way I was making records then was very loose. Two or three takes, pick the best one; everything was done live.'

As a producer, Thompson didn't see himself as another Phil Spector. Burned by the Gerry Rafferty experience, he kept it straight and simple. Talking to Max Kay in 1981, he thought his fault was being 'too enthusiastic to be a good producer. I'm not objective enough. My style tends to be too simple, but then that's the kind of production I like. The early Sam Phillips recordings all had it, they were straight and simple, but they were also exciting and atmospheric.'

Phillips was the man who invented rock'n'roll, with a little help from a teenage truck driver called Elvis Presley. On the records made in Memphis' sweltering Sun Studios in 1954 and 1955, Phillips can be heard coercing Elvis into ... something that, baby, we call rock'n'roll.

Loudon Wainwright III: 'Richard co-produced ... *More Love Songs* in 1986, with another friend of mine, Chaim Tannenbaum ... who is *so* Jewish ... So I was a little worried about Islam and ... Chaim. But they connected immediately, dug each other's writing and playing. I remember we'd work and go out to lunch, we were working out at Wapping, so we must have gone to the Bloom's out there, in Whitechapel. Of course as long as I've known Richard he's been a vegetarian ... occasionally he'll eat a piece of fish, but he's not a big burger guy. So I thought "Uh-oh ... Bloom's". But because it was kosher, he chowed down and had this huge thing of lamb. He didn't get all prissy, it was a case of when in Rome ..., or perhaps when in Tel Aviv. And because the animal had been butchered properly, he enjoyed a good slab of beef or whatever.

'Richard brought all those guys in for *More Love Songs* – Brass Monkey, Christine Collister, Mattacks, Martin Carthy. We felt that my records of the late 70s were too laboured, too worried over, too many concessions. As a producer, Richard would try and capture the energy of the songs, rather than convert the songs into something that would hopefully play on the radio ...'

During 1986, as well as some solo dates, a tour with the band to promote *Daring Adventures*, and a second folk club tour with John Kirkpatrick, Thompson also took to the road with Wainwright.

Loudon Wainwright III: 'We toured Australia and Japan together, the "Loud and Rich" tour. That was fun ... I had a pretty good following in Australia, he hadn't been there ever, so he opened for me. Then we went up to Japan, where he is huge! All these obsessive Japanese guitar players came out in droves. I was the opening act there. My whole thing is a word thing, and to see these guys out front practically taking notes ... Then coming backstage; the Japanese are, of course, so polite, and if you fuse that Japanese politeness with adulation, which Richard inspires anyway among guitar players and songwriters, I never saw such fawning.'

On its UK release, *Daring Adventures* picked up the usual clutch of superlatives accorded a Thompson release. *Time Out*, found Thompson 'yet again not only a writer and musician of consummate artistry, but a fellow of rare, simple integrity. A gem.'

In the second issue of *Q*, the rock magazine which was to define the music press' relationship with the 'rock aristocracy', David Hepworth, a staunch Thompson supporter of long-standing, wrote: '*Daring Adventures* has variety, melody, colour, drama, twisted humour, some of the best guitar playing likely to be heard this, or any other year, and occasionally the emotional force to pin you to the wall. It is, as I said, another Richard Thompson record.'

Back in his second home of America toward the end of 1986, Thompson was getting used to being marketed as a commodity by his parent

Richard Thompson

company. A 1986 *Billboard* profile was headlined 'Thompson is Quintessential Cult Artist', not a headline calculated to calm a record label. For a multinational conglomerate like Polygram, 'cult' is an anagram of 'no sales'.

Polygram's senior vice president of marketing Harry Anger was quoted in the showbiz bible as saying: 'The fact that Richard Thompson says he's not concerned with being a commercial success doesn't mean he wouldn't accept it if it should come . . .' Lapsing into buzz talk he outlined his marketing strategy for this 'quintessential cult artist' in anticipation of Thompson's American tour dates: 'We will attempt to motivate a buying pattern from the tour using alternative press, keying in on that AOR station in the individual market that plays Richard Thompson, and going after the college market both through college radio and newspapers. We will be consistently supporting the tour with airplay and targeted time buys keyed in with retailers who are aware of the importance of the artist.'

Richard: 'It's just about getting to the point now where alternative is big enough – it's a big enough minority for them to take notice. So folk alternative is almost a category now – but not quite. In America I can get on the radio now on Triple A format, which is Adult Album Alternative or something. There's actually a place for non-Pop, non-Rock, but interesting albums, people like Los Lobos, John Hiatt, the Cranberries would all go on Triple A. Which means that people who buy my records may finally be targeted – I think they actually know who they are now.

'I can see how people like me would be harder to market because we don't fit into categories that easily. I'm not trying to sound mysterious or special – although I am both mysterious and special! Major record companies are better at marketing the obvious stuff, and that's where the biggest audience is.

'It can be quite funny, meeting Bon Jovi or someone at Polydor, a meeting of aliens, people from a different planet. Rock and roll is a truly multi-generational music form – and I don't think necessarily I'm on the scrap heap these days.'

Chapter 23

THERE IS A STORY about the entertainer, the late Roy Castle, who was performing in a smoke-filled theatre sometime during the 1960s. True to form, Castle pulled out all the stops to try and win over the hard-to-please crowd. He sang, he told jokes, he tap-danced, he played the trumpet ... Finally, in a supreme effort to overcome the antipathy, Castle attempted to do something like break the UK tap-dance record while simultaneously juggling and playing the sousaphone. Barely into his record-breaking stride, a lone voice from up in the gods shattered Castle's confidence: 'Is there no end to your fucking talent?'

Diversity was Richard Thompson's game plan. With Polygram declining to take up the option following the lack of 'Thompsonmania' accorded to either *Across a Crowded Room* or *Daring Adventures*, the guitar/vocalist was confident that his manager Gary Stamler would come up with something. In the meantime, Thompson was footloose and fancy free.

Between labels he forged a working relationship with arranger and producer, Pete Filleul, who was gaining a reputation for his work with the BBC. Filleul left school and 'began to write songs, believing in the words of my father that I could be a "bloody Beatle" ... I tricked Decca Records into giving me a deal'. A spell with A Band Called O led to Filleul joining East of Eden for a year ('we had to play "Jig-A-Jig" every night. In Europe, we were billed as "the greatest folk-rock band in the world"!'). Sessions led to a spell with the Climax Blues Band, then work with Willy Russell on the musical drama *Blood Brothers*. Filleul's first BBC commission was *King of the Ghetto* with Dave Kelly. Ghetto producer Sally Head's next project was the acclaimed *Life and Loves of a She-Devil* in 1986, which many still recall in large part because of Christine Collister's haunting handling of Filleul's theme song.

Pete Filleul: 'I'd written "Warm Love Gone Cold" and they wanted to use it for *The Life and Loves of a She-Devil*, and when it came to record it, I wanted it to feel like one of those old Fairport songs ... and of course the way to achieve that was to have Richard playing on it.

'Richard had been a great hero to me ... and I thought if he does want to do it, I'll probably have to hire a massive studio and he'd arrive in his limousine. Little did I know. Within a fortnight, there's a knock at my door in East Dulwich, and Richard holding guitar, Fender amplifier and foot pedal comes in, sits in the utility room next to my studio, sets up his guitar, listens to the track, and worked out a part.'

The work on *She-Devil* led to the three-part drama series, *The Marksman*, which was the first full collaboration between Thompson and Filleul.

Pete Filleul: 'You're not actually tied to the constraint of the four-minute beginning and end piece of music, as opposed to writing thematically, perhaps having a musical idea attached to a character which you develop as the story develops. The extent to which the music supports the drama is also very interesting. But one of the most frustrating things that Richard would admit working in TV is that it takes a deuce of a long time and an awful lot of people that you have to be seen to respect the views of ... but that is the nature of the beast. My role deflects a lot of that away from him.'

The history of *The Marksman* was fraught, its depiction of urban violence was problematic at the best of times. But *The Marksman* attracted unprecedented publicity following the tragic events in Hungerford during August 1987. With a terrifying arsenal at his disposal, Michael Ryan ran amok in the small Berkshire town. Before his own suicide, Ryan left a trail of fourteen dead bodies. The subsequent showing of *The Marksman* that December was overshadowed by the Hungerford tragedy.

Thompson and Filleul collaborated next on another BBC series, *Hard Cash*, a four-part documentary series about 'the realities of life on the minimum wage'. The two men had begun working on incidental music for the series at the beginning of 1989, but impressed by the footage they had already seen, Filleul remembers them hitting 'upon the idea of expanding the project to record an album, including contributions from other songwriters, on the theme of exploitation at work'. *Hard Cash* was scheduled for airing on the BBC in March 1990.

Pete Filleul: '*Hard Cash* was never screened ... It was a documentary about the abolition of Wages Councils. It was a very political issue, and it was around the time that the BBC had come in for a lot of criticism from the government ... I think that this was perceived as the straw that might break the camel's back ... Initially, it was postponed ... There were a lot of legal issues, having worked with hidden cameras, we were accusing people of not paying the statutory rate ... It was after about eighteen months that we realised it wouldn't be shown.

'Richard really enjoyed it, probably because it was so quick ... It focuses the mind wonderfully. We had three days in the studio with the band, two for overdubs, four days for mixing ... It was a subject which has a lot of roots in traditional music anyway, and very many of the people who are involved would be interested, so why don't we ask them to write something for it? ... We ended up with a host of original material for a five- or six-part TV series, and we had two weeks to put the *Hard Cash* record together. He wrote "Mrs Rita" for June Tabor. Richard always does research ... He found a book in the library, *The Sweatshop Report* by Derek Bishton. There's a story in there about a woman in Birmingham accused of stealing two hundred pairs of knickers from her employer, Rita O'Connor Hosiery.'

The other new song Thompson contributed was the poignant 'Oh I Swear':

Can't run in a dead end street,
No wings upon your feet,
All your dreams are shackled to the ground.

Thompson also contributed 'Time To Ring Some Changes' with an extra two verses, including the scornfully anti-Thatcher:

Now listen here to the self-made man
He says why can't you if I can.
Can't you push buttons, can't you make plans?
It's time to ring some changes.

'The self-made man' was the living symbol of Thatcher's Britain. The man who, in Norman Tebbit's immortal phrase, 'got on his bike and looked for work'. This was the apogee of Thatcherism. The touching tale of how a grocer's daughter from Grantham, through her own efforts, and with no help from anyone else (certainly not the state, certainly not society – there was no such thing!) hauled herself up by her bootstraps, and became Prime Minister. Thatcher's belief in herself was so complete, that she was convinced everyone could do it. Everywhere you looked in the late 80s, there were self-made men, East End barrow boys turned asset strippers and the ubiquitous Yuppies. It was that uncaring 'greed is good' mentality which made the Thatcher years so unbearable for everyone but the selfish and the greedy.

Richard Thompson

In the name of greater efficiency and the market-led economy, hospitals were closed, pits were closed and entire communities emasculated, all because the figures didn't balance. The dole queues grew, and stretched back into memory, like the snaking lines of unemployed which so haunted the imagination from the 1930s. The dream ended with the recession of the 1990s. The self-made men watched pale-faced and chastened and wondered how they would pay the school fees and private health insurance now that fixed term contracts had become the norm.

Nowhere was the change more apparent than in the sweeping miles of empty office blocks which is Docklands. Thatcher's government believed that de-regulation of the City of London would make the capital a focus for financial consultants and investors from all over the world. In the end, they never came, and Docklands stands empty and echoing, vacant, like the enormous set for a re-make of Fritz Lang's *Metropolis* which will never get made.

The 1990s, the decade when the chickens came home to roost.

Hard Cash led to Thompson and Filleul collaborating on the soundtrack to the rarely seen 1991 film *Sweet Talker*. An engaging comedy starring Bryan Brown, who supplied the original story, and *Raiders of the Lost Ark* heroine, Karen Allen. *Sweet Talker* begins as a bargain basement hybrid of *Cool Hand Luke* and *The Sting*. Brown is a huckster who sets out to con the sleepy resort of Beachport, with a tale of a sunken sixteenth-century treasure ship. Amiable and undemanding, *Sweet Talker* is a satire on greed and people's willingness to be conned.

Thompson's vocal, 'Put Your Trust In Me', tops and tails the film over the credits. *Sweet Talker* went straight to video limbo. While its message 'You don't need anybody but yourselves' wasn't exactly original, the film is no worse than any one of a hundred comedies on your local video store shelf.

Pete Filleul: 'The film came about because the producer Taylor Hackford was a Richard Thompson fan. He had directed *An Officer and a Gentleman*, which was flavour of the year, and was setting himself up in LA to become a film-making mogul. At the time we were working with him, Taylor had four films in various stages of development, and was involved in massive distribution deals to get mega-quantities of money ... We weren't privy to that, but you'd read about it in *Variety*. In fact, there's a joke in [Robert] Altman's film *The Player*, at a board meeting, and somebody says "And, of course, there's a Taylor Hackford project". And this was a Taylor Hackford project.'

Hackford came to produce *Sweet Talker* on the back of two successful rock'n'roll movies, the Richie Valens biopic *La Bamba* and the Chuck Berry documentary *Hail! Hail! Rock'n'Roll*. Hackford's breakthrough came in 1982, when he directed the runaway Richard Gere success, *An Officer and a Gentleman*. He followed it with the critically panned, but box office-friendly, *Against All Odds* and *White Nights*.

Pete Filleul: 'Taylor Hackford liked Richard's stuff and contacted him through his manager, to see if Richard would be interested. He liked the script, but said he'd worked with me in England and that I was more used to working to picture ... Richard had seen a rough cut in LA, had gone in with a couple of basic ideas to put on the temp track. When they're doing editing, they create a temporary soundtrack, and it's the bane of all composers because very often the producer and the director fall in love with this music from the shelf ... It was important to get things of Richard's onto the temp track, three of which ended up being used. They appear in very rough forms, and cut by some music editor in the most ludicrous ways, who had no idea about Richard Thompson or that sort of music.

'Then we were given a schedule for the movie, and we were sent boxes of tapes, all with ten-minute sections of the film on ... We got this one bunch of videos and began to create a sequence against the original opening titles, so this cut refers to this musical change. About six weeks later, we hear that Taylor doesn't like the movie cut that way, he wants it cut another way, to tell a slightly different story ... "Beachport" did end up on the finished album and that was what was going to be the original title. Richard was fed up by the end of it with people faffing about, not knowing what they wanted, changing their minds expecting that the world would respond to their whims. He wanted to get on with his life, after vowing he'd never do another soundtrack.'

Even the press release for the soundtrack album of *Sweet Talker* couldn't disguise Richard's unhappiness at the way the project had sprawled: 'I gained a lot of experience with this project in regards to customising music for each rewrite as the film changed. *Sweet Talker* was quite a long project that took nearly a year to complete.'

There are familiar names scattered throughout the album credits (Mattacks, Nicol, Kirkpatrick, Zorn, Danny Thompson, Christine Collister). The album offers Thompson an opportunity to try out some uncharacteristic styles (Country & Western on 'Boomtown', muzak on 'Beachport') and unusual instrumentation (banjo on 'Sweet Talker').

Sweet Talker, the album, is a footnote to the Thompson catalogue, but is not without redeeming features. The opening track, 'Put Your Trust In Me' wouldn't have sounded out of place on 1988's *Amnesia*, and features some nice Duane Eddy-ish tremolo guitar, as well as a driving Thompson vocal. 'To Hang A Dream On' is brassy and punchy. 'Roll Up' is a jaunty jig with John Kirkpatrick's accordion to the fore.

Still between deals, a further Thompson collaboration came with the *Live, Love, Larf & Loaf* album by French, Frith, Kaiser and Thompson. The 1987 album was one of those records musicians make to keep themselves from going stir crazy. Everyone around them foams with enthusiasm and the reviews are enthusiastic if slightly baffled. (Why would Captain Beefheart's original drummer, Fairport Convention and Henry Cow founders and an 'accomplished innovative experimental guitarist' collaborate on a cover of the Beach Boys 'Surfin' USA'?) To further enhance this essentially aural joke, 'Hai Sai Oji-San' featured Thompson singing in Okinawan. *Live, Love* . . . is one of those musos albums, by musos for musos.

Thompson contributed 'a Neil Young kind of song', 'Killerman Gold Posse', about a gang terrorising passengers on the Circle Line. 'It was written before I did *Daring Adventures*,' Thompson told Colin Davies in *Hokey Pokey*, 'but . . . it wasn't the sort of thing that Polydor Records would jump up and down about.' Thompson also contributed the bible-black 'Drowned Dog Black Night', another powerful blinds-pulled down song complete with resonant solo. The album's final track was 'Bird In God's Garden', which Thompson had featured regularly on his 1977 'Islamic' tour.

French, Frith, Kaiser and Thompson, the Crosby, Stills, Nash and Young of the other world, resumed operations in 1990 with *Invisible Means*, which featured a stark and strongly traditional Thompson original, 'Begging Bowl'. FFK&T offered Richard an opportunity to let off steam and provided a forum for some slightly off-kilter songs of his own. He loved 'March Of The Cosmetic Surgeons' from the second FFK&T album, but like 'Psycho Street' which Thompson felt stretched him as a writer, it was the sort of song which alienated audiences. They're fine to hear in concert, providing shades of contrast, but soon pall once placed on record.

The 'Surfin' USA' of *Invisible Means* is the quartet's take on the traditional 'Loch Lomond', the age-old Scottish song which was long a firm favourite of Thompson's live set. Even if the vocal is a bit stiff, the ensemble manage to give us Lord Rockingham's XI colliding head-on with the riff of 'I Fought The Law' on a song so old its origins are lost in the mists of antiquity. Within that ragged ensemble he found space to push the musical parameters ever wider but there was too much discord, too many jagged edges for it to have much general appeal.

Solo

Richard: 'I love doing projects with other people, that's great, but I'm probably too selfish at this point. I'm too used to having my own way and being able to take solos as long as I want! I love doing projects, it's great to do a record and even a little tour or something – that can be great fun and very stimulating. It's important to be stimulated by stuff on the side as well, you can have your linear career, but it's great to have bits and pieces that you do with other people because it can really broaden you. It can make you look in other directions, it can surprise you and sometimes you can make unexpectedly good music.'

Back at the Mainframe, Gary Stamler had landed his client a deal with Capitol Records. Such Thompson favourites as the Band had been at home here as, more significantly, were his manager's prime clients Crowded House, who had signed to Capitol in 1986. Two Crowded House singles in the American Top Ten during 1987 had given manager Gary Stamler added muscle when it came to negotiating Thompson's contract that same year.

Richard: 'Hale Milgrim ... a cousin of Gary Stamler, came to Capitol Records and he's someone I'd known him for ten or twelve years when he was at Elektra. He's a huge music fan who started out in retail, someone who always came to my shows and he'd always come backstage, and suddenly there was this guy I knew who was the president of Capitol Records, and I have to say it made a difference.'

On the recommendation of Clive Gregson, John Martin looked after Richard's affairs in the UK.

John Martin: 'Richard's deals were done in America by Gary, he signed him to Polygram in the States, Capitol in the States ... It was always very difficult with Polygram in Britain, they were never interested, even less so in Europe, and they saw it all ... a bit similar to EMI with Any Trouble, they wouldn't have wanted them for this country, but they had to do it because the signing was in America ... There was never money for touring over here as there should have been.

'It all changed for the better when Gary did the deal with Capitol because, as luck would have it, one of Richard's biggest fans was the product manager at Parlophone, Tony Wadsworth. And Tony's best pal was Malcolm Hill, head of promotions, who was also a fan ... and so the two of them were a joy to work with because they had a lot of interest and a fair amount of clout. But they were also realistic people ... they committed more money to marketing Richard than most people would have done in this country, but they also knew that you were never going to sell half a million albums over here, so they weren't going to put their heads on the block.'

Richard Thompson

Pat Donaldson: 'Richard's always had a very good business sense, which he manages to keep at such a level that you're not aware of it ... You never notice Richard's business acumen. He knew what was rightfully his and what he should be getting, but that certainly wasn't something that was going to interrupt making music. I guess his priorities are in the right place: there's a time for making music, and there's a time for being a business person.'

Even with the muscle of Polygram behind him, playing the corporate game and taking support on sprawling American tours (REM, Suzanne Vega, Randy Newman, Bonnie Raitt, Crowded House); even with CD singles and concert videos, Richard Thompson had failed to crack the all-important American market. Pete Zorn and Dave Mattacks, who have trawled around the States with Thompson, trying to heighten his profile, had their own opinions about why Thompson still hasn't managed that major breakthrough.

Pete Zorn: 'For better or for worse, the one thing the American music industry does is to get a certain type of music to a certain type of audience, it knows where that audience is. Nobody knows where specific audiences are in the UK, which is why acoustic music is very much "Oh, go to the gig and buy a CD otherwise you don't have a chance". It's nothing to do with record stores, so the audience is out there somewhere. The people who are coming from AOR ... who have just heard of Richard, don't have to go to mail order, they can go to Capitol Records. The audience knows where the music is. If the record company can't find what sections of other audiences are coming over to Richard's music, and there are a lot of people coming over to it in the States, they at least have a clue where it can be found.'

Dave Mattacks: 'The thing with this type of music is that you get so far and you don't get any further. There is something about the way it sounds and the way people sing in this kind of music, that basically reaches a brick wall ... Even when you get a voice such as a Christine Collister which is much more listener-friendly in terms of the mainstream, they basically reach a block, and it doesn't go any further. And I don't really think there's any way round it.

'I think the fact that it is not, for want of a better phrase, American/ blues oriented, is a major obstacle to most people's subconscious listening and appreciation of it. The only way to get round it, and even then I don't think you do, is to do the lowest common denominator kind of thing, à la Pogues, where you shout and scream everything over a cod Irish accent and four to the bar on the bass drum ... The other aspect – of sabotaging one's own perceived career improvement – I think that may have gone on for a while in the 70s and 80s, but I certainly don't think it's going on with Richard now.'

Richard: 'I hate "rock", to tell you the truth. Real rock where you get fifteen thousand people and they're all swaying and holding their matches up. I have played to audiences of that size, but I don't like the scale of it. The mythic proportions to which rock has been built – it seems to me a very shallow culture and not something I really want to be part of. I'm really irritated by rock with a capital "R", I think it went past its sell-by date a long time ago. Certainly the stuff that gets signed, or gets on the radio and sells millions of copies, to me just seems absolutely banal. It's all been done before.

'The good stuff is the stuff people do in their garages and make up tapes and they get on college stations in America or the John Peel show here. But that's the stuff that doesn't get signed because it doesn't sound conventional enough maybe. But you have to consider rock'n'roll as a traditional form of music now, its been around for forty years which in the twentieth century is worth about four hundred years! So it is a traditional form, it's a kind of folk music – with a small F.'

America is coquettish in its attitude to British music. Prior to the Beatles, only Acker Bilk and the Tornados had made it to no. 1 on the American charts. America succumbed to Beatlemania, but then turned inward at the end of the 60s and throughout much of the 70s. The second British Invasion of the early 1980s did the business. But with the ubiquitous *Thriller*, the reliance on promo videos and the burgeoning MTV, America had little interest in, or affection for, British music.

America accounts for an estimated 40 per cent of total record sales, so its importance cannot be over-estimated in any artist's career. In *Mojo* in 1995, Bill Flanagan argued: 'No new British rock act has maintained any sort of success since 1986. A lot of this has to do with the US rise of rap and hip hop, country and grunge ... Ancient Brits such as Eric Clapton and Rod Stewart still fill their bank accounts with dollars, the Stones and Pink Floyd are quibbling over which of them set the all-time cash record for a US tour in 1994. There's no escaping the ugly truth: America still loves the old limeys, but has no appetite for the English stars of the last decade.'

Richard Griffiths, President of Epic Records, was quoted as saying: 'We don't have *NME* and *Melody Maker*, thank God, dictating to us what should happen this week ... What American radio does not want to hear is that band X is the next big thing out of England. They've heard it about Pulp and Blur and Manic Street Preachers and Ned's Atomic Dustbin and Suede and Echobelly and the Stone Roses ...'

Richard Thompson

Things went from bad to worse in the new decade; according to the chart book, *British Hit Singles*: '1994 was the worst year for British music in the US singles chart in living memory. Only one and one-third British hits featured in the year-end American Top 50, and they were both film songs from veteran stars ... The Swedish group Ace of Base did better than the entire British nation.'

The turnaround occurred during 1995, when Edwyn Collins, Simply Red, Everything But the Girl, Take That, Seal and Del Amitri all made a real, sustained impact on the American singles charts. There was never any likelihood that Richard Thompson could reach the mass market of Eurythmics or the Cranberries, but sustaining a core audience within that massive market was conceivable. Concentrating on college radio, emphasising Thompson's 'alternative' appeal, Capitol were convinced they could secure their artist a foothold.

Thompson himself was only too willing. With an American wife and manager, and with a record deal inked in the States, he was finally ready to undertake a whole new phase of his career. America offered enormous potential for Thompson, it was also a market which would take him on face value, without all the ex-Fairport Convention, folkie, doom and gloom baggage.

John Kirkpatrick had worked consistently with Richard Thompson for sixteen years by the time of the release of *Amnesia* in 1988, and was concerned by the Americanisation: 'I think those early records were Richard trying to work within the folk tradition, those are the records I prefer listening to. More recently, the last few with Mitchell Froom, they don't sound English. It's American session men, American producer ... He spends so much time in America that although he's still got a lot of Englishness about him and the way he writes, the sound of the records to me has lost a lot of what made his earlier records more interesting ...

'I don't think people would question his right to do what he wants to do. He'd still get loads of folkies going to his gigs ... A very high proportion of his audience when he plays in England have known him since Fairport. Then there's his rock audience, which is newer, younger. People still buy Richard Thompson records to learn the songs they can get up and sing in the folk clubs ... I suspect people are slightly disappointed that he doesn't feature that aspect of his work more prominently. There's always a bit of it. His records are just American pop records now. Despite the overdubs of acoustic instruments and early instruments that do give it a different colour ...

'It's an interesting thing this Americanisation of Richard Thompson.

I think he is under a lot of pressure, as far as making records goes, because he's been around for so long, and he's gradually started making it a bit in the States ... I think every time a record comes up they're saying, "okay give us a hit this time". Reading between the lines, I just get the feeling that there's more of that going on than he would probably like to admit ... I think he's happy to go along with it as well. I think he's got to the stage where he thinks "Oh bugger this, I've been at it all my life, I want the bloody hit single as well." '

Richard: 'I think in this country, I'm slowly shaking off the sixties hippie, folkie has-been image. In America it's been easier because I started with a fairly clean slate around 1981. I wasn't really known at all, so it was easier to walk in and be something new. I'm still treated as alternative in America, which is rather curious.'

Chapter 24

RICHARD: 'I just love needling Americans, but they don't get it at all. If you're going to write satirical songs or songs critical of society – then that's a fairly soft target and California is the softest target of all. It's totally outside, totally for show, what you look like and what car you're driving but it's quite interesting at the same time. I quite enjoy observing it because sometimes it's so ludicrous, but there's ludicrous things about Britain too, Britain's the opposite extreme, it's an old, rusty, pessimistic, ex-colonial aircraft carrier parked off Europe . . .'

While America has long been the ultimate goal for any performer, there are those who feared that in his determination to crack the American market, Richard Thompson was in danger of forsaking precisely what made him unique.

To penetrate the American heartland, sacrifices will always have to be made, rough edges smoothed off, compromises reached. The success of a record or movie in America has much to do with its lack of individuality, familiarity is appealing, and in their desire to tap into that massive market, most are happy to homogenize.

'Dire Straits to me are a very dilute band,' Thompson told *Q*'s Mat Snow, 'and it's the dilution that sells.'

America likes its originality in bite-sized chunks. The mega-albums are the ones which are so familiar, you're convinced you've already got them, the theme song of the American music industry is 'Send In The Clones'.

Rock'n'roll is now too big a term to embrace. The size, volume, impact and scale of the beast means that it has to be all things to all persons: rebellious and conformist; snotty and sincere; cultish and ballistic; nerdy and smooth. There is now a 40-year history to draw on. We have lived to see an American president name his daughter after a Joni Mitchell song, but do we really believe that what we see on MTV is part of that long tradition, rather than simple corporate desperation.

Thompson is too canny a player and too much of a realist to believe he could ever be successfully marketed to a Pearl Jam or a Green Day crowd. But there is an audience who respect REM which could tap into Thompson's music. Just shaving off a tiny slice of that audience would elevate Richard Thompson from cult figure into a major player.

The first step on that ladder was Thompson's new album *Amnesia*, for his new label Capitol, which was released in October 1988. David Sinclair's review in *Q* said it all: 'Another year, another label, another record, and *still* Richard Thompson awaits his just deserts. Surely there can be no other English performer able to boast such an authoritative and influential body of work while he remains such a proven commercial dud.'

The *Amnesia* sessions took place in Los Angeles in early 1988. Mitchell Froom was back behind the board and the top-notch American rhythm section of Jim Keltner and Jerry Scheff were retained. Clive Gregson and Christine Collister, John Kirkpatrick, Aly Bain and Phil Pickett made their contributions from the UK, recorded at the Kinks old studio Konk, in Tottenham. Around 30 songs were recorded for the album but, to date, titles such as 'Push And Shove' and 'Laughing Vigilante' remain tantalisingly unavailable.

'Turning Of The Tide' kickstarts the album into life. From its false start, through its world-weary vocal, familiar melody and atmospheric lyrics, it enters high on the Thompson Top Ten. Talking to *Hokey Pokey*, Thompson called 'Gypsy Love Songs' 'A true story, only the names have been changed. A musical *Day of the Locust*, my view of Hollywood.' 'I Still Dream' opens with the warm brass sound of the Fairey Engineering Band, but you doubt Thompson's sound-bite of the song as 'George Formby meets Bruce Springsteen'.

Thompson needed to court this new American audience. Ironic then that one of the tracks on his Capitol debut should be the scornful 'Yankee Go Home' ... Talking to *Hokey Pokey*, Thompson summed the song up: 'America's on the way out as Japan now buys the world. In Britain we understand this declining empires thing, so I thought I would offer a few words of consolation, to soften the blow.'

'Yankee Go Home' is a phrase familiar to anyone who grew up in Britain between 1942 and 1945 when millions of American GIs piled into the sceptred isle in preparation for D-Day. Compared to the dowdy-looking Brits, they offered film star glamour – 'they all looked like Clark Gable,' one infatuated girl of the time cooed. Not to mention their unlimited supplies of chewing gum, chocolate and nylons from the PX stores. Thompson quotes the most common complaint heard about the American servicemen during the Second World War, that they were 'over-paid, over-sexed and over here'.

Richard Thompson

American TV evangelism was the subject of 'Jerusalem On The Jukebox', a withering, scornful condemnation of the vapid values of Jimmy Swaggart and his ilk. Thompson fingers the superficiality of their 'beliefs'.

> In the bathroom mirror they try that Joan of Arc look again,
> Two parts Ingrid Bergman to one part Shirley MacLaine.
> The wounds of time kill you, but the surgeon's knife only stings ...

The Moral Majority behind the Republican right helped Reagan score two consecutive Presidential victories in the 1980s. Into the 1990s, they became an increasingly vocal voice in American politics. The babble and chatter became more strident, and was accompanied by an increase in extreme right-wing terrorist groups and murderous attacks on abortion clinics. And still the bile poured from the mouths of the TV evangelists who preached from their satellite pulpits in a world where 'God has the sharpest suit and the cleanest chin'.

Richard: 'Other songs are more about political or social commentary – I write a lot of songs about frustration – what people don't get from the twentieth century, where people feel inadequate – and what people get sold that doesn't fulfil them. What dreams people get sold by advertising, by governments, by countries and by social ideology that isn't ever going to do them any good – they're always going to fall short – and it just leaves them envious and jealous and inadequate.'

Tucked away as the penultimate track on *Amnesia*, 'Waltzing's For Dreamers' is undeniably one of Thompson's most beautiful and beguiling songs. Stylistically similar to 'Al Bowlly ...', the song sadly, inevitably, concludes that 'waltzing's for dreamers and losers in love'. The narrator has 'bet hard on love and lost everything'. There is no salvation in love, no safe haven in that turbulent, emotional ocean. The tune is as weary as the mood. It sounds like a hurdy-gurdy winding down, as in the background, just out of focus, skaters skim over a frozen Viennese lake.

'Pharaoh' is, at times, cumbersome and, at others, poignantly direct. Thompson's point is that ... 'plus ça change'. The pharaoh today may be clad in a striped suit, his pyramid an office block on the Isle of Dogs, but some things never change. The yoke and whip may have been replaced by BUPA and bonuses, but the fat cats still crack the whip, and it's the poor pyramid builders who forever labour under the lash:

> Call it England, call it Spain,
> Egypt rules with the whip and chain

Moses free my people again!
We're all working for the Pharaoh!

In his *Q* review, David Sinclair concluded: '*Amnesia* shows Thompson has forgotten none of his skills as a technically elite player, richly characterful singer, a literate and emotional songwriter and a truly original stylist. When will the world wise up to this remarkable man?' The magazine selected *Amnesia* as one of its albums of the year noting that 'few of his contemporaries can claim to celebrate twenty years of recording with something so substantial, so tough.' While in *Rolling Stone*, Jimmy Guterman caught the media mood, beginning his review 'Ho-hum, another first-rate Richard Thompson album.' Mal Peachey, writing in *Time Out*, called *Amnesia* 'a rare treat ... and far more worthy and hip than Chris Rea'.

Sales of *Amnesia* were respectable and the label did put some money into promoting the album, something which Thompson felt had been previously overlooked. But there were a series of cock-ups regarding single releases – 'Turning Of The Tide' and inexplicably 'Reckless Kind', were leaked rather than released. In the UK, *Amnesia* limped to a predictable no. 89 in the charts.

Thompson remained customarily rueful about his career. From his penthouse boardroom, *The Pharaoh* penned a further tongue-in-cheek biography for the Fairport reunion programme: 'Although this year has been an unspectacular one for Thompson Music and Leisure plc, it has been a time of quiet consolidation and satisfying growth. After our successful flotation in 1986, we are close to our target of six per cent worldwide profit on European holdings, and are confident of retaining our nine and a half per cent worldwide market return ...'

Thompson and producer Mitchell Froom had worked together well on two albums. Despite Thompson's reservations following *Sweet Talker*, Froom had landed him some work on the soundtrack for the neo-*noir Slam Dance*, which marked the big screen debut of Adam Ant. Froom also acted as honorary agent, securing gigs for Richard as guitarist on Crowded House records and converting Maria McKee into a fan. It was Froom who persuaded her to record Richard's 'Has He Got A Friend For Me' on her debut solo album.

Talking to *Hokey Pokey* soon after the release of *Amnesia* and during the recording of what would become *Rumor & Sigh*, Mitchell Froom enthused about Thompson: 'He's completely unique ... I've never worked on more than three records with anyone, but I think with Richard there is a good chance that he may be the first one, simply because the records are so fast to make. The time we've spent doing these three records is about the time it normally takes to do one record.'

Nancy Covey was in a perfect position to observe the changes in her husband's career. From her vantage point at McCabe's during the 1980s, she had watched the fluctuations of the US record industry: 'Gary Stamler was Richard's manager until recently. He'd got Crowded House going, and I think he was trying to help that along with Richard. I think the biggest change happened when Hale Milgrim became President of Capitol ... *Rumor & Sigh* got the big push. Hale Milgrim was a good friend of ours, he used to come to McCabe's. He was a major music fan, and a big Richard Thompson fan. And he said "I'm going to put money here and see what happens." And it helped. It doubled Richard's sales. By just doing interesting things, not doing the obvious, but by doing in-stores differently, you could hear a Richard Thompson record for free. Not your videos, we'd done that, and that obviously wasn't going to work for Richard. So he tried different things which he'd done before with Tracy Chapman while he was at Warner Brothers.

'I watch from the sidelines. I watch things going wrong. *Shoot Out the Lights*, when it was on Hannibal. I watched things being mismanaged. I was shocked. But I was never involved in that side of things. I've heard over the years that I've managed Richard, but that's not true. I've introduced him to people, but it's deadly, that pillow talk. That would be terrible.'

Richard: 'I don't care about what league I'm in, it doesn't matter. I really, really enjoy what I do right now. I don't want to do film scores, I don't want to open for Billy Joel. I'm quite happy with the set-up. What I want to do is write songs and make records and tour – tour with the band, tour solo. But all this stuff I'm doing now I just want to do more of it, I want to keep going and get it better and keep it interesting.

'Is everyone else doing their job? I think I'm doing my job, but I could probably do it better. But how's everyone else doing on their job? Is the record company doing a good enough job, could they do a better job? Probably they could. Do they need more of a kick up the backside? Probably they do.

'I've just hired a new manager who's probably going to do all that stuff outstandingly well, so I'm reasonably optimistic on that front. But this is what I like doing and if there are ways to make it better, good. You can always get more people to come to a concert and that always feels good, it feels like you're going somewhere. On the other hand, if there's only fifty people at a show you can still have a great time playing to those people. So in spite of what all the girls say, size isn't that important. But it is nice to feel you're going somewhere.'

Between *Amnesia* and *Rumor & Sigh* came events far from the music business, which would nevertheless stalk Richard Thompson over the ensuing years. In 1988, Booker Prize-winning author Salman Rushdie published *The Satanic Verses*.

On its publication, Rushdie's novel provoked outrage in Muslims the world over. Before the year was out, *The Satanic Verses* was infamous following violent demonstrations all over the United Kingdom. The book was banned in India and Rushdie was denounced in Pakistan, Saudi Arabia, Egypt and South Africa. Those who dared translate the blasphemous work were threatened and even murdered. Copies of Rushdie's book were publicly burned in scenes reminiscent of the Nazi book-burnings of the 1930s. The furore surrounding *The Satanic Verses* came to a head in February 1989, when the Iranian leader Ayatollah Khomeini pronounced a *fatwa* (death sentence) on Rushdie, who went into hiding and has lived under police protection ever since.

The cause of all this outrage was Rushdie's satirical treatment of various aspects of the Islamic faith in his novel. Raised a Muslim, Rushdie used his knowledge of Islam to subvert its most sacred symbolism. His fictional Imam was modelled on the Ayatollah Khomeini and his messianic figure 'Mahound' took his name from an ancient Western term of abuse for the Prophet. But the worst calumny came in a brothel scene, where Rushdie named the prostitutes after Mohammed's twelve wives. Rushdie also had his fictional creations question whether sections of the Koran might have been written by the Devil rather than the Prophet.

Fellow Muslims argued that Rushdie, with his personal experience of the faith, knew only too well how deeply offensive his book would be to believers. But *The Satanic Verses* is finally just a work of fiction, a mere pinprick against a millennia-old religion. The Christian Church, after all, survived Charles Darwin and *Monty Python's Life of Brian*.

The Western media had remained largely indifferent to the Islamic world until *The Satanic Verses* burned its way onto the front pages. From 1941, the Shah of Iran had ruled from his 'Peacock Throne' overseeing his country's economic expansion as Iran's supply of oil to the West increased. The opulent, Western-style court and courtiers, together with the Shah's growing reliance on brutal secret police, led to growing internal resistance centred around the country's religious leaders. The leading dissident Ayatollah Khomeini was exiled to France but continued to denounce the Shah's increasingly precarious government. By 1979, the Shah's position was untenable, and at the beginning of the year, he too flew into exile. The return of Ayatollah Khomeini in February 1979 was greeted by mass hysteria and rejoicing.

Ayatollah Khomeini oversaw his nation's 'Islamic Revolution', re-emphasising fundamental Islamic values. From early on, the Ayatollah's regime ran into problems with the West. The Shah was in America, undergoing treatment for the cancer which eventually killed him in 1980. Incensed at the Reagan government's refusal to return the Shah to Iran to stand trial, students held 63 Americans hostage in their embassy in Tehran for over a year.

Yusuf Islam – the artist formerly known as Cat Stevens – converted to Islam in 1977, and in 1989 was one of the first to condone the Ayatollah's *fatwa*. American band 10,000 Maniacs, who had included the Stevens' composition 'Peace Train' on their current album, asked that the track be removed from any subsequent pressings.

Richard Thompson knew he was on shaky ground. Talking to Marek Kohn of *The Independent* six months after the *fatwa*, Thompson commented on Yusuf Islam's endorsement of it: 'It's tricky. It's a minefield. I don't think there's anything clear-cut ... It's a can of worms, this one ... I believe up to a point in freedom of the artist ... the blasphemy laws in this country could certainly do with looking at. If they relate to Christianity, they should relate to other religions as well ... It [the book] was atrocious. And, in places, it really did upset me, actually. I did find it offensive.' Eventually forced into a corner and asked if Rushdie should be executed, Thompson prevaricated: 'If they handed me the gun ... I wouldn't shoot him.' That was to become Thompson's standard response to the Rushdie issue.

Richard: 'I think the reason [the *fatwa*] was said was for local consumption. I don't think the Iranian mullahs understand the West at all, they don't understand world politics – it's all for internal consumption – it's all for local votes and to continue the war that's been going on for about two thousand years inside Iran between the mullahs and the kings and the royal family. I'm not thrilled with Rushdie's book anyway – it was offensive to me actually, I mean, I wouldn't have killed him for it – I'd just have kind of slowly tortured him for a while and thrown him back!

'I didn't read the whole thing, it was so bloody boring. I read salient parts of it and I did find it offensive and I think he knew what he was getting into – I think he knew he was insulting a whole lot of Muslims – everybody actually. But he knew what he was doing and I think he has to accept the consequences.'

Such equivocation ignores the fundamental question of whether a writer's life should be under threat for what he wrote. While Richard Thompson and many others were genuinely offended by Rushdie's words, is that reason enough for the writer to be condemned to death?

Thompson is right when he says that Britain's blasphemy laws should be looked into. In a multi-cultural society protection should extend to all religions or to none. *The Satanic Verses* opened up a breach in an already uneasy and divided society. There are no easy answers or satisfactory compromises to be reached. But for over seven years, Salman Rushdie has had to live under the threat of death for writing a work of fiction. And that, to me, is another blasphemy.

Chapter 25

RICHARD: 'Suddenly with *Rumor & Sigh*, I sold twice as many records. I don't know what changed – I think it was a good record – it was a radio-worthy record and a marketable record, but I think the marketing budget definitely went up at that point and I got some attention at the record company.'

Rumor & Sigh was released in May 1991. To emphasise their commitment to marketing, Capitol organised a series of solo showcases in New York, Los Angeles, Toronto, Washington, Dallas, Atlanta and Ottawa. Talking to *Billboard*, Thompson called *Rumor & Sigh* 'the first record that's been really, truly promoted. Miracles can happen; the right people at the right place in a corporate structure', but Richard insisted that his priorities hadn't changed: 'The aim is to enjoy myself and try to be true to whatever ideals I have left.' *Billboard* concluded that 'it's not inconceivable that Thompson could bring this year's Bonnie Raitt-like breakthrough.'

Capitol's strategy paid off: *Rumor & Sigh* remains Richard Thompson's best-selling album ever. It reached no. 32 in the UK charts, an all-time high, and in America garnered Thompson a Grammy nomination. A professional musician of fifteen years standing, Thompson was gratified to find the record nominated in the 'Best Alternative Music Album' category. He lost out to REM and *Out of Time*, alongside fellow nominees Nirvana, Elvis Costello and Jesus Jones.

I talked to Thompson in Capitol's London office at the time of *Rumor & Sigh*. The interview took place right underneath *that* staircase on which the Beatles had posed for the cover of their first album in 1963. He was suitably modest about his achievements on the label: '*Amnesia* probably did worldwide, one hundred thousand, which I think is great "Wow! That's a Wembley Stadium full of people who've bought my record." The record company though, they don't even register unless it goes to a quarter of a million. So from a corporate point of view it's negligible, but I think it's pretty good going for an old folkie.'

Solo

For those who feared the further Americanisation of Richard Thompson, the spelling of the album title was all the confirmation they needed: *Rumor & Sigh*, what happened to the 'u'? Thompson sheepishly explained that the cover was painted in America and so he stuck with the American spelling. The title came from a poem by Alexander MacLeish ('Rumor and sigh of unimagined seas . . .'). MacLeish was a Pulitzer Prize-winning poet and playwright, who had died in 1982, but Thompson was not his first exposure to rock'n'roll. In 1969, Bob Dylan was approached to compose the music for a production of 77-year-old MacLeish's play *The Devil & Daniel Webster*. The play's producer regretfully declined Mr Dylan's submission. Mr Dylan graciously reworked the songs, and released them as *New Morning* the following year.

Thompson's willingness to play the record company game ensured the success of *Rumor & Sigh*, despite wanting to call 'I Feel So Good' the album's lead-off single, 'The Lost Sheep Returns To The Fold' ('but they thought that was a little too snappy'). Pressing all the right buttons (showcase gigs, lead-off single, promo video, sympathetic press coverage, synchronised touring to support the album release, radio plays . . .) all helped; but it was still the quality of the songs on the record which ultimately mattered. And great songs were something *Rumor & Sigh* had in abundance.

Whether performed solo, or as an acoustic interlude when touring with the band, the response to '1952 Vincent Black Lightning' is always phenomenal. Talking to me in 1991, Thompson admitted: 'Of all the songs I've ever performed, it goes down the best of the lot. That's of any song I've ever done live, anywhere! . . . So maybe the next album will be all ballads about British motorcycles – Triumphs, BSAs, Ariels.

' "Vincent" does tend to be the most popular, it always comes out on top on the Internet polls and college radio stations often say it was the most requested song over the year. And I've done these all-request shows where people will write requests at the door when they come in, then we have the bucket on stage and I have to play whatever comes out of the bucket. That's quite fun and it's also a market research tool, because afterwards you can hang onto the bucket and stick it all in the computer and see the level of requests and "Vincent" is always top there as well. It took me by surprise to find that people were that willing to listen to a ballad.

'I suppose I'd thought it was harder for people in the twentieth century to sit down and listen to a story in a song, but I was wrong. While it's a contemporary song it's got a very classical structure, a traditional ballad structure – which is a proven successful form. There's an attempt in the song to involve the listener in the story and the characters, and if the characters aren't appealing and people don't care about them, then they won't like the song or get the song, so it must succeed at that level.

'It's a hunt for mythology as well. A lot of the mythology of popular music is American – "The Midnight Special", "Going Down To New Orleans". And all those cars – "buy you a chevrolet". So romantic myth in song definitely crossed the Atlantic at some point. I think it had already done so by the 1920s, although you still had "A Nightingale Sang In Berkeley Square" or "Waterloo Sunset", but generally speaking the mythology of popular song has been in America, especially in the South.

'So being British, I've always tried to look for objects that have some kind of mythological appeal, that you can write about as a British songwriter. The Vincent is a fabulous beast, it really is a thing of fable and beauty and it's mythological, it's the lodestone around which the characters in the song revolve.'

Between them, Chuck Berry and Bruce Springsteen pretty much cornered the automotive imagery market. But Punk made English writers look to their own roots and prompted Tom Robinson to write a song about a 'Grey Cortina', while Ian Dury listed 'the Vincent motorsickle' as one of his 'Reasons To Be Cheerful' in 1979.

Marc Ellington: 'On "Vincent", that style of guitar playing is also very appealing to people ... it is 1918–1925, an American, Appalachian, style of guitar, almost Carter Family style ... It's a very interesting narrative on the whole position of "the hero". But in this case, the hero is not an individual, but a piece of machinery ... To understand the importance of something like a Vincent within the engineering heritage of this country is very important. Along with one or two other motorbikes, they were world beaters, it's been taken away by the Japanese now I suppose. But Richard sees the machine as the hero.'

Only 27 Vincents were ever manufactured, which makes it a convenient symbol for the decline of English manufacturing. The Vincent can be seen as emblematic of the value of individual craftsmanship in the face of mass production. In Thompson's adept hands, the ballad aches with the pressures of time, but still manages to be contemporary. With his inimitable eye for detail, Thompson is quick to point out that James Adie passing the keys of his machine to Red Molly was purely symbolic, as the motorcycle in question was kick-started!

'Read About Love', which opens the album, is a smutty memoir of an adolescent's obsession with sex. The song's protagonist swings between all the top-shelf smut and hardback science 'written by a doctor with a German name'.

'I Feel So Good' has the archetypal Richard Thompson opening: 'I feel so good I'm going to break somebody's heart tonight . . .' A ne'er-do-well is freed from prison and the song documents his bullying exultation at his freedom. Talking to Ken Hunt in *Folk Roots*, Thompson discussed the ambivalence which so often characterises his writing: 'Here's the dilemma for the listener . . . He's the protagonist of the song, and if you make someone the subject of the song, you're almost inevitably making him a hero. But he obviously isn't. Nor is he an anti-hero. You don't have any sympathy with him, but then he's no worse than the society that created him, and he might even be better. It's a very twentieth-century moral dilemma . . .'

'Grey Walls' was inspired by Colney Hatch Mental Hospital in Whetstone which Thompson passed on the bus as a teenager ('Absolutely, utterly depressing; black, dark despair . . .'). Chilling in its clinical description of electric shock therapy, the song had wider implications in the context of Margaret Thatcher's policy of closing down the old asylums and selling off their sprawling sites, without any real provision being made for the inmates.

The resignation of Margaret Thatcher in November 1990 had marked the end of an era in British political history. Singlehandedly, she had got rid of consensus politics, overseen a rise in state-sanctioned greed and created an economy which put profit before everything. The abiding legacy of Thatcherism was not the closure of mental hospitals, the de-recognition of trade unions . . . or any one of half a hundred crimes against its citizens: Thatcher's greatest calumny was in legitimising greed. She decreed 'there is no such thing as society', and proved it by de-constructing the welfare state which was set up for Thompson and his contemporaries in the post-war baby boom, and had been the safety net for successive generations.

Future generations would have to fend for themselves, Thatcher even privatised essential services which had been in public hands since 1945. In Harold Macmillan's telling phrase it was like 'selling off the family silver'. In the high-rise, champagne-swilling, anything-goes 1980s, Thompson had sounded a note of caution in his work. As in much of Bob Dylan's work at the same time, Thompson mourned the loss of spiritual values and bemoaned the tide of materialism which was so manifest.

A weak and divided Opposition, a greedy electorate and a tide in the affairs of men, all put Margaret Thatcher in power, and kept her there for eleven long and divisive years. Thompson's response was the belated 'Mother Knows Best', recorded on the day that Thatcher resigned, and reflecting the country's unwillingness to be ruled any longer by this hectoring harridan. In the final verse, the figure comes straight from the pages of the Brothers Grimm rather than the front door of No. 10 Downing Street:

> She says, bring me your first-born, I'll suck their blood
> Bring me your poor, I can trample in the mud,
> Bring me your visionaries, I can put out their eyes,
> Bring me all your scholars, I'll have them all lobotomised . . .

'I Misunderstood' is another of those sting-in-the-tail songs which Thompson relishes ('I thought she was saying good luck, she was saying goodbye . . .'). The twist recalls that employed by Elvis Costello on '(The Angels Wanna Wear My) Red Shoes': ('I said I'm so happy I could die; She said "Drop dead", then left with another guy . . .').

Rumor & Sigh wraps with 'Psycho Street', a challenging and largely unlistenable Thompson composition along the lines of 'Dance Of The Cosmetic Surgeons'. 'It's an experiment in song form,' Thompson told me in 1991. 'It's fairly radical. We weren't sure about putting it on the record, but Mitchell [Froom] and I really liked the beatnik backing, kind of cool. People really like it or dislike it – my wife hates it. I think that song is a one-off, but there are always possibilities about doing different things with songs.'

Talking to Ken Hunt in *Folk Roots*, Thompson admitted that the first couple of verses were written while he was thinking of Salman Rushdie and *The Satanic Verses*. On a lighter level, he also felt inspired to write an anti-*Neighbours* song, a protest against the ubiquity of the twice-daily Australian soap on British television.

Along with the song about the motorcycle, the other composition on *Rumor & Sigh* which still raises a smile is 'Don't Step On My Jimmy Shands'. The song is capable of being performed by Thompson in rollicking band style, or solo, when he feints with the crowd on the chorus. On record, the syncopated band version has all the drunken reeling of party revelry. Thompson was partially inspired to write the song by a story about the young Bob Dylan hogging the record player at a party, endlessly re-playing a Robert Johnson LP, 'Jimmy Shands' is a song for record-collecting nerds, by a self-confessed nerd.

Spending a lot of time in Scotland during his formative years, Thompson couldn't help but be aware of Scotland's premier accordionist, Jimmy Shand. Shand's influence on Thompson's own instrumental passages is well-documented and this song is a tongue-in-cheek tribute to Shand. Jimmy Shand MBE was born in 1908, and began recording in 1933; his unique style of playing and his two accordion, violin, piano, double bass and drum line-up became the standard bandstand set up for all practitioners of Scottish Country Dance.

Talking to me in 1991, Thompson was delighted that 'the Americans don't know what to make of it ... On one hand, he was a very corny musician, and hearing that stuff as a kid, I needed to purge it somehow. I love and hate aspects of the accordion and Scottish dance music.' Fans from around the world are convinced that on completing a tour, Richard Thompson cannot wait to get home, put his feet up, and relax by playing old 78s of Jimmy Shand, again and again and again. His London home is littered with rare records by the grand old man of Scottish dance, which fans press on him after shows around the world. Everything you could possibly ever want to know, and hear, about Jimmy Shand is to be found on the 1994 EMI CD *King of the Melodeon Men*.

Richard: 'Jimmy Shand was a pioneer of that style, he started that sound in the 30s and it became imitated and everybody ended up doing it and there were probably other bands that did it better in the end. It's kind of a cliché, and I have a love/hate relationship with it. It's all in there together – and that's what the song's about as well – love it and hate it at the same time. But people think Dennis Potter loves all that 30s music but he absolutely hated it – it was just a device.'

Thompson intended 'God Loves A Drunk' as a swipe at 'Mormons and Seventh Day Adventists, those people with the polyester suits, those people who are very clean and neat and clean-shaven, which means they're right with God.' He envisaged the song as being about spirituality, not necessarily equating devotion with sobriety, seeing the drunk, as he does in so many of his songs, as an outsider, an underdog, an outcast. 'God Loves A Drunk' continues Thompson's fascination with alcohol. A long-time teetotaller, although he did drink quite heavily in younger days on the road with Fairport, Thompson's portrait of the imbiber in this song is affectionate rather than scornful. In his 1973 song 'The World Is A Wonderful Place', Thompson writes that you 'envy the drunk' in a world which is plainly falling apart. It was around the same time that he wrote 'When I Get To The Border' ('say I drowned in a barrel of wine'), and 'Down Where The Drunkards Roll'.

Bernard Doherty: 'He was an aloof bloke. I suppose it's down to that horrible English thing of do you know someone if you don't get drunk with them? You don't meet someone for a cup of tea and get their life story. It's only when someone's had a bottle of wine that they're gonna let you know their inner feelings. Richard was a teetotaller from the day I met him . . .'

'God Loves A Drunk' reveals again Thompson's scorn for those semi-detached suburbanites. The pen-pushers and sober wage-slaves attract a particularly bitter brand of criticism from the writer who would like to think he has left suburban mediocrity far behind him, but is frustrated by how much of it remains within.

Clive Gregson: '*Rumor & Sigh*, I thought it was where his writing showed massive peaks and troughs. For Richard, there are no real howlers, he isn't ever going to write a Lieutenant Pigeon song . . . I think it had just run its course. Chris and I were really busy, we made the record, and we knew we couldn't make the tour. That was a really strange period for Richard, he ended up doing the tour with none of the usual suspects – basically an all-American band, with only Pat Donaldson on bass.

'Again, and it's fairly typical of Richard, *Rumor & Sigh* was the record Capitol went to town on, they really went for it . . . He was taking tour support, moving up into bigger venues, it was a big deal. It grieves me to say this, but I thought he went out with the worst band I've ever seen him with, the show I saw was so lacklustre . . . I think it was the essential Englishness of a lot of what Richard does had gone missing. They became a fairly functional mainstream rock band . . . They toured America, did a handful of UK shows, but when it came to a full British tour a few months later, and I'm only guessing, Richard got as many of the last band back – I did it, he kept Shawn [Colvin], DM, John K. That was good fun. It was like the last throes of that era really.

'*Rumor & Sigh* is his most successful record, shifted, what quarter of a million worldwide? But an expensive record to make, I don't know, £100,000 . . . I think if Capitol keep him, it's the same reason Warners kept Randy Newman and Ry Cooder . . . Richard lives half the year in the States, his wife is American, two of his sons are living there, and that's his biggest and most successful market . . .'

John Martin: 'I thought Richard was getting in a rut. I thought his approach to recording around 1990–91 . . . I felt basically it was time to make a change and record with new people, I thought a breath of fresh air would have been good, and a change of producer, not going back to the same gang of musicians. Richard would talk about wanting to do a new type of album, a new approach, but when it came to it, it would be exactly the same team, the same studios ... He would talk about recording perhaps a very much less electric, a more acoustic type of record, or at least a record that had a lot more space and percussion and different types of instrumentation, and he used to always talk about the idea of touring like that ... Lately he has done a much more stripped down type of thing, and I thought *Mirror Blue* was a pretty good sort of compromise. But years before that, he had a few more ideas, and probably it was the record company who said well, you can't really do it. You've got to go out and do rock tours, that's the way to success.'

Capitol's push paid off and *Rumor & Sigh* made its mark. Writing in the *NME*, Terry Staunton called the album 'Thompson's best record since *Hand of Kindness*', and singled out 'Vincent' as a 'contender for Thompson's best ever song'. To Thompson's delight, Staunton also found the album 'littered with a cast of characters David Lynch would kill for'. In *Folk Roots*, Colin Irwin wrote: 'This is Richard's most completely satisfying album for a long time. I know I always say that, but it's true – a tribute to the freshness and enterprise he still engenders and an example to forty-somethings everywhere.'

Q gave *Rumor & Sigh* its customary four-star review, and featured the album as one of its Best of the Year, following in *Amnesia*'s footsteps. In November 1991, Thompson also received the magazine's Best Songwriter Award at a ceremony held at EMI's legendary Abbey Road Studios.

Thompson toured to promote the album, a lengthy swing through North America and key UK dates during 1991. The opening act was Shawn Colvin, who was later to take up Christine Collister's role in the Thompson Band as well. Colvin became a stalwart of Thompson's live set up and later married his long-time sound engineer Simon Tassano. Coming in at the tail end of the female singer-songwriter boom of the late 80s, following on from Tracy Chapman, Michelle Shocked and Suzanne Vega – Colvin was a backing vocalist on Vega's breakthrough 'Luka'. Though she confessed to being a fairly late convert to Thompson's work, Colvin was making up for lost time with zeal.

As the year wound on, things seemed to be going up a gear in the Thompson camp. As well as the obligatory excellent reviews accorded *Rumor & Sigh*, the album actually appeared to be selling copies as well. And not just to the Richard Thompson diehards who would buy everything, from *Strict Tempo* to *Sweet Talker*, but tapping into a new audience, reared on REM and girding up for Nirvana.

Thompson's biggest gig of the year was in Seville, on 17 October 1991, when he appeared at the Guitar Greats celebration, as the special

Richard Thompson

guest of Bob Dylan. For Dylan-watchers, the occasion was up there with the Bard's disastrous Live Aid appearance. Thompson was asked to accompany Dylan on 'Boots Of Spanish Leather' and 'Across The Borderline', but when they reached the stage before an audience of millions, Bob appeared to have changed his mind and struck off into unrehearsed territory.

It was Dylan who opened the door for lyricists like Richard Thompson. It was Dylan who wrote many of the best songs in Fairport Convention's early repertoire. The opportunity to appear alongside Bob Dylan was too good to miss. But as Oscar Wilde cracked: 'beware of your dreams, in case they come true'.

Richard: 'It was the first time I'd met Dylan. I was asked to come in a day early to play in the band with him. They had a band with Simon Phillips on drums, Phil Manzanera on guitar, Jack Bruce on bass, Bruce Hornsby on keyboards – I thought great, that'd be nice. It was just to come in and play on "All Along The Watchtower" – we could only do one number. I got in in the afternoon and I was really tired, I was in the middle of a European tour, so I broke it and came from Amsterdam and I was going back to Rotterdam just to do this Seville thing. We did the rehearsal and Bob wasn't there so we just rehearsed without him and then I got a message from his tour manager asking if I could do some acoustic stuff with him.

'So I went up to the dressing room. It was kind of disappointing, because it was like he wasn't really there – he seemed socially very ill at ease and seemed totally unwilling to communicate, which was really disappointing because I really wanted to talk to him. I just kept hitting a brick wall and I thought, "oh well, if that's the way you want to be, to hell with it". I thought, oh, a pretentious, pompous, moody rock star, you know, I can't deal with it. So I was really disappointed. People said "well, some days he's like that and other days he's fine". The reports this year [1995] are that he's playing amazingly well after a while of being really not very good. So that's really good news. It must be hard being famous when you're only nineteen, and being the saviour of your generation. "Bob save us – what's the answer Bob"?'

Chapter 26

'RICHARD'S NOT A Top Ten act, he's not someone that huge resources can be ploughed into. But we've tried to work intelligently to broaden the crowd, so that the type of audience that likes Elvis Costello and intelligent rock is aware of Richard – and why they should be interested in his music.'

Promoter David Jones was talking to *Vox* in 1992 about Thompson's forthcoming 21-date solo acoustic UK tour. Thompson has always been able to divide his live work between solo acoustic and electric big band. Playing electric, Thompson was usually out there promoting a new album and reaching rock audiences. Playing solo, he was largely preaching to the converted, but he has always been very good at keeping in close touch with loyal fans.

Solo, Thompson travelled simply with Simon Tassano as tour manager/sound engineer. David Jones began booking the tour by the expedient of ringing prospective venues, and if they didn't know who Richard Thompson was, they didn't get the gig.

Jones' company, Serious Speakout, tackled Thompson's database direct, sending details of the tour directly to fans, or culling names from the mailing lists of venues Richard had played. 'What happens, we hope,' said David Jones, 'is that Richard's audience not simply be all the people who already know they'd like to see him, but also people that we've found.'

I saw Thompson on that 1992 solo tour at the Royal Festival Hall. Recently a father again for the fifth time, Nancy brought baby Jack along to see his dad at work. It was some time since I had seen him sustain a solo show, and I was struck by how much more confident and assured a performer he had become. It wasn't simply the chat and bonhomie which came across, but he genuinely seemed to relish performing, and was able to communicate that enthusiasm.

Standing solo, centre stage, there is nowhere to run, nowhere to hide. It is the ultimate test for a performer and his audience. Thompson's audiences have always been lively and likeable, they know he isn't all doom and gloom. They are not averse to a spot of misery on the night, but they know Richard will leaven the gloom with gags and offer a balanced show.

Richard: 'The best performances are where you can reach right into yourself. I think I get better at it – I think playing solo has been a revelation. I did odd solo things in the 70s, but having to work solo quite a lot has taught me a lot about being on stage and what an audience is and the respect with which you have to treat an audience.

'I probably figured at some point that I should be aggressive towards the audience in some way, I should go out to the audience and attack them. I think opening shows for rock bands was probably the point where I thought: I've got to shout at them, otherwise I'll go on and go off and they'll never have known I was even there. I played solo for Crowded House in Canada, where the audience was thirteen years old, which was quite difficult, but I usually won. So I'd shout at the audience and cajole them and at least try to annoy them or something. I suppose I've borrowed other people's personas to do it – it's a bit of Danny Thompson and a bit of Pat Donaldson and a bit of Loudon Wainwright as well, people who are kind of loud.'

It is a testament to Thompson's abilities as both songwriter and performer that so much of his material is versatile enough to work either with the benefit of an electric band, or lend itself to solo settings. But in Britain there is always the unwanted baggage, the inescapable shadow of Fairport Convention to reckon with. That Thompson chooses occasionally to work solo with a miked-up acoustic guitar shouldn't automatically exile him to folk hell. But while Bruce Springsteen can ditch the E Street Band, and everyone and his wife has jumped on the *Unplugged* gravy train, Richard Thompson has already been there and is wary of the pull of the past.

A trim and conventional figure onstage, Thompson always endeavours to put on a crowd-pleasing show. He will plug his current album – '1952 Vincent Black Lightning' was a dream for the 1992 solo shows. But over a couple of hours, he will also rove over his back catalogue, dusting down discarded gems and shining them up afresh. There are always songs he has fun with. 'Jimmy Shand' evokes a call and response, which brings a smile to his face.

Clive Gregson: 'I think the humour doesn't come across on his records, they tend to be a bit po-faced with the occasional aberration of humour. But I think onstage he is very likeable and very amusing, particularly solo.'

'Two Left Feet', freed from any rock'n'roll restraints with the band, is transformed. Thompson weaves over Fats Waller namechecking

Jackie Wilson's 'Reet Petite', Rene Magritte and Shredded Wheat in a rhyming frenzy. Solo, 'Two Left Feet' is one of the few occasions when Thompson will deviate from the familiar printed lyrics.

Richard: 'It's good to find new ways of doing old songs. It's a song that really works one way with a band and that's the only way you can do it. Or if I'm doing it solo, or I'm doing it with Danny maybe, there's ways to chop it up, it's loose enough that I can be all over the place and Danny can still find me occasionally. We can change verses, we can change instrumental pieces, you can slot different things in and out of it, you can change bar lengths, it can be any length at all, so we can have fun with it. It's good to have a few songs like that, that are really quite loose on stage, because then you can surprise yourself and other people every night by doing it slightly differently.

'If I'm playing solo, there are some songs where I get tied to the arrangement – if I'm not playing the arrangement then I'm not playing the song – something like "I Misunderstood", there's not a lot of variation I can put into it and still be true to it. So that's hard, you perform it like a classical music performance where you go through it and you express it in different ways, but you're basically playing the same notes. So it's nice to have a few things where you can just let it fly and see what happens.'

During the solo shows of the 90s, Thompson would dive back to a time before rock'n'roll with 'Don't Roll Those Bloodshot Eyes At Me', learned from an album by country singer Hank Penny; he also disinterred 'Rag Mop', courtesy of Bob Wills and the Texas Playboys. The rockabilly standard 'Hot Dog' was also regularly featured. A highlight of that Festival Hall show was his encore of the Who's 'Substitute', with Thompson flailing windmill-like over the guitar neck à la Pete Townshend.

Richard: 'The Who were our favourite band. I think they were the most impressive band you could see around London, we're talking 1965. By then, you had the Who, the Yardbirds, the Kinks, the Action, Gary Farr and the T-Bones. The Marquee Club was a good place to see these bands, but the Who were far and away the most impressive band you could see. They were stunning, great originality, so different, great visual ideas.

' "Substitute" I still do occasionally solo. It works really well solo, it's fun to do solo because you take away whatever the record was, which was that dynamic Keith Moon-type of thing, and strip it away and still make it very dynamic. The Townshend windmill effect is unbelievably hard to do – it's not hard to swing your arm round, but to hit the string occasionally, in the right order.'

Richard Thompson

It is salutary to remind yourself occasionally of Thompson's greatness. Like any performer made familiar by regular listening, you can take him for granted. But seeing Richard Thompson play live – even coasting – reminds you just how powerful a performer he is, and what a magnificent body of work there is to coast on.

Onstage, what you see is what you get.

Danny Thompson: 'The person who goes onstage and who comes offstage is the same person. Some people put an 'image' on stage, and they bring that image into their real life.

'There are people I've worked with who are talking like me one minute, then they go onstage and they say in that mid-Atlantic way "Now I'd like to do a number which is a kind of, it's a 'kind of' insight into the way . . ." And you're going "Who the bloody hell is this geezer all of a sudden?" And Richard is a million miles away from that. A man with no side at all. Maybe that gets on people's nerves; maybe they'd like to turn up and see these legendary people, with purple hats with cloaks, and deep, smouldering souls . . . well, hard luck!'

There are some performers who have been around for a mighty long time who, try as they might, never really change. They remain constant, on the level, and just occasionally, the fluctuating fads of the music industry intersect with that line. It happened to Leonard Cohen, for years the bard of the bedsit, the seigneur of black, polo-neck sweater wearers, diligently intoning the lyrics of 'Suzanne'. Then all of a sudden Cohen is hip, and at his 1988 Albert Hall concert on the back of *I'm Your Man*, bright-eyed, power-dressed Yuppies were stalking the amphitheatre, alongside the baffled, grey-haired originals, who had been bringing tea and oranges for over twenty years.

There is a caravanserai which has followed Thompson for thirty years. Those who recall, with dim affection, too many pints of beer slopping over their rugby shirt at Fairport gigs, as they marvelled at Thompson's unfeasibly fast guitar playing. Or maybe wandered into a folk club sometime in the early 1970s, to get away from the ubiquitous Ziggy-mania, and were transfixed by the translucent voice of the girl, and the shimmering guitar of the shaggy-headed cove to her left.

Then there are those who were caught unawares by Richard as the opening act at some stadium show and grew fascinated by the edgy character alone onstage. The one telling jokes one minute, then plunging like a bathysphere to the darkest depths of human emotion. Then rounding off his 40 minutes with a song about the terpsichorean hardships of being saddled with two left feet.

Thompson was making lots of new friends in America as a solo draw.

Solo

Early in 1992, Thompson joined Roger McGuinn for some solo shows. The two men would occasionally join together on Byrds' songs like 'Goin' Back' and 'The Ballad Of Easy Rider' which were familiar from early Fairport set lists.

Scottish-born David Byrne was a Thompson fan of long standing and the two men appeared together, also during early 1992. Each would take to the stage, and perform a selection of material – 'Vincent' went down a storm and Thompson also included a rare version of 'She Moved Through The Fair'. Byrne would delight with stripped-down versions of Talking Heads' hits – 'Psycho Killer', 'Road To Nowhere'. The fun lay in the choice of cover versions, like Neil Young's 'Rockin' In The Free World', Ewan MacColl's 'Dirty Old Town' and '?' and the Mysterians garage anthem '96 Tears'. Even Byrne was slightly baffled by Thompson's choice of encore at one of their final shows together – the Gallic Punk of Plastic Bertrand's 'Ca Plane Pour Moi', 'the sound of angry young Belgium' the *NME* commented on its 1978 release.

At the start of the 1990s, there was a legacy of bad feeling between Thompson and Joe Boyd. The trouble which had arisen over outstanding royalties from Thompson's stint at Hannibal Records, came to a head when Boyd decided to sell Hannibal to the American independent Rykodisc.

Joe Boyd: 'There was a period ... when Hannibal was in big financial trouble and relations were very difficult between Richard and myself, because I owed him a lot of royalties ... Basically, I paid Richard's royalties off, and in so doing, brought Hannibal to the point of bankruptcy ...

'*Shoot Out the Lights* and *Hand of Kindness* were primary assets, the main things that Rykodisc required ... That year of 1990, I was trying to keep the company alive, while paying a substantial amount to Richard every month, with an agreement that if I missed any payment, I had agreed that the ownership of the masters reverted to Richard, and I then would have had nothing to sell, and wouldn't have been able to pay everybody else their royalties.

'In the end an old girlfriend of mine lent me £5,000 ... so in the end, it all got paid. When Rykodisc took over, Richard and I were once again able to be friendly, but there were a few years during the last few years of Hannibal when it was difficult, and I don't blame him. I would have been outraged, I have no quarrel with his stance .... From his point of view, I was speculating with his royalties. I was trying to keep the label going – heating bills, paying salaries, going to Bulgaria and making records – while I owed him money. From my point of view, I knew that I had to keep doing that if I was to pay him money, that was the only chance I had – to keep the label going. I knew if I just stopped, the whole thing would collapse ... owing Richard a lot of money, which he would never see. That was my logic, but I can understand how slippery and arcane this logic can seem to an artist who's owed a lot of money.'

John Martin retained a watching brief on Thompson's activities in the UK. As well as the outstanding amounts from Hannibal, Thompson was understandably piqued about monies which Island owed him. These were royalties which stretched back over twenty years in some instances and Richard was determined to get some sort of financial justice.

John Martin: 'I worked a lot on the problems with Hannibal and Joe Boyd, identifying the debts and working out ways it could be resolved ... I worked as part of a team against Joe and we did force him into submission, if you like, and he had to pay a huge amount of money.

'The accountant had done audits in Island, and he was involved in getting Richard's back royalties. And because the Island thing was linked with Joe as well, he would directly deal with the Island people ... The accountant would be behind me being very heavy, threatening to take Hannibal to court for millions of pounds, and I'd be kind of saying "Well look, Joe, you've got to face this, you can't ignore this, what are you going to do? You've got to be a decent guy here, this is Richard we're talking about" – play on all that emotional stuff. The accountant was the one who got whatever was got out of Island ... And of course Island were to blame a lot with Joe because they'd never policed Hannibal on all the licences ... they'd let Joe get away with an awful lot.'

With *Rumor & Sigh* his best-selling album to date, Richard Thompson was in a strong position to apply some muscle. The dreamy teenager who never banked a cheque had matured into a responsible business man determined to rectify 25 years of financial ineptitude.

John Martin: 'At the beginning of the 90s, Richard had a very lucrative back catalogue publishing deal ... all his songs were got back from Island. Then Gary Stamler did a new deal and said you can't have any of the new material, but you can have all the back catalogue again, and by this time, Island Music was part of Polygram. So he did this great deal with Polygram Songs, a huge amount of money, as an advance, just for the back royalties ... So Richard was doing fine, he had an ongoing relationship with Capitol, he had his set-up with Hannibal and Island clarified ... money was beginning to come in. He was about to get his *Q* Songwriter's Award. He was back on TV, he was almost getting a *South Bank Show* all the time. He was that kind of bubbling under figure again.'

The Great Buried Treasure flag was being flown again. Typical was a Thompson profile by Pete Clark, which appeared in the London *Standard* of October 1993. Under the headline 'The best rock musician in the world – and he's never had a hit', Clark wrote: 'Richard Thompson is the best-kept musical secret there has ever been. To call him low-profile is an absurd hype. But he is arguably the most accomplished singer/guitarist/songwriter that the UK, and possibly the world, has ever produced.'

Joan (Richard's mother): 'It's surprising how many people do know of Richard. When we were living in Dumfries and my husband was retired – his parents had died, and for a few years he was steward of a club. We'd have dances, we used to have groups come from all over and my husband would always say "I don't suppose you've heard of Richard Thompson". And they had all heard of him – there wasn't a group who didn't know. That village is in the middle of nowhere. It was most strange.'

Over the years, journalists and broadcasters have continued to believe that if they get Thompson to confide his favourite songs, they would gain an insight into his tortured soul. It is a good shorthand method of gaining a fuller understanding of 'the man', like inspecting someone's record collection or bookshelves when you're visiting their house.

Thompson's musical tastes were formed in his youth, from his father's collection of jazz 78s and the classical music he heard daily working for Hans Unger, to his sister and her boyfriends' rock'n'roll favourites and the folk tradition he researched and absorbed during early Fairport days. All of these have remained constants, though he is reluctant to narrow his choices to a handful of favourites.

Richard: 'I think you'd get sick of any small number of records and I think your taste actually changes, stuff becomes flavour of the month and then goes out of fashion ... Unless you took some enormously long piece of music which you could never get through, but I hate Wagner so "The Ring" is out ... Perhaps you could take all the Beethoven symphonies. There wouldn't ever be enough music to keep you going – I really think that if you took eight gramophone records to a desert island you'd smash the lot in frustration within about a year.'

Despite the breadth of his tastes, for Thompson, as indeed for many of his age, Punk was the last great, seismic musical movement and he has few favourites much beyond the 1970s.

When asked for his favourite records, the same old names re-appear: the Comedian Harmonists (a pre-war German quintet), the Everly Brothers, Hank Williams, the Byrds, guitarist Thumbs Carlyle, the Band, Bob Dylan and Django Reinhardt ('the guitarist who had everything,' Thompson once told the *NME*, only to be trumped by Linda's comment 'except fingers').

Guesting on David Hepworth's GLR show in August 1991, Thompson listed his favourites as:

> Favourite Bob Dylan Song: 'Lily, Rosemary and The Jack Of Hearts'.
> Favourite Punk Record: Sex Pistols 'God Save The Queen'.
> Song You Wish You'd Written: Hank Williams 'My Sweet Love Ain't Around'.
> Record That Makes You Cry: The Five Blind Boys Of Alabama 'When God Dips His Pen'.
> All Time Favourite: Muddy Waters 'Mannish Boy'.

To David Cavanagh, in *Q* in 1994 when selecting further faves, Thompson added the Smiths ('narrow, but rewarding') and Elvis Presley's *The Complete Sun Sessions* ('I used to do "Trying To Get To You", but it's a really stupid thing to do, because you're never going to do it as well as Elvis.').

Pinned down again by *Q* a year later, on 'The Record That Changed My Life', Thompson admitted to *Scottish Dance Music* by Pipe Major John Burgess: 'It is both very soulful and kind of spine-chilling ... It requires a fairly exact kind of playing, the notes are very weighted. Each has a very specific emotional effect; none of it is wasted. There's a whole science of Scottish pipe composition as exacting as composing Indian ragas. And it swings.' (Topic Records released a John Burgess compilation, *King of the Highland Pipers*, in 1993.)

You can see the appeal to Thompson of the pipes. There is a dexterity to the playing which he would admire. Running deeper though is the emotion which the playing of a master piper can evoke. There is a melancholy in the laments which is among the most visual in all music. To hear a solitary piper play a lament is to comprehend the sad history of a whole nation. Many of Pipe Major Burgess' best-known recordings are laments, or pibrochs, which speak of battles lost or clans decimated. The English colonisation of Scotland, the Highland Clearances, the bloody and vengeful battle of Culloden, the romantic intrigue of the Prince across the water ... all are to be heard in the playing of a dexterous and resonant piper.

Solo

Marc Ellington has lived in Scotland since the early 70s. Since he stopped singing in the late 70s, he has become the Deputy Lord Lieutenant of Aberdeenshire and an advisor to the government on Historic Buildings. He lives at Towie Barclay Castle, where he believes Richard Thompson has spent every Hogmanay for the past twenty years.

Marc Ellington: 'I can remember when we were recording a record here with one of the best pipe bands we've got in Scotland, Richard was visiting. The Pipe Major was having difficulties working out harmonies for one of the songs, "The Bonnie Lass Of Fyvie-O" ... Richard discussed it with the Pipe Major, and within ten minutes they'd worked out an arrangement, which they still use to this day in competition. And I remember the amazement of everyone in the Pipe band that Richard wasn't a piping instructor.'

'One summer, in a pub on the Moray Firth, and the landlord remembered hearing somewhere – probably from Ian Sutherland who lives in the village – that Richard played the guitar, and he produced this old, battered nylon Mexican guitar with one string missing and said "Go on Richard, play us a song". And of course there's nothing worse for someone than to have it thrust into your hand. Richard grabbed the thing, and it was amazing – he went through every Scottish ballad worth singing, a few of his own songs I'd never heard, a selection of Abba hits, Jimmy Shand favourites and the odd Chuck Berry duck walk across the tables ... It ended with Richard backing the landlord singing "My Way". Four hours of musical bliss.'

Richard: 'I've always enjoyed Scottish music – especially pipe music – because it's so stirring somehow, it's very haunting, that drone just does something to you. I've always felt that the Scottish culture has been more important to me than the English. If I'd ever had a choice, I would have played football for Scotland rather than for England. It just moves something in me. I love English music as well and Irish music – it's all part of the mélange – the family's got roots all over the place. The most magical music imaginable ... Scottish music had quite a big influence on me, but less of the accordion dance music – I really like the pipe music and the songs – the ballads, the whole vocal style.'

Although he divides his time between London and Santa Monica, and stresses his Scottish roots there is something comfortingly, abidingly English about Richard Thompson. The side of Thompson which relishes the quirky and decidedly off-kilter habits and traditions which populate England, his England, seems to underpin the best of what he writes. But while his recent records have been criticised for sounding too American, one positive consequence of the time he has spent in the States, has been an unbuttoning of his English reserve.

Nancy: 'I think it enabled him to lighten up, performing in the States. He was able to be himself and I would encourage him to do that . . . I think a load was lifted off him from his situation here, not just personal, but everything else that kind of held Richard down.'

LA gives him the distance to observe his homeland with objectivity and affection. It was from his exile in Switzerland and France that James Joyce recreated the Dublin of his youth. In the same distant way, from the vantage point of Pallisades Park, Thompson recalls Box Hill and the Hog's Back of his England. It's worth remembering that from early in his career Thompson's avowed intent was to create a uniquely English brand of rock'n'roll: 'The English are a different race, there's no question about that, and it's a good thing to write about that.' His deep fascination with the English folk tradition which was nurtured on *Liege & Lief* and has threaded through his entire career is still a source of endless inspiration.

Richard: 'It's the main place I still learn from, because there's so much of it, I still find stuff in it. Instrumentally and lyrically, it's a big source for me still, and it has been all the way through. I've never stopped learning from it . . . I'm always looking at traditional music just for ideas or language.'

Recent partner Danny Thompson shares Richard's preoccupation with the music of England: 'I've got this thing about "English" music, people shout about the pipes and the Celts, which is great. The English are very lax about waving their own flag. All our great composers, like Elgar, Vaughan Williams, there is a unique Englishness about our culture and our music, which never gets mentioned.'

The two men have been working on 'The Industrial Project' for a number of years, but seem to be enjoying the research so much that the earliest likely date for release is early 1997.

Richard: 'The research is great and takes you to places you're not expecting to go, literally and metaphorically. There's some stuff for the record that I'm supposed to be doing with Danny which has and will take us to all sorts of pieces of industrial archaeology and has already taken us through endless libraries – just to find out all this stuff that we're going to leave out.'

Writing his idiosyncratic songs, Thompson revels in researching the background, whether about conditions in the slave-labour sweatshops of the North, or the type of suspension attached to an MGB-GT. And once he's got that handle, he has to try and distil a 90-minute film, a

250-page novel or an hour-long television drama into a five-minute song. That is the challenge. That is the talent.

Danny: 'Richard being Richard he came from a completely different angle, instead of writing about ships going down the slipway, he wrote about a saboteur working in the machine shed ... womens' rights. The more personal aspects of what the revolution was all about.

'Pastoral society, with hamlets, church steeples, everyone saw the fruits of their labour. They worked with tools they'd made, with animals they'd looked after, lived off the land. It seemed pretty stable ... From that, you go to this amazing Industrial Revolution, where the church steeples are replaced by chimneys, where there is a need for the Salvation Army to be born; where timetables come into being, when people don't see the end of their labours, are treated like slaves.

'For the music, a new rhythm came into the world, industry brought in all these new rhythms ...'

Chapter 27

THE BOX SET began life as a vinyl obituary. To satisfy the insatiable desires of diehard fans of dead rock'n'rollers like Buddy Holly and Eddie Cochran. The deceased's record label gathered together the greatest hits, sprinkled the set with alternative takes, demos, unreleased tracks and live performances and then sat back to count the takings. Soon after Elvis Presley's death in 1977, RCA offered up the eight-album *Elvis Aron Presley* to his fans; a cardboard and vinyl tombstone to mark a career long gone.

As with most things rock'n'roll, the change came courtesy of Bob Dylan. *Biograph*, released in 1985, was a Dylan Greatest Hits, but with eighteen previously unreleased (though widely bootlegged) tracks. Dylan had himself compared bootleggers to phone-tappers. The success of *Biograph* made the record industry sit up and take notice and appreciate – perhaps for the first time – that fans bought inferior quality bootlegs not as a snub, but so they could accumulate and appreciate every facet of an artist's career.

Eric Clapton's six-album *Crossroads* retrospective in 1988 marked the turning of the tide. Polydor Records marketing executive George McManus told me: 'I think the Clapton box was the landmark. When it came out ... people in the industry were ringing me up and asking for one so they could copy it! Until then, you simply put all the artist's available albums in a cardboard box, maybe with a booklet, and released it. *Crossroads* had twenty or thirty per cent unreleased or unavailable material, along with Eric's best-known work, all chronologically sequenced. After *Crossroads*, I think the other labels realised what they had in their vaults, which led to the Led Zeppelin, Byrds and Jethro Tull boxes.'

Crossroads certainly opened the floodgates, established artists now insisted upon a box set to set the seal on their status. When it worked, it worked brilliantly well, Bob Dylan's 1991 *The Bootleg Series* was exemplary; but Lou Reed's cobbled together, pretentiously titled

Solo

Between Thought and Expression was not. Following *Crossroads*, box sets of varying degrees of excellence by established acts such as Crosby, Stills and Nash, Rod Stewart, Bob Marley, Sandy Denny, Yes, Elton John, the Clash and Phil Spector were all made available.

Certain names however were missing from the box set bonanza – Van Morrison, the Rolling Stones, Bruce Springsteen ... and Richard Thompson. Thompson is a reluctant nostalgist but he was coaxed into a suitably retrospective mood, and with no new album to occupy his time, he dutifully sat down and sifted through his back catalogue.

When it comes to releasing material which he had never intended to be heard, Thompson is not enthusiastic. Talking to me about the second *Doom & Gloom* tape, compiled by *Flypaper*, Thompson conceded: 'Well the Doom and Gloom stuff – I don't care if this stuff comes out. I'd rather it didn't, but it was supposed to be a way to finance the newsletter (*Flypaper*) – which I think is a good idea, it's a good service which people seem to appreciate.'

As you would expect, with an artist who has been performing and recording for nearly 30 years, Thompson has been a favourite target of the bootleggers. Over the years, various Fairport bootlegs have surfaced, notably *Heyday*, a cassette of the band's BBC radio sessions from the late 1960s, which was eventually released officially in 1987.

Bootlegs stir up all the old arguments. The artist receives no recompense but then the only people who buy bootlegs are hardcore fans who have bought everything official anyway. The artist has no say in what is released on bootleg, but then again sometimes the artist is not the best judge of what to release. Bootlegs are often poor quality recordings, but do you remember some of the first generation CDs put out by the majors ...?

Through the magic of bootlegging, Thompson fans can now get to hear the intriguing Gerry Rafferty production of *Shoot Out the Lights* (*Rafferty's Folly*), and compare it with the officially sanctioned Joe Boyd release. With Thompson insisting on the withdrawal of *Small Town Romance*, the only official release of a solo and acoustic performance, fans have been only too grateful for the dozen or so bootleg live CDs.

Richard Thompson with Danny Thompson Live at Crawley 1993 was the first salvo in a new strategy to thwart the bootleggers. Thompson has negotiated with Capitol one extra album release per year outside his contract, to act as a tour souvenir. Crawley was the first and there are plans for an official live Big Band CD sometime during 1996.

Richard: 'What we've done at this point is to strike a deal with EMI to let us stick out one thing a year, which hopefully I can get increased because it doesn't solve the problem. What I'd like to do is every time we do a major tour, I'd like to have something out after it and that would begin to combat the bootleg problem. I've got fifteen CD bootlegs out, and you don't get paid for them, nobody asks you, they're unlicensed. So people are just ripping you off – they're stealing from you. So if there is a demand to be satisfied, if that's the case then I'd rather satisfy it myself. Crawley was the first step in getting something live out. So if people need it, there it is.'

It is a nice, thoughtful idea, which fans are bound to appreciate. Thompson's sleeve notes for the Crawley release took the form of a broadside against bootleggers: 'The recording is . . . part of our recent policy to regularly release live recordings. This is in an effort to stop inferior bootleg versions of the same thing appearing in shops, mail-order catalogues and on market stalls. As you probably know, artists and composers receive no royalty from bootlegs.'

In December 1993, Thompson revealed to *Hokey Pokey* that he'd nixed the release of a Richard and Linda album culled from BBC sessions of the 1970s: 'I really don't like the idea of it. It's not financially beneficial to me and it's not relevant to what I'm doing now. I don't need live performances out there on sale, especially stuff that isn't first rate—if it was first rate, I might think of releasing it myself.'

It was partly pressure from fans at *Flypaper* and *Hokey Pokey*, partly record company encouragement and partly Thompson's own determination to quell the bootleggers, which led to the release of a Richard Thompson box set in 1993. The situation with Joe Boyd resolved, Thompson's three CD retrospective *Watching the Dark* was subsequently released on Hannibal.

Joe Boyd: 'Part of the settlement under which I got twelve months to pay him his royalties was that I would withdraw *Small Town Romance*, which I think is a shame as it's a really good record, but he was uncomfortable with it. Once he started on *Watching the Dark*, Ed Haber dealt with Richard, I spoke to him a few times during the process to make sure he was happy with the way it was going. Everything that was on that record is something Richard agreed could be on the record . . . I'd personally like to have seen some of the earlier things on there, things where he played longer solos, but he likes it. It's a good package. My main contribution was the running order, which some people complain about, but as a listening experience, I think it works . . .'

Richard: 'I thought that was an interesting idea to do. You see if you don't do things then other people will do them without asking you –

like an ex-record company who've got some of the material can phone up Island and say, license me this, license me that and they can put out their own thing. So it's better to be involved and co-operate with people you like and get it out there before the wolves start knocking at the door. So I was quite happy with that, I think they did a good job. It was a reasonable selection of material, as the reviews pointed out, it attempted to satisfy the completists on one hand and be a "greatest hits" compilation on the other.

'There's loads of studio stuff from the last ten or twelve years, there's leftover album tracks from almost every record. But they might not have vocals on necessarily, I don't think they're completed. But most of the earlier studio stuff has been pretty well plundered. Though Fairport at Goldstar, that would be a good one.'

Talking to Pete Clark in *The Standard* about his past being disinterred so publicly, Thompson was self-effacing: 'I suppose it's quite flattering. But being English, it's flattering and embarrassing at the same time. If you're English, you have to be embarrassed by everything.'

Watching the Dark was a compromise with the bulk of the criticisms maintaining that it was too much 'greatest hits' and not enough 'rare and unreleased'. There was the accumulated work of three decades to choose from, yet almost half the material on the box set was already available on official releases. Many fans felt short-changed.

Watching the Dark was intended for collectors who already had every official release. A single CD Greatest Hits is an appealing prospect – twenty toe-tapping Thompson tunes on one disc. Perhaps one of the *Watching the Dark* discs could have accommodated that, with the remaining two discs devoted to demo recordings, rare cover versions from concerts, electric versions of acoustic songs, and vice versa . . .

Unfortunately, there doesn't seem much likelihood of demos appearing further on down the line.

Richard: 'I really try not to demo anything – I try and keep it in my head and I play stuff to Mitchell for instance. He and I do just sit down before a record and I'll play stuff or we'll do a duet, he'll play organ and I'll play guitar, so there must be some priceless versions there somewhere! But that's about as far as it goes, I don't like doing demos, because sometimes they're better than the record and then what's the point of doing the record? Sometimes you can hit the spirit on a demo and you can have a problem living up to it.'

It was that element of spontaneity which Bruce Springsteen struck on his 1982 *Nebraska* album. After carrying round a demo in his back pocket for four months, Springsteen found he simply couldn't replicate their grainy authenticity and so he released the demo. Unsurprisingly, *Nebraska* is Richard Thompson's favourite Springsteen album.

There was much on *Watching the Dark* to recall Howard Carter's awestruck description of what he saw on opening Tutankhamen's tomb: 'Wonderful things'. The eighteenth-century song 'Bogie's Bonnie Belle' reminds you just what an effective teller of stories Thompson is, accompanied only by his own guitar. Thompson's fondness for the Scottish ballad tradition is well known, and his rendition captures all the drama and passion of the genre. 'Bogie's Bonnie Bell' is an aching companion piece to Fairport's 'Matty Groves', telling of a love across the class divide which can never be sanctified, because Isabelle 'was of noble kin'.

Highlights from the 23 newly available tracks also included the inexplicably withheld 'Crash The Party', which finally crashed through the door. Thompson had featured the song regularly as an encore during his tours with a band. The song always arrived like a drunken reveller at Hogmanay and allowed Thompson the space to indulge his James Burton fantasies.

Richard: 'I thought it was a trivial song to commit to vinyl. It seemed a bit lightweight, too upbeat to end up on one of my records. It was designed as an encore song for the stage. I played it to Mitchell and he thought it was a bit too lightweight and I agreed.'

The live 'Calvary Cross' and 'Shoot Out The Lights' are powerful reminders of the strength of Thompson's guitar playing when stretched to snapping point in performance. Indeed, much of *Watching the Dark* seems aimed at the Thompson aficionados who revel in the howling feedback and reverb frenzy of his electric playing. They are rewarded by extended workouts on 'When The Spell Is Broken', 'I Ain't Going To Drag My Feet No More' and 'Tear-Stained Letter'. The Swarb-less 'Sailor's Life' from 1969 and Gerry Rafferty-produced *Shoot Out the Lights* tracks are interesting souvenirs rescued from the archives, and it is nice to hear Richard play the hurdy gurdy he had built himself on 'Poor Wee Jockey Clarke'.

For all its flaws and omissions, *Watching the Dark* is worth having for one track alone, the only existing version of one of Thompson's most riveting and haunting songs, 'From Galway To Graceland'. Just when you think you've heard enough shrieking guitar solos and enough variations on 'Wall Of Death', the song comes upon you with all the coiled mystery of Thompson on the edge.

'From Galway To Graceland' is a story full of sympathy and perception, but told with cool objectivity and a fine eye for detail. The tragic tale of a fan wholly obsessed with Elvis Presley, who flees her home looking 'pretty in pink', humming 'Suspicion', her favourite Presley song, sporting her 'Elvis I Love You' tattoo. The tragic figure posts a silent, determined, demented vigil by the King's grave at Graceland. Unable to accept the finality of Elvis' death, the girl from the West Coast of Ireland sits, day after day, silent and accusing. Obviously deeply disturbed, there is a fine line to be drawn between the emptiness of her own barren life and her worship of the dead King of rock'n'roll. Crazy as it is, just how much emptier would her life be without that obsession?

A dark and disturbing tale, painting a bleak picture of fandom and hero worship – the song ends, not as you'd hope, with a souvenir bracelet and happiness back in Galway, but with 'handcuffs this time'. Thompson's mournful vocal injects every atom of tragedy into the song, the end is simply heartbreaking:

Blindly she knelt there, and she told him her dreams,
And she thought that he answered, or that's how it seems.
Then they dragged her away, it was handcuffs this time,
She said 'My good man, are you out of your mind?
Don't you know that we're married? See I'm wearing his ring' . . .

Marc Ellington: 'You take a song like "From Galway To Graceland", his complete understanding of the obsession that people can develop for individuals . . . To see that and understand that, that ability to empathise with people in their moment of despair, says an awful lot about the strength and the basic health of the man.'

The subject of hero worship is something Thompson has touched on before. He is circumspect about his own heroes and the dangers of hero worship: 'It depends on who your heroes are, you've got to pick the right heroes. I've got heroes, I've got spiritual heroes and I've got musical heroes. I'm not sure I go for the heroes of popular culture – and I'm not sure that what I like about Elvis would be what everybody else would like about Elvis, I'm not sure I'd go for the flared trousers and rhinestones, for me that wasn't the pinnacle of Elvis. I think he peaked earlier.'

Thompson knows that he too is the object of fandom, hardly on the scale of Elvis, but there are those who seek him out because they feel that somehow, he has articulated their own innermost thoughts. He is rightly wary and knows how and when to avoid those sort of fans.

Marc Ellington: 'Go on the tube with Richard and you'll see the one loony that spots him and sits opposite him and stares. His power over

Richard Thompson

people is amazing, through what they've got from his music. I think in many cases they're getting it wrong ... With people listening so often on Walkmans, I think that relationship of the person on record is so much deeper and so much more profound. I think people form a relationship with that person simply because there's the exclusion of outside life. Probably the Kurt Cobain syndrome of kids getting so plugged into it in an isolated sense. Richard's been a victim of that too, because I would think if there are strange people listening to his stuff, that is the stuff they will listen to again and again and again.'

As a songwriter, Richard Thompson refuses to accept what's on the surface, and scratches instead deep beneath the skin, until blood is drawn. Thompson is far more concerned with the entrails of a relationship than its superficial beauty. He wants to get his hands dirty. Richard Thompson is not interested in politely detailing the first flush of passion, the cordial deepening of a relationship, the growing old gracefully.

Richard: 'I don't think human nature is straightforward or that a relationship follows the lines of the romantic myth, it just isn't that way, it's much more complicated than that and every relationship is different.'

Thompson's territory is a turbulent, choppy ocean of emotion. He sails a tiny boat, bobbing on a sea of turmoil, lashed by waves, beneath a sky which is always slate-grey. The songs of Richard Thompson are morse-code messages, tapped out from behind the enemy lines of love and romance. They send dots and dashes into the cold, still night, picked up by monitors in dark, underground bunkers.

Richard: 'You write what moves you. I grew up listening to the Everly Brothers and all that mournful stuff like "Ebony Eyes" and Scottish ballads. You get into that whole folk thing and it's all kind of miserable, everybody's getting murdered and it's all very sad. I really like all the sad stuff. Not because I'm miserable – I just think it makes great music, it's really good stuff, it doesn't make you sad, it's just fun to listen to, it's so moving. It's just an enjoyable experience.

' "The Old Hoose" by Lady Nairne is a really sad song, but it has a wonderful kind of nobility. It's the nobility of the human spirit, I think, that is what I get out of sad songs. That's why the greatest sad songs are in major keys, like *Orfeo ed Euridice* by Gluck, which is unbelievably moving and sad and tragic. But it's like this jolly major tune, it's so dignified.

'It's not to do with whatever your mood is. I've always been a fairly optimistic, fairly happy, reasonably contented person I think – so if I write a sad song, it's not because I'm sad necessarily . . . but it's life, you can't escape life. Life's terrible, you've got money stuff, you got woman trouble, all that sort of stuff. There's one thousand and one ways that life chips away at you, and eventually it gets you. You're going to end up in the little box, a lunchbox for worms.

'So you do sing about hard times and you do sing about sad experiences – not necessarily when you're sad, but sometimes you just reflect on the sad times. It's something that moves people, like when you hear a heartfelt piece of soul music like "Dark End Of The Street" or "When A Man Loves A Woman" and you think "Yeah, I know what you mean".'

Thompson can seem disingenuous when he passes off his darkest and most sombre songs simply as 'observations' about 'characters'. Of course not all his songs are cut from the cloth of despair, and of course, the character who 'feels so good' that he's going to break somebody's heart tonight is not actually the composer. But there is a constancy, a wilful return to the dark end of the street, which only confirms the casual listener's impression of him and his work; a determination to dissect, rather than embrace, which many find off-putting.

Nancy: 'I tend to think that Richard sees the reality of life, because you've always got those two sides, and being a cynical English person . . . that's what Richard talks about. I don't think he's particularly dark. He seems to have a good grasp of the range of human emotions and he talks about those things . . . It's funny because I don't see him as all that bleak, but I read about it all the time.'

As a songwriter, only Elvis Costello can match Thompson's intensity, writing about twisted emotions, love, pain, skewered relationships, the whole damn thing. Thompson and Costello are strange bedfellows. The angry young man of Punk and the revered and esteemed father figure of English folk rock. But craftsmen both. Each recognises the other's strengths. Costello has covered two Thompson songs 'The End Of The Rainbow' and 'Withered And Died', typically two of the bleakest in the catalogue, songs which stretch tautly across the jugular.

Richard: 'I was asked to appear on *Goodbye Cruel World* and I would have liked to have done it, but I think I was just in the wrong country. But in the end he struggled through, he managed to play something – he's a good guitar player – a self-effacing sort of chap. What he played was really good, I don't know that I could have done any better. I do admire him, I think you have to say he's the most interesting songwriter generally in the pop world. As a pop writer he's the most interesting and the most hard to keep up with because he writes so much stuff. I actually struggle to hear everything, but I do hear everything.

'I used to do a solo version of "Pump It Up", which was quite fun – just to strip it down and take it somewhere else. I like a lot of his songs, yeah. I can think of about a dozen that would be quite fun to tackle.'

A good Thompson song burrows deep into your soul. It won't let go. There is something disturbing there which entices you. A dark and twisted vision which gives the songs their originality; their undeniable, idiosyncratic and remarkable Richard Thompson quality. But it is the very darkness and malevolence that keeps them from a wider audience.

'From Galway To Graceland' is a good example, a song about misplaced emotion, the sheer pointlessness of hero-worship. And a final verse which finds the song's central figure, its 'heroine', forcibly removed from Elvis Presley's graveside in handcuffs. This is not the sort of material which some big-hatted, big-hearted country and western star would be happy covering.

Thompson is nowhere near as sentimental as his audience about his songs. To him, they are often diary entries of long ago; somebody else's diary, written in somebody else's hand. I spent some time with him, trying to pin down the fate of one particular song, long-rumoured, and not even available on poor-quality bootleg. Thompson furrowed his brow, vaguely recalled the song in question, and dismissed it with an unsentimental shrug as 'rubbish', and moved on.

Richard: 'I like to treat writing in a lot of different ways. One of the really good ways to think about it is as a job, but it's not just a job, so you have to have other ways of thinking about it as well. You wear different hats, there's the job hat: when nothing is happening creatively so it's time to go to work and I just blast through and I'll write anything and see what happens just to get the tap unrusted. And then there's times when you get the poetic feeling, and you have to think of yourself as a poet and far too sensitive to be treating it as a job.

'There are other times when I think of it as a craft – that's the part you can really work on and hone, by studying and reflecting on what the song form is. You're looking at other songwriters and poets, and looking at melody and seeing what works and what doesn't and how you can fit it all together, and that's definitely a part you can polish. Also I think while you're working on the craft, that will give you ideas. I always remember when I used to paint, when I was at school, I used to really enjoy painting, and sometimes the creative time was actually priming the canvas in white and while you were priming it, you'd almost painted the picture in your head. Just being involved in the craft process can sometimes be the inspiration – it just puts your mind into the right state to be receptive.

'I'm a bit of head person, I do a lot in my head. Musically I don't always work at an instrument – I can hear most of it and it's a good place to be writing music if you can because it's so loose and you're not nailing it down so much. It can float more, you can allow the music to float longer before you really pin it down, so in theory that should take you to other places.'

Thompson is understandably nervous about describing the writing process. It's as if you are caught talking about it, the magic's gone, and all you're left with is the technique, just the nuts and bolts, but none of the actual inspiration.

Clive Gregson: 'One of the things I've never talked to Richard about is writing songs. I've held him in awe since I was about eighteen. Richard doesn't need to collaborate. He's very, very complete. I think outside of Lennon and McCartney, he's the greatest English songwriter full stop.

'I think there are songs that come out of the air and are special and there are other songs ... If you're spannering it together, that craft of songwriting is the least interesting in many ways. I think Richard like many songwriters is very capable of doing that, we all know where the chorus should come. It's actually not that much to do with songwriting, as a conduit of expression ... I think Richard is actually at his best when he breaks all the rules.'

Reluctant to talk about the inspiration, Thompson is also loathe to reveal what the songs are actually about ('But what are your songs *about?*' people kept asking Bob Dylan: 'Oh, some are about five minutes, some are about six minutes ...'). But when it comes to the mechanics, the actual process, Richard is happy to talk about the physical translation, from head to paper.

Richard: 'A lot of people who write seem to have a writing fetish – fairly obsessed with stationery shops ... I do like that French paper, cross hatched, with four-hole ringbinders. The trouble is, that once you start using that system, you can only buy it in France and Belgium, so I have to play in France or Belgium at least once a year to restock.

'I like to work on a double-page spread where there's lots of room, so you can start in one place and you can be writing tangentially up here or down there and you have quite a large visual area, rather than a spiral notebook where there's no room to go sideways. I like to go sideways when I'm writing rather than writing in a line or a logical sequence. You can tidy up later. You can edit it all down later on. But

Richard Thompson

as your mind is being fertile, it's good to be able to go where it wants to for a while.

'I just use the old Uniballs. But I do keep a pen and mini notepad in my pocket at all times, because that stuff never comes back if you miss it, the overheard conversations or the stuff when you're driving. It's very hard to hang on to that stuff and stuff you wake up with, you have to get it down really quickly or it's gone, as is the nature of the human mind.'

Nancy: 'I think basically Richard is writing all the time. I think eighty per cent of the time, Richard is writing, singing, thinking. Most of the time his eyes are moving, and he's gone. And I think all the time he's looking ... I don't think there's any song that absolutely, exactly happened – but sometimes I'll hear a song and think I remember seeing that person walking down the street and he created that story out of that. He has a little notebook, little things will get jotted down all the time. He's best when he has a span of time, then he can sit down like he's going to an office. But in his breast pocket you will always see a pen and there is always a notebook. And when he's in a writing phase, right before an album, then one could have an interrupted meal. When he's on a roll, then it happens more and more ...'

'He would never say "Hey honey, like this one?" No. Absolutely not. We don't talk about it as a song, if I refer to it, I say "Do you need to work?" ... I think it's kind of like, you open the oven door on the soufflé, you don't want to do that too early, it might fall. It's kind of a fragile thing. I don't know exactly what it is, but you kind of need to leave it. That probably comes back to why we get along, because I'm not involved musically. So we don't talk about it, we don't have to break that bubble.'

Linda: 'The main bulk of the writing always took place for an album. Throughout our married life, he just went off to another room with his guitar all the time, so you never knew if he was practising the guitar – which he did a lot – or whether he was working on songs. He was quite secretive about it, I think sometimes it was tough to even show me the songs.

'Going in to record an album, there'd maybe be four or five songs that dropped by the wayside. But then there would be a lot more that he threw away. The bleak ones were very bleak, but he never wrote anything too personal about himself, which I always thought was a great shame. I think he was just scared to do that. To open a can of worms. He would never write a song saying "I love you" or "I hate you" or whatever. He would never make it personal. Or maybe those were the ones he threw away.'

A constant reiteration from Thompson is that as a writer, he is merely the conduit for the song. The actual 'inspiration' comes from somewhere else. Certainly, he is reluctant to discuss the inspiration for his songs. He will happily discuss the mechanics, but what comes to him and into his head alone, that's his turf, that's his exclusive territory.

When I interviewed Thompson in 1977, he told me: 'I'm just collating other people's ideas and putting them into a digestible form, the music isn't from me.' He said he was seriously thinking of putting a bibliography on the next album sleeve 'so that people could go to the source, which avoids it being a magic process whereby the person with the knowledge withholds it from the other people and there's no transmission of how it's done.'

Talking to Colin Irwin in *Melody Maker* in 1978, Thompson was emphatic: 'I don't believe in writing songs. It's all bullshit, no one writes the songs. They all come from something else. One just gets the PRS, that's all.' Thompson hates the autobiographical reading of his songs. 'At the bottom of every record there should be a disclaimer,' Thompson told Bill Flanagan, 'saying: "The views expressed by the singer are not necessarily those of the songwriter." '

Richard: 'I'm just not sure where the join is. I think I do, but it probably gets embellished a little bit. I think stuff gets fictionalised sometimes to make it more interesting. Or sometimes you fall for a rhyme that suddenly makes the song more interesting, but definitely leads you away from the truth – the cold hard truth. Then you get into strange fictional truth, which is often a little bit more exciting and sometimes it's more amusing or cutting.

'Sometimes a song or a piece of art is larger than life in order to reflect it. In order to tell the truth, sometimes you exaggerate or overdraw, and in a song, you've only got three minutes and two verses to put it across, so you do have to paint boldly. I think you can be subtle in the editing, in what you leave out, so you just have the pithy phrases and leave lots out, but it's still big strokes . . .

' "Sally Go Round The Roses" – there's the other eight verses which explain that she was a horticulturist or something. But if you leave a lot to the imagination that can sometimes make an interesting song and you can still tell the story.

'I like to experiment to keep it fresh. I think songwriting is too interesting, and there are too many places it could go, just to say I'm going to write this kind of song, this pithy, dry, terse Hemingway sort of song and I'm not going to write this complex Dylanesque ballad or this bouncy pop song.

Richard Thompson

'Songwriting is too interesting and too much fun to limit yourself to one style. Songwriting is fun and if you're enjoying yourself when you're writing it, that's something that comes across in the quality of the song. Enjoyment is a really big part of the process, even in writing a bleak song – it's a satisfying process.'

While he mistrusts the probing of his inspiration, Thompson welcomes interpretation. Talking to Paul Zollo in *Song Talk* about 'The King Of Bohemia', Thompson confirmed: 'It's named after a pub actually . . . There was one journalist who thought the song was about Dylan. They thought that Dylan was the King of Bohemia. They had this whole theory, which I thought was quite good. I was almost encouraged to take it up.'

Clive Gregson: 'I remember we were on the bus once, and John Kirkpatrick said "What's 'Calvary Cross' about, Richard?" He said "It's just music, innit?" . . .'

John Kirkpatrick: 'He's never expounded "musical philosophy" at a recording session or on the road. It's the sort of thing he'd say in an interview, because that's the sort of thing you have to say in interviews.'

Technically, Thompson is attracted by the discipline of songwriting – the need to condense, to distil, the challenge to cram everything into three verses. By honing everything to the bone, you are concentrating the detail, ignoring the fleshy luxury. It is the songwriter-as-cameraman approach, dollying the camera to a specific mark, with a specific angle to make a specific point.

Richard: 'I think the song form is really interesting – there's so much you can do with it – people are willing to listen to them – there's outlets for it, you can put it on the radio or you can put it in your car. You can listen to it at home or go to a concert. So there's all kinds of places where people will listen to that particular form. We haven't really explored the limits of it, and the styles – there's so much that can be done with it, it's fascinating what you can do, what you can say, how simple you can make it and how complex. So I'm glad I'm in this field.'

All Thompson has learned about the craft of songwriting, about detail, about compression and broad brush-strokes, was applied to his best-loved song of all, '1952 Vincent Black Lightning'.

Richard: 'It's classic storytelling in a ballad form which is fun, I like doing that. There's also a kind of shorthand storytelling which is I suppose more cinematic, you're just cutting a part out of the story, or you're chopping it up, doing it in a much more editorial style – you might chop out the middle and the end of the story. You're bursting through the door, *cinema-verité* style, and you're just recording what

Cambridge Folk Festival, 1981
Courtesy Jo Lustig Management; Edward Haber Collection

The last duo tour, Glen Cove, NY, 1982. Left to right: Linda, Simon Nicol, Richard, Dave Mattacks (partially obscured), Pete Zorn
Photo: Paul L. Kovit

Double exposure from the 1982 tour
Photo: Paul L. Kovit

Out-take from *Hand of Kindness* album cover photo session. Left to right: Simon Nicol, Clive Gregson, Dave Mattacks, John Kirkpatrick, Pete Zorn, Dave Pegg, Pete Thomas, and Richard Thompson
Photo: Bill Gill, courtesy Hannibal Records/Rykodisc U.S.A.

Left Richard moonlighting
Photo: Frank Kornelussen

Below Cropredy rehearsal for *Full House* line-up. Left to right: Swarbrick, Pegg, Thompson, and Nicol
Photo: Paul L. Kovit

Thompson live on stage in 1985
Photo: Frank Kornelussen

Backstage at McCabe's in 1984. Left to right: Elvis Costello, Nancy Covey and Richard Thompson

Double exposure, at the Towne Crier, Beekman, NY, 1983
Photo: Paul L. Kovit

Thompson band, 1988. Left to right: John Kirkpatrick, Christine Collister, Richard, Pat Donaldson, Clive Gregson
Photo: Gabe Sonnino

With David Byrne at the Town Crier, March 7, 1991
Photo: © Warren Ogden

With Roger McGuinn, c. 1990
Photo: Gabe Sonnino

With Henry Kaiser,
late '80s
Photo: Gabe Sonnino

At Central Park, New York, NY, early '90s
Photo: Gabe Sonnino

With Danny Thompson, early '90s
Photo: Gabe Sonnino

The McThompson twins, backstage at Cropredy in 1995
Photo: Sylvía Thompson

goes on in the middle, and suggesting everything else. The keyhole effect – describing one meeting or one room – from that you ascertain the rest of the story. Which isn't a bad idea if you've only got three minutes of a popular song. But I'm beginning to think that people actually like ballads like to listen to them and that's influenced the number of verses I've been writing lately – I've got a sixteen verser coming up on the next record. That's leaving out as much as possible – that's really cramming!'

All manner of themes, subjects, emotions and topics jostle for attention in the songs of Richard Thompson. The concerns of his faith are evident, the decay in society's values. There is his life in Santa Monica and Finchley. The zig-zag of an emotional rollercoaster. The fascination of things mechanical and architectural, graphic and cerebral. Thompson's interests take him across the board, but where he goes when he vanishes to write, is a solitary place.

He applies himself rigorously to the process of writing, to creating those characters, and then, the worst bit, disposing of them because there isn't room:

Richard: 'You have to try and make them like that. You don't have time for the character development of a novel unfortunately – so you get straight in there and deal with broad strokes, so it's a little cruder. You almost have to have the same kind of character development in your head and then discard ninety-eight per cent of it – just to make whatever two lines you write about somebody real. *You* have to know all the background and then *not* use it. I had to know as much as possible about Vincent motorcycles, and then not use it, leave out all the verses with the technical jargon, because it's too boring for normal people! Whatever you write about, you have to know it very well, as well as you can. Then because it's just a song, you have to ditch it.

'I think a lot of popular music is actually recycling semi-clichés into new phrases or sayings, and it seems quite valid if you take half a well-known phrase and mix it up with a few others. You actually make a song out of it and it kind of works. So I think one does deal in clichés in popular song in a way that a poet wouldn't dare touch, but as a songwriter you can get away with it. You sometimes have to have ear-catching things people half remember and that makes it easier somehow. It just seems to be part of the style, I'm not inventing anything, I'm good at ripping anything off.'

Chapter 28

NANCY: 'I watch a show like everybody else would and I forget I'm married to him. Richard on stage, the personality, the jokes, that really is very much Richard. That's just over the years Richard coming out of his shell and becoming who he was at home and becoming lighter ... Richard on a good night doing 'Calvary Cross' or 'Tear-Stained Letter', or one of those guitar solos – when they really get there, that gets me. I get teary – I think this is the guy I live with. When he goes off on another planet.'

From being a shy and hesitant performer, literally hiding behind the amplifier in the early Fairport days, Thompson has become more confident and assured in dealing with an audience. Verbally, he feints and jests, orchestrating the evening with consummate ease.

More importantly, in performance Thompson adds muscle. Live, there are chunky interpretations of songs which sound fragile on disc. With a band blazing behind him, his guitar flailing and soaring to fresh heights of electric mystery and mastery, Thompson puts flesh onto bare and bleached bones.

Over the years, I've seen Thompson perform on stages of various sizes. The first time ever I saw his face was from half a mile away at the 1970 Bath Festival of Blues and Progressive music. It was the year after Woodstock, but the film was scheduled to open in London around the time of the Bath festival.

Thanks to the expectations raised by Woodstock and the Isle of Wight, rock festivals were now seen as a gathering of the tribes. The roads surrounding Shepton Mallet were jam-packed with weekend hippies, festival-goers, drop outs. The Hell's Angels (UK branch, the ones who'd done such a good job policing Hyde Park for the Stones the summer before) were acting as unofficial chauffeurs, and it was the Angels who biked Fairport onto the site that afternoon, hours late.

For me the abiding memory of Bath 1970 was Fairport. I'd been aware of them in a tangential sort of way; they occupied a periphery, along with the John Barleycorn-era Traffic and pre-Bowie Mott the Hoople. *Liege & Lief* was too recent to be recognised as a seminal album, the one that broke down the barriers between 'folk' and 'rock'. It was just the most recent Fairport Convention album, which had been quite well reviewed in *Rolling Stone*. But that was six months ago. This was Fairport now.

From my site on the hill, I could vaguely discern that (in the argot of the times) there was no chick singer with them, the blonde had quit. The vocals ebbed and flowed up the hill. It wasn't epiphany, it was pleasant background music for a summer's afternoon. Then the band slipped in a section of jigs and reels and as they sailed through 'Dirty Linen' and 'Flatback Caper', Fairport took the crowd with them.

Since then I've seen Richard Thompson play to half-empty rooms, in smoky venues in suburban London. Wonderful evenings, where he mixed traditional material with a choice selection from his own burgeoning back catalogue.

Whether in the back room of the Half Moon in Putney or the sweeping stage of the Royal Festival Hall, Thompson applies the same concentration and commitment to his performance. Acoustic or electric, subdued or electrifying, he is a consummate performer. His performances all the more remarkable now as you consider his development from that nervous and awkward teenager to the assured professional of today.

Soon after his performance at Cropredy, in the August of 1995, I saw Thompson back in front of a band again. He was headlining the Guildford Folk and Blues Festival. Summer was drawing to a close and there was a definite chill in the air as he took to the stage before a crowd of a few thousand on the Sunday night. He proceeded cautiously, there are obvious differences between Thompson acoustic and electric: solo, he tends towards the introspective, he's friskier with a band. There is a relish in the way he attacks the electric guitar and whips it into shape.

Beginning with selections drawn from *Mirror Blue*, his latest album, Thompson took time finding his feet. Then during 'I Can't Wake Up To Save My Life' Thompson played his ace, an electric solo as tortured as a Bacon painting.

'The Way That It Shows' was hallmark Thompson, like Mr Pooter in *Diary of a Nobody*, baffled at receiving an insulting Christmas card, the object of a Thompson 'love song' must have mixed feelings. Here was the desolate territory of emotional no-man's land, observed from a hot-air balloon. All is never what it seems, Thompson spots the flaws,

Richard Thompson

penetrates the artifice, seeing 'glycerine in the tear, rouge in the blush'. It is a mission behind enemy lines, operating under deep cover in occupied territory. Thompson soon identifying the 'chink in your armour . . . [the] crack in your defences'.

Thompson is now warmed up, the playing is more flexible, the player visibly more relaxed. Guitar runs of ferocious intent pebble-dash the cold night air. As the intensity of his playing increases, Thompson's face becomes the canvas on which the emotion is etched. During a fearsome solo, the electricity waving and soaring, Thompson is rapt, somewhere between agony and ecstasy, his face as pained as a martyr's at the stake.

Thompson manages to combine skill and dexterity with emotion and commitment in his playing. It is, even after all these years, an awesome combination.

As he plays, you can see that the music elevates him, even as it flows from his hands, it spins out and off to another place. As he plays, as the solos spin and bob and weave across the crowd, Thompson looks part ecstatic, part constipated.

'Tear-Stained Letter' lightens the load. It is one of Richard's great upbeat songs. He makes fun sound fun. Even if it is hard to reconcile a song which deals in the highly charged emotion of tears and scars with Thompson's obvious exuberance. The carnival atmosphere is heightened by the sight of Pete Zorn, playing a saxophone which looked like it had dropped out of a Christmas cracker.

All efforts at typecasting Thompson as poet of the open vein and chronicler of the emotional down and out, are undone when he announces that the subject of his next song is 90 years old this year. A familiar roar greets the frivolous and ever so silly 'Don't Sit On My Jimmy Shands'. Evoking an immediate call and response, Thompson is manifestly delighted at the crowd's willingness to share the silliness of the song.

As a player, Thompson avoids blues clichés. As he stretches himself on electric guitar, he remains one of the few 'guitar heroes' to eschew the blues. His American influences are worn proudly and loudly on his sleeve, yet in his playing today are still the seeds of Thompson's early determination to create and pursue a defiantly English brand of rock'n'roll.

'Shoot Out The Lights' steamrollered across the night, heavier than lead, Thompson's solo had all the agony of souls crying out from purgatory. Dave Mattacks' drums sounded a fusillade – a firing squad. And all the while, Thompson going all the way along the neck, and on into the unknown.

Solo

A crowd-pleasing 'Wall Of Death' began to bring it all back home. It's all about taking risks, of raging against the dying of the light. Standing three-quarters on to the microphone, Thompson's favoured beret made him look like he'd just strolled in from the 7th Arrondissement.

'Hokey Pokey' was reworked and delivered as a heavy metal feast. A step back to the baseline and Thompson unleashed a fearsomely intense solo, jagged and serrated, but each note as precisely placed as an acupuncturist's needle. Thompson seemed to enter a trance-like state, spilling out hypnotic notes, riffing in a spellbinding manner.

As he tightens his grip around the guitar neck, Thompson's veins are pumping, the adrenalin is flowing. From the body come the notes, and the noise, but the spirit comes from somewhere else. Somewhere deep within, a place Richard Thompson knows all about, but to which he can never guarantee returning. It is his ability to create and sustain tension with his hallmark whiplash guitar, which consistently elevates his playing.

'Al Bowlly's In Heaven' came next. In the wake of the VJ Day celebrations and precisely half a century on from the end of the last war, Thompson's song struck a chord. Conjuring up images not only of down and outs sleeping rough on the streets of London, but also of the victors limping back to their new Jerusalem.

Thompson is a regular visitor to his past in live performance. Unlike David Bowie, there is no arbitrary cut-off from what has been. The opportunity to promote a new album is always taken, but he is not prissy about going back. He has always provided good value for fans, encouraging requests, consulting the Internet, paying attention to fanzine lists, so that a Richard Thompson show is shaped as much by the punters as the performer.

During 1995, Thompson was to be heard playing favourites as far back as 'Now Be Thankful' from Fairport, circa 1970, 'I Want To See The Bright Lights Tonight', 'The Sun Never Shines On The Poor', 'Hokey Pokey' and 'Dimming Of The Day'. He shuffles old favourites into the deck with the casual ease of a card sharp. To stave off boredom, Thompson will dip back into the record collections of Big Muldoon and Joe Boyd, will dust down fragments of songs last heard under the covers on Radio Luxembourg, and will bowl a googly come encore time.

John Kirkpatrick: 'You see I didn't have that rock'n'roll background, when I was gigging with Richard and Linda, and they'd be saying we'll do some Jerry Lee Lewis for the encore, I didn't have a clue what they were talking about. I learned my rock'n'roll by having to play it on

Richard Thompson

Richard's encores. At the beginning I was completely at sea, I didn't know the chord changes. I didn't know what a 12-bar meant ... It was rather unnerving, playing a solo when you don't even know what the chords are.'

It can be unnerving up there alongside Thompson when he goes soaring off to a stratosphere far removed from the concert stage. Even if you're in the band, it can be disconcerting.

Pat Donaldson: 'You rehearse things, and that's how they are. He doesn't fly off the handle as far as arrangements go. But he extends himself as a guitar player, the song is the song, and he sings it, but as an instrumentalist, that's one of the great joys of working live with Richard. There are times when I just want to stop and listen to him play – well, you can't because you're supposed to be accompanying him. The things that come out of that amplifier are just extraordinary – a mind that is whirring, then his flights of fancy, he's way out on a limb, he's right at the end of the branch, and it's liable to crack at any moment.'

It is impossible to pinpoint where Thompson goes when he starts soloing, and he himself has only the vaguest of ideas.

Dave Pegg: 'Richard goes off on a tangent during the guitar solos. I'm a very straight bass player, I just play the root notes, with occasional bits of filling in, I can never go off with Richard. If it was Jaco Pastorious and Richard you'd get some fantastic music. If he had somebody playing with him who could pick up on where he was going ... I think it's better that way, where everybody plays straight and keeps to some organised pattern ... Richard sometimes does go off on these extended cosmic things ...

'The guitar playing is devastatingly original and there is nobody else in the world who plays like Richard, especially when he plays electric guitar ... it's like something that has come completely out of his head, although he has all these influences – he can play country, rock'n'roll, jigs and reels until the cows come home. But when you listen to a Thompson solo, it's not even a mixture of any of the roots, it's something that's completely off the top of his head, and that's what is so great about him. It's not safe, it doesn't have any boundaries, he'll go off, and sometimes doesn't come back.'

Pete Zorn: 'We rehearsed the last tour for three days, and that was with the technicals and everything. We literally had run through every song we were going to do by the end of the first day, then it was working with lights and the sound. The soundchecks turn into the most obscure Hank Marvin instrumental ever. That's where you blow the carbon out, have a bit of fun. He now has an idea of a show instead of a set, I think the mistake was trying to break down all that material into two sets with a break in between . . .

'I think he has a starting point, which has the same shape each time, but then he takes it where he feels he wants it to go. So much of this is internal, I can only guess. Things are ticking over a lot, in the first week of a tour, once he makes the decision what the order is, and gets the order right. Last year (1994) was the best set I've heard him do. The right combination of each period, and you tell someone it's two hours fifteen minutes every night, on the dot, and it's "Oh, I thought it was just over an hour". So once he gets a shape he can be comfortable with, and not have to worry about, then you see each song change a little each time, you get that internal dynamic of the set.'

As a guitarist, Thompson is inimitable. There is no one quite like him. The appeal is non-verbal, the artistry beyond art; you can construct and de-construct the song lyrics, but his playing seems like an instinctive and intuitive tapping into a force he does not necessarily comprehend, but can only convey.

Richard: 'That's the idea and it's a bad night if that doesn't happen. The good times are always when the music takes over and you're just a kind of vehicle – I don't know where it comes from.

'Some of the songs we do with the band are open ended in terms of soloing – and it's my band, so I get to play as long as I want! There's an intellectual process that goes on when you're improvising pieces and a losing of yourself as well, so you prepare for improvising: you practise your scales and your riffs and your licks, and you have your own cliches that you throw in whenever you can.

'I'm still a long way short of imagination in terms of guitar playing – there's things I'd like to be able to play . . . Just technical things that I'm maybe not fast enough for, or haven't done enough homework on to do. You hear things in other fields, like the jazz field or the classical field and you think amazing, I wish I could do that. So perhaps you start aspiring towards that and you apply it to your own style.

'It's more usually skill things though – you think that's something I could really improve on, whereas you listen to Charlie Parker and think that's amazingly imaginative, but how do you rationalise that, what kind of spirit do you need to play notes like that, how do you get that inspired? Hank Williams always said – how do I aim emotion with that intensity? What kind of megaphone do you have to put your emotions through to get it that hard and concentrated and coming straight at you? He knows where that place is and it's like a laser and he cuts your head off with it.'

Richard Thompson

Simon: 'Richard can play with a freedom which astonishes me ... When he starts going off on these melodic fantasies, he's unconstrained. He really is a free-flowing musician. It's too good for music. You fall into another dimension of appreciation. It becomes visual ... He has always had that attitude to music.

'He does put on a bit of a face when he's playing: he shuts his eyes and he puts his head back. I don't know how much of that is a habit and how much is an affectation ... I think since he's been living in America he's become a more strongly visual performer. He is more strikingly dressed, more confident, more assured in how he wants to look, both onstage and offstage. But you need to be, it goes with the territory. You've gotta grab 'em by the throat in the first five minutes, otherwise you've had it. He has become a bit more ... defined.'

Muna: 'I'd see him on stage, but we'd joke about it. He used to close his eyes and there was no contact with the audience. He's a lot better now. He jokes and he's really funny. He used to be so remote and moody. But he wasn't at home. It's not "moody" moody, it's just being in a different world, which I was always quite aware of, he was just doing his music.'

It isn't just the audience that Thompson leaves open-mouthed with his abilities. The musicians standing either side of him onstage are equally in awe of his playing.

Clive Gregson: 'I think he is still the best guitar player I've seen in any context, because he's got astonishing technique, on so many different disciplines. Few people can play rockabilly and make it sound that authentic, few people can play jazz, the folk idiom, the Celtic idiom, out-and-out rock'n'roll, just about the only thing I've never heard him have a go at is heavy metal ... He's a brilliant improviser, totally off the top of his head. I've seen him do things where you know that he's flying completely by the seat of his pants. He's also not afraid of making mistakes, which I really admire, which not a lot of guitar players do – him and Neil Young.'

With the deletion of *Small Town Romance*, and the substitution of the sub-standard *Live at Crawley*, there is a real gap in the Thompson oeuvre, where a good live album should be.

Clive Gregson: 'One thing Richard has never done and which is long overdue is a really killer live record, and I've often thought, suggested it on a few occasions too, that the Jackson Browne *Running on Empty* approach would suit Richard. A bunch of new songs, get the right band, go out and play fourteen or fifteen shows, record the lot and pick the best performances. I think you'd have an absolutely killer Richard record. In many ways, it would be more cost effective than the records he makes, which are not cheap by the time you've schlepped backwards and forwards across the Atlantic.'

Danny Thompson, who began accompanying Richard in concert regularly during the 1990s, still marvels at 'the governor's' abilities onstage.

Danny Thompson: 'You come to hear a great songwriter, accompanying himself, unbelievably on his guitar. The other thing in a world of a million guitar players, to stick a record on and go, "Oh that's Richard Thompson". That in itself is enough, forget the songwriting ... I stand onstage sometimes and think this song is giving me the goosebumps, not because of any personal feelings, but because it's such a devastating song, which sounds like a traditional song, but which he wrote, then I'm aware of what he's playing ... The other bonus is: the next night, it's different. It's not like cabaret ...

'He's quite capable of going into "Purple Haze", or "Ferry Cross The Mersey", or a Bob Wills tune ... His musical knowledge and experience is vast. He's not just a one-genre geezer. His ears are not painted on ...'

Rarely has Thompson been unnerved when performing, although the cool facade did crack while on tour in Scandinavia in 1983, as he told Ken Hunt in *Swing 51*: 'I'd been playing in discos, and they'd stop the disco for an hour and stick me on, which wasn't always very popular with the clientele, because I was playing acoustic. I think at the end of the tour, I was doing a good proportion of Buddy Holly and Abba numbers, just to create some kind of reaction in the audience ...

'In some town, up in the Arctic Circle, one wild Friday night, I was up there singing with my eyes closed, and I opened them, and there was a guy about six inches away from me with a knife a few inches from my throat. He said ... "Why don't you play something normal?" So I nodded to him and said "Yes, absolutely ..." I was in the middle of a number at the time, which I finished, all the while thinking, "what's a normal number?" I can't remember what the next number I did was, but it must have been normal because I didn't see him again.'

Driving Richard and Linda to gigs around the country during the 1970s, Bernard Doherty saw a lot of Richard on and offstage: 'We'd go on these long journeys, and I remember I had the ultimate Chuck Berry Greatest Hits, "Nadine", "No Particular Place To Go" and I remember Richard saying the great thing about Chuck Berry's solos, the first part was very simple, but the last four bars he'll dive over the edge, you'll lose him, but he'll come straight back in. And I remember we got to this gig, and every solo Richard did that night was a Chuck Berry ...

Richard Thompson

He could do Hendrix, I saw him in a dressing room once, he just did these incredible Hendrix licks.'

Over the years, Thompson has defined his stagecraft and his onstage persona. Playing with a band, he has gained in confidence by trying to tackle some of rock music's sacred cows head-on.

Richard: 'It's one of the stances of rock music that you don't really say anything to the audience, you can shout at the audience and say we love you and all that sort of stuff, but you don't really talk to them, you talk down to them from your rock podium. Actually talking to the audience doesn't happen too much with bands, but solo you have to unless you're going to be a real arrogant bastard or incredibly rude, which can work. I've tried that sometimes to be the aloof, arrogant one, just to see what happens and sometimes you go down better that way! People think "oh he's great, so weird and mysterious" – so that can be good.

'I think I started trying to be aggressive and sometimes conversational and sometimes tell jokes and things on stage, just as a way to soften the audience up and once they're softened up you can just slip the knife in between their ribs. You can hit them harder with the quiet song that hits home, when they're not expecting it.

'There are some songs that even sound like they're going to be funny songs – like "God Loves A Drunk" – sometimes the audience titter at the first couple of lines and then having tittered they're already in too far to get out and they have to listen to the rest of it and it gets darker and darker and they're stuck there, because they've been lured in. So it can be a useful device to confuse an audience in that way and it's part of the fun of doing it.'

Following his deal with Polygram in 1985, Thompson could afford to tour regularly with a band to help promote the latest album. Piling into a minibus, Richard Thompson went out to search for America. He was capable of pulling a decent crowd at prestige venues in Boston, Minneapolis, New York, Chicago and San Francisco. But to reach into and make an impact on the American heartland, Thompson had to settle for playing support, which could prove a disillusioning experience.

Clive Gregson: 'We did a couple of shows opening for REM, which was hilarious. They asked for Richard to do it. This was 1986, they were just really breaking big. Cincinatti and Cleveland, Civic Centres seven or eight thousand. One of the weirdest gigs I've ever done in my life. They were fans ... We went on and it was full. They hated us beyond belief. There were about six people in the front going "Richard we love you" ... Then REM went on and they were crap, and the audience weren't bothered about them either ... They'd heard they were the happening band, and were only there to buy the T-shirt ... I think Richard would rather go on and play two hours of his own stuff to a hundred people, than thirty-five minutes under very trying circumstances with crap sound and the audience hating you in front of Megadeth.'

Many friends, musicians and admirers have commented on Thompson's greater confidence in front of an audience these days. Many attribute Richard's increased assuredness to his wife Nancy, but that 'confidence' in front of a crowd is something he has worked hard at.

Richard: 'I think it's true of a lot of artists actually – off-stage they're bad communicators, shy, you know, they stutter, Peter Gabriel or somebody. There are so many artists you meet who claim they're shy – Danny Thompson claims he's shy, he seriously thinks he's a shy person. But there's a lot of performers who achieve their adequacy on the stage – that seems to be the way that they fulfil themselves – and off-stage they go back to being shuffling wrecks – mere shadows of men. I've certainly counted myself among that small legion.

'I don't think I'm a performer in that sense, but it's something I enjoy doing, I like being on stage and I like working *with* the audience, the audience is very important to the show, whatever's going to happen.

'There's a kind of person who's on the shy side, for whom going on stage is actually quite difficult – there are people who vomit every show. Elvis says he throws up all the time before he goes on stage, Tommy Steele still throws up before he goes on stage. But they want to be up there and they want to do it, but there's this nervousness about doing it.'

Touring with Richard Thompson has rarely been a 'sex and drugs and rock and roll' cocktail. Mature and sensible chaps with mature and sensible hairstyles, the rock'n'roll frenzy was not for Thompson and crew. 'Scrabble' was how Christine Collister remembered those long trawls criss-crossing the American Midwest.

Dave Mattacks: 'All the tours I've done with Richard the past few years I've always had a good time, there's always fun. But it's not archetypal TV sets out of windows, falling over staggering, it's not that kind of thing. It could be silliness in a restaurant in the middle of nowhere in America, it could be a game in some bowling alley. It's things like watching *A Fish Called Wanda* when it came out in the middle of nowhere in America, and laughing at the jokes, and no one else in the audience getting them and coming out hysterical afterwards. Just friends having a good time together instead of "whoa", pulling birds ... But that's not to say it's a po-faced bunch of twerps sitting

Richard Thompson

around reading dictionaries, or sitting in the back of the van reading the Koran.'

Danny Thompson: 'When we're on tour, and I think this helps our relationship, instead of trying to find a McDonald's, we look for a mini-golf course. A lot of Scrabble, you know, you arrive at a gig at three o'clock, do the soundcheck, then there's five hours to kill before you're on.'

And always, there are the local radio interviews, the station idents, the close encounters with regional press to be endured. Thompson will grit his teeth, smile, and go through it all again. All in the hope of selling a few more albums, or shifting a few more tickets to that night's show. Richard has been doing this sort of thing most of his adult life. There aren't many flankers that can be worked on him, and he does enjoy putting the boot on the other foot.

Pete Zorn: 'We arrived at a gig, sometime in the late 70s . . . and the inevitable man with the machine, some young spark from the local radio station is there, who thought he had a new angle. The guy says "Now Richard, every interview starts with me asking you a question, just to be different Richard, let's begin with you asking me a question." So Richard turned to him and smiled and said "All right, where have all the liberals gone?" I thought this is going to be some interview.'

To alleviate the boredom of travelling, Thompson frequently takes the wheel of the band's tour bus during those long hauls down the American highways. He enjoys travelling, it gives him a fresh perspective on who he is, where he's been and where he's going. Away from the wheel though, an American tour with Richard Thompson doesn't exactly read like like an excised chapter from a Led Zeppelin memoir.

Pete Zorn: 'It's a strange sort of travelling club. It's very calm on the bus. Richard and company have the back lounge, if you want to watch television or videos, you do it in the front. It's a kind of travelling obscurists' reading society. There's high-level Scrabble going on in the back lounge. He has very quiet pursuits. He and Danny talk about Islamic stuff.

'Richard always gets the most out of touring. You can go to Muncie, Indiana, and he'll know that there's a museum there that has the world's second-largest ball of string, or something. He'll know, because he's been so much round the States. So he knows, oh yes, next week I'm going to be there, that's the place for coffee.'

Richard: 'In terms of touring there's things called budgets. You can tour and life can be hell, you can be sharing a room with someone who snores prodigiously or someone with vile drug habits; you can be crammed in a really uncomfortable van, doing ridiculously long drives, doing horrible gigs to no people. I understand why the odd musician commits suicide, it can be really, really horrible.

'You can also be stuck touring in your legend, you can be marooned playing pubs and bars forever, which is a kind of hell in that it just repeats forever. But if you're lucky and careful, touring can be fun, and it is right now. We are just about at the point where if the band goes out, we can now afford to tour America in a bus – quite a nice bus. We can only afford one bus at the moment, the next step is you get two, you get the crew bus and the band bus so the crew can go ahead. At the moment we still have to get up at six o'clock in the morning!

'It's fun, because you're working with people that you like, you're not in a band with four people you hate – I've never been in that position, but that can happen – you just hate your fellow musicians. But because it's a pleasant social situation, it's really fun, the last band tour we did in the States was really enjoyable and it wasn't too tiring, we were out for at least two months but it was really manageable.'

During the mid-90s, Thompson has toured with a stripped-down band (Danny Thompson, Pete Zorn and Dave Mattacks) which keeps the costs down. Working just with Danny is cheaper still.

Clive Gregson: 'You see him with Danny now and it's so different. It's quite a slick show now, which I find strange for Richard, I always thought the shows were very ramshackle. That maybe changed when we were with the band, it became more of a presentation if you like.'

Richard: 'There's never enough money to tour with a band, especially in Europe – we lose money. In America we can plan it so that we just about make money. But there's more stuff we need, so if we can earn more money on the road then we can get that second bus, we can pay the musicians real wages, we can start carrying a lighting rig and all the things that are important to create that special moment. If I play solo I do fine, I earn a good living, but playing solo has diminishing returns without the high profile record release and without the band tour – which you need just to keep it at that level. If you just play solo, then it sort of slips back into clubland.'

Danny Thompson: 'I think he's as successful as he wants to be. In order to go further, do you have to be like Springsteen, be that living legend? And be that person? . . . I think because of his honesty, the fact that finishing a piece like "Shoot Out The Lights", with a devastating guitar solo, instead of standing there with his foot up on the monitor, and the light fading. He'll suddenly say "Bloody Maggie Thatcher" and blah blah blah. Because he's so self-effacing, purposely defusing this kind of precious atmosphere. It's like: there we are, that was deadly serious, meanwhile, we're all real people, let's get on with it.'

There's a joke about a man lost in New York, who asks a passer-by how to get to Carnegie Hall, to be told 'Practise!'

Richard: 'Just in terms of keeping your fingers working, keeping your calluses up, you have to play on a regular basis. You can miss the odd day, that's not a disaster. But in terms of keeping limber you really have to be playing, you can be watching cricket at the same time. Sometimes when you're watching the cricket you can come up with something in a rather unconscious way, that might be something of a good song or a good riff. Your fingers find something without you really thinking about it.'

Muna: 'He was always playing the guitar . . . To this day, if you're trying to watch television, he's sitting playing, and you're going "Dad!", and he doesn't realise, because to him it's second nature.'

Nancy: 'He is always playing. If we're watching TV he'll be playing, he just always plays. Right before going on the road, then he needs to sing to get his voice going. I don't know if you'd call it practising . . . He just loves to play, he plays all the time.'

Last word to the man who began it all.

Big Muldoon: 'My wife wanted to buy me an anniversary present, a guitar from a shop in Tottenham Court Road, and we asked Richard to come along and help us choose it. It was a fake Gibson, Richard tried it out, and it was amazing, everyone in the shop drifted over, so he said this sounds all right, you have a go. I thought, Oh no, the humiliation again, here we are back on the North Circular . . .! He plays the guitar faster than I can listen to it.'

Chapter 29

> Or when the moon was overhead,
> Came two young lovers lately wed;
> 'I am half sick of shadows', said
> The Lady of Shalott

THE TITLE OF Richard Thompson's 1994 *Mirror Blue* album came from Alfred Lord Tennyson's epic poem 'The Lady of Shallot'. The lady of the title spends her life staring at the 'mirror blue' of the record title, preferring illusory romance to the reality of life. And when confronted by the reality, 'the mirror crack'd from side to side', and death comes to The Lady of Shallot.

Tennyson's poem did much to alert the Victorians to the romantic chivalry of the Arthurian legends. 'Shallot' was a corruption of 'Astolat', an island which legend has it used to occupy the site where Guildford now stands.

In a nationwide 1995 poll, 'The Lady of Shallot' was voted the country's second-favourite poem, following Rudyard Kipling's 'If . . .' Half remembered as a kind of Victorian soap opera, Tennyson's poem celebrated courtly virtue and helped consolidate the Arthurian myth. The poem has also been interpreted as representing the divide between life and art, the gap between commitment and distance. So plenty there for Richard Thompson to get his teeth into.

The sessions for *Mirror Blue* were underway by the beginning of 1993, but the album was not released until January 1994. The delay was due to changes at the top of Capitol Records when Thompson champion Hale Milgrim was replaced by Gary Gersh. Talking to *Hokey Pokey*, Thompson reflected: 'The president of Capitol changed and they fired people down the line – it happens a lot in the record industry. With that sort of structural change it takes at least six months to get straight again, and it seemed best to wait until they'd got the company back in the right shape – it was a mutual decision.'

Richard Thompson

Thompson was keen on the unorthodoxy of *Mirror Blue*. He particularly relished the deconstruction of the standard rock'n'roll drum sound. The rhythms were staccato, the drums of Pete Thomas were dismantled. Every artist is more enthusiastic about his new album than revisiting half-forgotten records of a quarter of a century before, but Thompson really did envisage the album as a breakthrough, tearing away from the standard concept and conceit of rock'n'roll, and trying something radical and fresh in a stale old form.

Richard: 'I thought it was a sort of deconstruction of the rock rhythm section in some ways. It was a radical record – and a brave record – it was off the back of the records Mitchell and Tchad [Blake] did with Suzanne Vega and Los Lobos and the couple of records Tchad did with Tom Waits. All of which I thought were terrific records and they all had a kind of character to them – a sound that was really trying to strip away some clichés, like why have a snare drum, why the backbeat? And just looking at the song and seeing what does the song need, what's going to work?

'Because we worked in a small studio, we got to the point of actively disliking digital echo, so we said we just won't have any – we hadn't got any plates or chambers here so we just won't have any echo, so there isn't any. There's a bit of tape echo on the voices and that's about it. There's kind of room sound, but there's no reverberation.'

Thompson's enthusiasm for the playing of Pete Thomas was heartfelt. Thomas had occupied the drum stool of Elvis Costello's Attractions since their inception in 1977. He had served his apprenticeship in the pub-rock follies of Chilli Willi and the Red Hot Peppers, as well as a stint with singer-songwriter John Stewart.

Richard: 'The reason we selected Pete Thomas to play the drums was because he was someone who was happy to experiment with his kit and would also happily be sound-checking it for hours and would still have the energy when it came to Take One. So Pete might be in there for six hours just mucking around with tins of Heinz beans or washboards, just figuring out grooves on a fairly strange selection of percussion and finding a comfortable way that he could play it, which wasn't always sitting at a drumstool, sometimes having it across a piano stool or something. So that was a lot for him to be thinking about and a lot of time setting that up. But because of his stamina, he was always fresh for a few takes.

'He doesn't hit it that hard, it's more in the nuance of the wrist. He's also a pop drummer which I thought was good, he comes from pop rather than rock and I'm actually kind of sick of rock with a capital "R". If anything could be said to be clichéd at this point, it's rock rather than pop. I'm thinking of the stadium thing and the metal thing and then all that "attitude" stuff – the Pearl Jam thing, and all the grunge – it all seems quite pretentious to me. I'd rather have Abba or something, I'd definitely rather have Crowded House or Blur . . .'

That reliance on percussion, on re-inventing a rock rhythm section of bass and drums, obviously dictated the sound of the finished record. In conversation, you can feel Thompson's enthusiasm for the freedom he felt was offered by *Mirror Blue*. But too often, the album sounded like one of Tom Waits' junkyard constructions which, by the time of *Bone Machine*, had Waits sounding like a blind panel-beater trying to find his way out of a metal coffin.

The songs on *Mirror Blue* to which the fans responded most were the touching, solo 'King Of Bohemia' and the similarly structured, lengthy narrative of 'Beeswing'. Elsewhere, the clutter obscured the quality.

After nearly 30 years, you can see why Richard Thompson wanted to flex his creative muscle away from the standard twelve song; bass, drum, guitar, crumhorn rock'n'roll album. He has rocked and he has rolled. He has been busy doing it while others of lesser ability have soared passed him. By now, and by rights, he should be entitled to try whatever he wants, with whoever he wants. And, in equal measure, he should be able to take it on the chin, if the reviews or comments from those who have assiduously followed his snaking trail, don't match his own vision of the finished record.

By his own admission, Thompson lacks the discipline for the sustained creativity of a novel. Family and close friends speak highly of the quality of Richard's painting, though it remains publicly unseen. His prose efforts have been limited to sleeve notes (*Full House, Henry the Human Fly*), and while he tinkers in private over short stories, his territory is the song, and the collection of songs he gathers together and sequences on an album. As a bonus, you also get some scorching guitar and impassioned singing, but the album stands or falls by the quality of the songs which Thompson has fashioned for his new release.

Clive Gregson: 'I think his last few records are fatally compromised by a lot of things, and I . . . can only assume that it's some kind of external pressure. But I don't believe that Richard has ever really been that bothered about making records. It's not the real thing for him, I think he's one of those people who loves to write songs, and that's the creative process, and then the recording is a necessary evil to get them out . . .'

The loyalty of Thompson's fans has never been in doubt, they have stuck with him, through thin and thin, and though they might find fault

Richard Thompson

in *Mirror Blue*, that doesn't mean they won't be there next time out, they are entitled to an opinion.

An overwhelming pall hung over the album. Its deconstruction seemed wilful, without any substance to replace what had been taken away. For all its avowed newness, there was a feeling that we had all been here before. A Richard Thompson album is a rare treat, always familiar, but never a copy.

Mirror Blue's 'Fast Food' is that rarest of things, a Richard Thompson song which failed to register, a song as disposable as its subject matter. 'Mingus Eyes' was a further look at hero worship and role modelling, which Thompson had dealt with so much more effectively on 'From Galway To Graceland'. 'Mascara Tears' and 'Taking My Business Elsewhere' just seemed so insubstantial in the Richard Thompson scheme of things.

Incapable of making a wholly duff album, Thompson still played his aces: 'King Of Bohemia' was a rebuttal of the sentiments in 'The End Of The Rainbow' twenty years before. The song began life as 'Jack Straw's Castle', a pub near Thompson's Hampstead home, and a familiar location for gay Londoners. To avoid confusion, the composer altered the title to 'King of Bohemia' . . . a pub near Thompson's London home.

'Beeswing' is exactly the type of song Richard Thompson fans love to get their teeth into, a solo folkie ballad, this time dealing with the 1960s. There are echoes here of George Orwell's *A Clergyman's Daughter*, in the tale of a girl who falls from grace. To his credit, Thompson refuses to romanticise his memories of 'the Summer of Love', and adroitly lays the blame:

> And they say her flower is faded now
> Hard weather and hard booze,
> But maybe that's just the price you pay
> For the chains you refuse . . .

'Beeswing' is a song firmly lodged in Thompson's subconscious, he tried writing another song of the same title before, but abandoned it, instead taking the name for his song publishing company.

Marc Ellington: 'If you listen to a song like "Beeswing", you can actually hear that not only is he writing a song about this girl, but he understands clearly the alienation of travelling people, and the difficulty of people adapting to a changing society. There's no one else writing like this. Ewan MacColl wrote a song called "The Travelling People", which simply just placed this mass of people who are culturally so important within European history – travelling people, gypsies – and he just said "I'm a freeborn man of the travelling people..." and all that, but what Richard could do because he understands how society operates and understands alienation of cultural groups, he was able to take this one person and tell a bigger story.'

'Easy There, Steady Now' had Thompson back on the familiar stalk of the psycho let loose. Talking to David Cavanagh in *Mojo*, Thompson spoke of the song's inspiration: 'I think human minds don't vary that much from one person to another. I think everyone contains all the bits. You can be Mozart or you can be Jack the Ripper, the potential is all in there somewhere. But being human beings, we have morality and there are triggers to stop us doing bad things and lead us to do good things.'

'The Way That It Shows' was like a late night stroll down the familiar hallways of a seedy, downtown motel. Behind each numbered door, betrayal, infidelity and bruised romance lurk in vacant shadow.

Mirror Blue divided Thompson's long-time fanbase like no other record. Maybe it was the lack of guitar on record, although that was well represented on the long and winding fade of 'The Way That It Shows'. Maybe it was the fact that Thompson's songs at times sounded like they were struggling under a skip of discarded cutlery...

Fans hoping to get their own Richard Thompson Garden Icon, as pictured on the album's cover, were also to be sadly disappointed:

Richard: 'They made eighteen and I told them they had to destroy them all. The whole idea of it was that it was an anti-icon icon, the whole idea was that there shouldn't be any, but they were dying to make thousands of them as promos.'

As ever, there was much to relish on *Mirror Blue*, but there seemed to be an element missing from the finished album. Maybe it was all that wilful deconstruction which explained the poor reception. *NME*'s Danny Frost wrote: 'Swamped by thundering, know-nothing drums and suffocating sonic shimmer, *Mirror Blue* is one of the most heavy-handedly produced records you'll ever hear. The songs themselves peek out all too rarely from beneath a swathing blanket of reverb, and Thompson's strengths – his vulnerability, intimacy, the pin-sharp thrusts and parries of his guitar – are all very nearly negated.'

In *Q*, David Hepworth's review dipped below the customary four stars: 'In reprising the sound and shape of *Rumor & Sigh* for *Mirror Blue* ... he and Froom have wandered near the border that separates the polished from the pat ... The belated appearance of the dark and vivid "From Galway To Graceland" ... suggests that over the last few

Richard Thompson

years this end of Thompson's repertoire has been neglected in favour of wooing radio programmers with the kind of rock sound they feel comfortable with.'

The most controversial opinion of *Mirror Blue* was that of long-time collaborator Clive Gregson, who reviewed the album for *Mojo*. Nailing his colours to the mast early on, Clive admitted that Thompson was 'my all-time favourite guitarist, and arguably the finest living English songwriter. Richard has never made anything resembling a bad record. His weakest offerings still stand head and shoulders above most artists' finest hours ... I'd rather have any Richard Thompson record than the combined output of U2, REM and Dire Straits.' So far, so good, but where Gregson put noses out of joint was in his assertion that '*Mirror Blue* is not a great record by Richard's own very high standards.'

Musicians who have worked with Richard Thompson over the years tend to remain loyal – friends in the studio and admirers of the work. Many said how privileged they felt to work with him and even long-term collaborators spoke of their pleasure at being asked to work with him again.

John Kirkpatrick: 'Going to do a session for Richard is like having acupuncture, afterwards you feel "Bloody hell, that was fantastic".'

Pat Donaldson: 'I think people take Richard a lot more seriously sometimes than he actually is. He's a well-rounded human being. My memories of working with Richard Thompson are happy ones ... and it's always a pleasure. It's a thrill to play with the man.'

Dave Mattacks: 'There were times during that 1994 tour with Richard, three-and-a-half months here and in the States, that were absolute magic, some of the happiest times I've spent onstage with anybody. It was just tremendous and I don't have that with anybody else. Even knowing Richard for all these years, you don't lose your awe with someone that genuinely talented. I'm not walking about doffing me cap, but I have a real respect for Richard. He is one of the greatest songwriters and guitar-players and singers and I think he's a great bloke. I like him even more now. There was a period, the Sufi period, when let's just say I had a bit of difficulty relating to him. Now he's more devout, more into it than ever he was, but his way of dealing with it is much more mature, and I respect him even more for that.'

Today, over twenty years after his conversion to Islam, Richard Thompson still sees its effect on his life as: 'Total ... What you believe changes how you deal with life completely. I just have a philosophy that I apply to everything, which is great, that means you don't have to think about it, it's all decided ... In terms of Islam, in twenty years I've got it more in perspective. So I live life as a Western rock'n'roll musician – which is what I am for my sins – and I try to be a reasonable human being, that's all.'

Muna: 'I always remember my dad praying, loads of times in the day ... He was just a very severe person about religious things. Not so much any more actually, since he met Nancy ... it's not so prominent, but it's always there.'

Nancy: 'I'm married to a Muslim ... Being a Muslim you have to marry a believer. He could not marry an atheist, but I'm not. I'm a Christian, but I'm a believer in God, so that's okay. He wouldn't be drawn to someone who was an atheist, because he's a strict Muslim. He still is. He's never missed a prayer that I've ever known. He could be coming home at 6 a.m. from the Bottom Line in New York and he'll still do his prayers ... The thing is, I think he learned, as people do, when you first convert to something, you're telling everybody about it, and it actually turns people off. So he doesn't do that ...

'Richard would say that when he became a Muslim, that was who he was ... that's kind of who Richard is. Sure, he can appreciate good things, but if you had a fire, he'd walk away and he wouldn't cry, he'd be absolutely fine. When my mother and I are fighting over who's gonna have my grandmother's stuff, he says "It doesn't matter". And I think that's probably how he's always been. I think being a Muslim suited him, I'm not sure it changed him.'

Few though – even among the most regular collaborators – speak of Thompson as a close friend. There was warmth when colleagues spoke of working with Thompson, but even those who had enjoyed long and – on record, at least – fruitful relationships with him were cautious. The warmth was evidently there, but it was the warmth of a fire observed through a frosted window.

Clive Gregson: 'I've known Richard since 1980, and he's a hard person to get to know in the way that you would know your best friend. He is basically a very private person ... I think he works at that, to be honest. I think it's that that has kept him fairly sane through periods of abject rejection and all the stuff musicians go through, I think he keeps his own counsel.'

Dave Mattacks: '*Strict Tempo* is the last time I played with him on record. I'm kind of torn between thinking how come I'm good enough to do the tours and I'm not good enough to do the record. The other side is, great, I get to play with Richard ... I am disappointed that on his major records over the past few years, I haven't got a call to do it. Everyone else seems to except me ... I never get a look in. I'm caught between being paranoid, thinking that I'm not good enough, but then again if I'm not good enough he wouldn't ask me to do the tours. If I'm honest, I am disappointed, because without taking anything away from Pete Thomas or [Jim] Keltner or any of the other excellent drummers that he has on his records, I think I play in a certain way that hopefully is not uncomplementary to him, and I'd like to get the chance to put that on a CD.'

John Kirkpatrick: 'I think he is a solitary individual. Essentially, I don't think he actually needs anybody, he's very self sufficient. His faith has given him most of what he needs and anything else is a bit of a bonus ... Most of the time he's very jolly and fun to be with, then all of a sudden he'll shut down and he's not there ... Going from one extreme to another at the flick of a switch ... I think he likes to achieve a distance between people.'

Richard and Linda's eldest daughter Muna confirmed that her father was not the most outwardly emotional of men: 'He's not openly affectionate, he's quite reserved in all areas ... We all knew that he loved us in his own way, as kind of a quiet, unsaid thing. I don't think any of us doubted it, but we didn't see him very much. It was a long-distance relationship a lot of the time. He is fairly self-sufficient, definitely. He only lets people know as much as he wants them to know. I don't think ever, in my life, he's really ever lost control. I should think I've seen him cry once. He's the sort of person who can tell you off, or look at you, and you just shake. I remember being so fearful of him, because he's one of those people who commands authority and respect, without ever raising his voice. He's very self-contained.'

Linda: 'I don't ever remember Richard's dad praising, or even alluding ... I don't think he ever could have said 'Well done' or whatever. He would say things to us like "Why don't you do things that people will listen to? Like that nice Shirley Bassey." I'm sure his father loved him. I come from a Scottish family myself and they find it very hard to show any love, and often their way of showing it is to criticise you, in the mistaken belief that that will make you do better.'

Talking to those who I would have expected to include themselves in the category of close friends, there was evidently still a distance, a reserve, a feeling of cordiality rather than intimacy. There was awe and respect in abundance but little sense of reciprocal affection. Richard Thompson remains, in Churchill's words, 'a riddle wrapped in a mystery inside an enigma'.

Simon Nicol has certainly known Thompson as long as any musician, and remains one of his oldest friends, I asked Simon if he really knew

Richard: 'We're from very similar backgrounds. We are north London, middle class, grammar school kids of the same age who have been involved in the same "big fish in a small pond" music for about the same length of time . . . I wouldn't say that I know him in the sense that I could predict his next move in any given situation, or that I really understand how he feels about a third party. I know I love him and I love what he does, and he's closer to me than much of my family, even though we don't have to be in each other's pockets on a weekly basis to do that. But I wouldn't necessarily say that he loves me. But I don't need him to. It's not one of those demanding kind of relationships. I'm really pleased that I still do get to work with him occasionally, and I'm astonished at how much he carries on improving . . . I wouldn't expect him to be verbal. Because of our shared background, if you wanted to come up with a category of person who's unlikely to be effusive or eloquent about their emotions, that would be your starting place.'

Richard Thompson is not remote or intimidating. But if you were to make up a psychological profile of a remote, rather austere man, who had difficulty communicating his real emotions, the photofit would reveal someone rather like Richard Thompson. He is as much a product of his genes and his environment, his upbringing and his education, as any middle-class English boy child, born in the immediate aftermath of the Second World War.

Linda: 'I obviously can't speak for now, but in my experience I think he is . . . detached. He is cool, very cool. There is nothing very emotional or hysterical or anything like that. A pretty cool customer . . . I think a lot of that has to do with his upbringing and his family, but also that whole . . . if you were a boy, you weren't allowed to cry. Boys don't cry. You just accepted that. You never praised a child to his face, you could do it behind his back, in case they got big-headed. And of course that caused a lot of children a lot of pain.'

It was while touring America with Fairport in 1970 that Richard formed a relationship with Liz Gordon, which resulted in the birth of Richard's first child Jesse.

Richard: 'I get on with Liz very well these days, she's a very nice lady, a professor of French literature. Poor Jesse, look what he had to grow up with! I suppose it was on the first Fairport tour that we met – she was a hippie in those days, an amateur chanteuse – she sang Russian folk songs. You could get away with anything in those days!

'I wasn't really in touch with Jesse until he was about twelve – when it seemed like a good idea to get in touch. Up to that point I didn't have a very good relationship with Liz so it was hard to find a line of approach, but it seemed that it would be a good idea to get to know him and spend some time with him and it worked really well.

'He's integrated into the family now – he's a great kid and gets on well with my other kids. They didn't know about him before and that all had to come out in some crisis, but it all worked out in the end.'

Pete Zorn: 'I think he's divided his life into two compartments: there's Richard at home, and Richard at work, whether that's in the studio, at the office, whether he's dealing with musicians or dealing with touring, the business side of it, that's one Richard. And that's the Richard we all know. There's no difference between him at a board meeting and him in a recording studio . . .

'The more you work with Richard, the more you get worried about how little you know about him. He's very much here and now, don't bother me about what happened years ago . . . From what I gather, life with Fairport was very similar to what we were doing in the late 70s: van touring. In a sense, all you had to do was look around you to see what it was like, one-star hotels, very, very long drives, you manhandled the gear yourself, broke it down yourself. So it was pointless to ask. It was just like *that*, but with a different group of people.'

Chapter 30

SOMEWHERE IN THE HIGH echelons of Capitol Records in Los Angeles, someone decided that the word was ... Richard Thompson. As early as 1991, with sales of *Rumor & Sigh* on the up, plans were underway for a Richard Thompson Tribute Album. The word went out: 'Do you want to pay homage to Richard Thompson?' And back came the yeah, yeah, yeahs. But these things take time ...

With *Watching the Dark* released during 1993, Thompson was becoming accustomed to looking back over his shoulder and letting the hosannas of tribute flood over him. After years of protraction and negotiation, *Beat the Retreat* was finally released in 1995. 'Songs by Richard Thompson' were interpreted by among others, REM, Bonnie Raitt, Los Lobos, David Byrne, June Tabor, Martin Carthy and Maddy Prior.

The tribute album thing took flight when, in 1987, Manchester's Imaginary Records began releasing entire albums of contemporary acts paying tribute to a seminal artist or band – Thompson himself contributed a cover of 'Here Without You' to the label's Byrds tribute. That same year, Jennifer Warnes' Leonard Cohen tribute, *Famous Blue Raincoat* ('Jenny sings Lenny' to its friends) not only began the Cohen revival, but lent a degree of credibility to the whole tribute concept.

The climate was right for a tribute explosion. The dream album for a record company to market is a Greatest Hits package. Take a handful of familiar titles by a favourite act; sprinkle with a few cover versions; lightly fricassee with freshly recorded duets, and you have the perfect package to sell to a captive audience. In the UK during the months leading up to Christmas (the last quarter accounts for something like forty per cent of the year's total record sales), the charts are filled with Greatest Hits and Best Ofs ... The extra running time of CDs provides the perfect opportunity to digest an artist's career into one convenient, bite-sized chunk.

Richard Thompson

The problem is, that a Greatest Hits package only really works while there are hits to be had. You can regurgitate and re-shuffle, but doing it more than twice a decade is risky. The success of MTV's *Unplugged* phenomenon was as much a function of the familiarity of the material as hearing it re-interpreted acoustically. (The lack of electricity was, in any case, conveniently overlooked by the time Bruce Springsteen came to record his contribution.) In the cosily nostalgic culture of the 1990s music industry, any alternative approaches to familiar-but-new packaging were instantly appealing. And so it was that the tribute record came to be. Familiar songs by familiar artists, but all in fresh new combinations. It was indeed a marketing man's dream come true.

By the time Richard Thompson's tribute, *Beat the Retreat* was finally released in 1995, the world had already seen whole albums devoted to the work of Arthur Alexander, Doc Pomus, Leonard Cohen (thrice), Elton John, Jimi Hendrix, Curtis Mayfield ... It had seemed such a good idea at the time, but eyebrows were raised and questions asked when entire albums were devoted to the inspirational work of the Carpenters, Kiss and the Hollies.

There was no doubting the sincerity of the artists involved, but too often it seemed they were chosen because they shared a label, rather than for any heartfelt desire to pay tribute. It was also a case of round up the usual suspects – Sinead O'Connor, REM and Elvis Costello seemed to do little but pay tribute throughout much of the 90s.

Richard: 'There's versions I've enjoyed. I really like Swan Arcade singing "The Great Valerio", I thought that was very interesting, they basically sang the chords from the version I did, vocally which was quite exciting. I liked Sandy's version of "For Shame Of Doing Wrong", that was very nice. If anybody covers your song that's really an achievement and an honour, it doesn't matter who they are, that someone could be bothered to like your song enough to record it, that's absolutely fantastic. Sometimes other people's versions are so close to your own that it's hard for you to get much out of it as a writer.'

Capitol's Tony Wadsworth, long-time Thompson champion, told *Music Week*: 'The album is a logical continuation of what we've been doing since Richard arrived at Capitol. He has gained the respect of a wide variety of musicians, from cutting edge performers like Bob Mould to traditional English musicians, and we aim to get a wider recognition of his work.'

Thompson himself had mixed feelings about the finished album. Talking to Dinosaur Jr's Jay Mascis (who tackled 'I Misunderstood' on the tribute album) in *Interview* magazine in December 1994, he joked: 'Actually, I thought it was going to be a tribute in the Roman sense, where they send a couple of princesses as hostages and pay me so much gold a year.' When pressed as to what he felt about having a whole album full of artists paying tribute to his talent, Thompson niftily sidestepped: 'It's like being bitten in the dark by a beautiful woman who's pretending to be a small but persistent insect ... It's like being taken to the zoo when you were a kid and discovering that the animals really can talk ... It's like finding out on your mother's deathbed that she really was a geologist.'

Beat the Retreat, from its dour cover in, sounds less like a tribute, than an obituary. No one involved seems to savour the songs, there is little relish in any of the performances, and even the mighty sound weak: the pairing of James Burton and June Tabor on the title track should be a solid-gold sound, but somehow ... REM sound like they were being force fed mogadon while cutting 'Wall Of Death' ... X and Dinosaur Jr sound like they just cranked the amps up to eleven and let rip ...

The album has its moments: Los Lobos duly do the business on 'Down Where The Drunkards Roll'; David Byrne hijacks the riff from 'Suspicious Minds' and almost welds it onto 'Just The Motion'; Beausoleil take 'Valerie' on a diverting cajun journey through the bayoux, and the Five Blind Boys of Alabama make 'Dimming Of The Day' as near to a gospel experience as you can get on a compact disc in the 1990s.

A far less star-studded, yet more worthy Richard Thompson tribute had already been put together in 1993, by fanzine founder Colin Davies. All proceeds from *Hokey Pokey*'s *The World is a Wonderful Place*, went to local south London charities and there was a real enthusiasm from the participants for their chosen Thompson track. 'Look what they've done to my songs, ma' was the caption on the photo of a grimacing Thompson.

Highlights included Christine Collister's spectral 'How Will I Ever Be Simple Again'; Plainsong's 'From Galway To Graceland'; Clive Gregson getting a second crack at his all-time favourite Richard song 'Dimming Of The Day'; ex-Lone Justice bassist Marvin Etzioni on the obscure Thompson original, 'It Don't Cost Much' and Ron Kavana's bleary take on 'I Want To See The Bright Lights Tonight' ... Of special interest was the title track, unlisted on the sleeve, but which appears magically and mysteriously as Track 13. Linda Thompson sings a wonderful, bleakly ironic Richard composition:

How does it feel to be nothing?
How does it feel to be small?

Richard Thompson

> Pull hard on that wine,
> It's the end of the line,
> Oh the world is a wonderful place

The song sounds as though it could happily have slotted onto the *Bright Lights* album. It was in fact a demo, written for a 1973 play by a friend of the Thompsons, Barbara Gordon.

Another low-key tribute around the same time was folk singer Dave Burland's 1992 homage, *His Master's Choice: The Songs of Richard Thompson*, to which 'The Master' himself contributed guitar. Burland is a soft-voiced Yorkshire singer who'd been singing Richard's songs since the late 60s, and this was a well-chosen selection of folk club favourites ('The New St George', 'The Old Changing Way', 'Poor Ditching Boy' etc). Affectionate and heartfelt, it made a refreshing alternative to the glitzy *Beat the Retreat*.

The tributes ringing in his ear, Thompson just gets on with his professional life – writing and recording, touring and promoting.

Richard Thompson is happy enough with his lot, aware of his position, but equally aware of just what he's up against. He has played the game the way he's been told and he's kicked against it. He's been with majors and he's been with minors. He has friends in high places but he recognises that his career here is in stasis, and whatever he does, however hard he tries, being able to move on up seems, inexplicably, beyond his control.

Though in recent years a more ambitious side of Thompson has been revealed, those who know him well feel that he is still ambivalent about 'The Big Time'. He would undoubtedly welcome wider recognition for his work (and a second tour bus), but is reluctant to sacrifice the anonymity of what is a very pleasant lifestyle.

Clive Gregson: 'I think in terms of commercial success, he likes to be accepted, and he likes to make a living and he's doing okay. More important to him, I think, is the fact that people in the know know he's the greatest... I think Richard's a bit perverse about this, that if something stands a chance of being commercially acceptable to the Great Unwashed, he will shoot himself in the foot and take a bit of a left turn...'

Muna: 'I think he's turned down a lot of things that could have been his "stairway to stardom", because he wants to do his own thing and remain sincere to his music, which is great. But in the same breath, he's been doing it for years, and I think even he's thinking it's time he reaped some sort of reward.

'I think he'd just hate to be famous. He likes pottering around and doing the gardening, he's a very basic person. He likes the basic things in life, and I think he'd just find it horrendous to be hunted down in the streets; that to him, is a nightmare.'

Richard: 'The last solo tour I did earlier this year [1995], attendance suddenly doubled, things just suddenly went bang for no reason I could quite figure out, suddenly we did incredible business and sold out the whole tour. It was a huge leap and I don't know why ... I got on the Radio One playlist with the last album, which was quite an achievement.

'What are your choices? You could not tour. You could do an album and not tour, you could not do an album and tour, or you could not do an album and not tour, those are the choices! I think the important thing is how you do you do the album and how you tour. So you can radically re-think what it is you do – say, right this record is going to be a totally different concept, we are going deconstruct what we do or something. In terms of what you do on stage and how you tour – that can also be changed a lot if you want to. So it doesn't have to be a conveyor belt or this closed inevitable cycle that you're trapped in.'

Professionally, it is in performance that Richard Thompson really feels he comes alive. On a good night, Thompson makes a unique connection between the performer and his audience. It is what he does and has been doing for all of his adult life.

Richard: 'It's communication. You try to play from the heart and you try and play to the heart. I suppose that what you really want to do is move people, not all the time and not every song maybe, but in the show you want to move people. And at the end of the night you want people to come out feeling different, hopefully feeling more expanded somehow or feeling richer.'

The most obvious change in Thompson's approach to performance in the 1990s, came with his regular appearances alongside double bassist, raconteur and fellow Muslim, Danny Thompson. The men had known each other since the 1960s, 'but being in rival bands (Fairport *v* Pentangle), we always had to cross the road to avoid actual contact,' Richard noted.

A decade older than his guitarist chum, Danny Thompson's career had begun in the mid-50s skiffle boom and proceeded through British jazz, R&B and comprehensive session work. As well as working with Donovan, Nick Drake, Tom Paxton, Sandy Denny and Rod Stewart, over the years Danny also played bass on sessions for Matt Monro, Cliff Richard and Engelbert Humperdinck. Best known for his work

Richard Thompson

in Pentangle, Danny remained with the folk supergroup until 1972 then forged a long and fruitful partnership with John Martyn. Session work paid the bills and kept Danny busy, and he formed his own group, Whatever, in 1987. His friendship with Richard began before their partnership.

Danny Thompson: 'When he asked me to work in a duo, I wasn't sure, I thought it would affect the friendship. But he said "Oh we'll try four or five gigs in Italy, see how it goes. We'll have some food, we'll take the families. If there's a hiccup, that'll be it."

'We started playing tennis before we really started playing together ... He's an aggressive player. He plays to win. He tends to let you make mistakes; he tends to hang back. I tend to go for the killer shots. I do the Jimmy Connors "Yeah", which rattles him a bit. He gets rattled at any sort of exaggerated victory demonstration ... He doesn't do the jumping over the net thing, but he loves to win.'

Tennis opponents and ornithologists together, the Thompsons formed an easygoing partnership onstage. Danny's subtle and nimble bass fingering perfectly underscores Richard's dexterous guitar playing. If there is a tendency to muso noodlings between the two, it is offset by the between-songs patter, which has all the cut and thrust of a Mutt and Jeff routine.

Richard: 'If there's something in Swing tempo – if it's me and Danny – I like to throw in something from the 40s or 50s that he can play proper swing bass to and that we can improvise over – something that's fairly up and the audience can get off on it, perhaps even a bit humorous.'

The Thompson Twins were captured together on disc in 1995 on the limited edition *Live at Crawley* CD. Originally broadcast on the very grown-up BBC Radio Three, the eleven-song set on CD was representative of the duo's stage set, but with time pressing, the banter was surgically reduced. Away from the concert stage, the two Thompsons are regular opponents, either across the tennis net, on the merciless mini-golf course or the green baize of the snooker table. They are united in concert, and in cricket.

Danny Thompson: 'We play cricket together. He's a pretty good all-rounder. A good slow, spin bowler ... Bats about six. He fields long hop. Our first game, against the team from *Miss Saigon*, he took three wickets, twenty-odd runs, ran a bloke out.'

Rolling into 1995, with *Beat the Retreat* and *Mirror Blue* right behind him, Richard Thompson found himself again in exalted company, when *The Guardian* profiling, 'Guitar Heroes' in January 1995, put him up there with Jimi Hendrix, Jimmy Page, Eric Clapton and Jeff Beck.

Solo

'Britain's best relatively obscure guitarist' was back across the Atlantic, to begin recording something like his fifteenth album of new material, and his fifth with Mitchell Froom producing, for release in Spring 1996. In January 1994, Thompson had told David Cavanagh in *Mojo*: 'The next album I'm planning is a very commercial record, well, in my mind commercial, no doubt in the reference terms of the world, hopelessly outdated. I'm going to do a real 60s-style commercial record, sort of the Searchers meets the Chieftains. Three-minute pop songs, harmony choruses, the works. That's the concept. It'll probably sound like all my other albums.'

Thompson's first double album is a package which offers something for everyone, from the scorching electric Richard to the sensitive, acoustic Thompson. *you? me? us?* displays, once again, Thompson's astonishing diversity, a record which veers from the sweeping folk balladry of 'Woods Of Darney' to the jagged, enticing pop of 'Am I Wasting My Love On You?'

Simon Nicol: 'It's a great vibe working with Richard in the studio at the moment, with Mitchell Froom, and Keltner. It's corny, but it is fun to play. Everybody thinks it's special. You know, you might do something else to pay the rent, but this is what you do for fun.'

Richard: 'I think I've got more idea of what's needed to be a songwriter and to be a performer and a musician. I can do it better now. Nostalgists may differ, but I still think I'm getting better. I've got more understanding of what I do and I'm more creative now, I write more stuff now – I've found out how to do it.'

The first CD, subtitled *Voltage Enhanced*, begins with the subdued 'Razor Dance', but only really gets underway when Thompson kicks in with the familiar 'I'm A Man' riff which prefaces 'She Steers By Lightning'. The electricity is muted on this disc, but it is evident on the coiled menace of a song like 'Dark Hand Over My Heart'.

'Put It There Pal' is Thompson at his most spiteful ('the sun shines out of your arse' he spits at one point). A venomous vocal and a bitter, spiky guitar give the song a distinctive menace. 'Business On You' namechecks the novel *A Town Like Alice* and Delius, and the atmosphere is enhanced as Thompson's electric guitar is stalked by his mandolin.

'Bank Vault In Heaven' benefits from a snarling solo and Christine Collister's eerie backing vocals, which hover like a raincloud over the song. 'The Ghost Of You Walks', a lightly picked acoustic piece which incongruously closes the electric half of the proceedings. The Ghost Walks is theatrical slang for 'we are going to be paid'.

Richard Thompson

The second disc, 'Nude', will appeal to those who relish the Richard Thompson of 'Vincent', 'Beeswing' and 'King Of Bohemia', with haunting, poignant pieces such as 'She Cut Off Her Long Silken Hair' and 'Woods Of Darney'.

The opening track, 'Baby Don't Know What To Do With Herself' is as close to the blues as Thompson has hitherto sailed. Sounding like it was left off Bob Dylan's first album, the song has Thompson listing the options for the girl in his world – wiping 'her tears on a rusty nail' or resting her cheek on 'a cold steel rail'.

Even by Thompson's standards, 'Sam Jones' is a wallow down among the dead men. A hovering, vulture-like contemplation of war and its aftermath. While Ingmar Bergman had Death playing chess in *The Seventh Seal*, Thompson's figure of Death is the homely named Sam, who has visited the battlefields of the Boyne and Culloden in search of bones:

> ... all picked over, clean as a whistle,
> No sign of meat on and no sign of gristle

Even as he rests Sam dreams of:

> Roomsful of skeletons a-dancing the quadrille,
> Rows and rows of skulls singing 'Blueberry Hill'

The concluding 'Woods Of Darney' is a mournful memoir of the generation laid waste by the First World War. Reminiscent of Eric Bogle's powerful 'No Man's Land', 'Woods Of Darney' has Thompson in reflective mood: a photograph of a fallen comrade's girl becomes a lucky charm, the girl an obsession:

> And my hands may be rougher, and my tongue may be coarser,
> But I knew I could give you a love good as his

'Woods Of Darney' winds down the record, calm and contemplative, a worthy addition to Thompson's body of work, as indeed is the whole album. After nearly 30 years of making music, he is still obviously capable of bringing something fresh to the feast.

This latest album will however do nothing to scupper the prevailing image of Richard Thompson as poet of the open vein. 'Sam Jones' is so wilfully in-yer-face woeful it's almost like hearing Thompson say 'You think I've been bleak before? You ain't seen nothin' yet . . .!'

Richard: 'I get complaints that there's too much death in songs and really, you know, I'm a pretty spiritual person, I really see death as a door rather than an end . . . I just see it as a way into the next room. You know, perhaps death is just a metamorphosis – so I'm quite comfortable with that but other people maybe aren't. But, hey, that's their problem.

'I mean, the Middle Ages was all full of memento mori and all that kind of stuff. You were taught, and you wanted, to remember death. It was a thing that was important to you, not to get too carried away with all the illusory stuff, because life was pretty short and pretty serious and you were going to get carried off by the plague in a couple of minutes, so enjoy life in the right perspective.'

Hokey Pokey reader Dave Leeke was amused when his computer spellchecker did not recognise 'Thompson', offering 'Tombstone' as an alternative. It seems appropriate; most people seem to imagine that Richard Thompson spends most of his waking moments lounging in a cemetery, with his Thesaurus open at 'misery'.

And yet, Richard Thompson doesn't dangle new-born babies by their ankles from high-rise windows, though he is quietly, confidently capable of writing a song about someone who does. More chillingly, Thompson understands what drives them to do it. His perception of the dark side of the psyche mirrors that of novelist Ruth Rendell, a similarly placid and pleasant middle-class writer. Both live quiet lives of understated Englishness and confound all expectations with their compelling dissections of the nature of evil.

Marc Ellington: 'I think the songs are "Dark and Twisted" in the sense of looking at characters and individuals. It's really by looking at the extremes of life that you define the centre of it ... Richard's looking at all these disasters around the edges, and all these people that are falling off the edges, to define the centre. But that doesn't mean that that's *his* centre ... There is the paradox that we all love Van Gogh, the troubled, strife-ridden artist expressing their inner problems ... I don't think that's the case as far as Richard's concerned. I don't believe that there's anything dark or strange that I've seen there ... and I think as much as anyone, I would have seen that. It just ain't there, at all.'

Linda: 'I don't think he is the cheeriest person in the world, or maybe he is but not when I see him. We do see each other, to do with the children, he was here this morning to collect Kammy. I would love to be friendlier with Richard, but he's just not a person for that. I remember once we did a show at Drury Lane and afterwards some ex-girlfriend of his had travelled down from Newcastle or something, she was at the stage door, and he wouldn't let her in ... That's him. When he burns a bridge, he does, and torches the town just to be sure.'

Loudon Wainwright III: 'I always like the dark things on record, so

Richard Thompson

I was personally surprised that he was so light-hearted and funny, but yeah, I know. I remember saying to various friends and girlfriens "You got any Richard Thompson?" And they'd go "Oh Jesus, not him, that's the kind of a guy I don't want to go out and have dinner with".'

Dave Pegg: 'He is one of the most up people you could hope to meet. Most of the time he seems to have perpetual happiness, which is unusual in someone who is a musician. He's a cheerful soul. He's a worker, he won't whinge if he's stuck in the van for seven hours going up and down the New Jersey Turnpike.'

Nancy: 'I didn't know all the history of Richard Thompson. I knew none of the baggage . . . Richard is a very nice, kind person with a good sense of humour. That was who I knew. I didn't know about all this other "doom and gloom" stuff, and that's probably why we got along so well. I didn't know the Richard Thompson mystique, which has been with him since he was seventeen years old . . .'

Richard: 'Once people have a perception of you it's very hard to change that – and perhaps you never do, you just have to live with it. So a lot of stuff in print seems to me pretty spurious, it doesn't bear any relation to the music or to me. It's just words that you write and an image that's projected and it doesn't really matter at the end of the day.'

Ever onward, this self-effacing, quiet and retiring individual continues to accrue critical adulation and incremental record sales. In conversation, articulate and amusing, self-deprecating and wry, Thompson gives the illusion of revelation, but in fact, is a past master of disguise. Thompson is evasive, a master dribbler, who can bypass what he wants to avoid with ease and dexterity.

'If I was as successful as Neil Young,' Thompson told Justine Picardie in *The Independent on Sunday* in January 1995, 'I wouldn't have to do any interviews, and no one would have to know anything, and that would be fine. But the fact is, I have to deal with the media, so I have to answer questions about myself . . . and I'll keep fending them off. I'll keep lying as much as possible to preserve my sanity.'

He is entitled to say that. He has heard all the questions a hundred times before and has diligently, courteously, replied to them all. It is hard to believe that the diffident character, painfully answering questions, is the musician capable of targeting your emotions with the devastating certainty of an Exocet.

Nervily loquacious, Richard Thompson also trawls through the abattoir of emotion, which has produced some diverting results. To look at, you wouldn't think he posed a threat, but on the record, there is something politely subversive about the man. While he may kebab emotional turmoil with his songs, Richard Thompson always prefaces the operation with a polite 'Do you mind . . .?'

Talking to both his wives, Linda and Nancy, I was surprised at just how capable Thompson was of sealing off his creative side even from them. A loving husband, a fond parent, a dutiful son, and yet . . . The creative element of Richard Thompson, that tiny percentage of the whole, which is perhaps the most interesting part, the reason why people have bought his records and studied his songs for nearly 30 years, remains a closed book. The bit of Richard Thompson which makes those decisions – which articulates all that bitterness and despair and chronicles the angst – is beyond our reach, perhaps beyond even his comprehension. That aspect of Richard Thompson remains a sealed room.

In the aftermath of a murder, the police seal off the site. Before removing the corpse, a white shape is drawn around it, the body is then removed. You get the outline of the victim at the scene of the crime, but the nature and the fibre of the man remain hollow and empty, the content tantalisingly unknown.

What there is to treasure forever is there on the records – all those wonderful songs, ranging from the teenage impression of mortality on 'Meet On The Ledge' to the wary look at hero worship on 'From Galway To Graceland'. Wonderful, wonderful songs.

There is a diffidence, a reluctance to accept the praise regularly heaped upon him, which is an engaging feature of his personality. Try congratulating him on his music, try articulating its effect on you over the years, and you feel as though you have just made an indecent suggestion to a Cardinal. 'Gosh . . . Golly . . . Mm' . . . says Richard Thompson.

As I finished my final interview soon after Richard's appearance at Cropredy in the summer of 1995, we sat and watched the cricket on the television. He was obviously pleased that the red light had clicked off my cassette, and that his part of the ordeal was over. From now on, it was up to me to try and make sense of a life that he, after all, had only lived.

'That should do,' he smiled. We sat and watched the end of an inconclusive over. 'Course,' the smile reappeared, 'ask me the same questions in a couple of hours, and you'd get another completely different set of answers.' He paused as if to consider the situation. 'They'd probably be true too.'

We shook hands, and Richard went off to join Nancy, who had been looking after Jack. The residents of the Banbury hotel paid no attention

Richard Thompson

to the father, mother and son in the lobby. Richard was reluctant to discuss future plans, fearful that it might jeopardise them. He was pretty certain though, and was willing to reveal, that the Thompson family would spend the afternoon visiting a a nearby wildfowl sanctuary.

Richard Thompson's songs meanwhile lurk behind locked doors, through the keyhole, in through the out door, up the down staircase... Glimpses of light in a surround of darkness. Just a random read through the lyrics of *Rumor & Sigh*, reveals heartbreak, heartbreaking misunderstanding, disillusion, bitterness, lies, wounds, jealousy, death... And that was his best-selling album.

The music of Richard Thompson helps you blow your troubles away while reflecting the anguish which brought you to the dance.

For all his ability to tug you into the light, it is to the dark you are drawn. Slowly, inexorably, there is a horrible fascination which leads you to the precipice:

Let me ride on the wall of death one more time,
Let me ride on the wall of death one more time,
You can waste your time on the other rides,
But this is the nearest to being alive,
O Let me take my chances on the wall of death...

In the end, you are spared, to ride 'one more time'. On the ride, and against the odds, comes the hope.

Afterword

THE SUN IS PLAYING hide and seek with the first clouds Oxfordshire had seen all through that long, hot summer of 1995. A few specks of rain even sent a rainbow bridge over the field in the normally sleepy village of Cropredy.

Richard Thompson and Fairport are inexorably linked in the public eye, even though he only made five albums with them and quit the band a quarter of a century ago. Although his career has long since eclipsed Fairport's, Thompson still comes out to play a useful opening bat for the band – 'but we can only afford Richard every two years now,' jokes Johnny Jones, Cropredy's indefatigable stage manager.

Fifteen years after Fairport split for positively the last time, and fourteen years on from the first Fairport reunion, rather like the Last Night of the Proms, the music is almost incidental to the event which is Cropredy.

By the time it gets dark, it's difficult to reconcile the fresh-faces which stare from Fairport album sleeves with the venerable gents onstage. But as Fairport lumber toward their 30th birthday in 1997, Cropredy 95 drew nearly 20,000 fans to the field. The weather determines the size of the Saturday 'walk-up', but there is a hard core of around 15,000 who will attend come rain or shine. For them, it's forever Fairport.

What draws them still to Fairport is a sort of tribalism, a sense of belonging, of identifying with the band. Increasing crowds have led to tighter security and better organisation in recent years, but members of Fairport, past and present, stroll around the festival site throughout the weekend and there is little distance between the band and the fans.

More abstractly, there is an underlying empathy with Fairport. The band who suffered so much, who saw members plucked prematurely, and tragically, from their ranks. You think automatically of Sandy Denny, who died in 1978, but there's also Martin Lamble who so few knew – Fairport's first 'proper' drummer, he played on three albums and then died in the 1969 road crash which nearly finished the band.

Afterword

Then there was the Dutch lorry driver who died in 1971 when his vehicle plunged into the house where Fairport were living.

It all comes round again. The fans return to Cropredy every August to witness a much-loved band, a band who have suffered, but who have survived against all the odds. For all its frivolity and obvious bonhomie, fuelled by Wadworth's excellent ale, sunshine sometimes and the irresistible dance rhythms of Fairport, Cropredy is part Glastonbury, part seance and part revivalist meeting.

Listening to Simon Nicol – the founder member whose house gave Fairport its name – sing 'Crazy Man Michael' late on that Saturday evening in 1995, conjures up memories of poor, long gone Sandy. It's a song suffused with all that familiar Fairport melancholy, written by Richard Thompson in the immediate aftermath of the 1969 crash which killed Martin Lamble and also took Thompson's girlfriend, Jeannie Franklyn.

'Crazy Man Michael' floats across the field of fellow-travellers uniting them in the not so recent past of Muswell Hill and the late 60s, of *Oz* and *International Times*, Pink Floyd and Hyde Park free concerts and the Roundhouse. Memories – real or virtual – of a time past and full of promise, when the future lay bright and shining ahead. Hearing Simon sing this song is to hear the past, but also to know it too far gone and irredeemable.

Cut to the chase, and the next number is Simon again, singing another Richard Thompson song, 'How Many Times' which Fairport recorded on their 1985 *Gladys' Leap* album, but which Thompson himself has only reluctantly recorded. It's a jump cut across the crowded decades. The link is Richard Thompson.

Diehard Fairport fans relish the gloom and pessimism of Thompson's most moving songs, but the old Doom and Gloom-meister skittishly wrong-footed the fans during his sunny Saturday afternoon spot. This was the 1995 model Richard, appearing onstage in a kilt of the Cameron clan, complete with tam o'shanter set at a jaunty angle.

Those who value the symbolism of Thompson's songs above all, appreciated the fact that, during the driest British summer since records began, the rain began to fall just as Thompson launched into 'Wall Of Death' . . .

The bekilted Thompson began his set in the only way possible, with a cheery 'Don't Sit On My Jimmy Shands', the part put-down, part homage to the Scottish accordionist whose polkas, waltzes and reels were an integral part of his adolescence.

The set drew largely on Thompson's solo albums, those lugubrious songs, eloquent on disc, but made all the more so by Thompson's guitar, vocal. A new song 'Cold Kisses', trawled the familiar territory of love-song-as-threat, the relationship damned by a line about 'being behind enemy lines'.

'Turning Of The Tide' was the opening track of Thompson's 1988 *Amnesia*, his first album with EMI Records. The song furtively visits the tawdry docks and bar-room brawls of Jacques Brel with attendant 'cheap perfume' and 'creaking bed in a hotel room'. Aficionados and symbol-seekers nod sagely at the title and chorus, Thompson's fascination with the pull of the moon on the tide having been noted twenty years before on 'Dimming Of The Day', and again, more recently in 'the old and waning moon' on 'King Of Bohemia'.

The bridge speaks of a 'shabby' dress – apt and atmospheric and not a word heard much in rock'n'roll. Elvis Costello, a long-time Thompson admirer, wrote 'Shabby Doll' in 1982, and 'shabby' somehow seems to sum up the tarnished achievements of Thatcherism and the tawdry legacy of the long-gone 1980s. One of Thompson's rare, overtly political songs on 1992's *Rumor & Sigh* caricatures Margaret Thatcher as 'Mother Knows Best'. *Rumor & Sigh* – far and away Thompson's best-selling album – also delivered the song which has become the most requested of the 240-odd recorded during a professional career of nearly 30 years: '1952 Vincent Black Lightning'. At Cropredy last year, the song revved up and roared away with the honours.

Some ridiculously fluid fingering introduced the ballad, a contemporary reworking in traditional form of a Bonnie and Clyde narrative. 'Vincent' is the shy son of a policeman, his nose pressed against the steamed-up transport cafe windows of Thompson's teenage years. The push-bike adolescent, enviously imagines the leather boys doing the ton on their greasy motorcycles as they tear over the Hog's Back near Guildford, or roar down to Boxhill.

Certain death is an important part of the ballad tradition. The song's real impact comes in the last verse, the romance doomed from the word 'go', but the cumulative detail and accumulating tragedy accelerates into the unknown, and at least the hero knows he'll be in good company:

> Said young James, in my opinion,
> There's nothing in this world
> Beats a 52 Vincent and a red-headed girl.
> Now Nortons and Indians and Greeves won't do
> They don't have a soul like a Vincent 52 ...

As the precise detailing of the story draws us toward the inevitable tragic end, the song moves up an emotional gear:

Afterword

> I see angels on Ariels in leather and chrome,
> Swooping down from Heaven to carry me home . . .

The yearning to return home is probably universal and definitely something of a cliché, but the vividness of Thompson's particular vision sharpens the familiar emotional tug into a pang. Home, the destination in every down-home country and western tune, the promised land of all the best folk songs, the emotional centre at the heart of the darkest blues material. 'Home' is where every bar singer, R&B shouter, pop stylist and cheap, lounge-lizard crooner knows they can get a response.

The home to which James Adie goes is that mythic place whose pull we never escape, but to which we can never return, the whole of humanity in exile from Eden. But in Thompson's words even the stalest sentiments are made fresh.

The Sunday following Fairport's sprawling Saturday night set is traditionally given over to a barbecue. The band past and present, crew and visitors, gather in the garden of one of the many pubs near Cropredy. It's an opportunity for everyone concerned with putting on the festival to unwind.

The crew talk in tongues, their conversation dwelling on rigs and generators, running order and calamities – narrowly avoided or otherwise. The band too have done their bit, in every conceivable permutation, and with more line-ups than Brixton police station, Fairport have rung the changes. In a set which is the folk-rock equivalent of *Gone with the Wind* without the Intermission, Fairport have kept everyone happy. Now is their time to relax.

Highlight of the afternoon is a lengthy and incomprehensible game of Aunt Sally, played out in the back garden of the pub. The origins of the game go back too far, lost in the mists of antiquity. Created and played regularly in less politically correct times, the written rules run: 'A game in which sticks or cudgels are thrown at a figure of an old woman's head mounted on a pole, the object being to hit the nose of the figure, or break the pipe stuck in its mouth.'

It seemed a highly appropriate game to be associated with the very English Fairport Convention, particularly after imbibing sufficient amounts of ale. 'It's an excuse to drink a lot,' confirmed Simon Nicol cheerfully.

Pleasantries exchanged, teams were picked. Corralling Nancy Covey's Festival Tours visitors into one team, it is decided to be a grudge match, UK versus USA. Fairport's American guitarist Jerry

Afterword

Donahue was caught between a rock and a hard place – his passport said 'USA', but the Fairport connection was equally strong. In the end, birthright took precedence over band loyalty and Donahue manfully wielded a cudgel on behalf of the USA.

The British team captain took matters in hand. Richard Thompson applied the same intensity to commanding his Aunt Sally team that Sunday afternoon as he had applied to playing 'Wall Of Death' the day before. Keeping a steady nerve and marshalling his troops well, Thompson's captaincy ensured a close victory for the UK team.

The public face of Richard Thompson is confident if somewhat diffident. An admired songwriter, assured singer, and guitarist whose fluency is envied by mentors, peers and disciples. Onstage, there is no denying the intensity of a Thompson performance, or the jagged and frayed emotion he brings to his songs, which ebbs and flows over the evening. But the territory which Thompson inhabits in his songs is a Pinteresque landscape of betrayal, deceit, mixed emotions and clumsy conclusions. Rather like life, in fact.

In person, Richard Thompson seems maladroit in unfamiliar company and there is a protective screen surrounding him, frequently physical. Wife Nancy can spot someone waiting to tell Richard they wish all his songs were like 'The End Of The Rainbow' with practised ease and keep them tactfully at arm's length. Thompson himself is deft at avoiding those keen to disinter a past he regards as long gone. For him, the old songs are little more than jottings in a long-forgotten notebook, or juvenilia wrapped in a ribbon bow of childhood.

He is capable of eyeballing a situation he's not comfortable with and stepping aside, both literally and conversationally. But once he knows the conversation won't dwell on lyrical analysis of songs he wrote half a lifetime ago, he eases into amiable social mode – an engaging conversationalist with a broad sweep of interests far removed from rock'n'roll.

Get Thompson on gardening and you're dug in for the evening. Cricket is another enthusiasm, arcane radio shows from the 1950s, the guitar solos of James Burton . . . you can while away a whole summer.

As the night winds down though, and the conversation follows its uncharted course, you find yourself glancing at Thompson, and thinking 'This is Henry the Human Fly; this man wrote the songs which are as much a part of the fabric of my life as poor dress sense and Scalextric'.

A biography of Richard Thompson is, of course, much more than the story of one man. Thompson's career has twisted and turned for nearly

Afterword

30 years. Beginning in the hazy underground of alternative London in 1967, when Fairport's colleagues included Pink Floyd, Thompson has left his trail, like a snail's silvery spoor, over the whole history of British rock'n'roll.

A jukebox stocked only with Richard Thompson songs is one of the few Wurlitzers which wouldn't run out of steam. For fresh thousands every year, there is a sense of delighted discovery. In his work they find a depth and substance manifestly lacking in the superficiality of end-of-millenium pop pap.

It's a strange and disconcerting thought, but then, as he approaches his 50th birthday, and as he commits personal and discreet memories to the clinical and indiscreet mechanisms of a tape recorder, Richard Thompson cannot help but reflect what a long, strange life it has been.

With so much looking back, inevitably you are drawn to look forward. For Thompson there is an immediate future visible. It is about three feet tall, it is his son Jack. Almost simultaneously, Thompson became a father for the fifth time, and a grandfather – when his first daughter Muna gave birth to a son.

For those who know the man only through his work, there is a constant, magnetic pull of the tide that is Richard Thompson's past. It's all there already, that life; on record and disc: in tatty and battered LPs, dragged around from bedsit to first flat, or in shiny, pristine CDs, neatly lined up on IKEA units. But then, like everyone else's life, the picture can change and distort, or shatter and re-align. Nothing is ever quite what it seems, you can never fully form a picture from what a man says on record.

Things change, but what remains essentially the same is the talent, held forever in that work. The composer may grow weary of his old songs, believing they dog his every footstep forward; a millstone, dragging him backwards into the past. But coming back to that marvellous body of work, you are struck again – and again and again – by its innate, inimitable quality.

There is something timeless and wonderful about Richard Thompson's music, from his fledgling first steps with Fairport Convention, to the assured music he has made since his split with Linda.

What remains so encouraging about Thompson's work, is that even with a career spanning three decades behind him, he is still capable of progressing, of always going one step beyond what is expected of him. That is the wonder. That is the pleasure. This is the man.

Discography
by Colin Davies

1. Main album releases.
2. Other compilation/live albums with Richard Thompson as main artist or band member.
3. Fan club cassettes.
4. Full albums of cover versions of Richard Thompson songs.
5. Mandolin/guitar tuition tapes featuring Richard Thompson.
6. Main studio/live single/e.p. releases.
7. Main promo-only single/e.p. releases.
8. Albums featuring Richard Thompson (sessions).
9. Single/e.p. releases featuring Richard Thompson (sessions).
10. Compilation albums featuring Richard Thompson.
11. Promo-only compilation albums featuring Richard Thompson.
12. Videos featuring Richard Thompson.
13. Recorded songs written by Richard Thompson.
14. Recorded songs co-written by Richard Thompson.

Note: Catalogue numbers are generally given as UK LP.
CD re-issues are only mentioned where extra tracks were included (or tracks removed) on that re-issue.

1. MAIN ALBUM RELEASES
(includes recordings where Richard is solo or band member and soundtracks)

Year	Artist	Title	Label	Cat No.
1968	FAIRPORT CONVENTION	**Fairport Convention**	Polydor	582 035
1969	FAIRPORT CONVENTION	**What We Did On Our Holidays**	Island	ILPS 9092
	(released in USA as Fairport Convention)		A&M	SP 4185
1969	FAIRPORT CONVENTION	**Unhalfbricking**	Island	ILPS 9102
1969	FAIRPORT CONVENTION	**Liege & Lief**	Island	ILPS 9115
1970	FAIRPORT CONVENTION	**Full House**	Island	ILPS 9130

Discography

Year	Artist	Title	Label	Catalog
1972	THE BUNCH	Rock On	Island	ILPS 9189
1972	RICHARD THOMPSON	Henry The Human Fly	Island	ILPS 9197
1972	ASHLEY HUTCHINGS/ RICHARD THOMPSON/DAVE MATTACKS/JOHN KIRKPATRICK/BARRY DRANSFIELD	Morris On	Island	HELP 5
1974	RICHARD & LINDA THOMPSON	I Want To See The Bright Lights Tonight	Island	ILPS 9266
1975	RICHARD & LINDA THOMPSON	Hokey Pokey	Island	ILPS 9305
1975	RICHARD & LINDA THOMPSON	Pour Down Like Silver	Island	ILPS 9348
1976	FAIRPORT CONVENTION	Heyday (cassette only)	—	
1976	RICHARD THOMPSON	Guitar, vocal (part live)	Island	ICD 8
1976	FAIRPORT CONVENTION	Live At The L.A. Troubadour (live 1970)	Island	HELP 28
1978	RICHARD & LINDA THOMPSON	First Light	Chrysalis	CHR 1177
1979	RICHARD & LINDA THOMPSON	Sunnyvista	Chrysalis	CHR 1247
1981	RICHARD THOMPSON	Strict Tempo	Elixir	LP 1
1982	RICHARD & LINDA THOMPSON	Shoot Out The Lights	Hannibal	HNBL 1303
	(re-issued on CD 1986 + one bonus track)		Hannibal	HNCD 1303
1983	RICHARD THOMPSON	Hand Of Kindness	Hannibal	HNBL 13
	(re-issued on CD 1986 + 1 bonus track)		Hannibal	HNCD 1313
1984	RICHARD THOMPSON	Small Town Romance	Hannibal	HNBL 1316
	(re-issued on CD 1986 + 3 bonus tracks)		Hannibal	HNCD 1316
1985	RICHARD THOMPSON	Across A Crowded Room	Polydor	825.421.1
	(1 bonus track on CD issue)			
	(CD re-issued 1992 less the bonus track)		Beat Goes On	BGO LP/CD 139
1986	FAIRPORT CONVENTION	House Full (live at LA Troubadour 1970)	Hannibal	HNBL 1319
1986	RICHARD THOMPSON	Daring Adventures	Polydor	829.728.1
	(re-issued 1992)		Beat Goes On	BGO LP/CD 138
1987	FAIRPORT CONVENTION	Heyday (CD of 1976 cassette but varied track list)	Hannibal	HNBL 1329
1987	FRENCH, FRITH, KAISER, THOMPSON	Live Love Larf & Loaf	Rhino	70831
1987	PETER FILLEUL & RICHARD THOMPSON	The Marksman (TV soundtrack)	BBC	REB 660

Discography

1988 FRENCH, FRITH, KAISER, THOMPSON (3 bonus tracks on CD issue)	Live Love Larf & Loaf	Demon	FIEND CD102
1988 RICHARD THOMPSON	Amnesia	Capitol	48845.1
1990 VARIOUS ARTISTS	Hard Cash	Green Linnet	
1990 FRENCH, FRITH, KAISER, THOMPSON (3 bonus tracks on CD issue)	Invisible Means	Windham Hill	3049 1094
1991 RICHARD THOMPSON	Sweet Talker (film soundtrack)	Capitol	EST 2170
1991 THE GPs (reissued 1996)	Saturday Rolling Around (live 1991)	Woodworm HTD Records	WRCD 014 HTDCD 53
1991 RICHARD THOMPSON	Rumor & Sigh	Capitol	95713.1
1993 RICHARD THOMPSON	Watching The Dark (3 x CD RT retrospective)	Hannibal	HNCD 5303
1994 RICHARD THOMPSON	Mirror Blue	Capitol	81492
1995 RICHARD THOMPSON WITH DANNY THOMPSON	Live At Crawley 1993	Whatdisc	WHAT 2CD
1996 RICHARD THOMPSON	you? me? us?	Capitol	33704
1996 RICHARD THOMPSON	two letter words: Live 1994	Flypaper	FLYCD 006

2. OTHER COMPILATION/LIVE ALBUMS WITH RICHARD THOMPSON AS MAIN ARTIST OR BAND MEMBER

1976 RICHARD THOMPSON	(Canada) Live (More Or Less)	Island	ILPS 9421
1982 FAIRPORT CONVENTION	Moat On The Ledge (live 1981)	Woodworm	WR 001
1983 FAIRPORT CONVENTION	(cassette) The Boot (live 1983)	—	
1987 FAIRPORT CONVENTION	(cassette) The Other Boot (live 1986)	—	
1988 FAIRPORT CONVENTION	(cassette) The Third Leg (live 1987)	—	
(US Version has five extra tracks including A Sailor's Life on which RT appears)			
1993 FAIRPORT CONVENTION	25th Anniversary Concert (live 1992: 2 × CD)	Woodworm	WRD CD022
1996 LINDA THOMPSON	Dreams Fly Away	Hannibal	HNCD 1379

3. FAN CLUB CASSETTES (Subscribers only)

1985 RICHARD THOMPSON	Doom & Gloom From The Tomb Vol. 1	Flypaper	FLYC 001

Discography

| 1991 | RICHARD THOMPSON | Doom & Gloom II (Over My Dead Body) | Flypaper | FLYC 003 |

4. FULL ALBUMS OF COVER VERSIONS OF RICHARD THOMPSON SONGS

(*indicates featuring Richard Thompson or Richard & Linda Thompson)

1992	DAVE BURLAND	His Master's Choice*	Road Goes On Forever	RGF 009
1993	VARIOUS ARTISTS	The World Is A Wonderful Place* (track 13: not credited on album sleeve)	Hokey Pokey	HPR 2003.2
1995	VARIOUS ARTISTS	Beat The Retreat	Capitol	EST 2242

5. GUITAR/MANDOLIN TUITION TAPES FEATURING RICHARD THOMPSON

| 1976 | RICHARD THOMPSON (USA) | The Guitar Of Richard Thompson (3 × cassette + booklets) | Homespun Tapes Ltd | |
| 1983 | NILES HOKKANEN & RICHARD THOMPSON (USA) | The Electric Mandolin (Mandolin Theory, Technique/ Improvisation) (a double cassette/book mandolin tutor) | | 08 |

6. MAIN STUDIO/LIVE SINGLE/E.P. RELEASES (7"/12"/CD)

(includes recordings where Richard is solo, or duo/band member)

1968	FAIRPORT CONVENTION	(7") If I Had A Ribbon Bow/If (Stomp)	Track	604020
1970	FAIRPORT CONVENTION	(7") If (Stomp)/Chelsea Morning	Polydor	2058 014
1968	FAIRPORT CONVENTION	(7") Meet On The Ledge/Throwaway Street Puzzle	Island	WIP 6047
1968	FAIRPORT CONVENTION	(7") (USA) Fotheringay/I'll Keep It With Mine	A & M	1108
1969	FAIRPORT CONVENTION	(7") Si Tu Dois Partir/Genesis Hall	Island	WIP 6064
1970	FAIRPORT CONVENTION	(7") Now Be Thankful/Sir B. McKenzie's Daughter's Lament For The 77th Mounted Lancers	Island	WIP 6089

Discography

Year	Artist	Title	Label	Cat. No.
1970	FAIRPORT CONVENTION	Retreat From The Straits Of Loch Knombe, In The Year Of Our Lord 1727, On The Occasion Of The Announcement Of Her Marriage To The Laird Of Kinleakie (7") (Germany) Now Be Thankful/Guinness Book Of Records	Island	6014031

(B-side is actually Sir B. McKenzie's ... with joke title as song title is 'reputedly' the world's longest single title)

Year	Artist	Title	Label	Cat. No.
1972	THE BUNCH	(7") Let There Be Drums (flexi issued with LP)	Island	WI 4002
1972	THE BUNCH	(7") When Will I Be Loved/Willie & The Hand Jive	Island	WIP 6130
1974	RICHARD & LINDA THOMPSON	(7") I Want To See The Bright Lights Tonight/When I Get To The Border	Island	WIP 6186
1975	RICHARD & LINDA THOMPSON	(7") Hokey Pokey (The Ice Cream Man)/I'll Regret It All In The Morning	Island	WIP 6220
1978	ALBION BAND	(7") Poor Old Horse/Ragged Heroes	Harvest	HAR 5156
1978	RICHARD & LINDA THOMPSON	(7") Don't Let A Thief Steal Into Your Heart/First Light	Chysalis	CHS 2278
1979	RICHARD & LINDA THOMPSON	(7") Georgie On A Spree/Civilisation	Chrysalis	CHS 2369
1982	RICHARD & LINDA THOMPSON	(7") Don't Renege On Our Love/Living In Luxury	Hannibal	HNS 703
1984	RICHARD THOMPSON	(7") (Germany) Tear Stained Letter/Where The Wind Don't Whine	Teldec/Hannibal	76.12988
1985	RICHARD THOMPSON	(7") You Don't Say/When The Spell Is Broken	Polydor	POSP 750
1988	RICHARD THOMPSON	(7") Turning Of The Tide/Pharaoh	Capitol	CL 516
1988	RICHARD THOMPSON	(7") Reckless Kind (album)/Turning Of The Tide (live)	Capitol	CL 550
1989	RICHARD THOMPSON	(CD) Reckless Kind (album)/Turning Of	Capitol	CDCL 550

Discography

1989 RICHARD THOMPSON	The Tide (live)/Jerusalem On The Jukebox (live) (12") Reckless Kind (album)/Pharaoh (live)	Capitol	12CL 550
1991 RICHARD THOMPSON	Can't Win (live) (7") I Feel So Good/Harry's Theme	Capitol	CL 617
1991 RICHARD THOMPSON	(CD) I Feel So Good/Harry's Theme/Backlash Love Affair	Capitol	CDCL 617
1991 RICHARD THOMPSON	(7" & CD) Read About Love (album)/I Feel So Good (solo live)	Capitol	CL 638 & CD638
1991 RICHARD THOMPSON	(CD) Read About Love (album)/I Feel So Good/I Misunderstood/Choice Wife (3 × solo live)	Capitol	CDCL 638
1991 RICHARD THOMPSON	(7") I Misunderstood (album)/1952 Vincent Black Lightning (album)/Now That I'm Dead (live solo)/Waltzing's For Dreamers	Capitol	CL 651
1991 RICHARD THOMPSON	(CD) I Misunderstood (album)/1952 Vincent Black Lightning (album)/Now That I'm Dead (live solo)/Waltzing's For Dreamers	Capitol	CDCL 651
1992 RICHARD THOMPSON	(CD) (Holland) I Misunderstood (album version)/I Misunderstood (live): (official Dutch Rumor & Sigh tour single)	Capitol/EMI	7243 8802752 6

7. MAIN PROMO-ONLY SINGLE/E.P. RELEASES (7"/12"/CD)
(includes recordings where Richard is solo, or duo/band member)

1983 RICHARD THOMPSON	(7") Wrong Heart Beat/Devonside	Hannibal	HNS 704
1983 RICHARD THOMPSON	(12") The Wrong Heartbeat/Tear Stained Letter/Hand Of Kindness	Hannibal	HNPRO 1
1985 RICHARD THOMPSON	(12") (USA) You Don't Say/You Don't Say	Polydor	PRO 338.1

Discography

1985 RICHARD THOMPSON	(12") (USA) **When The Spell Is Broken** (album)/**When The Spell Is Broken** (live)	Polydor	PRO 348.1
1986 RICHARD THOMPSON	(7") (Germany) **Shoot Out The Lights/The Great Valerio/Don't Tell Secrets** (all live versions: single Polydor 5202 also issued free with Daring Adventures LP in Germany)	Polydor	885 422 7
1986 RICHARD THOMPSON	(12") (USA) **Valerie/Valerie** (Edit)	Polydor	PRO 438.1
1986 RICHARD THOMPSON	(7") (Australia) **Valerie/Valerie** (Edit)	Polydor	885 467-7
1986 RICHARD THOMPSON	(12") (USA) **Nearly In Love** (album)/**Nearly In Love** (version No.2)	Polydor	PRO 465.1
1988 RICHARD THOMPSON	(CD) **Turning Of The Tide/Pharaoh**	Capitol	DPRO 79388
1988 RICHARD THOMPSON	(12") **Turning Of The Tide/Turning Of The Tide** (2 × album version)	Capitol	SPRO 79408
1991 RICHARD THOMPSON	(CD) **Easy There, Steady Now** (album)/**Easy There, Steady Now** (edit), **Goin' Back** (live), **God Loves A Drunk** (live)		
1991 RICHARD THOMPSON	(CD) (USA) **I Feel So Good**	Capitol	DPRO 79730
1991 RICHARD THOMPSON	(CD) (USA) **I Misunderstood** (album)/**I Misunderstood** (acoustic)/**I Feel So Good** (acoustic)/**1952 Vincent Black Lightning** (acoustic)/**Now That I'm Dead** (acoustic)/**The Choice Wife** (acoustic)	Capitol	DPRO 79078
1991 RICHARD THOMPSON	(12") (USA) (track list as above CD)	Capitol	SPRO 79104
1991 RICHARD THOMPSON	(cassette) **Live In Ventura** (7 Sept 1991)	Capitol	
1991 RICHARD THOMPSON	(CD) **I Misunderstood**	Capitol	DPRO 79967
1991 RICHARD THOMPSON	**Read About Love**	Capitol	DPRO 79885

Discography

1991 RICHARD THOMPSON	(CD) **The Hannibal Sampler**	Hannibal	VRCD 1303
(13 tracks incl. Richard & Linda and Fairport tracks)			
1992 VARIOUS ARTISTS	(CD) Ferrington Guitars sampler for CD issued with Ferrington Guitars book (Jonathan Cape and Callaway Editions)		
1993 RICHARD THOMPSON	**I Can't Wake Up To Save My Life/Shoot Out The Lights** (live)/**1952 Vincent Black Lightning** (live)	Capitol	DPRO 79854
1993 RICHARD THOMPSON	(CD) **Watching The Dark** (7-track sampler)	Hannibal	VRCD 5303
1993 RICHARD THOMPSON	(7") (USA) **I Can't Wake Up To Save My Life** (jukebox single)/**Easy There, Steady Now**	Capitol	S718043
1994 RICHARD THOMPSON	(CD) (USA) **I Can't Wake Up To Save My Life** (album)/**Shoot Out The Lights/1952 Vincent Black Lightning** (2 × live)	Capitol	DPRO 79854
1994 RICHARD THOMPSON	(Germany) **I Ride In Your Slipstream**	Capitol	P 519 383
1994 RICHARD THOMPSON	(CD) (USA) **Easy There, Steady Now** (album)/**Easy There, Steady Now** (edit)/**God Loves A Drunk/Goin' Back** (2 × live)	Capitol	DPRO 79364

8. ALBUMS FEATURING RICHARD THOMPSON (SESSIONS)

1969 MARC ELLINGTON	Marc Ellington	Phillips	SBL 7883
1969 NICK DRAKE	Five Leaves Left	Island	ILPS 9105
1969 DUDU PUKWANA AND THE SPEARS	(South Africa) Dudu Pukwana And The Spears	Quality	LTJ S232
1970 NICK DRAKE	Bryter Layter	Island	ILPS 9134
1970 GARY FARR	Strange Fruit	CBS	S 64138
1970 AL STEWART	Love Chronicles (RT appears as Marvyn Prestwick)	CBS	S63460
1970 IAN MATTHEWS	Matthews Southern Comfort	Uni	UNLS 108

Discography

Year	Artist	Title	Label	Catalog
1971	IAN MATTHEWS	If You Saw Thru' My Eyes	Vertigo	6360 034
1971	SANDY DENNY	The North Star Grassman & The Ravens	Island	ILPS 9165
1971	MARC ELLINGTON	Rains/Reins Of Changes	B&C	CAS 1033
1971	STEFAN GROSSMAN	Those Pleasant Days	Transatlantic	TRA 246
1971	MIKE HERON	Smiling Men With Bad Reputations	Island	ILPS 9146
1971	SHELAGH McDONALD	Stargazer	B&C	CAS 1043
1971	JOHN MARTYN	Bless The Weather	Island	ILPS 9167
1971	MICK SOFTLEY	Streetsinger	CBS	64395
1971	SHIRLEY COLLINS AND THE ALBION COUNTRY BAND	No Roses	Pegasus	PEG 7
1972	SANDY DENNY	Sandy	Island	ILPS 9207
1972	JOHN KIRKPATRICK	Jump At The Sun (RT appears as Agnes Mirren)	Trailer	LER 2033
1972	IAN MATTHEWS	Tigers Will Survive (RT appears as Woolfe J. Flywheel)	Vertigo	6360 056
1972	MIKE & LAL WATERSON	Bright Phoebus	Trailer	LES 2076
1973	JOHN MARTYN	Solid Air	Island	ILPS 9226
1973	SANDY DENNY	Like An Old Fashioned Waltz	Island	ILPS 9258
1973	FAIRPORT CONVENTION	Rosie	Island	ILPS 9208
1973	ANDY ROBERTS	Urban Cowboy	Elektra	K42139
1974	JOHN CALE	Fear	Island	ILPS 9301
1975	HARVEY ANDREWS & GRAHAM COOPER	Fantasies From A Corner Seat	Transatlantic	TRA 298
1975	MARC ELLINGTON	Marc Time	Transatlantic	XTRA 1154
1975	MIKE HERON	Mike Heron's Reputation	Neighbourhood	NBH80637
1975	GEOFF MULDAUR	Is Having A Wonderful Time	Reprise	K 54046
1976	BRIAN PATTEN	Vanishing Trick	Tangent	TGS 116
1977	SANDY DENNY	Rendezvous	Island	ILPS 9433
1978	JULIE COVINGTON	Julie Covington	Virgin	V 2107
1978	THE ALBION BAND	Rise Up Like The Sun	Harvest	SHSP 4092
1979	NICK DRAKE	Fruit Tree (3 × LP set)	Island	NDSP 100
1979	RALPH McTELL	Slide Away The Screen	Reprise	K 56599
1979	GERRY RAFFERTY	Night Owl	United Art's	UAS 30238
1981	ARIZONA SMOKE REVIEW	Thunderin' On The Horizon	Rola	R 006

Discography

Year	Artist	Title	Label	Cat. No.
1981	MURRAY HEAD	How Many Ways	Music Lovers	MLP 101
1981	VIVIAN STANSHALL	Teddy Boys Don't Knit	Charisma	CAS 1153
1981	DAVE SWARBRICK	Smiddyburn	LOGO	1029
1981	DAVID THOMAS & THE PEDESTRIANS	The Sound Of The Sand & Other Songs Of The Pedestrian	Rough Trade	ROUGH 30
1982	MARTIN CARTHY	Out Of The Cut	Topic	12TS 426
1982	RALPH McTELL	Water Of Dreams	Mays	TG 005
1983	ANY TROUBLE	Any Trouble	EMI-America	ST17096
1984	ANY TROUBLE	Wrong End Of The Race (double LP)	EMI-America	AMLS 24 0120 3
1983	T-BONE BURNETT	Proof Through The Night	Side Effects	FIEND 14
1983	DAVE SWARBRICK	Flittin'	Spindrift	SPIN 101
1983	DAVID THOMAS & THE PEDESTRIANS (with RT)	Variations On A Theme	Rough Trade	ROUGH 60
1983	LOUDON WAINWRIGHT III	Fame And Wealth	Demon	FIEND 5
1983	J. J. CALE	No. 8	Mercury	MERL 22
1985	FAIRPORT CONVENTION	Gladys' Leap	Woodworm	WR 007
1985	FOLK OCH RACKARE	(Sweden) Rack Bag	Amalthea	AM53
1985	THE GOLDEN PALOMINOS	Visions Of Excess	Celluloid	CELL 6118
1985	LOUDON WAINWRIGHT III	I'm Alright	Demon	FIEND 54
1986	(Music From The BBC-TV Series)	The Life & Loves Of A She Devil	BBC	REB 615
1986	NICK DRAKE (re-issue + extra album Time Of No Reply)	Fruit Tree (4 × LP set)	Hannibal	HNBX 5302
1986	NICK DRAKE	Time Of No Reply	Hannibal	HNBL 1318
1986	THE ELECTRIC BLUEBIRDS	The Electric Bluebirds	Making Waves	SPRAY 105
1986	ASHLEY HUTCHINGS	An Hour With Ashley Hutchings And Cecil Sharp	Dambuster	DAM 014
1986	DAGMAR KRAUSE	Supply & Demand	Hannibal	HNBL 1317/D
(released in Germany (in Deutsch) as Angebot & Nachfrage)				
1986	RALPH McTELL	Bridge Of Sighs	Mays	TPG 009
1986	FAIRPORT CONVENTION	Expletive Delighted	Woodworm	WR 009
1986	THE DEEP SEA JIVERS	Raptures Of The Deep Mermaid	MMD	101
1986	LOUDON WAINWRIGHT III	More Love Songs	Demon	FIEND 79

Discography

1987	JULIAN DAWSON & THE FLOOD	(Germany) As Real As Disneyland	Polydor	831607
1987	JOHN KIRKPATRICK	Blue Balloon	Squeezer	SQZ 124
1987	SAEKO SUZUKI	Studio Romantic (Japan)	Dear Heart	MIL 1030
1988	TAM REID	(cassette) King Of The Bothy Ballad Singers	Ross	CWGR 119
1988	CHARLIE ALLAN	(cassette) The Auld Folks On The Wa'	Pedigree Cattle	ARDO 107
1988	CROWDED HOUSE	Temple Of Low Men	Capitol	EST 2064
1988	MICHAEL DUCET & CAJUN BREW	Hot Cajun Rhythm 'n' Blues	Special Delivery	SPD 101
1988	MITCHELL FROOM	Slam Dance (film soundtrack)	Island	ISTA 15
1989	MARIA McKEE	Maria McKee	Geffen	WX 270
1989	SYD STRAW	Surprise	Virgin America	VUSLP 6
1989	LOUDON WAINWRIGHT III	Therapy	Silvertone	ORE 500
1989	VARIOUS ARTISTS	Time Between – A Tribute To The Byrds	Imaginary	ILLUSION 004
(1 × bonus track on CD issue)				
1990	VARIOUS ARTISTS	Circle Dance	Hokey Pokey	ConeD
1991	BEAUSOLEIL	Cajun Conja	Demon	FIEND 704
1991	THE GOLDEN PALOMINOS	Drunk With Passion	Venture-Nation	VE 905
1991	HENRY KAISER	We Hope You Like Our New Direction	Reckless	RECK 21
1991	VARIOUS ARTISTS	Bringing It All Back Home (2 × LP)	BBC	REF 844
1991	WILLIE NILE	(USA) Places I Have Never Been	Columbia	CK 44434
1991	BONNIE RAITT	Luck Of The Draw	Capitol	EST 2145
1992	THE GOLDEN PALOMINOS	Drunk With Passion	Venture	VE 905
1992	SUZANNE VEGA	99°F	A&M	540 012.2
1992	SHAWN COLVIN	Fat City	Columbia	COL 467961 2
1992	JENNIFER WARNES	The Hunter	Private	261 974
1992	CHRIS HARFORD	Be Headed	Elektra	9 61364-2
1993	ROBERT PLANT	Fate Of Nations	Esperanza/ Fontana	514.867.2
1993	STEPHEN FEARING	The Assassin's Apprentice	True North (Canada)	TNK 84
1993	NILES HOKKANEN	(USA) (cassette) On Fire & Ready	Mando- crucian	MD 003
1994	THE ASHLEY HUTCHINGS BIG BEAT COMBO	Twangin' N' A-Traddin	HTD	HTDCD25

Discography

1994 DANNY CARNAHAN & ROBIN PETRIE	Cut & Run	Fledg'ling	FLE 1006
1994 TREVOR LUCAS & SANDY DENNY (Australian Fanzine issue)	Trevor & Sandy – Together Again (The Attic Tracks Vol. 4)	Fiddlestix	FOF 6
1994 EVERYTHING BUT THE GIRL	Amplified Heart	Blanco Y Negro	96482.2
1994 BONNIE RAITT	Longing In Their Hearts	Capitol	CDEST 2227
1996 BOO HEWARDINE	Baptist Hospital	Blanco Y Negro	0630-12045-2
1996 NORMA WATERSON	Norma Waterson	Hannibal	HNCD 1393

9. SINGLE/E.P. RELEASES FEATURING RICHARD THOMPSON (SESSIONS)

1970 IAN MATTHEWS	Colorado Springs Eternal/The Struggle	UNI	UNS 513
1971 IAN MATTHEWS	Hearts/Little Known	Vertigo	6059 048
1971 GARY FARR	Revolution Of The Season/Old Man	Boulder CBS	S 5430
1971 IAN MATTHEWS	Reno Nevada/ Desert Inn	Vertigo	6059 048
1972 IAN MATTHEWS	Da Doo Ron Ron/ Never Again	Philips	6006197
1972 SANDY DENNY	Listen Listen/ Tomorrow Is A Long Time	Island	WIP 6142
1972 MIKE & LAL WATERSON	Rubber Band/Red Wine & Promises	Transatlantic	BIG 507
1973 FAIRPORT CONVENTION	Rosie/Knights Of The Road	Island	WIP 6155
1973 FAIRPORT CONVENTION	(Australia) Rosie/ Knights Of The Road	Island	K 5028
1977 JULIE COVINGTON	Only Women Bleed/Easy To Slip	Virgin	VS 196
1977 SANDY DENNY	Candle In The Wind/Still Waters Run Deep	Island	WIP 6391
1978 JULIE COVINGTON	(I Want To See The) Bright Lights/A Little Bit More	Virgin	VS 225
1979 ALBION BAND	Pain & Paradise/Lay Me Low	Harvest	HAR 5175
1980 JOHN KIRKPATRICK	Jogging Along With Me Reindeer	Dingles	SID 226
1981 ARIZONA SMOKE REVIEW	All Fall Down/Border Song	Rola	R 006
1981 VIVIAN STANSHALL	Calypso To Collapso/ Smoke Signals At Night	Charisma	CB 382

Discography

Year	Artist	Title	Label	Catalog
1984	ANY TROUBLE	(7" single) Baby Now That I've Found You/Bricks & Mortar	EMI-America	EA 166
1984	ANY TROUBLE	(12" E.P.) Baby Now That I've Found You/Bricks & Mortar Does He Call Your Name	EMI-America	(12)EA166
1984	T-BONE BURNETT	Behind The Trapdoor	Demon	VEX 3
1984	ANY TROUBLE	Open Fire/Coming Of Age	EMI-America	EA 173
1985	LOUDON WAINWRIGHT III	Cardboard Boxes/Colours	Demon	D 1039
1986	LOUDON WAINWRIGHT III	Unhappy Anniversary/The Acid Song	Demon	D 1044
1986	CHRISTINE COLLISTER	(7" single) Warm Love Gone Cold/Cavatina	BBC Records	RESL 199
1986	CHRISTINE COLLISTER	(12" E.P) Warm Love Gone Cold	BBC	12RSL 199
1986	THE DEEP SEA JIVERS	Deep Sea Jiving/Raptures (Palais Mix)	Mermaid	MMD 201
1986	RALPH McTELL	Bridge Of Sighs/Blind Arthur Goes To Adelaide	Mays	
1986	ELECTRIC BLUEBIRDS	Tell It Like It Is/Wake Me, Shake Me	Making Waves	SURF 117
1987	LOUDON WAINWRIGHT III	Your Mother And I	Demon	D 1052
1988	CROWDED HOUSE	Sister Madly/Marilyn In The Slums	Capitol	CL 513
1987	JULIAN DAWSON & THE FLOOD	(12" e.p.) Slipping Away	Polydor (Germany)	885 954-1
1990	CLIVE GREGSON & CHRISTINE COLLISTER	The Great Provider/Good With My Hands	Special Delivery	SPEC 45005
1992	JENNIFER WARNES	Rock You Gently/Lights Of Louisiana	Private	115 391
1993	TIM FINN	Persuasion	Capitol	CDCLS 692
1994	EVERYTHING BUT THE GIRL	Rollercoaster (E.P)	Blanco Y Negro	NEG 69
1995	BOO HEWARDINE	Worlds End/Sad Cowboy	Blanco Y Negro	NEG83CD
1996	BOO HEWARDINE	Joke/Black Cat/Auctioneers/Fire Dogs	Blanco Y Negro	NEG86CD
1996	BOO HEWARDINE	Joke/First Day In Hell/Buzz Aldrin/I Miss You	Blanco Y Negro	NEG86CDX
1996	BOO HEWARDINE	(cassette) Joke/Black Cat	Blanco Y Negro	NEG86C

Discography

10. COMPILATION ALBUMS FEATURING RICHARD THOMPSON
(in all sorts of guises)

Year	Artist	Title	Label	Cat. No.
1968	VARIOUS ARTISTS	Pop Party (3 × LP box set)	Polydor Special	236517/8/9
1969	VARIOUS ARTISTS	You Can All Join In	Island	IWPS 2
1969	VARIOUS ARTISTS	Nice Enough To Eat	Island	IWPS 6
1970	VARIOUS ARTISTS	Backtrack 2	Track 99	2407002
1970	VARIOUS ARTISTS	Pop Party (single LP off 1968 box set)	Polydor	2682001
1970	VARIOUS ARTISTS	(USA) Friends	A & M	SP 8021
1970	VARIOUS ARTISTS	Bumpers	Island	IDP 1
1972	FAIRPORT CONVENTION	History Of Fairport Convention	Island	ICD 4
1972	FAIRPORT CONVENTION	(USA) Fairport	Chronicles A & M	SP 6016

(also includes tracks from Sandy Denny, The Bunch and Fotheringay)

Year	Artist	Title	Label	Cat. No.
1975	VARIOUS ARTISTS	Rare Tracks	Polydor Special	2482274
1975	VARIOUS ARTISTS	Over The Rainbow	Chrysalis	CHR 1079
1975	VARIOUS ARTISTS	The Electric Muse	Island/Trans-atlantic	FOLK 1001
1978	VARIOUS ARTISTS	The Greater Antilles Sampler	Antilles	AX 7000
1980	VARIOUS ARTISTS	It Ain't Me Babe	Polystar	BOBTV 1
1980	IAN MATTHEWS	Discreet Repeat (2 × LP)	Rockburgh	ROCD 109
1983	VARIOUS ARTISTS	(Australia) Folk With Poke	Island	L37944
1985	VARIOUS ARTISTS	Feed The Folk (track = re-mix of The Dundee Hornpipe/The Poppy Leaf originally on Strict Tempo album)	Temple	FTP 01
1985	SANDY DENNY	Who Knows Where The Time Goes (4 × LP box set)	Island	SDSP 100
1985	SANDY DENNY	Who Knows Where The Time Goes (3 × CD set)	Hannibal	HNCD 5301
1986	DAVE SWARBRICK	When The Battle Is Over	Conifer	CRFC 528
1987	SANDY DENNY	The Best Of Sandy Denny	Hannibal	HNCD 1328
1987	VARIOUS ARTISTS	Island Story (2 × LP)		
1987	VARIOUS ARTISTS	Island Life (2 × LP set)	Island	ISL 25
1988	VARIOUS ARTISTS	Back On The Road	Stylus	SMR 854
1988	VARIOUS ARTISTS	New Routes	Stylus	SMD 97
1988	VARIOUS ARTISTS	Island Life (7 × LP box set)	Island	IBX 25

Discography

Year	Artist	Title	Label	Catalog
1989	GERRY RAFFERTY	Right Down The Line	United Artists	UAG 30333
1989	VARIOUS ARTISTS	(Canada) Ben & Jerry's Newport Folk Festival '88 Live	Alcazar	ALC 105
1990	VARIOUS ARTISTS	(Canada) Ben & Jerry's Newport Folk Festival '88 Live Vol. 2 – Mementos	Alcazar	ALC 113
1990	VARIOUS ARTISTS	Tell It Thru The Song (3 × LP/3 × CD)	Teledisc	TELLY 48
1991	IAN MATTHEWS	(USA) Orphans & Outcasts Vol. I – 1969–1979	Dirty Linen	CDL 102
1991	VARIOUS ARTISTS	Best Of TV Themes	Pickwick	PWKS 645
1991	VARIOUS ARTISTS	Out Of Time	Imaginary	ILL CD 031
1991	VARIOUS ARTISTS	All Through The Year	Hokey Pokey	HPR 2002.2
1991	THE GOLDEN PALOMINOS	A History: Vol. 1 (1982–1985)	Demon	MAUCD 625
1991	IAN MATTHEWS	(USA) Orphans & Outcasts Vol. I	Dirty Linen	CDL 102
1991	VARIOUS ARTISTS	The Best Of Mountain Stage Vol. 1	This Way Up	514 494.2
1991	VARIOUS ARTISTS	(USA) Turn Of The Decade	Red House	RHRCD 336
1991	VARIOUS ARTISTS	Children Of The Revolution (3 × LP/CD set)	Teledisc	TELCD 51
1991	VARIOUS ARTISTS	A Little On The CD Side: Vol. 3 (sampler issued with *Musician* magazine)		
1991	VARIOUS ARTISTS	The Bob Dylan Songbook	Connoisseur	VSO PMC 158
1992	LOUDON WAINWRIGHT III	Fame & Wealth/I'm Alright (2 × LP reissue on CD)	Demon	FIENDCD 711
1992	VARIOUS ARTISTS	(Holland) 2 Meter Sessie: Vol. 3	Varagram/ Radio Records	515 698
1992	FAIRPORT CONVENTION	25th Anniversary Pack (4 × album re-issue collection)	Island	FCBX1
1992	VARIOUS ARTISTS	Nice Enough To . . . Join In	Island	IMCD 150
1992	VARIOUS ARTISTS	One And Only – 25 Years Of Radio 1 (2 × CD)	Band Of Joy	BOJCD 25

Discography

1992	VARIOUS ARTISTS	(CD issued with Ferrington Guitars book published by Jonathan Cape & Callaway Editions – ISBN 0-224-03557-6. RT performs **The Job Of Journeywork** – see also promo singles)	
1992	VARIOUS ARTISTS	Folk Heritage II	Music Club	MCD 049
1992	VARIOUS ARTISTS	(Belgium) **Update Live**	(Studio Brussel)	ART 004-2
1992	RALPH McTELL	Silver Celebration	Castle Co's	CCSCD 329
1993	VARIOUS ARTISTS	(Germany) **Tanz & Folkfest Rudolstadt '92**	hei-deck	(no cat no)
1993	VARIOUS ARTISTS	Tell It Thru' The Song	Tellydisc	TELCD 48
1993	VARIOUS ARTISTS	The Folk Collection	Topic	TSCD 470
1993	AL STEWART	To Whom It May Concern (2 × CD)	EMI	CDEM 1511
1994	NICK DRAKE	Way To Blue – An Introduction to Nick Drake	Island	PY 899
1994	VARIOUS ARTISTS	Folk Routes	Island	IMCD 197
1994	ASHLEY HUTCHINGS	The Guv'nor Vol. 1	HTD	HTDCD23
1994	VARIOUS ARTISTS	(USA) **Broadcasts Vol. 2** (107.1 KGSR Radio Austin radio station release)		
1994	VARIOUS ARTISTS	(USA) **ONXRT: Live From The Archives Vol. 2** (93XRT Chicago radio station release)		
1994	VARIOUS ARTISTS	In Our Own Words – Vol. 1	Razor & Tie	2813
1994	VARIOUS ARTISTS	(USA) **KBCO Studio C: Vol. 3**		
1995	VARIOUS ARTISTS	Live At The World Cafe Volume 1		WC9501
1995	VARIOUS ARTISTS	(USA) **KFOG 104.5/97.7 Live From The Archives II**		ARCH 2-2
1995	VARIOUS ARTISTS	Essential Folk	Nectar	NTRCD 030
1995	VARIOUS ARTISTS	Folk Heartbeat	Emporio	EMPRCD 595
1995	VARIOUS ARTISTS	(USA) **The Bottom Line**	Nectar	NTMCD 501
1995	ASHLEY HUTCHINGS	The Guv'nor Vol. 2	HTD	HTDCD29
1995	ASHLEY HUTCHINGS	The Guv'nor Vol. 3	HTD	TDCD38
1995	VARIOUS ARTISTS	Global Gumbo	Rhino	R2 77208

Discography

1995	SANDY DENNY/ TREVOR LUCAS	Sandy Denny, Trevor Lucas And Friends The Attic Tracks 1972–1984	Raven (Australia) Special Delivery (UK)	RVCD 46 SPDCD1052
1995	VARIOUS ARTISTS	(USA) Troubadours Of British Folk Vol. 2	Rhino	R2 72161
1995	VARIOUS ARTISTS	(USA) Troubadours Of British Folk Vol. 3	Rhino	R2 72162
1996	VARIOUS ARTISTS	(Germany) Tanz & Folkfest Rudolstadt 1995	hei-deck	RUCD 96-1

11. PROMO-ONLY COMPILATION ALBUMS FEATURING RICHARD THOMPSON
(in all sorts of guises)

1971	VARIOUS ARTISTS	Pop Power	Polydor	3574 002
1971	VARIOUS ARTISTS	Super Groups	Polydor	3574 003
1973	VARIOUS ARTISTS	The Hit Sounds Of Merrie Melodies (2 × LP)	Warner Bros	PRO 550
1975	FAIRPORT CONVENTION	Tour Sampler	Island Tour	ISS2
1986	VARIOUS ARTISTS	Island Life: Media Sampler	Island	MP1
1991	VARIOUS ARTISTS	Route 91	Capitol	DPRO 79416
1992	NICK DRAKE	(USA) Nick Drake: The Hannibal Sampler	Hannibal	VRCD 4434
1993	VARIOUS ARTISTS	(USA) Medium Rare (Rykodisc compilation)	Rykodisc	VRCD 0001
	(features RT live version of Skull & Crossed Bones)			
1994	VARIOUS ARTISTS	Where Are My Headphones – Live From Studio A Vol. Two (Columbus, Ohio Radio Station)	WCBE-FM	90.5
1994	VARIOUS ARTISTS	Eleven Years & Counting	Ryko/ Hannibal	VRCD 9401
1994	RICHARD THOMPSON	Mirror Blue (promo of whole album)	Capitol	TENNYSON 1

12. VIDEOS FEATURING RICHARD THOMPSON

1982	FAIRPORT CONVENTION	Fairport Convention: Cropredy 30th August 1980 (live recording of FC and their guests: time 53 mins)	Videotech	

Discography

1982 FAIRPORT CONVENTION	Reunion Festival: Broughton Castle 1981* (live recording 15 August 1981)	Videotech	
1981 VARIOUS ARTISTS	Rock Guitar – A Guide To The Greats	Longman Video	
1983 FAIRPORT CONVENTION	A Weekend In The Country (live recording 13/14 August 1982)	Videotech Videotech	
1983 RICHARD THOMPSON (+band) (released in UK 1986)	Across A Crowded Room (USA) (84 mins)	Sony	
	Across A Crowded Room (UK) (84 mins)	Hendring	HEN 2 038 E
1986 FAIRPORT CONVENTION	Cropredy Capers (65 mins) (live recording 8/9 August 1986)	Intech Video	
1987 FAIRPORT CONVENTION	It All Comes Round Again (documentary + Cropredy Festival 1987: 1 hr 50 mins)	Island Visual Arts	IVA 002
1987 FAIRPORT CONVENTION	In Real Time (Cropredy Festival 1987 only: 56 mins)	Island Visual Arts	
1991 FAIRPORT CONVENTION	Live At Maidstone 1970 (includes Matthews Southern Comfort: 32 mins)	Musikfolk	MF01
1993 FAIRPORT CONVENTION	Live At Broughton Castle 1981 (re-issue of*: 109 mins)	Musikfolk	MF 03
1994 IAN MATTHEWS (USA)	Compass And Chart Vol. 1 (RT on only one track – **Reno Nevada**)	Perfect Pitch	

13. RECORDED SONGS WRITTEN BY RICHARD THOMPSON

(also showing album on which they first appeared and other artists who have covered song)

A Blind Step Away (Live Love Larf & Loaf)
   JUNE TABOR
A Bone Through Her Nose (Daring Adventures)
A Commercial Proposition
   MATTHEWS SOUTHERN COMFORT
A Heart Needs A Home (Hokey Pokey)
   DENNIS TRACEY
   PHIL HARE
   TONY TRISCHKA & SKYLINE

   SHAWN COLVIN & LOUDON WAINWRIGHT III
   RUNAWAY EXPRESS
A Poisoned Heart And A Twisted Memory (Hand Of Kindness)
Al Bowlly's In Heaven (Daring Adventures)
Albion Sunrise
   ALBION COUNTRY BAND
   ENGLISH AIR

Discography

Am I Wasting My Love On You (you? me? us?)
The Angels Took My Racehorse Away (Henry The Human Fly)
   DAVE BURLAND
   HEDGEHOG PIE
Baby Don't Know What To Do With Herself (you? me? us?)
Baby Talk (Daring Adventures)
Backlash Love Affair (Rumor & Sigh)
Back Street Slide (Shoot Out The Lights)
Bad News Is All The Wind Can Carry (Doom & Gloom II)
   BRASS MONKEY
Bank Vault In Heaven (you? me? us?)
Beachport (Sweet Talker)
Beat The Retreat (Pour Down Like Silver)
   JUNE TABOR
Beeswing (Mirror Blue)
Begging Bowl (Invisible Means)
Boomtown (Sweet Talker)
Borrowed Time (Sunnyvista)
Both Ends Burning (Hand Of Kindness)
Burns' Supper (you? me? us?)
Business On You (you? me? us?)
Cajun Woman (Unhalfbricking)
   THE ASHLEY HUTCHINGS ALL-STARS
The Calvary Cross (I Want To See The Bright Lights Tonight)
   HOME SERVICE
   ROBYN HITCHCOCK
Can't Win (Amnesia)
Cash Down Never Never (Daring Adventures)
The Choice Wife (First Light)
Civilisation (Sunnyvista)
   IAN MATTHEWS
Cold Feet (Henry The Human Fly)
   THE BUSHWACKERS
Cold Kisses (you? me? us?)
Crash The Party (Watching The Dark)
Dark Hand Over My Heart (you? me? us?)
Dead Man's Handle (Daring Adventures)
Devonside (Hand Of Kindness)
Died For Love (First Light)
   DOLORES KEANE

Dimming Of The Day (Pour Down Like Silver)
   ANY TROUBLE
   DAVE BURLAND
   BONNIE RAITT
   MARY BLACK
   LINDA RONSTADT
   DANNY CARNAHAN & ROBIN PETRIE
   FIVE BLIND BOYS OF ALABAMA
   CLIVE GREGSON, EDDIE READER & BOO HEWARDINE
   THE DIXIE DARLINGS
   CHRIS MILES
   PHIL COOPER & MARGARET NELSON
   RUNAWAY EXPRESS
   RUDE GIRLS
Don't Let A Thief Steal Into Your Heart (First Light)
   THE POINTER SISTERS
   HENRY KAISER BAND
Don't Renege On Our Love (Shoot Out The Lights)
Don't Sit On My Jimmy Shands (Rumor & Sigh)
Don't Tell Secrets (ep only)
Don't Tempt Me (Amnesia)
Down Where The Drunkards Roll (I Want To See The Bright Lights Tonight)
   TONY ROSE
   HANS THEESSINK (Austria)
   TELHAM TINKERS
   FRASER & BRUCE
   JOHN LEONARD & JOHN SQUIRE
   CHRIS & CARLA
   FUNGUS
   LOS LOBOS
   MARTIN & JESSICA SIMPSON
   DAVE BURLAND
   FIONA JOYCE
   BRIAN DEWHURST
   JIM MAGEEAN & JOHNNY COLLINS
   TOM LEWIS
   PHIL COOPER & MARGARET NELSON
Drowned Dog Black Night (Live Love Larf & Loaf)
The Dune Ship (Sweet Talker)

Discography

Easy There, Steady Now (Mirror Blue)
The Egypt Room (Hokey Pokey)
The End Of The Rainbow (I Want To See The Bright Lights Tonight)
  ELVIS COSTELLO
  TREVOR LUCAS
  TOM ROBINSON
Farewell Farewell (Liege & Lief)
  MARY BLACK
  MADDY PRIOR & MARTIN CARTHY
  ATWATER-DONNELLY
  CHRISTINA HARRISON
Fast Food (Mirror Blue)
Fire In The Engine Room (Across A Crowded Room)
First Light (First Light)
For Shame Of Doing Wrong (Pour Down Like Silver)
  SANDY DENNY
  SPUD
  MAE McKENNA
  MAGGIE HOLLAND & JOHN MOORE
  SYD STRAW & EVAN DANDO
  PETER BLEGVAD
  YO LA TENGO
  BARBARA BEEMAN BAND
  LOOSE DIAMONDS
For The Sake Of Mary (Mirror Blue)
From Galway To Graceland (Watching The Dark)
  PLAINSONG
  IAN MATTHEWS
  RON KAVANA
Genesis Hall (Unhalfbricking)
  X-TAL
  JUNE TABOR
Georgie On A Spree (Hokey Pokey)
  SWAN ARCADE
The Ghost Of You Walks (you? me? us?)
Ghosts In The Wind (Across A Crowded Room)
God Loves A Drunk (Rumor & Sigh)
  NORMA WATERSON
The Great Valerio (I Want To See The Bright Lights Tonight)
  MAGGIE HOLLAND
  SWAN ARCADE
  BACKWOODS JAZZ
  MADDY PRIOR & MARTIN CARTHY
  MADOU (Belgium)
  FATIMA MANSIONS
Grey Walls (Rumor & Sigh)
Gypsy Love Songs (Amnesia)
Hand Of Kindness (Hand Of Kindness)
Hard Luck Stories (Pour Down Like Silver)
  ROY BAILEY
  MELANIE HARROLD
  THE BUSHWACKERS
  DAVE BURLAND
  FLASH COMPANY
Harry's Theme (Sweet Talker)
Has He Got A Friend For Me (I Want To See The Bright Lights Tonight)
  DEIGHTON FAMILY
  MARIA McKEE
Hide It Away (you? me? us?)
Hokey Pokey (The Ice Cream Song) (Hokey Pokey)
House Of Cards (First Light)
  DAVE BURLAND
How I Wanted To (Hand Of Kindness)
  BARBARA BEEMAN BAND
  CARIN KJELLMAN
  MARTIN & JESSICA SIMPSON
How Many Times Do You Have To Fall (Small Town Romance)
  FAIRPORT CONVENTION
How Will I Ever Be Simple Again (Daring Adventures)
  RUA
  BATTLEFIELD BAND
  CHRISTINE COLLISTER
  DAVE BURLAND
  COLCANNON
  PHIL COOPER, MARGARET NELSON & PAUL GOELZ
I Ain't Going To Drag My Feet No More (Across A Crowded Room)
I Can't Wake Up To Save My Life (Mirror Blue)
I Feel So Good (Rumor & Sigh)
I'll Regret It All In The Morning (Hokey Pokey)
I Misunderstood (Rumor & Sigh)
  DINOSAUR JUNIOR
  SALLY BARKER
I Ride In Your Slipstream (Mirror Blue)
I Still Dream (Amnesia)

Discography

I Want To See The Bright Lights Tonight (I Want To See The Bright Lights Tonight)
  JULIE COVINGTON
  WEDDINGS, PARTIES, ANYTHING
  BARRENCE WHITFIELD WITH TOM RUSSELL
  RON KAVANA
  DAVE BURLAND
  TIM BROADBENT
Jealousy (Doom & Gloom I)
Jennie (Daring Adventures)
Jerusalem On The Jukebox (Amnesia)
Jet Plane In A Rocking Chair (Pour Down Like Silver)
  ENGLISH AIR
Justice In The Streets (Sunnyvista)
Just The Motion (Shoot Out The Lights)
  DAB HAND
  CARIN KJELLMAN
  HAPPY TRAUM BAND
  DAVID BYRNE
  WILLIAM PINT
Keep Your Distance (Rumor & Sigh)
Killerman Gold Posse (Live Love Larf & Loaf)
Killing Jar (Invisible Means)
  ELAINE MORGAN
King Of Bohemia (Mirror Blue)
The Knife Edge (Strict Tempo)
  THE HOKEY POKEY STRINGS
Layla (First Light)
The Little Beggar Girl (I Want To See The Bright Lights Tonight)
  PANZIE POTTER
Little Blue Number (Across A Crowded Room)
Living In Luxury (Shoot Out The Lights – original CD only)
Lonely Hearts (Sunnyvista)
Long Dead Love (Daring Adventures)
Love In A Faithless Country (Across A Crowded Room)
Love Is Bad For Business (Small Town Romance)
  MEN & VOLTS
Lover's Lane (Daring Adventures)
Madness Of Love (Doom & Gloom I)
  ADAMS, FRENCH, KAISER & WEST
  POLLY BOLTON

  GRAHAM PARKER
Man In Need (Shoot Out The Lights)
March Of The Cosmetic Surgeons (Invisible Means)
Mary And Joseph (Henry The Human Fly)
Mascara Tears (Mirror Blue)
The May Day Psalter (Circle Dance)
Meet On The Ledge (What We Did On Our Holidays)
  FAIRPORT CONVENTION
  NOEL MURPHY
  PRELUDE
  IAN MATTHEWS
MGB-GT (Mirror Blue)
Mingus Eyes (Mirror Blue)
Missie How You Let Me Down (Daring Adventures)
Modern Woman (recorded but not released)
Mother Knows Best (Rumor & Sigh)
Mrs Rita
  JUNE TABOR
Mystery Wind (Rumor & Sigh)
Nearly In Love (Daring Adventures)
Never Again (Hokey Pokey)
  SHIRLEY & DOLLY COLLINS
The New St. George (Henry The Human Fly)
  ALBION COUNTRY BAND
  JOHN COY
  DAVE BURLAND
  BEGGARS' HILL
  TAVERNERS
Night Comes In (Pour Down Like Silver)
  JUNE TABOR & THE OYSTER BAND
  FULL MOON FAIR
Nobody's Wedding (Henry The Human Fly)
No Man's Land (What We Did On Our Holidays)
  THE NEW SEEKERS
No's Not A Word (you? me? us?)
Oh I Swear (Hard Cash)
The Old Changing Way (Henry The Human Fly)
  BATTLEFIELD BAND
  BOB DAVENPORT
  DAVE BURLAND
Old Man Inside A Young Man (Hokey Pokey)

Discography

Painted Ladies (Henry The Human Fly)
Peppermint Rock (Invisible Means)
Pharaoh (Amnesia)
    HELL BENT & HEAVEN BOUND
    THE HOUSE BAND
The Pitfall/The Excursion (guitar, vocal)
The Poor Boy Is Taken Away (Pour Down Like Silver)
The Poor Ditching Boy (Henry The Human Fly)
    IAN MATTHEWS
    FAIRPORT CONVENTION
    ALISTAIR RUSSELL
    FUNGUS
    GEORGE WILSON
    PHIL COOPER & KIRK CHILTON
    DAVE BURLAND
    BEGGARS' HILL
    KATE DELANEY & GORDON McINTYRE
Psycho Street (Rumor & Sigh)
Put It There Pal (you? me? us?)
Put Your Trust In Me (Sweet Talker)
Rainbow Over The Hill (Rise Up Like The Sun)
    THE ALBION BAND
Razor Dance (you? me? us?)
Read About Love (Rumor & Sigh)
Reckless Kind (Amnesia)
    VICTORIA WILLIAMS
Restless Highway (First Light)
Roll Over Vaughn Williams (Henry The Human Fly)
Roll Up (Sweet Talker)
Sam Jones (you? me? us?)
Saturday Rolling Around (Sunnyvista)
    ARIZONA SMOKE REVIEW
    STEWED MULLIGAN
Shady Lies
    MARC ELLINGTON
    IAN MATTHEWS
Shaky Nancy (Henry The Human Fly)
    DAVE BURLAND
Shane And Dixie (Mirror Blue)
She Cut Off Her Long Silken Hair (you? me? us?)
She Steers By Lightning (you? me? us?)
She Twists The Knife Again (Across A Crowded Room)
Shine On Love (Across A Crowded Room original CD only)
Shoot Out The Lights (Shoot Out The Lights)
    BOB MOULD
    X
Sisters (Sunnyvista)
    THE FRASER SISTERS
Small Town Romance (Small Town Romance)
    ASHLEY HUTCHINGS
    BOBBY SUTCLIFF
Smiffy's Glass Eye (Hokey Pokey)
    THE DIXIE DARLINGS
Speechless Child (Doom & Gloom I)
Strange Affair (First Light)
    HOLLY TANNEN
    JUNE TABOR & MARTIN SIMPSON
    SHUSHA
    NO RIGHT TURN
Streets Of Paradise (Pour Down Like Silver)
The Sun Never Shines On The Poor (Hokey Pokey)
    PATTI O'DOORS
    TREVOR LUCAS
    FUNGUS
Sunnyvista (Sunnyvista)
Sweet Surrender (First Light)
Taking My Business Elsewhere (Mirror Blue)
Tale In Hard Time (What We Did On Our Holidays)
Tear Stained Letter (Hand Of Kindness)
    JO-EL SONNIER
    WES McGHEE
    NICOLETTE LARSON
    PATTY LOVELESS
    ALBERT LEE & HOGAN'S HEROES
    THE CONQUERORS
Time To Ring Some Changes (Small Town Romance)
    THE ALBION BAND
    SWARBRICK & NICOL
    JOHN COY
    JOHN & CHRIS LESLIE
    SPIRIT OF THE WEST
To Hang A Dream On (Sweet Talker)
Traces Of My Love (Sunnyvista)
Train Don't Leave (you? me? us?)
Turning Of The Tide (Amnesia)
    BOB MOULD

Discography

Twisted (Henry The Human Fly)
Two Left Feet (Hand Of Kindness)
   FILE
Valerie (Daring Adventures)
   MARSHALL CRENSHAW
   TREVOR LUCAS
   BEAUSOLEIL
1952 Vincent Black Lightning (Rumor & Sigh)
   DAN PLEWS
   GREG BROWN
   BURACH
Walking On A Wire (Shoot Out The Lights)
   TREVOR LUCAS
   NEW ST GEORGE
   KNOTS & CROSSES
   THE BIS-QUITS
Walking Through A Wasted Land (Across A Crowded Room)
Wall Of Death (Shoot Out The Lights)
   BUSHWACKERS
   REM
   PETE & MAURA KENNEDY
Waltzing's For Dreamers (Amnesia)
   FOUR MEN & A DOG
   LEAPY LEE (promo)
   THE KEITH HANCOCK BAND
   DAVE BURLAND
   PHIL COOPER & MARGARET NELSON
   NASHVILLE BLUEGRASS BAND
   THE BARLEYCORN
The Way That It Shows (Mirror Blue)
We Sing Hallelujah (I Want To See The Bright Lights Tonight)
   JOHNNY COLLINS
   HOME SERVICE
   PHIL COOPER & MARGARET NELSON
   SHAWN COLVIN & LOUDON WAINWRIGHT III
Wheely Down (Henry The Human Fly)
   IAN KEARY & IVOR CUTLER
When I Get To The Border (I Want To See The Bright Lights Tonight)
   ARLO GUTHRIE
   ALISTAIR RUSSELL
   LUCY KAPLANSKY
When The Spell Is Broken (Across A Crowded Room)
   BONNIE RAITT
   HARROLD & BLANCHFLOWER
   AL KOOPER
Where The Wind Don't Whine (Hand Of Kindness) (on CD only)
Why Do You Turn Your Back? (Sunnyvista)
Why Must I Plead (Rumor & Sigh)
Withered And Died (I Want To See The Bright Lights Tonight)
   DAVE BURLAND
   BRAM TAYLOR
   ELVIS COSTELLO
   CROWS
   HEDGEHOG PIE
   ROBYN HITCHCOCK
Woods Of Darney (you? me? us?)
Woman Or A Man (Small Town Romance)
   MICHAEL DOUCET & CAJUN BREW
The World Is A Wonderful Place (The World Is A Wonderful Place)
The Wrong Heartbeat (Hand Of Kindness)
Yankee Go Home (Amnesia)
You Don't Say (Across A Crowded Room)
You Dream Too Much (Rumor & Sigh)
You're Going To Need Somebody (Sunnyvista)
   THE BLUE AEROPLANES

NOTE: RT also credited with Improvisation/That Little Thing/Hendrix-type solo on **The Electric Mandolin** (mandolin tutor)

Discography

14. RECORDED SONGS CO-WRITTEN BY RICHARD THOMPSON
(also showing album on which they first appeared and other artists who have covered song)

RT & IAN MacDONALD
If (Stomp) (Fairport Convention)

RT & PAUL GHOSH & ANDREW HORVITCH
Decameron (Fairport Convention)
Sun Shade (Fairport Convention)

RT & GEORGE PAINTER & ASHLEY HUTCHINGS
The Lobster (Fairport Convention)

RT & ASHLEY HUTCHINGS
It's Alright Ma, It's Only Witchcraft (Fairport Convention)
Throwaway Street Puzzle (guitar, vocal)
If It Feels Good, You Know It Can't Be Wrong (Heyday)

RT & ASHLEY HUTCHINGS & SANDY DENNY
The Lord Is In This Place ... How Dreadful Is This Place (What We Did On Our Holidays)

RT & IAN MATTHEWS
Book Song (What We Did On Our Holidays)

RT & DAVE SWARBRICK
Crazy Man Michael (Liege & Lief)
  SILVER BIRCH
  THE BUSKERS
  VIKKI CLAYTON
  THE IRISH TRADITION
  SUNDOWN
  GENERAL HUMBERT
  DANNY O'FLAHERTY
  NORTHEAST WINDS
  TERESA DOYLE
  FIONA JOYCE
  SEANNACHIE
  NEW ST GEORGE
  BETSY McGOVERN
  CEILI'S MUSE

Walk Awhile (Full House)
  ZULUS
Sloth (Full House)
  JACOBITES
  WATERSHED
  NIKKI SUDDEN & DAVE CUSWORTH
Doctor Of Physick (Full House)
Now Be Thankful (History Of Fairport Convention)
Sickness & Diseases
  FAIRPORT CONVENTION
The Journeyman's Grace
  FAIRPORT CONVENTION
Poor Will & The Jolly Hangman (guitar, vocal)

RT & DAVE SWARBRICK/SIMON NICOL/DAVE MATTACKS
Sir B. McKenzie's Daughter's Lament For The 77th Mounted Lancers Retreat From The Straits Of Loch Knombe, In The Year Of Our Lord 1727, On The Occasion Of The Announcement Of Her Marriage To The Laird Of Kinleakie (Fairport 'Live' Convention)

RT & DAVE PEGG/DAVE SWARBRICK/SIMON NICOL/DAVE MATTACKS
Matthew, Mark, Luke & John
  FAIRPORT CONVENTION

RT & LINDA THOMPSON
Pavanne (First Light)
  SWARBRICK & NICOL
  BACKWOODS JAZZ
  JUNE TABOR
Did She Jump Or Was She Pushed (Shoot Out The Lights)

RT & DAVID THOMAS
Bird Town
  DAVID THOMAS & THE PEDESTRIANS

Discography

RT & DAVID THOMAS & PHILIP MOXHAM
The Birds Are Good Ideas
DAVID THOMAS & THE PEDESTRIANS
Sound Of The Sand
DAVID THOMAS & THE PEDESTRIANS

RT & DAVID THOMAS & ANTON FIER
Yiki Tiki
DAVID THOMAS & THE PEDESTRIANS

RT & DAVID THOMAS & ANTON FIER & JOHN GREAVES
The New Atom Mine
DAVID THOMAS & THE PEDESTRIANS

RT & DAVID THOMAS & ANTON FIER & EDDIE THORNTON
Man's Best Friend
DAVID THOMAS & THE PEDESTRIANS

RT & T-BONE BURNETT
Welcome Home Mr Lewis
T-BONE BURNETT

RT & PETER FILLEUL
My Time (The Marksman)
Gordon (The Marksman)
Rude Health (The Marksman)
Night School (The Marksman)
Cornishe Pastiche (The Marksman)
Crossing The Water (The Marksman)
On Yer Eyes (The Marksman)
Don't Ever Change (The Marksman)
Up There (The Marksman)
Persuasion – instrumental version (Sweet Talker)
TIM FINN
Conviction (Sweet Talker)
Sweet Talker (Sweet Talker)
False Or True (Sweet Talker)

RT & TIM FINN
Persuasion
TIM FINN

RT & PETER FILLEUL & CRAIG CHARLES
The Marksman (The Marksman)

RT & PETER FILLEUL & PHIL WRIGHT
Gutters On The Run (The Marksman)

RT & HENRY KAISER
Tir-Nan-Darag (Live Love Larf & Loaf)

RT & MARVIN ETZIONI
It Don't Cost Much (The World Is A Wonderful Place)
MARVIN ETZIONI

NOTE: This discography was compiled by Colin Davies, with reference to a Richard Thompson discography by David Suff that appeared in *Hokey Pokey*, (#28), the RT newsletter Davies operated. CD thanks for their help Ian Rennie, David Thomas, Brian New, Derek Harding, Wayne Smith, Stephanie Maine, Sian Wynne, John Falstaff, Patrick Humphries, Tom Spruce, Phil Daniels, John Martin. If you have any additions or corrections, please write to *Hokey Pokey*, Field Corner, Millham Lane, Dulverton, Somerset, England, TA22 9HQ. Please send an S.A.S.E. if a reply is required.

Bibliography

Brewer's Dictionary of Phrase and Fable, 15th Edition, Revised by Adrian Room (Cassell, 1995)
British Hit Albums, 6th Edition, Paul Gambaccini, Tim Rice, Jo Rice (Guinness, 1994)
British Hit Singles, 10th Edition, Tim Rice, Paul Gambaccini, Jo Rice (Guinness, 1995)
Days in the Life: Voices From the English Underground, 1961-1971, Jonathon Green (Heinemann, 1988)
The Eagles: The Long Run, Marc Shapiro (Omnibus, 1995)
The Electric Muse: The Story of Folk into Rock, Dave Laing, Karl Dallas, Robert Shelton, Robin Denselow (Methuen, 1975)
Folk Song in England, A. L. Lloyd (Panther, 1969)
The Guinness Encyclopedia of Popular Music, 2nd Edition, Edited by Colin Larkin (Guinness, 1995)
High Fidelity, Nick Hornby (Victor Gollancz, 1995)
In Session Tonight: The Complete Radio 1 Recordings, Ken Garner (BBC Books, 1993).
The London Encyclopedia, Edited by Ben Weinreb and Christopher Hibbert (Papermac, 1993)
London's Rock Landmarks, Marcus Gray (Omnibus, 1985)
London's Rock Routes, John Platt (4th Estate, 1985)
Never Again, Britain 1945-1951, Peter Hennessy (Vintage, 1993)
The Penguin Book of Folk Ballads, Edited by Albert R. Friedman (Penguin, 1977)
Richard Thompson: 20 Years of Doom and Gloom, Clinton Heylin (Privately printed, 1987)
The Woodworm Era: The Story of Today's Fairport Convention Fred Redwood and Martin Woodward (Jeneva, 1995)
Written in my Soul: Conversations With Rock's Great Songwriters, Bill Flanagan (Omnibus, 1987)

Lyric Permissions

'1952 Vincent Black Lightning'
'King Of Bohemia'
'Time To Ring Some Changes'
'Rainbow Over The Hill'
'The Way That It Shows'
'Oh I Swear'
'Jerusalem On The Jukebox'
'Waltzing's For Dreamers'
'Pharaoh'
'I Feel So Good'
'Read About Love'
'Mother Knows Best'
'From Galway To Graceland'
'The World Is A Wonderful Place'
'Beeswing'
'Sam Jones'
'The Woods Of Darney'
  Written by Richard Thompson
  © Beeswing Music
  Lyrics reproduced by kind permission of the publisher.

Lyrics of 'Telling Me Lies' are reproduced by kind permission of Linda Thompson.

'Hokey Pokey'
'I'll Regret It All In The Morning'
'The Egypt Room'
'The Sun Never Shines On The Poor'
'Modern Woman'
'Woman Or A Man'
  Written by Richard Thompson
  © Bee Bee Music
  Lyrics reproduced by kind permission of the publisher.

'Walking On A Wire'
'Shoot Out The Lights'

'Wall Of Death'
'When The Spell Is Broken'
'I Ain't Going To Drag My Feet No More'
'Valerie'
'Missie How You Let Me Down'
'Nearly In Love'
'Al Bowlly's In Heaven'
  Written by Richard Thompson
  © PolyGram Music Publishing Ltd.
  Lyrics reproduced by kind permission of the publisher.

'Meet On The Ledge'
'Roll Over Vaughn Williams'
'Poor Ditching Boy'
'Painted Ladies'
'Wheely Down'
'End Of The Rainbow'
'When I Get To The Border'
  Written by Richard Thompson
  © Warlock Music Ltd.
  Lyrics reproduced by kind permission of the publisher.

'Pavanne'
  Written by Richard Thompson & Linda Thompson © PolyGram Music Publishing Ltd.
  Lyrics reproduced by kind permission of the publisher.

'Poor Will And The Jolly Hangman'
  Written by Richard Thompson & Dave Swarbrick © Warlock Music Ltd.
  Lyrics reproduced by kind permission of the publisher.

Index

A&M Records 67, 76, 77, 102
Abbott, Kingsley 39
'Al Bowlly's In Heaven' 248–9
Albion Band 35, 76, 181–3, 194
Albion Country Band 128–30
'Albion Sunrise' 130, 147
Altham, Keith 43
America, British music in 261–2
American music industry 260–62, 264–5
Andersen, Eric 56, 213
Andrew, Geoff 251
Andrews, Bernie 55
Angel, The (Little Hadham) 98–9, 106, 108–9, 114–17, 122, 124–5
'Angels Took My Racehorse Away, The' 131, 133, 134
Any Trouble 226–7, 236, 259
Arcadians, The 12–13
'Atom Heart Mother' 102
Attlee, Clement 13–14

'Baby Don't Know What To Do With Herself' 336
Bain, Aly 265
'Baker Street' 192, 194
'Ballad of Easy Rider' 88, 178, 179
Band, The 63, 78–9, 87, 98, 107, 111, 112, 135, 259
'Bank Vault In Heaven' 335
Barbican Preview Concerts 207
Bath Festival of Blues & Progressive Music 102–3, 306–7
Battle of the Field, The 129–30
Beat Instrumental 57, 62
Beat the Retreat 329–31
Beatles 38, 40, 42, 43, 45, 63, 132, 135, 205

'Beeswing' 321, 322
Betteridge, David 143, 144
Billboard 252, 272
'Birmingham Water Buffalo Club, The' 113
'Blackwaterside' 64
Blackwell, Chris 142, 144
Blake, Tchad 320
Blossom Toes 42
'Bone Through Her Nose, A' 247
'Book Song' 63, 65
bootlegs 292–3
Bowdler, Thomas 83
Bowlly, Alick 248–9
box sets 292–4
Boyd, Joe
  Fairport Convention recordings 37, 43–4, 52, 59, 75–6, 79, 87, 91, 114–15
  Hannibal Records 199, 201, 206, 208–9, 225–6, 228, 285–6, 294
  and Linda Peters 121, 122, 123, 175, 239
  Richard & Linda recordings 181, 184, 199, 201, 202, 206
  Richard's solo recordings 224, 225–6, 228, 232–3
  at Warner Brothers 115, 123
Braceland, Jack 44
Bramham, Harvey 72–3
Branson, Richard 125, 184
brass bands in pop music 146–7, 182
Brass Monkey 76, 237, 251
'Bright Lights' (single) 162
Britten, Benjamin 86
Broadwood, Lucy 83–4
Bron Agency 161, 162
Brothers in Arms 243, 244–5

Index

Broughton Castle 200, 210
Brown, Geoff 141, 155, 156, 226
Brown, Joe 4
Bruce, Jack 280
Bryden, Bill 238
Buckley, Tim 50
Bunch, The 125–6, 138, 152
Burland, Dave 332
Burns, Robert 90
Burton, James 24, 122, 134, 240
'Business On You' 335
Byrds, The 50, 102, 329
Byrne, David 285

'Cajun Woman' 56, 64, 68, 70
Cale, John 159
'Calvary Cross' 146, 163, 164, 178, 180, 182, 296, 304
Cambridge Folk Festival 163–4
Campbell, Alex 62
'Candle In The Wind' 175
Capitol Records 259, 265, 272, 278, 286, 293, 319, 329
Carruthers, Ben 52
Carthy, Martin 71, 79, 86, 129, 200, 211, 237, 251
Cash, Johnny 50, 56
'Cash Down Never Never' 247
Cashbox 239, 246
Castle, Roy 253
Cavanagh, David 288, 323, 335
Chieftains, The 160, 187
Child, Francis James 82, 86, 90
Chipping Norton Studios 195, 197, 203
'Choice Wife, The' 187
Chrysalis Records 177, 185–6, 189–90, 193, 197
circus-inspired songs 205
'Civilisation' 190
Clapton, Eric 100, 187, 292
Clark, Gene 50
Clark, Pete 287, 295
Cocker, Joe 49
Cohen, Leonard 48, 49, 56, 58, 284, 329, 330
Collins, Shirley 126, 128
Collister, Christine 224, 227, 233, 236, 243, 251, 257, 265
Colvin, Shawn 278, 279
'Come All Ye' 89
compact discs 244, 250

Compleat Dancing Master, The 130
Conway, Gerry 123, 126, 236, 243
Cook, Betsy 195, 205, 238, 240
Cordell, Denny 45
Cornwell, Hugh 28, 29
Costello, Elvis 24, 40, 149, 238, 242, 249, 272, 276, 299, 315, 320, 330, 343
Cousins, Dave 53
Cousins Club 53, 121, 142
Covey, Nancy 207, 210–11, 216, 217–18, 221–3, 229, 268
Covington, Julie 184–5
'Crash the Party' 296
'Crazy Man Michael' 5, 90–91, 106, 121
Cropredy 4–6, 35, 69, 114, 199–200, 217, 341–5
Crowded House 267, 268, 282
Curd, John 161

'Dargai' 171
'Dark End of the Street' 178, 179
Davenport, Bob 211
Davies, Colin 258, 331
'Dead Man's Handle' 246–7
Denny, Alexandra Elene Maclean (Sandy) 76, 93, 121, 172–3, 330
background 53–4
death 105, 193
Fairport Convention 5, 53–5, 57, 66, 94–6, 122
Fotheringay 35, 115, 123, 139, 236
Happy Blunderers 123
North Star Grassman and The Ravens, The 64, 123
onstage 57, 66
Rendezvous 93, 175, 181, 193
singing 6, 54–5, 66, 123
songwriting 68, 89, 185, 193
Denselow, Robin 94, 126, 141, 226
'Deserter, The' 82, 84, 90
d'Etchingham, Humphrey 124
'Devonside' 224
Dexter, Jeff 46
'Did She Jump Or Was She Pushed' 188, 193
'Died For Love' 187
'Dimming of the Day' 146, 170, 171, 235, 331
Dire Straits 244–5

Index

Disc & Music Echo 59, 68, 115–16, 135
Doherty, Bernard 57, 158, 160, 162, 166, 192–3, 206, 313
Dominion Theatre 231
Donahue, Jerry 229
Donald, Timi 144, 191
Donaldson, Pat 124, 126, 131, 144, 172, 227
Donegan, Lonnie 20, 36, 52
'Don't Let A Thief Steal Into Your Heart' 187, 189
'Don't Renege On Our Love' 196, 202
'Don't Step On My Jimmy Shands' 276–7
Dorfsman, Neil 243
'Down Where The Drunkards Roll' 138, 146, 147, 331
Dr K's Blues Band 36, 38
Draheim, Sue 129
Drake, Nick 59, 115, 123, 124, 134, 158, 193, 230
Dransfield, Barry 128
Dunn, Alan 237
Dyble, Judy 41, 47, 48, 51, 52, 201
Dylan, Bob 29, 30, 43, 50, 52, 56, 63, 64, 68–70, 78–9, 86–7, 121, 139, 141, 162, 179, 200, 272, 276, 292, 301

Eagles, The 111, 112, 135
Eaglin, Snooks 23
'Easy There, Steady Now' 323
Eclection 72, 75
Egan, Joe 192
'Egypt Room, The' 156
Eight Feathers Boys Club 53
Electric Dysentery, The 36
Electric Muse, The 87, 126
Elixir Records 199
Ellington, Marc 112, 191, 288–9
Elliott, Jane 105
'End Of The Rainbow, The' 146, 148–9, 150, 299
Essex Music 50
Ethnic Shuffle Orchestra, The 36, 37, 38
Evans, Mick 176
Evening Standard 73, 287, 295
Everly Brothers 56, 126, 205

Fairey Engineering Band 243, 265
Fairport Convention
American tours 101–2, 109–14
band formed 38–9, 41, 45
Boyd signs up 44, 46
cover versions 49–51, 62–3, 64
Denny joins 53–4
drinking 110, 111, 114
Dyble leaves 52
earnings 46, 54, 67
at Farley Chamberlayne 79–80, 88–9, 92
first record 46–7
folk-rock music 88, 91, 139, 181
gigs 38–47, 66–7, 72, 92, 113–14
influences 35, 78
and Led Zeppelin 113–14
living in The Angel 98–9, 106, 108–9, 114–17
M1 accident 72–6
Mattacks joins 79
Matthews dismissed 66
onstage 40, 48, 57, 66
play college circuit 49, 61, 70, 114
and politics 60
popularity 96–7
Radio 1 sessions 55–6, 179
return after split 99
reunions 4–6, 35, 69, 114, 199–201, 217, 341–5
split (1969) 93–6
Thompson leaves 115–17
traditional songs 62, 64–6, 68, 80, 82, 101, 109
Fairport Convention (albums)
Angel Delight 106
Babbacombe Lee 160
Fairport Convention 51–2, 56–7
Full House 82, 99, 101, 102, 103, 104–8, 114, 321
Gladys' Leap 194
Liege & Lief 71, 82, 84, 87, 88–92, 93–6, 104, 109, 116, 138, 179, 181
Unhalfbricking 64, 67–71, 75, 90, 91, 92, 96, 112
What We Did On Our Holidays 56, 60–61, 62–5
Fairport House 34–5, 37, 47
Fame & Wealth 227
Family 42, 49, 55, 56, 75
'Farewell, Farewell' 89–90
Farina, Richard 48, 50, 56, 86, 88
Farley Chamberlayne 79–80, 88–9, 92

376

Index

'Fast Food' 30
Fate Of Nations 114
Feldman Music 64
Filleul, Pete 253–7
Finchley Press, The 46–7
'Fire in the Engine Room' 234
Flanagan, Bill 235, 247, 248, 261, 303
'Flee as a Bird' 178, 180
Flypaper 58, 91, 188, 233, 234, 293
Flywheel, Wolf J. 64
folk music 30–31, 63, 80, 81–8, 139
Folk Roots 12, 275, 276, 279
Fotheringay 35, 115, 123, 139, 236
'Fotheringay' 63
Foundations, The 226
Frame, Pete 65
Frank, Jackson C. 53, 86
Franklyn, Jeannie 72–3, 75, 76, 91, 156
Frater, Shawn 38
French, Frith, Kaiser & Thompson 258
Frey, Glenn 111–12
Friends 91–2
'From Galway to Graceland' 3, 133, 296–7, 300, 331
Froom, Mitchell 233, 242–5, 265, 267–8, 295, 320, 335
Frost, Danny 323
Full House 56
Fuller, Malcom 24, 25
Fusion 67

garage music 231
Genockey, Liam 195
'Georgie on a Spree' 156
Gersh, Gary 319
Ghosh, Paul 51
'Ghost of You Walks, The' 335
Gilbert, Jerry 141, 158
Glastonbury 103
'God Loves a Drunk' 277–8
Goddard, Lon 67
'Going, Going Gone' 199–200
Goldstar Studios 102
Goon Show 17, 27
Goossens, Sidonie 157
Gordon, Liz 327
GPs 199–200
Graham, Bill 76
Grant, Peter 114
Grease Band 49
'Great Valerio, The' 147, 205, 330

Grech, Rik 56
Green, Jonathon 44, 46
Green, Richard 43
Gregson, Clive 164, 171, 203, 224, 226–7, 233, 236, 243, 259, 265, 324
'Gresford Disaster' 182
'Grey Walls' 275
Guardian, The 141, 226, 334
Guildford Folk & Blues Festival 307
Guterman, Jimmy 267
Guthrie, Woody 30, 87
Guv'nor Volume 1, The 37
Guv'nor Volume 3, The 50

Habibiyya 152
Hackford, Taylor 256–7
Half Moon, Putney 199, 243, 307
Hamilton IV, George 50
Hampstead Heath 3–4, 20, 58–9, 135, 205
Hannibal Records 199, 201, 206, 208–9, 225–6, 228, 285–6, 294
Happening 44 Club 44
Happy Blunderers 123
Hard Cash 182, 254–5
Hardin, Glen D. 50
Hardin, Tim 49–50
Hardy, Phil 158
Harris, Emmylou 24
Harris, Sue 129, 189
Hart, Tim 87
'Has He Got A Friend For Me?' 140, 146
Hawkins, Dale 24
Hayes, Eric 80
Hayman, Preston 176
'Heart Needs a Home, A' 157, 158, 178
Hendrix, Jimi 45–6, 63, 100, 123, 330
Henley, Don 111
Hennessy, Peter 14
Henry, Stuart 55
Hentoff, Nat 86
Hepworth, David 229, 251, 288, 323
Heron, Mike 115, 124
Heyday 56, 57, 293
Heylin, Clinton 101
Hill, Malcom 259
His Master's Choice: The Songs Of Richard Thompson 332
Hogan, Peter 28

377

Index

Hokey Pokey 47, 52, 180, 258, 265, 267, 294, 319, 331, 337
Hokey Pokey (album) see Thompson, Richard & Linda (albums)
'Hokey Pokey' (song) 155, 158
Hokey Pokey (trio) 140, 142, 149
Home Service 239
Hopkins, John 'Hoppy' 44, 60
Hornby, Nick 146–7
Hornsby, Bruce 240, 279
Hornsey College of Art 26, 27, 28, 29
Horsman, Bill 27
Horvitch, Andy 51
House Full 112
'How I Wanted To' 225, 226
'How Many Times Do You Have to Fall' 194, 227
'How Will I Ever Be Simple Again?' 246, 248, 331
Hoxne 166–7, 173
Humperdinck, Engelbert 43
Hunt, Ken 193, 197, 201, 225, 234, 235, 275, 276, 313
Hutchings, Ashley (Tyger) 89, 124, 126
  Albion Country Band 128–30
  background 35–8
  Fairport Convention 5, 33, 38, 63, 66, 73, 94–5
Hyde Park concert 92

'I Ain't Gonna Drag My Feet No More' 233
'I Feel So Good' 273, 275
'I Misunderstood' 276
'I Want To See The Bright Lights Tonight' 5
'I'll Keep It With Mine' 56, 64, 214
'I'll Regret It All In the Morning' 155–6
I'm Alright 250
Ian Campbell Folk Group, The 71, 97
'If (Stomp)' 51
If Man But Knew 152
If You Saw Thru' My Eyes 124
Incredible String Band, The 42, 44, 47, 59, 102, 106, 121
Independent, The 270
Independent on Sunday 154, 338
Interview 330
Invisible Means 258
Irwin, Colin 49, 141, 181, 186, 188, 189, 226, 233, 235, 279, 303

Island Records 45, 57, 59, 101, 124, 132, 136, 142–4, 160, 177–8, 286
'It'll Be Me' 179
'It's Alright Ma, It's Only Witchcraft' 52

'Jack O'Diamonds' 52
'Jack Straw's Castle' 4, 322
Jansch, Bert 62
Jefferson Airplane 45, 52, 62, 79, 96, 102
'Jerusalem on the Jukebox' 266
'Jet Plane in a Rocking Chair' 171
John, Elton 122, 330
Johnson, Blind Willie 65
Jones, David 281
Jones, Max 28
Jones, Nick 28, 29, 43, 52

Kassan, Brian 246
Keltner, Jim 243, 265, 335
Kendall, Paul 177
Kenis, Linda see Thompson, Linda
Kenis, Steve 239–41
Khomeini, Ayatollah 269–70
King, Jason 78
'King of Bohemia, The' 149, 304, 321, 322
Kirkpatrick, John 11, 64, 184
  Albion Band 35, 76, 181–3, 194
  Albion Country Band 128–30
  Brass Monkey 76, 237, 251
  Jump at the Sun 124
  with Richard & Linda 162, 164, 180, 189, 190, 195
  with Richard, solo 131, 207, 224, 243, 251, 257, 262, 265, 278
  Richard Thompson Big Band 227
Kiss the Girls and Make Them Cry 156
Knebworth 114
Knopfler, Mark 243, 244–5
Kohn, Marek 270
Konk Studios 265
Kornelussen, Frank 58, 91
Kribbet, Jeff 38

'Lady of Shallot, The' 319
Lake, Steve 157–8
Lamble, Martin Francis 6, 39, 56, 65, 73, 341–2
Larson, Neil 185, 189

378

Index

'Layla' 187
Leadon, Bernie 111–12
Led Zeppelin 97, 102, 113–14
Ledge, The (Pothole Tree) 4, 58–9
Lee, Albert 229
Lee, Leapy 59
Leopold Antiques 159
Let It Rock 158
Lewis, Richard 38, 39
Life and Loves of a She-Devil, The 254
Lincoln Festival 123
Lindley, David 229
Little Hadham 98–9, 102, 108
Live, Love, Larf & Loaf 258
Live at the LA Troubadour 112
Lloyd, A. L. (Bert) 70, 79, 83, 85, 92, 95
'Lobster, The' 51
Lock, Graham 189
Loder, Kurt 235
Logan, Nick 67
London Zoo 30
'Lonely Hearts' 190–91, 192
'Long Dead Love' 248
Love Chronicles 114, 124
'Love In A Faithless Country' 233
Lucas, Trevor 72, 125, 126, 147, 184
Lustig, Jo 141–2, 143, 158, 159, 160, 166, 177, 185–6, 193, 202, 216

'M1 Breakdown' 51
Macauley, Tony 122, 226
MacDonald, Ian see Matthews, Ian
MacFarlane, Ruari 236, 243
MacGowan, Shane 231
Mackie, Rob 155, 162
MacKinnon, Angus 180, 206
MacLeish, Alexander 273
 Manzanera, Phil 280
'Marcie' 50
Marksman, The 254
Marley, Bob 144
Martin, John 229, 259, 286
Martyn, John 113, 121, 123, 124, 155
Mascis, Jay 330
'Mason's Apron' 101
Mattacks, Dave 124, 127, 128, 251
 Fairport Convention 79, 94, 113
 GPs 199–200
 with Richard & Linda 162, 164, 180, 201, 211, 215

with Richard, solo 198, 207, 257, 278, 308, 315, 324–5
Matthews, Ian 45, 51, 63, 64, 66, 184
Tigers Will Survive 64
Matthews Southern Comfort 35, 124, 139
'Matty Groves' 89, 101
Mayall, John 100, 102
McCabe's 207, 210, 211, 221, 222–3, 268
McGuinn, Roger 285
McKee, Maria 267
McManus, Ross 40
McTell, Ralph 199–200
Means, Andrew 135
'Meet On The Ledge' 3, 5, 6, 29, 57–9
Melody Maker 25, 28, 38, 43, 46, 48, 49, 52, 59, 67, 75, 107, 115, 123, 126, 135, 141, 142, 155, 157, 181, 186, 189, 226, 233, 235, 261, 303
Mendelsohn, John 70
Middle Earth Club 47, 48
Mighty Baby 176
Milgrim, Hale 259, 268, 319
Miller, Mandy 17
'Million Dollar Bash' 69
Mirren, Agnes 124
'Missie How You Let Me Down' 246, 247–8
Mitchell, Joni 50, 51, 64, 92
'Modern Woman' 193–4
Mojo 145, 261, 323, 324, 335
'Mole In A Hole' 157
More Love Songs 250–51
Morris On 125, 128–9
'Mother Knows Best' 276, 343
'Mr Lacey' 63, 178
Muldoon, Big see Roberts-Miller, Richard
Murphy, Hugh 194, 195, 238
Music Week 330
Musician 206, 235, 247

National Theatre 76, 182, 238–9
Neal, Peter 45
needletime restrictions 40, 55
Nelson, Rick 24, 111, 113
'Never Again' 76, 156, 185
New Colours 64
New Seekers, The 64
'New St George, The' 129–30, 138, 332

Index

Newmark, Andy 185, 189
Newport Folk Festival 75–6, 87
Nicol, Simon 76–7, 184, 257
   Albion Country Band 128–30
   background 35, 37–8
   Fairport Convention 38, 40, 48, 57, 73
   Hokey Pokey 142, 149
   with Richard & Linda 195, 196, 201, 211–12, 215
   Richard Thompson Big Band 227
'Night Comes In' 164, 170, 171, 178, 180, 182
Night Owl 192, 193
'1952 Vincent Black Lightning' 3, 273–4, 279, 304–5, 343–4
NME 42, 43, 67, 107, 115, 135, 145, 156, 168, 189, 261, 279, 285, 288, 323
'No Man's Land' 63–4, 65
No Roses 126–7, 129
'Nobody's Wedding' 131, 133
North Bank Youth Club 36, 37
'Nottamun Town' 64–5
Notting Hill Free School 44
'Now Be Thankful' 106

Ochs, Phil 29, 50, 72, 76–7, 86, 105, 111
'Old Changing Way, The' 133, 332
Oldfield, Mike 140–41
Oldham, Andrew 40
Olympic Studios 71, 202
Omaha Rainbow 204, 217
One Clear Moment 238–9
Ostin, Mo 238
Over the Rainbow 155
Oz 46

'Painted Ladies' 133–4
Parsons, Gram 24, 112, 134, 230
'Pavanne' 188
Peachey, Mal 267
Peel, John 55, 68, 69, 141, 144, 155, 261
Pegg, Dave (Peggy)
   Fairport Convention 97–9, 113–14
   GPs 199–200
   Happy Blunderers 123
   with Richard & Linda 164, 180, 189, 193, 201
Penhallow, John 41

'Percy's Song' 69
Peters, Linda *see* Thompson, Linda
'Pharaoh' 266–7
Phillips, Sam 250
Phillips, Simon 280
Picardie, Justine 154, 338
Pick of the Pops 18, 30
Pickett, Phil 195, 243, 265
Pink Floyd 41, 43, 45, 47, 63, 75, 102, 186
Plant, Robert 114
Platt, David 50
Platt, John 92
Pogues, The 230–32, 235, 260
Polydor 229, 232, 252, 292
Polygram 229, 252, 253, 286
'Poor Ditching Boy, The' 133, 135, 138, 182, 332
'Poor Will & The Jolly Hangman' 5, 106–7, 114, 178
Powell, Roger 176
Presley, Elvis 24, 124, 243, 250, 292
Prestwick, Marvin 124
'Psycho Street' 276
Punk music 175, 177, 186, 229, 230
Purple Flange, The 108
'Put It There Pal' 335
Pyramid, The 45

Q 229, 251, 264, 265, 267, 279, 286, 288, 323
Quartermain, Mick 58
Queen Elizabeth Hall 163

Radio Luxembourg 18, 36
Radio 1 40, 42, 55–6, 141, 161, 179
radio programmes 17–18, 20
Rafferty, Gerry 192–3, 194–7, 201
'Rainbow Over The Hill' 182, 183
Ralfini, Brenda 68
Raphael, Neil 39
'Read About Love' 274–5
Record Mirror 67, 107, 115, 135
Reed, Lou 206
Reprise Records 136
'Reynardine' 82, 89
Richard, Cliff 179–80
Richard & Linda Thompson *see* Thompson, Richard & Linda
Richard Thompson Big Band 227
Rise Up Like the Sun 181–3

Index

Roberts, David 24, 25
Roberts-Miller, Richard (Big Muldoon) 23–4, 27, 30, 39, 49, 134
rock'n'roll 18–20
'Roll Over Vaughn Williams' 132–3
Rolling Stone 1, 70, 80, 92, 103, 107, 145, 206, 235, 267, 307
Rolling Stones 27–8, 40, 42, 45, 60, 63, 73, 141
Ronstadt, Linda 110, 111, 112, 213, 214, 216
Roundhouse 57, 65, 67, 75, 162
Royal Festival Hall 49, 92, 281, 283, 307
Rush, Elizabeth 243
Rushdie, Salmon 269–71, 276
Russell, Tom 204, 217
Ryan, Michael 254
Rykodisc 285

'Sailor's Life, A' 66, 70–71, 77, 80, 91, 187
'Sam Jones' 336
San Francisco 207, 214
Santa Cruz 213–14
Savile Theatre 47
Scheff, Jerry 243, 265
Seekers, The 124
Seville 279–80
Sgt Pepper 38, 42, 51, 63, 158
'Shaky Nancy' 134
Shand, Jimmy 277
Sharp, Cecil 82–4
'She Moves Through The Fair' 56, 64–5
Sheene, Dave 189
Shipston, Roy 115–16
Shirt Sleeve Studio 158
'Si Tu Dois Partir' 64, 69–70, 143
'Silver Threads & Golden Needles' 111
Sinclair, David 265, 267
'Sir B. MacKenzie' 101, 106
'Sir Patrick Spens' 82, 101, 105
Slam Dance 267
'Sloth' 101, 105, 106, 214
'Smiffy's Glass Eye' 156
Smith, Norman 'Hurricane' 43
Snow, Mat 264
Song Talk 304
Sound Techniques Studios 46, 145, 161
Sounds 135, 158
Sour Grapes 149–50

Sparks, Steve 70
Speakeasy, The 46
St Aloysius School 25
St Michael's Church Hall, Golders Green 38
St Peter's Church, Westbourne Grove 65
Stamler, Gary 229, 242, 253, 259, 268, 286
Staunton, Terry 279
Stealer's Wheel 192
Steeleye Span 35, 87, 89, 94, 108, 139, 158, 159, 186
Stewart, Al 124, 162
Still Waters, The 36
Straight Music 161
'Strange Affair' 187–8, 189
Street Life 155, 180
'Streets of Paradise' 170–71
'Sun Never Shines On The Poor, The' 156–7
'Suzanne' 49, 56, 58, 92
Swarbrick, Dave 125, 227
  collaboration with Thompson 5, 88, 105–6, 114
  Fairport Convention 70–71, 79, 88–92, 93–4, 96–7, 100–101
Sweeney's Men 89
'Sweet Little Rock'n'Roller' 178, 179
Sweet Talker (film) 256–7
Swinburn, Wally 201
Swing 51 193, 197, 234, 235, 313
Symonds, David 55, 56

'Tale In Hard Time' 64
Talent Selection Group 55
'Tam Lin' 82, 90, 101
Tams, John 182–3, 238–9
Tannenbaum, Chaim 250
Tassano, Simon 228, 279, 281
Taylor, Graeme 183
'Tear-Stained Letter' 3, 225, 226
Thatcherism 255–6, 275–6
Thomas, David 180
Thomas, Pete 225, 227, 320
Thompson, A. C. 12
Thompson, Adam (Teddy, son) 154, 166, 168
Thompson, Danny 228, 257, 290, 315, 317, 333–4
Thompson, Jack (son) 281, 346

381

Index

Thompson, Jesse (son) 327–8
Thompson (née Rawlins), Joan (mother) 11–12, 13
Thompson, John (father) 11–12, 14, 16–17, 20, 22, 26, 29, 67
Thompson, John Templeton (great-grandfather) 12–13
Thompson, Kamila (daughter) 221
Thompson (née Peters), Linda 54, 121–2, 125, 129, 158, 238, 331
see also Thompson, Richard & Linda
and Boyd 121, 122, 123, 175, 239
dysphonia 155, 240
and Islam 151–4, 165–7
marriage with Richard 137, 210–17
marriage with Steve Kenis 239–41
Thompson, Muna (daughter) 166, 346
Thompson, Pamela (Perri, sister) 12, 16, 18–19, 23, 26–8, 29, 30, 73, 179
Thompson, Richard John
see also Fairport Convention; Thompson, Richard & Linda
accordion playing 64
Albion Country Band 128–30
and American bands 111–12
American tours 206–9, 222, 236–7, 314–17
Americanisation 243, 262–3, 273
apprenticed to Hans Unger 32, 41, 43
birth 12
cult status 232, 252
Dr K's Blues Band 36, 38
drinking 277–8
and drugs 60
Dylan, accompanies 280
early childhood 13, 14–15, 20
English rock'n'roll 127–8, 135
Ethnic Shuffle Orchestra, The 36, 37, 38
Fairport Convention, leaves 115–17
folk clubs, playing 31
French, Frith, Kaiser & Thompson 258
GPs 199–200
guitar, learns 22, 23–5
guitar playing 100–101, 310–12, 318
Happy Blunderers 123
homes 3, 14, 15–16, 27, 31, 49, 79, 98, 117, 152, 166–7, 173, 217–18
imagination 26
Islamic faith 150, 151–4, 163, 165–9, 173–4, 177, 187, 204, 270–71, 324–5
and Jeannie Franklyn 72, 75, 76, 91, 156
and Judy Dyble 47, 52
Linda, first collaboration 125–6
Linda, marriage break-up 210–17
Linda, meets and marries 121, 129, 137
and Liz Gordon 327
Los Angeles, first visit 76–7
Loud & Rich tour 251
M1 accident 73, 75
and money 125
musical influences 18–19, 20, 29–31, 32, 287–9
Nancy Covey, meets and marries 210–11, 216, 217–18, 223, 229
onstage 40, 48, 57, 66, 100, 306–14, 333
personality 324–8, 337–9
political songs 234
psyche 336–7
record producer 250–51
relationships 324–8
Richard Thompson Big Band 227
royalty payments 285–6
session work 123–4, 129, 158–9, 226–7
shyness 15, 16, 40
solo tours 237, 281–5
songwriting 5, 29, 51, 62–3, 68, 77, 109, 162, 290–91, 298–305
stutter 1, 15
Swarbrick collaborations 5, 88, 105–6, 114
train spotting 21, 97–8
TV and film music 254–7
vegetarian diet 121, 140
at William Ellis School 26–8, 28–30, 31–2, 58
Thompson, Richard (albums)
Across A Crowded Room 230, 232–7
Amnesia 262, 265–7, 272, 279, 343
Anglian Heritage 201
Crosscuttin' 201
Daring Adventures 243–52
Guitar, Vocal 88, 157, 164, 168, 177–80
Hand of Kindness 223–7, 233, 285
Henry the Human Fly 115, 116, 127, 130, 131–7, 138, 154, 168, 321

Index

I Remember Wally Swinburn 201
Mirror Blue 3, 30, 149, 279, 319–24
Richard Thompson with Danny Thompson Live at Crawley 1993 293–4, 334
Rumor & Sigh 267, 268, 272–9, 340, 343
Small Town Romance 182, 194, 208, 227–8, 293, 294
Strict Tempo 197–9, 207
Sweet Talker 257–8
Swinburn Garland, A 201
Watching the Dark 70, 178, 203, 294–7
Thompson, Richard & Linda
  American tour 211–16
  critical acclaim 159
  gigs 161–5, 175–7, 189, 194
  Hokey Pokey 142, 149
  onstage 139–40, 160, 172, 213, 214, 216
  play folk clubs 138–40
  Sour Grapes 149–50
  Sufi band 175–7
Thompson, Richard & Linda (albums)
  First Light 175, 186–90
  Hokey Pokey 76, 140, 154–8, 166
  I Want to See the Bright Lights Tonight 116, 139, 140, 142–9, 151, 154, 155
  Pour Down Like Silver 151, 164, 168, 170–72, 193
  Rafferty album 194–7, 202–3, 206, 293
  Shoot Out the Lights 64, 137, 193, 196, 201, 202–6, 208–9, 211, 215, 216–17, 285
  Sunnyvista 175, 190–91, 192, 201
Thriller 230, 261
Tilbrook, Glen 191
Tim Turner's Narration 36, 41
Time 37, 216, 239
Time Out 206, 226, 251, 267
'Time To Ring Some Changes' 182, 183, 188, 227, 255
'Time Will Show The Wiser' 51
Times, The 226
Tobler, John 51
Top Gear 55
Top of the Pops 42, 64, 70
Track Records 45

Traffic 101–2, 111, 144, 149, 165, 172
tribute albums 329–32
Troubadour, The (Earls Court) 53, 121
Troubadour, The (Los Angeles) 77, 110–13
'Turning of the Tide' 343
Twangin' 'n' A-Traddin' 35–6

UFO Club 41, 44
underground bands 41–2, 45–6, 55, 59
Unger, Hans 32

'Valerie' 245, 246, 248, 331
Vance, Tommy 52
videos, promo 230, 261
Virgin Studios 125
Vogue 19
Vox 281

Wadsworth, Tony 259, 330
Wainwright III, Loudon 110–11, 214, 223, 227, 250–51
'Walk Awhile' 104–5
'Walking On a Wire' 203, 204
'Walking Through a Wasted Land' 234
'Wall of Death' 197, 202, 205
'Waltzing's For Dreamers' 59, 266
Ward, Ed 107
Warlock Music 68
Warner Brothers 115, 123, 136, 238
Warnes, Jennifer 240
'Washington At Valley Forge' 37
Waterson, Mike 127, 157
Way of Life 97
'Way That it Shows, The' 323
'We Sing Hallelujah' 138, 147, 182
Weeks, Willie 185, 189
Welch, Chris 59, 107
'Wheely Down' 134
'When I Get To The Border' 146, 147, 277
'When The Spell Is Broken' 233
'When Will I Be Loved?' 126, 138
Whiteman, Ian 150, 152, 176
Who, The 283
Who Knows Where the Time Goes 53
William Ellis School 26, 28–30, 31–2, 58
Williams, Richard 142–3, 149, 158, 177–9
Wilson, Brian 233

383

Index

Wilson, Tony 48
Winner, Langdon 38
Winwood, Muff 142–4
Winwood, Steve 101, 150, 189
Witchseason 44, 46, 48, 59, 68, 121, 123, 124
'Withered & Died' 146, 299
Woffinden, Bob 145, 156
'Woman Or a Man' 200–201, 227
Wood, John 43, 47, 71, 145, 158, 177
Wood, Roy 4, 5
Wood, Royston 127–9
Woodley, Bruce 124
'Woods of Darney' 336
Woodworm Studios 193
World is a Wonderful Place, The 331–2
Wrong End of the Race 226
Wyvill, Brian 3–4, 38, 58–9

'Yankee Go Home' 265
Yardbirds, The 100
You Can All Join In 59
'You Don't Say' 232, 233

Zig Zag 51, 65, 144, 150, 163, 177
Zollo, Paul 304
Zorn, Pete 192, 195, 201, 207, 211–12, 215, 223–5, 227, 257, 308, 315